# THE BRITISH TOMMY
## IN NORTH WEST EUROPE, 1944-1945

### VOLUME TWO
### ORGANISATION, ARMAMENT AND VEHICLES

Jean BOUCHERY

Drawings by Jean-Marie MONGIN
Translated from the French by Alan McKAY

*HISTOIRE & COLLECTIONS - PARIS*

# TABLE OF CONTENTS

**INTRODUCTION** — 6
The British Army in 1944

**1 - The ORGANISATION of UNITS, the 21st ARMY GROUP** — 8
The order of Battle of the larger formations, organisational tables.
Description of the different Corps and Services.

**2 - The ARMS and the SERVICES** — 28

**3 - INDIVIDUAL and UNIT ARMAMENT** — 62
Hand guns, machine carbines, rifles, Bren gun, machine guns, PIAT, mines, explosives, grenades.

**4 - ARMOUR** — 82

**5 - ARTILLERY** — 100

**6 - TRANSPORT VEHICLES** — 114

**7 - TACTICAL MARKINGS of VEHICLES and MACHINES, CAMOUFLAGE** — 122

**APPENDICES** — 134

**BIBLIOGRAPHY** — 140

# D-DAY TO VE-DAY
# THE BRITISH TOMMY

The first volume was dealt with dress, equipment and insignia used by the campaigning Tommy; this second volume deals with the important chapters on individual and group armament, as well as the different material used by the various arms and services of the front-line units.

Moreover - and this is the principal link with the first volume - the order of battle and the organisation of the different formations engaged in the Northwest Europe theatre of operations enable us to locate the exact position of the units that were incorporated in these formations. All units are listed in the appendix of this book.

Let us conclude this introduction by saying that these pages, by means of the numerous tables showing the markings, give us the opportunity of identifying the origin of the units to which vehicles and machines were affected with a degree of precision when consulting period documents.

This is one of the major elements of this second volume which concludes this vast fresque given over to The British Soldiers.

*Jean Bouchery.*

*Above:*
**Normandy June 1944. Tommies of the 3rd Infantry Division settling down on the rear of this Flail Sherman *"Mellerstang"*, belonging to the 1st Lothians and Border Horse (79th Armoured Division).**
*(Imperial War Museum)*

# THE BRITISH ARMY

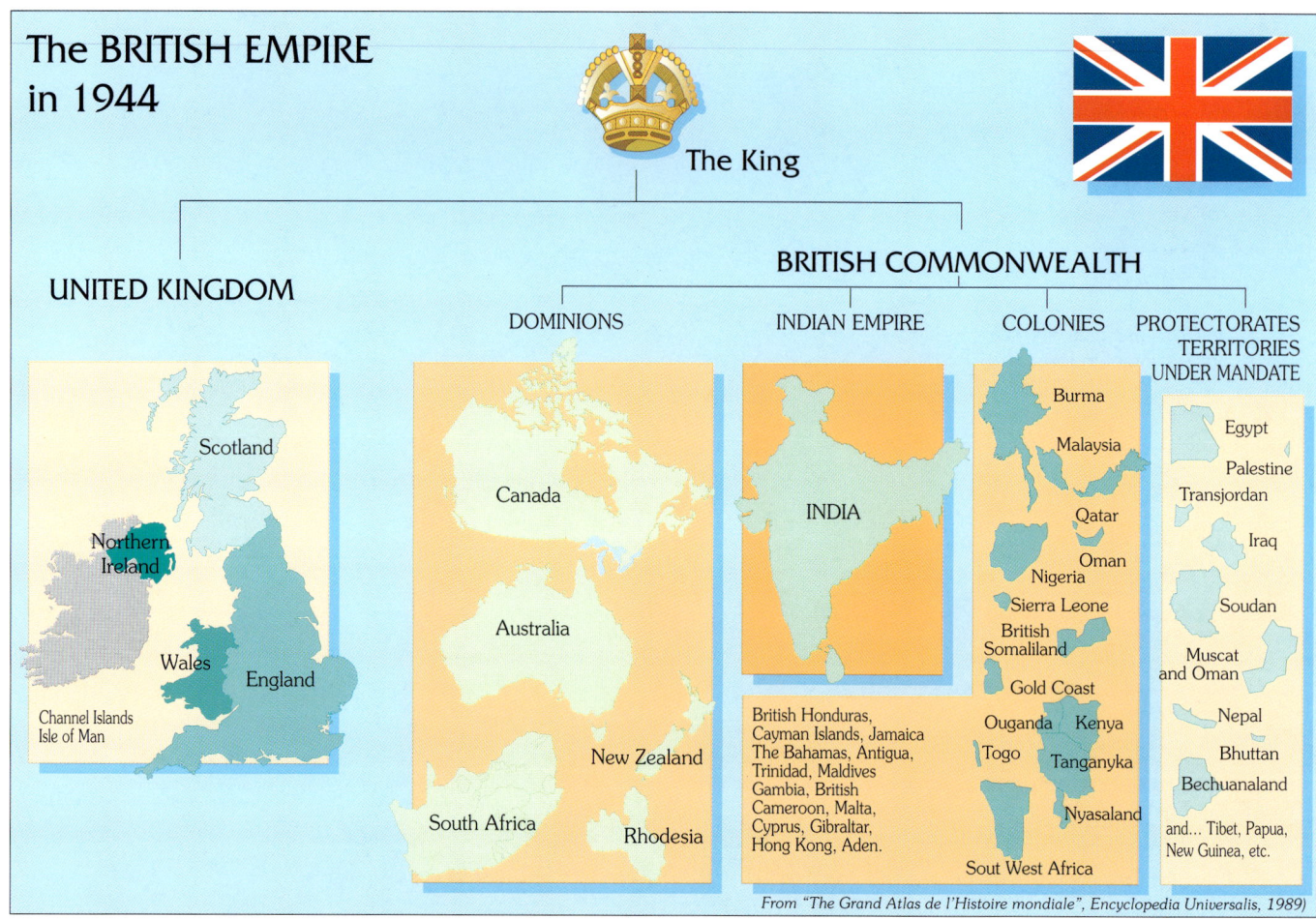

*From "The Grand Atlas de l'Histoire mondiale", Encyclopedia Universalis, 1989)*

# 1. The Organisation of the Army

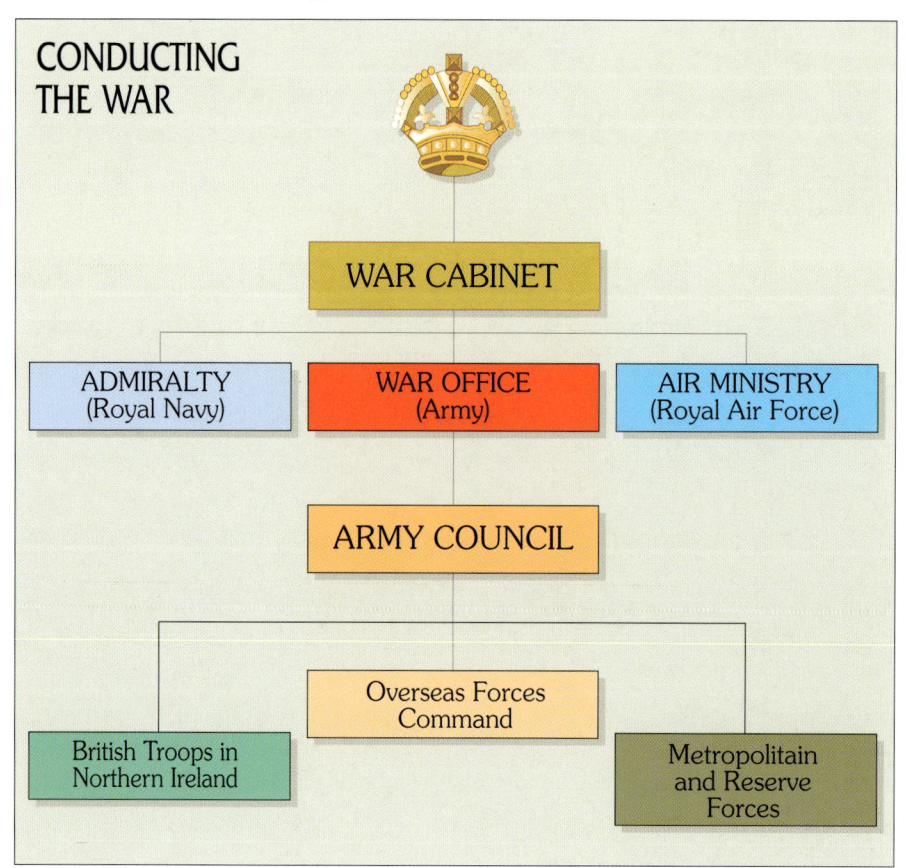

*Opposite:*
A succinct organogram of the conduct of the War and of the chain of command:

- The Armed Forces (the Three Services), the Royal Navy, the Army and the Royal Air Force were responsible to three different authorities: the Admiralty, the War Office and the Air Ministry. These three authorities' action was co-ordinated by the War cabinet.

- the War Cabinet. A temporary organisation created for the duration of the War, it directed the conflict with relation to the Empire. The Chief was Winston Churchill, Prime Minister and Defence Minister, assisted by a secretariat, an Imperial Defence Committee and the Committee of the Chiefs of the General Staff, presided by Sir Hastings Ismay, the Prime Minister's military assistant and personal representative.

- the War Office. This ministry included both military and civilian personnel. The highest ranking officer was the Chief of the Imperial General Staff, General Sir Alan Brooke.

- the Army Council. The Army was placed directly under the responsibility of the Army Council whose Chairman was the Secretary of State for War. This organisation was made up of ten members, of which five were military. The Army Council defined the Army's general policy: personnel management, Training, Equipment and Armament Supply, and payment authority. It was not responsible for the running of the War; this was the responsibility of the Prime Minister, Defence Minister.

# THE ARMY IN PEACE-TIME

## The Regular Army

The Army was entirely professional and was made up of volunteers aged from 18 - 31 who had signed on for 7 years, their contract being renewable at the end.

It was about 250 000 strong; a part of this force served overseas.

## The Territorial Army

The reserve was made up of volunteers who signed on for 4 years. On top of their ordinary civilian occupations, these men carried out 35 days' military instruction a year (plus 10 days during the first year) of which a fortnight was spent in a training camp.

## The Supplementary or Special Reserves

This reserve included men who were mainly specialists and who had already spent time in the Army and who were kept in reserve after returning to civilian life. These men could be called up individually or in already made up units.

# THE WAR-TIME ARMY

After May 1939, Parliament voted a law instituting compulsory military preparation for men aged 20 - 24.

On 3rd September 1939, at 11.15 local time, Great Britain declared war on Germany and compulsory conscription for men of 18 to 41 was established by the National Service Act (1).

The different peace-time notions of the Army gave way to a single entity: the British Army, a generic term applied to all land forces.

---

(1) With the exception of the 6 Northern Irish counties where recruitment was done on a voluntary basis; nevertheless about 70 000 Irishmen joined the ranks of the British Army.

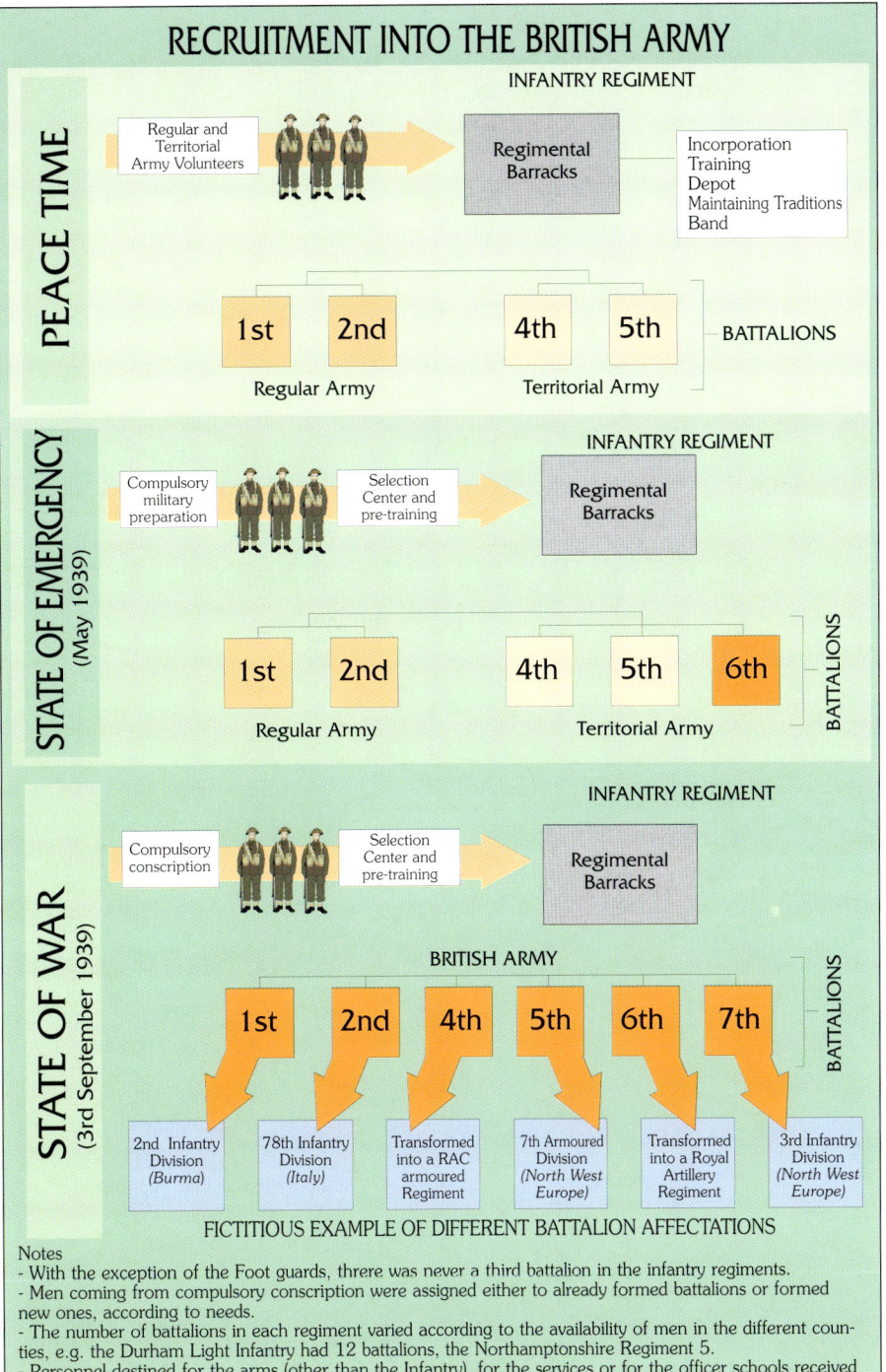

Right.
Map of the sector of operations of the 21st Army Group during the campaign in Northwest Europe, from June 1944 to May 1945.

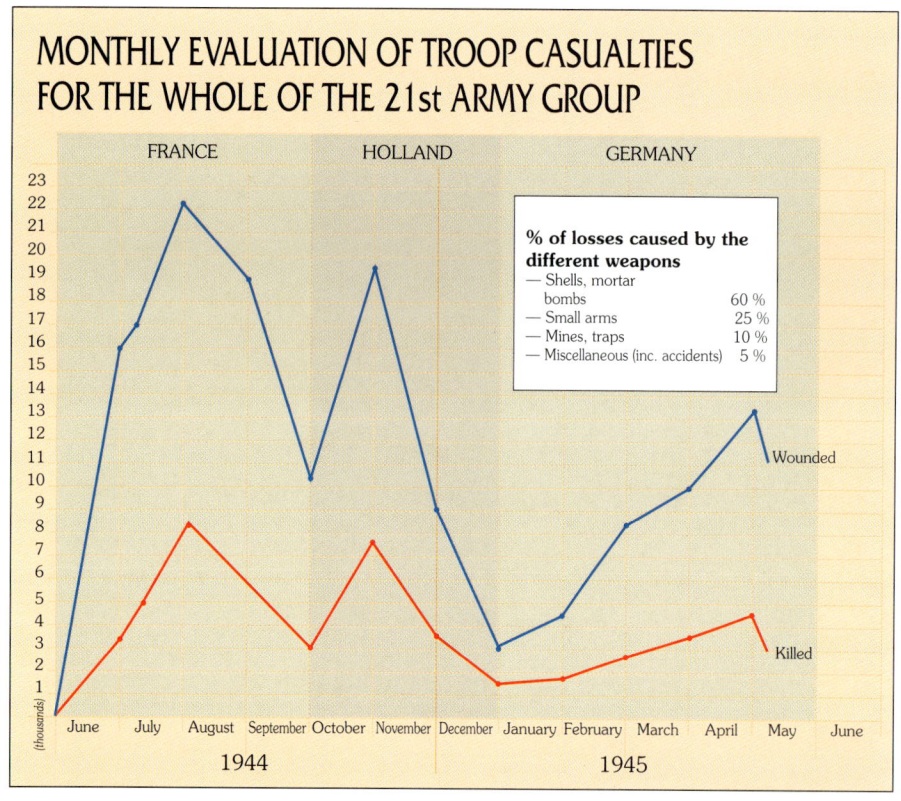

**MONTHLY EVALUATION OF TROOP CASUALTIES FOR THE WHOLE OF THE 21st ARMY GROUP**

% of losses caused by the different weapons
- Shells, mortar bombs — 60 %
- Small arms — 25 %
- Mines, traps — 10 %
- Miscellaneous (inc. accidents) — 5 %

### TOTAL STRENGTHS and LOSSES

The total strength of the land forces present in the theatre of operations in Northwest Europe only

as at 8th May 1945 — **835 208 men**

**Losses per division from 6th June 1944 to 1st October 1944**
(killed, wounded, missing)

|  |  |
|---|---|
| Guards, armoured division | 3 385 |
| 7th armoured division | 2 801 |
| 11th armoured division | 3 825 |
| 3rd infantry division | 7 342 |
| 15th infantry division | 7 601 |
| 43rd infantry division | 7 605 |
| 49th infantry division | 5 894 |
| 50th infantry division | 6 701 |
| 51st infantry division | 4 799 |
| 53rd infantry division | 4 984 |
| 59th infantry division | 4 911 |
| 1st Airborne | 7 212 |
| 6th Airborne | 4 457 |

**Total losses in men from 6th June 1944 to 7th May 1945**
(British troops only)

| | |
|---|---|
| Killed or died from wounds | 30 276 |
| Wounded | 96 672 |
| Missing or taken prisoner | 14 698 |
| Total | 141 646 |

*Opposite Left*
Normandy, June 1944. In the streets of the village of Bretteville-l'Orgueilleuse, a jeep from the Military Police passes another jeep, probably a communications Jeep, belonging to an anti aircraft division. Both belong to the 12th Corps, as shown by the leaves and the tree trunks, symbolising the green counties of Kent and Surrey where the units of the Corps had been assembled.
(IWM)

*Opposite Right*
Normandy, 21st June 1944. Prime Minister and Defence Minister, Winston Churchill talking with General Montgomery, commanding the 21st Army Group, regrouping at that date all the Allied land forces committed on the Continent, since 6th June 1944.
(IWM)

# Normal English Measurements

## VARIOUS MEASUREMENTS

| Volume | | Length | | Weight | |
|---|---|---|---|---|---|
| 1 Pint | 0.568 litre | Inch | 2.54 cm | Ounce (oz) | 28.35 gr |
| 1 Quart | 1.136 litre | Foot | 30.5 cm | Pound (lb) | 0.453 kg |
| 1 Gallon | 4.546 litre | Yard | 91.4 cm | Ton | 1 016.04 kg |
| | | Mile | 1608.64 m | | |

### LADEN WEIGHT OF VEHICLES

**CWT** (*Hundredweight*) = 50.80 kg

| | |
|---|---|
| 5 CWT | **250 kg** (jeep) |
| 8 CWT | **400 kg** |
| 10 CWT | **500 kg** |
| 15 CWT | **750 kg** |
| 30 CWT | **1 500 kg** |

Above these weights, the weight is expressed in TONS, roughly equivalent to the metric tonne: 1 016.04 kg

### CALIBRES
EXPRESSED IN INCHES

**1 Inch** (In.) = 2, 539 cm

| | |
|---|---|
| .303 inch | 7,7 mm |
| .380 inch | 9 mm |
| 2 inches | 50,8 mm |
| 3 inches | 76,2 mm |
| 3.7 inches | 94 mm |
| 4.2 inches | 106 mm |
| 4.5 inches | 114,3 mm |
| 5.5 inches | 139,7 mm |
| 8 inches | 203 mm |

### CALIBRES
TERMS OF THE WEIGHT OF THE PROJECTILE

**1 pound** = 0 kg 453

| | |
|---|---|
| 2 pounder | 40 mm |
| 6 pounder | 57 mm |
| 17 pounder | 76,2 mm |
| 25 pounder | 87,6 mm |

# THE 21st ARMY GROUP

# CHAPTER 1 — The 21st ARMY GROUP
## 1. The Organisation of the Allied Command

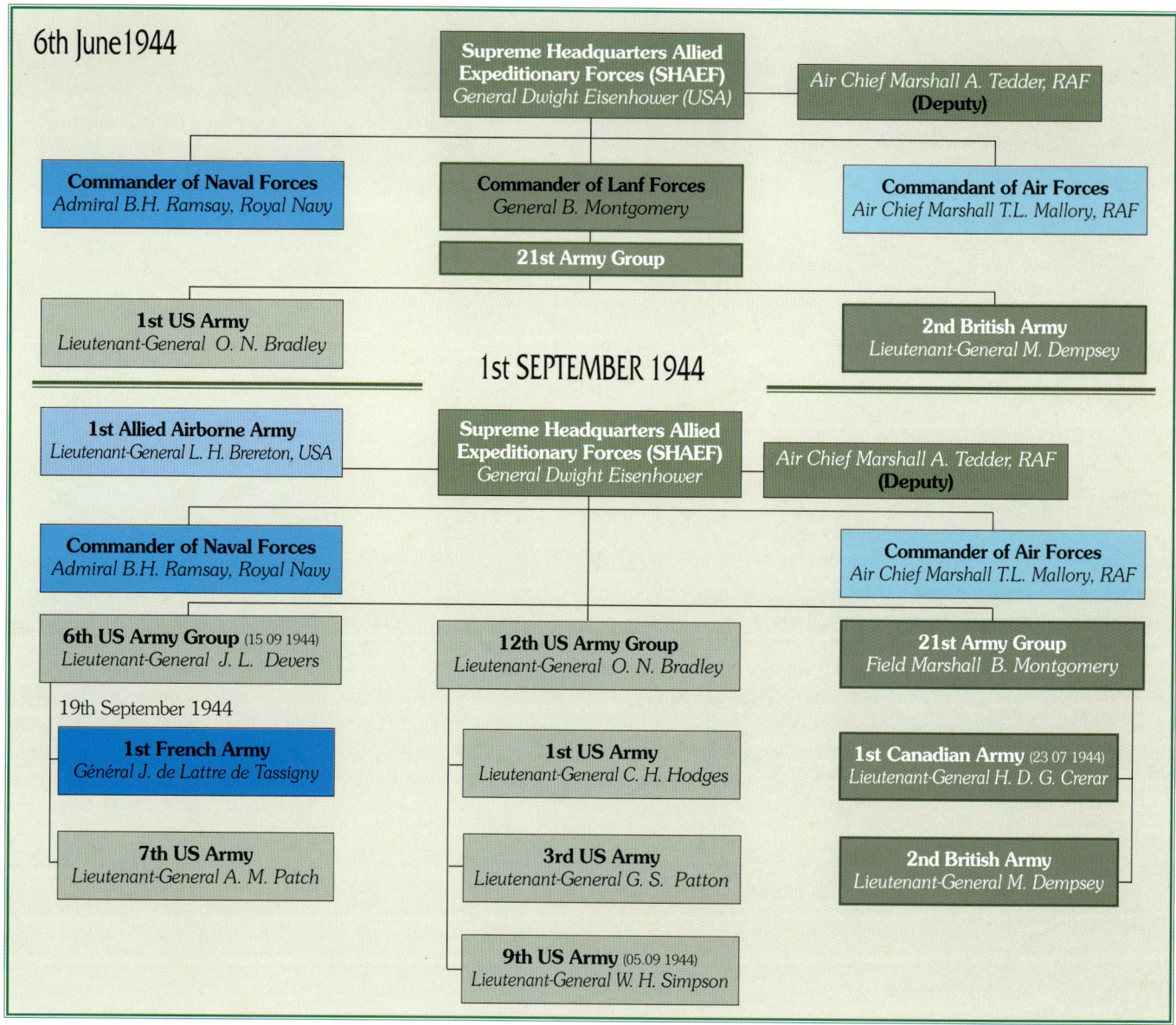

## BREAKDOWN OF 21st ARMY GROUP'S PERSONNEL
### (August 1944)*

### ARMS

| | |
|---|---|
| Royal Artillery | 18 % ** |
| Infantry (incl. Airborne Troops) | 14 % |
| Royal Engineers | 13 % |
| Royal Armoured Corps | 6 % |
| Royal Corps of Signals | 5 % |
| **TOTAL** | **56 %** |

### SERVICES

| | |
|---|---|
| Royal Army Service Corps | 15 % |
| Pioneer Corps | 10 % |
| Royal Electrical and Mechanical Engineers | 5 % |
| Royal Army Medical Corps | 4 % |

### SERVICES (cont.)

| | |
|---|---|
| Royal Army Chaplain's Department | |
| Royal Army Ordnance Corps | |
| Royal Army Pay Corps | |
| Royal Army Veterinary Corps | |
| Royal Army Educational Corps | 10 % |
| Intelligence Corps | |
| Army Physical Training Corps | |
| Army Catering Corps | |
| Corps of Military Police | |
| Military Provost Staff Corps | |
| **TOTAL** (for the Services) | **44 %** |

\* Percentages based on 660 000 men
\*\* The relative strength of the Artillery resulted from doctrines evolved from World War One experience.

*Left.*
General Crocker, commanding the 1st Corps at the outset of Operation Goodwood, 18th July 1944, watching his divisions advancing at a few kilometres from Caen.
(IWM)

*Right.*
A Staghound armoured car moving towards the front during Operation Goodwood. The white number 44 on a green background below a white rectangle indicates a reconnaissance regiment attached to an Army Corps
(IWM)

## The Army in N-W Europe: commands, strengths, means

| Group, unit | Average strength | Symbol | Under the command of a |
|---|---|---|---|
| Army Group | 600 000 | | Field Marshall |
| Army | 150 000 | | General |
| Corps * | 60 000 | | Lieutenant-General |
| Division | 15 000 / 18 000 | | Major-General |
| Brigade | 3 500 | | Brigadier |
| Battalion Regiment (RAC, RA) | 850 | | Lieutenant-Colonel |
| Company, Squadron | 130 | | Major |
| Platoon | 37 | | Lieutenant or 2nd Lieutenant |
| Section | 10 | | Corporal / Bren Group — Lance Corporal |

9

# PRINCIPAL BRITISH UNITS AND GROUPS COMMITTED ON THE CONTINENT

From 6th June 1944 to 1st September 1944 *(from « Victory in the West », volumes I and II, Major L. F. Ellis)*

## 21st ARMY GROUP

General Montgomery — Commander in Chief
Major General de Guinguand — Chief of Staff

- **1st Special Service Brigade**
Nos 3, 4, 6 Army Commandos, No 45 (Royal Marine) Commando
- **4th Special Service Brigade**
Nos 41, 46, 47, 48 (Royal Marines) Commandos
- **Armoured Support Group**
1st, 2nd Royal Marine Armoured Support Regiments
- **Special Air Service**
1st Special Air Service Regiment, 2nd Special Air Service Regiment
3rd French Parachute Battalion, 4th French Parachute Battalion (2e et 3e RCP)

### GHQ and ARMY TROOPS
*General Headquarters units and general army reserve groups*

- **79th Armoured Division**
- **Independent Brigades**
4th Armoured Brigade, 6th Guards Armoured Brigade,
8th Armoured Brigade, 27th Armoured Brigade,
31st Armoured Brigade, 33rd Armoured Brigade
34th Armoured Brigade, 56th Infantry Brigade

### ROYAL ARMOURED CORPS

- **GHQ. Liaison Regiment RAC ('Phantom')** — *Reconnaissance*
- **2nd Armoured Replacement Group** — *Armour and Replacement delivery units*
- **2nd Armoured Delivery Regiment**
- **25th Canadian Armoured Delivery Rgt.**
(The Elgin Regiment)

### ROYAL ARTILLERY

- **HQ. Anti-Aircraft Brigade Regiments**
74th, 76th, 80th, 100th, 101st, 105th,
106th, 107th
- **Heavy Anti-Aircraft Regiments**
60th, 86th, 90th, 99th, 103rd, 105th, 107th,
108th, 109th, 112th, 113th, 115th, 116th,
121st, 146th, 165th, 174th, 2nd Canadian — *Anti-Aircraft Defence*
- **Light Anti-Aircraft Regiments**
20th, 27th, 32nd, 54th, 71st, 73rd, 93rd,
109th, 112th, 113th, 114th, 120th, 121st,
123rd, 124th, 125th, 126th, 127th, 133rd,
139th, 149th
- **Searchlight Regiment**
41st
- **HQ Army Groups Royal Artillery (AGRAs)**
3rd, 4th, 5th, 8th, 9th, 2nd Canadian
- **Heavy Artillery Regiments**
1st, 51st, 52nd, 53rd, 59th
- **Medium Artillery Regiments**
7th, 9th, 10th, 11th, 13th, 15th, 53rd, 59th,
61st, 63rd, 64th, 65th, 67th, 68th, 72nd, 77th,
79th, 84th, 107th, 121st, 146th, 3rd Canadian,
4th Canadian, 7th Canadian
- **Field Artillery Regiments**
4th RHA, 6th, 25th, 86th, 147th, 150th,
191th, 19th Canadian

### ROYAL ENGINEERS

- **HQ. Army Group Royal Engineers**
10th, 11th, 12th, 13th, 14th, 1st Canadian
- **GHQ Troops Engineers**
4th, 7th, 8th, 13th, 15th, 18th, 48th, 59th
- **Airfield Construction Groups**
13th, 16th, 23rd, 24th, 25th
- **Army Troops Engineers**
2nd, 6th 7th, 1st Canadian, 2nd Canadian,
2nd, 3rd Battalions Royal Canadian Engineers

### ROYAL CORPS OF SIGNALS

- **21st Army Group Headquarters Signals**
- **2nd Army Headquarters Signals**
- **1st Canadian Army Headquarters Signals**
- **Air Formation Signals**
No11, No12, No13, No16, No17, No18
- **1st Special Wireless Group ' R' Force**
- **Beach Signals**
B 10, B 13

### INFANTRY

- **Headquarters protection units**
4th Battalion The Royal Northumberland Fusiliers (MG)
1st Canadian Army Headquarters Defence Battalion (Royal Montreal Regiment)

### ARMY AIR CORPS

- **Glider Pilot Regiment**
1st Glider Pilot Wings, 2nd Glider Pilot Wings

## LINES OF COMMUNICATION AND REAR MAINTENANCE AREA

- **Headquarters Lines of Comunication**

|  |  |
|---|---|
| Nos 11, 12 Lines of communication areas | |
| Nos 4,5,6 Lines of communication Sub-Areas | |
| Nos 7, 8, Base Sub-Areas | |
| Nos 101, 102, 104 Beach Sub-Areas | |
| Nos 5, 6, 7, 8, 9, 10 Beach Groups | |
| Nos 10, 11 Garrisons | |
| Nos 2,3,5,6 Railway Construction and Maintenance Group | Royal Engineers |
| No 3 Railway Operating Group | Royal Engineers |
| No 1 Canadian Railway Operating Group | Royal Engineers |
| Nà 1 Railway Workshop Group | Royal Engineers |
| Nos 2, 6, 8, 9, 10, 11 Port Operating Group | Royal Engineers |
| Nos 1, 2, 4, 5, Port Construction and Repair Group | Royal Engineers |
| Nos 3, 4 Inland Water Transport Group | Royal Engineers |
| No 2 Mechanical Equipment (Transportation) Unit | Royal Engineers |
| Bomb Disposal Units | Royal Engineers |
| Nos 2, 12 Lines of Communication Headquarters Signals | Royal Corps of Signals |
| No 1 Canadian Lines of Communication Headquarters Signals | Royal Corps of Signals |
| 5th, 8th Battalions The King's Regiment | Infantry |
| 7th Battalion The East Yorkshire Regiment | Infantry (disbanded 12 1944) |
| 2nd Battalion The Hertfordshire Regiment | Infantry (disbanded 11 1944) |
| 6th Battalion The Border Regiment | Infantry (disbanded 08 1944) |
| 1st Buckinghamshire Battalion The Oxf. and Bucks. Light Infantry | Infantry |
| 5th Battalion The Royal Berkshire Regiment | Infantry |
| 18th Battalion The Durham Light Infantry | Infantry |
| — Liaison Officers | |
| — Civil Affairs | |
| — Press Correspondants | |

## 2nd ARMY

*Lieutenant. General Dempsey, General Officer Commanding-in-chief*

### I Corps — Lieutenant. General Crocker
The Inns of Court Regiment, ( Armoured Cars) RAC
62nd Anti-Tank Regiment, Royal Artillery
102nd Light Anti-Aircraft Regiment, Royal Artillery
9th Survey Regiment, Royal Artillery
I Corps Troops Engineers, Royal Engineers
I Corps Signals, Royal Corps of Signals
16th Casualty Clearing Station, 32th Casualty Clearing Station, RAMC

### VIII Corps — Lieutenant. General O'Connor
2nd Household Cavalry Regiment ( Armoured Cars) RAC
91st Anti-Tank Regiment, Royal Artillery
121st Light Anti-Aircraft Regiment, Royal Artillery
10th Survey Regiment, Royal Artillery
VIII Corps Troops Engineers, Royal Engineers
VIII Corps Signals, Royal Corps of Signals
33rd Casualty Clearing Station, 34th Casualty Clearing Station, RAMC

### XII Corps — Lieutenant. General Ritchie
1st Royal Dragoons ( Armoured Cars) RAC
86th Anti-Tank Regiment, Royal Artillery
112th Light Anti-Aircraft Regiment, Royal Artillery
7th Survey Regiment, Royal Artillery
XII Corps Troops Engineers, Royal Engineers
XII Corps Signals, Royal Corps of Signals
23rd Casualty Clearing Station, 24th Casualty Clearing Station, RAMC

### XXX Corps — Lieutenant. General Bucknall
Lieutenant. General Horrocks (à/c 04.08.44)
11th Hussars (Armoured Cars) RAC
73rd Anti-Tank Regiment, Royal Artillery
27th Light Anti-Aircraft Regiment, Royal Artillery
4th Survey Regiment, Royal Artillery
XXX Corps Troops Engineers, Royal Engineers
XXX Corps Signals, Royal Corps of Signals
3rd Casualty Clearing Station, 10th Casualty Clearing Station, RAMC

## 1st CANADIAN ARMY

*Lieutenant General Crerar*

2nd Canadian Armoured Brigade

### II Canadian Corps
2nd Canadian Infantry Division
3rd Canadian Infantry Division
4th Canadian Armoured Division

## ALLIED FORMATIONS

1st Polish Armoured Division
Royal Netherlands Brigade (Princess Irene)
1st Belgian Brigade
Czechoslovakian Armoured Brigade
1st, 2nd, 3rd Polish Parachute Battaloins

## AIR OBSERVATION POST SQUADRONS

- **83rd Group RAF**
Nos 652, 653, 658, 659, 662 Squadrons
- **84th Group RAF**
Nos 660, 661 Squadrons

# PRINCIPAL BRITISH UNITS AND GROUPS COMMITTED ON THE CONTINENT

From 1st September 1944 to 8th May 1945 *(from « Victory in the West », volumes I and II, Major L. F. Ellis)*

## 21st ARMY GROUP

General Montgomery — Commander in Chief
Major General de Guinguand — Chief of Staff

### GHQ and ARMY TROOPS
*General Headquarters units and general army reserve groups*

- **Army Air Corps**
  1st Wing The Glider Pilot Regiment
  2nd Wing The Glider Pilot Regiment
- **Special Air Service**
  1st Special Air Service Regiment, 2nd Special Air Service Regiment * — *(Belgian Special Air Service Regt.)*
  2nd French Parachute Battalion, 3rd French Parachute Battalion (2e et 3e RCP)
- **79th Armoured Division**
- **Independent Armoured and Infantry Brigades**
  4th Armoured Brigade, 6th Guards Armoured Brigade,
  8th Armoured Brigade, 34th Armoured Brigade,
  115th Brigade, 116th Brigade - Royal Marine (20.02.1945)
  305th Brigade**, 306th Brigade**, 308th Brigade**
  1st Commando Brigade, 4th Commando Brigade

### ROYAL ARMOURED CORPS
- **GHQ. Liaison Regiment RAC** ('Phantom') — *Reconnaissance*
- **2nd Armoured Replacement Group** — *Armour and*
- **2nd Armoured Delivery Regiment** — *Replacement delivery units*
- **25th Canadian Armoured Delivery Rgt.** (The Elgin Regiment)

### ROYAL ARTILLERY
- **HQ. Anti-Aircraft Brigade Regiments**
  31st, 50th, 74th, 75th, 76th, 80th, 100th, 101st, 103rd,
  105th, 106th,107th, 5th Royal Marine
- **Heavy Anti-Aircraft Regiments**
  60th, 64th, 86th, 90th, 98th, 99th, 103rd, 105th, 107th, 108th
  109th, 110th, 111th, 112th, 113th, 115th, 116th, 118th,
  132nd, 137th (mixed), 139th (mixed),146th, 155th (mixed),
  165th, 174th, 176th, 183rd, 3rd Royal Marine, 2nd Canadian — *Antttti-Aircraft Defence*
- **Light Anti-Aircraft Regiments**
  4th, 20th, 26th, 32nd, 54th, 71st, 73rd, 93rd, 109th,
  113th, 114th, 120th,123rd, 124th, 125th, 126th, 127th,
  133rd, 139th, 149th, 150th 4th Royal Marine
- **Searchlight Regiments**
  1st, 2nd, 41st, 42nd, 54th
- **HQ Army Groups Royal Artillery (AGRAs)**
  3rd, 4th, 5th, 8th, 9th, 17th, 59th, 1st Canadian, 2nd Canadian
- **Super Heavy Artillery Regiments**
  3rd, 61st
- **Heavy Artillery Regiments**
  1st, 32nd, 51st, 52nd, 53rd, 56th, 59th
- **Medium Artillery Regiments**
  3rd, 7th, 9th, 10th, 11th, 13th, 15th, 51st, 53rd, 59th,
  61st, 63rd, 64th, 65th, 67th, 68th, 69th, 72nd, 77th,
  79th, 84th, 107th, 121st, 146th, 1st Canadian, 2nd Canadian,
  3rd Canadian, 4th canadian, 5th Canadian,7th Canadian
- **Field Artillery Regiments**
  4th RHA, 6th, 25th, 32nd, 86th, 90th (ex 50th Division),98th, 110th*,
  116th*, 147th, 150th*, 166th, 191th*, 11th Canadian,19th Canadian
- **Survey Regiments**
  11th

### ROYAL ENGINEERS
- **HQ. Army Grous Royal Engineers (AGREs)**
  8th, 10th, 11th, 12th, 13th, 14th, 18th, 1st Canadian
- **GHQ Troops Engineers**
  2nd, 4th, 7th, 8th, 13th, 15th, 18th, 19th, 48th,
  50th (ex 50th Division), 59th (ex 59th Division),
- **Airfield Construction Groups**
  13th, 16th, 23rd, 24th, 25th
- **Army Troops Engineers**
  2nd, 6th 7th, 1st Canadian, 2nd Canadian,
  2nd, 3rd Battalions Royal Canadian Engineers

### ROYAL CORPS OF SIGNALS
- **21st Army Group Headquarters Signals**
- **2nd Army Headquarters Signals**
- **1st Canadian Army Headquarters Signals**
- **No 5 Headquarters Signal (SHAEF)**
- **Air Formation Signals**
  No11, No12, No13, No 14, No 15, No16, No17, No18
- **1st Special Wireless Group**

### INFANTRY
- **Headquarters protection units**
  4th Battalion The Royal Nortumberland Fusiliers (MG)
  1st Canadian Army Headquarters Defence Battalion (Royal Montreal Regiment)

---
\* Units removed from operations during the campaign
\*\*Reinforcement units made up of transfered artillery regiments. They were engaged in April 1945

## LINES OF COMMUNICATION AND REAR MAINTENANCE AREA
*Zone des étapes et dépôts*

- **Headquarters Lines of Comunication** — Major-General Naylor
  Nos 11, 12 Lines of Communication areas — Major General Surtees (01.01.1945)
  Nos 4, 5, 6, 9, 15, 16, 17, 18, 19, 20, 21
  (ex No 101 Beach Sub-area) Lines of communication Sub-Areas
  Nos 7, 8, Base Sub-Areas

|  |  |
|---|---|
| Nos 2, 3, 5, 6 Railway Construction and Maintenance Group | Royal Engineers |
| Nos 3, 4, 7 Railway Operating Group | Royal Engineers |
| No 1 Canadian Railway Operating Group | Royal Engineers |
| Nos 1, 3 Railway Workshop Group | Royal Engineers |
| Nos 2, 6, 8, 9, 10, 11 Port Operating Group | Royal Engineers |
| Nos 1, 2, 4, 5, 6 Port Construction and Repair Group | Royal Engineers |
| Nos 2, 3, 4 Inland Water Transport Group | Royal Engineers |
| Nos 2, 12, 13, 17 Lines of Communication Headquarters Signals | Royal Corps of Signals |
| No 1 Canadian Lines of Communication Headquarters Signals | Royal Corps of Signals |
| 5th, The King's Regiment | Infantry |
| 1st Buckinghamshire Battalion The Oxf. and Bucks. Light Infantry | Infantry |
| 18th Battalion The Durham Light Infantry | Infantry |
| 600th, 601st, 606th, 607th, 60!th, 609th, 611th, 612th, | Royal Artillery * |
| 613th, 614th, 616th, 617th, 619th, 623rd, 625th, 630th, | Royal Artillery * |
| 631st, 637th Regiments | Royal Artillery * |

## 2nd ARMY
*Lieutenant. General Dempsey, General Officer Commanding-in-chief*

**I Corps** — Lieutenant. General Crocker
The Inns of Court Regiment, Royal Armoured Corps *(Armoured Cars) RAC*
62nd Anti-Tank Regiment, Royal Artillery
102nd Light Anti-Aircraft Regiment, Royal Artillery
9th Survey Regiment, Royal Artillery
I Corps Troops Engineers, Royal Engineers
I Corps Signals, Royal Corps of Signals
16th Casualty Clearing Station, 32th Casualty Clearing Station, RAMC

**I Airborne Corps *** — Lieutenant. General Browning
I Airborne Corps Signals, Royal Corps of Signals — *Corps Troops*

**VIII Corps** — Lieutenant. General O'Connor Lieutenant-General Barker (02.12.1944)
2nd Household Cavalry Regiment *(Armoured Cars) RAC*
91st*, 63rd Anti-Tank Regiment, Royal Artillery
121st Light Anti-Aircraft Regiment, Royal Artillery
10th Survey Regiment, Royal Artillery
VIII Corps Troops Engineers, Royal Engineers
VIII Corps Signals, Royal Corps of Signals
33rd Casualty Clearing Station, 34th Casualty Clearing Station, RAMC

**XII Corps** — Lieutenant. General Ritchie
1st Royal Dragoons *(Armoured Cars) RAC*
86th Anti-Tank Regiment, Royal Artillery
112th Light Anti-Aircraft Regiment, Royal Artillery
7th Survey Regiment, Royal Artillery
XII Corps Troops Engineers, Royal Engineers
XII Corps Signals, Royal Corps of Signals
23rd Casualty Clearing Station, 24th Casualty Clearing Station, RAMC

**XXX Corps** — Lieutenant. General Horrocks
11th Hussars *(Armoured Cars) RAC*
73rd Anti-Tank Regiment, Royal Artillery
27th Light Anti-Aircraft Regiment, Royal Artillery
4th Survey Regiment, Royal Artillery
XXX Corps Troops Engineers, Royal Engineers
XXX Corps Signals, Royal Corps of Signals
3rd Casualty Clearing Station, 10th Casualty Clearing Station, RAMC

## 1st CANADIAN ARMY
*Lieutenant General Crerar*

| | |
|---|---|
| 1st Canadian Armoured Brigade | Transfered from italian front (03 1945) |
| 2nd Canadian Armoured Brigade | |

**I Canadian Corps et** — Transfered from italian front (03 1945)
**II Canadian Corps**

| | |
|---|---|
| 1st Canadian Infantry Division | Transfered from italian front (03 1945) |
| 2nd Canadian Infantry Division | |
| 3rd Canadian Infantry Division | |
| 4th Canadian Armoured Division | |
| 5th Canadian Armoured Division | Transfered from italian front (03 1945) |

## ALLIED FORMATIONS

1st Polish Armoured Division
1st Polish Parachute Brigade
Royal Netherlands Brigade (Princess Irene)
1st Belgian Brigade
Czech Armoured Brigade — *Transfered to the IIIrd US Army in April, after the siege of Dunkirk*

# 2. The Divisions

These form the main structure fighting of the British Army. These groups will be examined after a short introduction and a brief panorama of the arms and services.

## The division level

Operating within an Army Corps, where they were most frequently grouped as two Infantry divisions accompanied by an Armoured Division, these large groups form the High Command main fighting tool.

During the campaign, divisions could be transfered from one corps to another depending on the needs of the battle.

Each division in the line, roughly 16 000 men was supported by 25 000 men spread throughout the various support groups, army corps, army, lines of communication and maintenance areas.

This ensemble of 41 000 men was called the divisional level. 8 000 vehicles and miscellaneous machines (roughly one vehicle for 5 men.) were at its disposal.

Three types of divisions were committed in the North-West Europe campaign:

## Infantry Division

The organisation of this large group was based on three infantry brigades of three battalions each.

A large contingent of support services enabled the battle to be sustained over a long period.

## Armoured Division

As a striking force, the armoured division consisted of an armoured brigade of three tank regiments and a mechanised infantry battalion transported by half-tracks.

The main part of the accompanying infantry consisted of an infantry brigade of three battalions transported by lorries.

The Armoured Reconnaissance regiment, effectively a fourth tank regiment, enabled four seperate fighting groups of an armoured regiment and an infantry battalion to be constituted.

The real reconnaissance function was carried out by the Army Corps Reconnaissance Regiment or by the regimental reconnaissance troops.

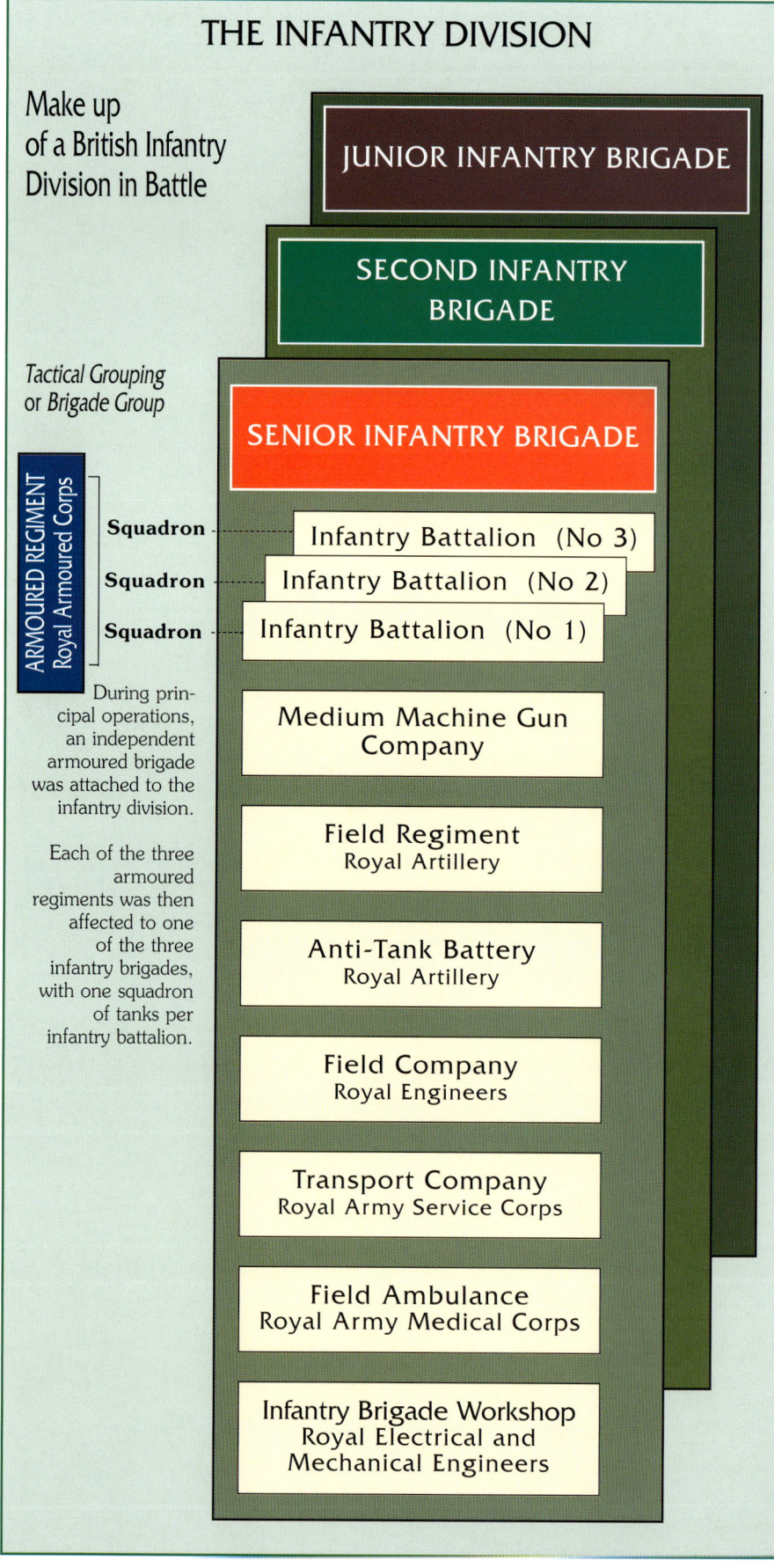

## Airborne Division

The Airborne division was organised principally in the same way as the infantry division with three brigades made up of three battalions each.

Two of these brigades were parachutists, and the third was made up of glider-borne infantry battalions.

Each brigade of the Airborne Division included support elements which were attached to it and which were either parachuted or air transported by glider. In general, two-thirds of the division could be transported by air.

The remainder and the heavy equipment came by sea or land.

The parachute regiments were entirely made up of volunteers.

# 3. The Infantry Divisions

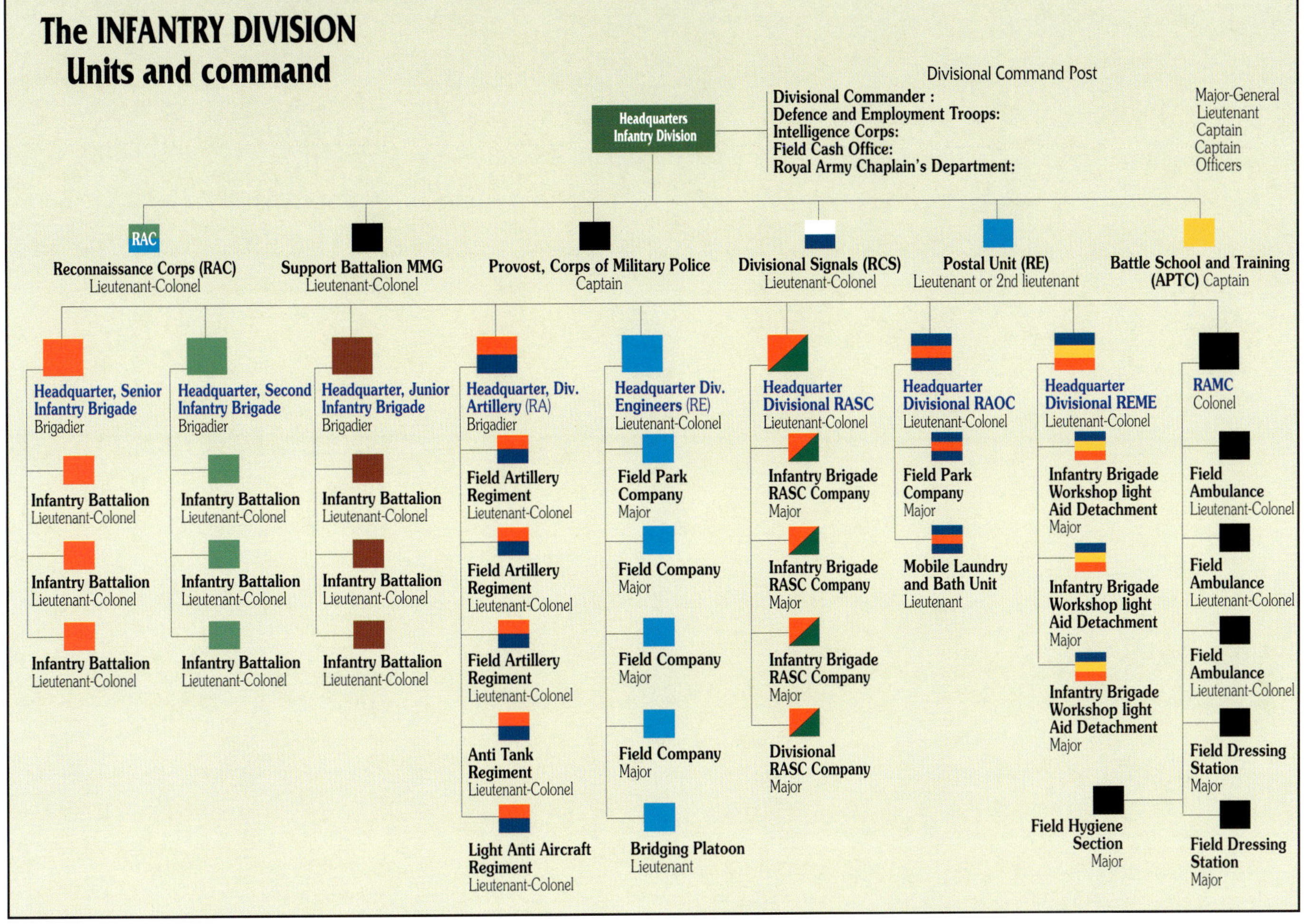

## The INFANTRY DIVISION
### Units and command

**Divisional Command Post**
- Divisional Commander: Major-General
- Defence and Employment Troops: Lieutenant
- Intelligence Corps: Captain
- Field Cash Office: Captain
- Royal Army Chaplain's Department: Officers

**Headquarters Infantry Division**

- **Reconnaissance Corps (RAC)** — Lieutenant-Colonel
- **Support Battalion MMG** — Lieutenant-Colonel
- **Provost, Corps of Military Police** — Captain
- **Divisional Signals (RCS)** — Lieutenant-Colonel
- **Postal Unit (RE)** — Lieutenant or 2nd lieutenant
- **Battle School and Training (APTC)** — Captain

**Headquarter, Senior Infantry Brigade** — Brigadier
- Infantry Battalion — Lieutenant-Colonel
- Infantry Battalion — Lieutenant-Colonel
- Infantry Battalion — Lieutenant-Colonel

**Headquarter, Second Infantry Brigade** — Brigadier
- Infantry Battalion — Lieutenant-Colonel
- Infantry Battalion — Lieutenant-Colonel
- Infantry Battalion — Lieutenant-Colonel

**Headquarter, Junior Infantry Brigade** — Brigadier
- Infantry Battalion — Lieutenant-Colonel
- Infantry Battalion — Lieutenant-Colonel
- Infantry Battalion — Lieutenant-Colonel

**Headquarter, Div. Artillery (RA)** — Brigadier
- Field Artillery Regiment — Lieutenant-Colonel
- Field Artillery Regiment — Lieutenant-Colonel
- Field Artillery Regiment — Lieutenant-Colonel
- Anti Tank Regiment — Lieutenant-Colonel
- Light Anti Aircraft Regiment — Lieutenant-Colonel

**Headquarter Div. Engineers (RE)** — Lieutenant-Colonel
- Field Park Company — Major
- Field Company — Major
- Field Company — Major
- Field Company — Major
- Bridging Platoon — Lieutenant

**Headquarter Divisional RASC** — Lieutenant-Colonel
- Infantry Brigade RASC Company — Major
- Infantry Brigade RASC Company — Major
- Infantry Brigade RASC Company — Major
- Divisional RASC Company — Major

**Headquarter Divisional RAOC** — Lieutenant-Colonel
- Field Park Company — Major
- Mobile Laundry and Bath Unit — Lieutenant

**Headquarter Divisional REME** — Lieutenant-Colonel
- Infantry Brigade Workshop light Aid Detachment — Major
- Infantry Brigade Workshop light Aid Detachment — Major
- Infantry Brigade Workshop light Aid Detachment — Major
- Field Hygiene Section — Major

**RAMC** — Colonel
- Field Ambulance — Lieutenant-Colonel
- Field Ambulance — Lieutenant-Colonel
- Field Ambulance — Lieutenant-Colonel
- Field Dressing Station — Major
- Field Dressing Station — Major

## INFANTRY DIVISION
### Armament and transport

Total Strength of the division: **18 347 officers and men.**

#### Armament

| | |
|---|---:|
| Pistols, revolvers | 1 011 |
| Rifles | 11 254 |
| Sten guns | 6 525 |
| Bren guns | 1 262 |
| Vickers machine guns | 40 |
| 2 in. mortars | 283 |
| 3 in. mortars | 60 |
| 4.2 in. mortars | 16 |
| PIATs | 436 |
| 20mm AA Cannon | 71 |
| 40mm cannon | 36 |
| 40mm self-propelled cannon | 18 |
| 25 pounder gun | 72 |
| 6 pounder anti-tank gun | 78 |
| 17 pounder anti-tank guns | 32 |

#### Vehicles and machines

| | |
|---|---:|
| Motor-bikes | 983 |
| Miscellaneous light vehicles, Jeeps | 495 |
| Armoured Cars | 31 |
| Scout-cars | 32 |
| Bren gun carriers, half-tracks | 595 |
| Ambulances | 52 |
| 15 cwt trucks | 881 |
| 3 ton trucks | 1 056 |
| Various tractors | 205 |
| Trailers | 226 |

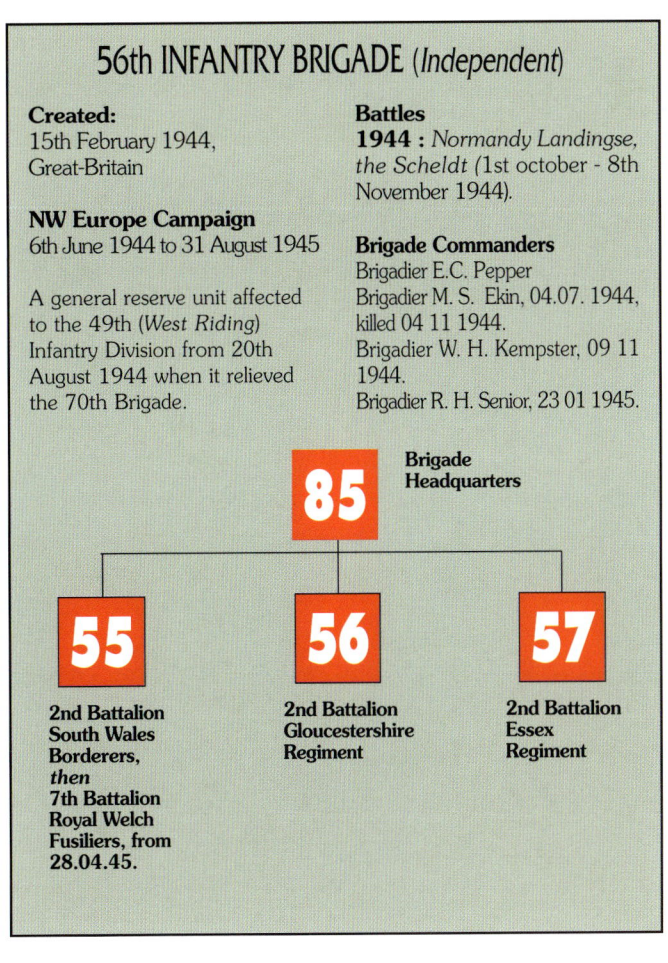

## 56th INFANTRY BRIGADE (*Independent*)

**Created:**
15th February 1944, Great-Britain

**NW Europe Campaign**
6th June 1944 to 31 August 1945

A general reserve unit affected to the 49th (*West Riding*) Infantry Division from 20th August 1944 when it relieved the 70th Brigade.

**Battles**
**1944:** *Normandy Landingse, the Scheldt* (1st october - 8th November 1944).

**Brigade Commanders**
Brigadier E.C. Pepper
Brigadier M. S. Ekin, 04.07.1944, killed 04 11 1944.
Brigadier W. H. Kempster, 09 11 1944.
Brigadier R. H. Senior, 23 01 1945.

**85** — Brigade Headquarters

- **55** — 2nd Battalion South Wales Borderers, then 7th Battalion Royal Welch Fusiliers, from 28.04.45.
- **56** — 2nd Battalion Gloucestershire Regiment
- **57** — 2nd Battalion Essex Regiment

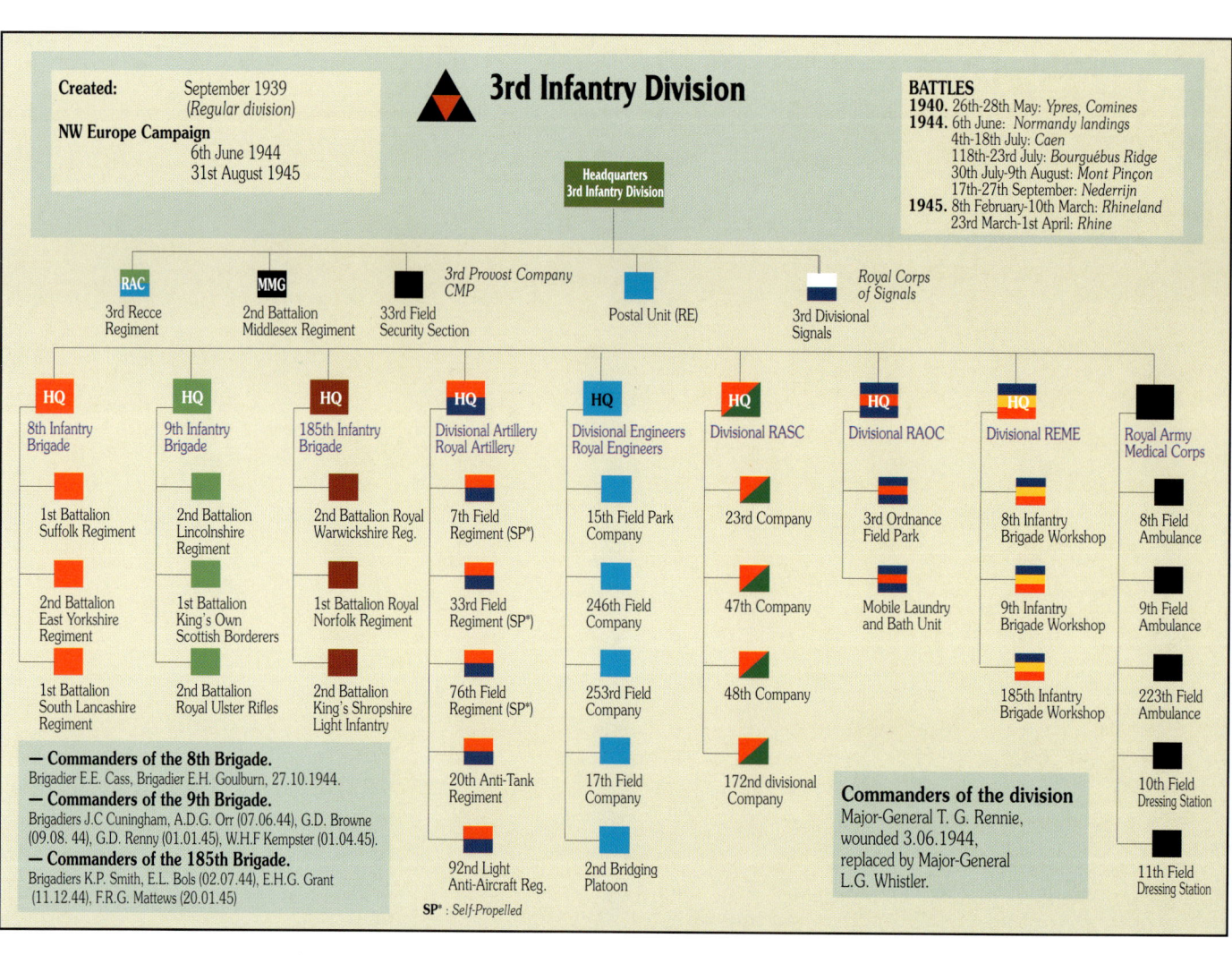

# 3rd Infantry Division

**Created:** September 1939 *(Regular division)*
**NW Europe Campaign**
6th June 1944
31st August 1945

**BATTLES**
**1940.** 26th-28th May: *Ypres, Comines*
**1944.** 6th June: *Normandy landings*
4th-18th July: *Caen*
118th-23rd July: *Bourguébus Ridge*
30th July-9th August: *Mont Pinçon*
17th-27th September: *Nederrijn*
**1945.** 8th February-10th March: *Rhineland*
23rd March-1st April: *Rhine*

**Headquarters 3rd Infantry Division**

- RAC — 3rd Recce Regiment
- MMG — 2nd Battalion Middlesex Regiment
- 3rd Provost Company CMP
- 33rd Field Security Section
- Postal Unit (RE)
- Royal Corps of Signals — 3rd Divisional Signals

### 8th Infantry Brigade
- 1st Battalion Suffolk Regiment
- 2nd Battalion East Yorkshire Regiment
- 1st Battalion South Lancashire Regiment

### 9th Infantry Brigade
- 2nd Battalion Lincolnshire Regiment
- 1st Battalion King's Own Scottish Borderers
- 2nd Battalion Royal Ulster Rifles

### 185th Infantry Brigade
- 2nd Battalion Royal Warwickshire Reg.
- 1st Battalion Royal Norfolk Regiment
- 2nd Battalion King's Shropshire Light Infantry

### Divisional Artillery Royal Artillery
- 7th Field Regiment (SP*)
- 33rd Field Regiment (SP*)
- 76th Field Regiment (SP*)
- 20th Anti-Tank Regiment
- 92nd Light Anti-Aircraft Reg.

### Divisional Engineers Royal Engineers
- 15th Field Park Company
- 246th Field Company
- 253rd Field Company
- 17th Field Company
- 2nd Bridging Platoon

### Divisional RASC
- 23rd Company
- 47th Company
- 48th Company
- 172nd divisional Company

### Divisional RAOC
- 3rd Ordnance Field Park
- Mobile Laundry and Bath Unit

### Divisional REME
- 8th Infantry Brigade Workshop
- 9th Infantry Brigade Workshop
- 185th Infantry Brigade Workshop

### Royal Army Medical Corps
- 8th Field Ambulance
- 9th Field Ambulance
- 223rd Field Ambulance
- 10th Field Dressing Station
- 11th Field Dressing Station

— **Commanders of the 8th Brigade.**
Brigadier E.E. Cass, Brigadier E.H. Goulburn, 27.10.1944.
— **Commanders of the 9th Brigade.**
Brigadiers J.C Cuningham, A.D.G. Orr (07.06.44), G.D. Browne (09.08. 44), G.D. Renny (01.01.45), W.H.F Kempster (01.04.45).
— **Commanders of the 185th Brigade.**
Brigadiers K.P. Smith, E.L. Bols (02.07.44), E.H.G. Grant (11.12.44), F.R.G. Mattews (20.01.45)

**Commanders of the division**
Major-General T. G. Rennie, wounded 3.06.1944, replaced by Major-General L.G. Whistler.

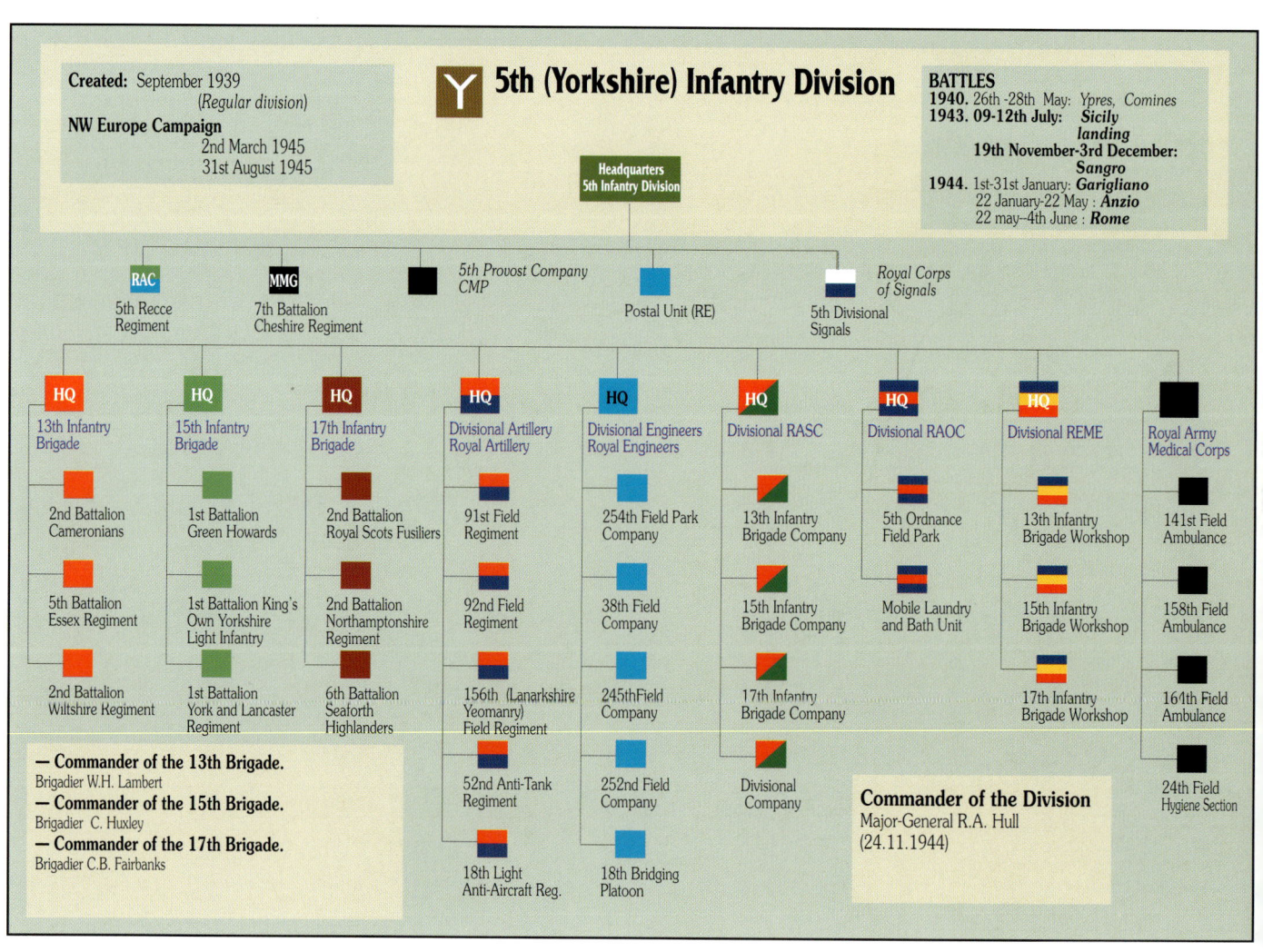

SP*: *Self-Propelled*

---

# 5th (Yorkshire) Infantry Division

**Created:** September 1939 *(Regular division)*
**NW Europe Campaign**
2nd March 1945
31st August 1945

**BATTLES**
**1940.** 26th-28th May: *Ypres, Comines*
**1943.** 09-12th July: *Sicily landing*
19th November-3rd December: *Sangro*
**1944.** 1st-31st January: *Garigliano*
22 January-22 May: *Anzio*
22 may-4th June: *Rome*

**Headquarters 5th Infantry Division**

- RAC — 5th Recce Regiment
- MMG — 7th Battalion Cheshire Regiment
- 5th Provost Company CMP
- Postal Unit (RE)
- Royal Corps of Signals — 5th Divisional Signals

### 13th Infantry Brigade
- 2nd Battalion Cameronians
- 5th Battalion Essex Regiment
- 2nd Battalion Wiltshire Regiment

### 15th Infantry Brigade
- 1st Battalion Green Howards
- 1st Battalion King's Own Yorkshire Light Infantry
- 1st Battalion York and Lancaster Regiment

### 17th Infantry Brigade
- 2nd Battalion Royal Scots Fusiliers
- 2nd Battalion Northamptonshire Regiment
- 6th Battalion Seaforth Highlanders

### Divisional Artillery Royal Artillery
- 91st Field Regiment
- 92nd Field Regiment
- 156th (Lanarkshire Yeomanry) Field Regiment
- 52nd Anti-Tank Regiment
- 18th Light Anti-Aircraft Reg.

### Divisional Engineers Royal Engineers
- 254th Field Park Company
- 38th Field Company
- 245th Field Company
- 252nd Field Company
- 18th Bridging Platoon

### Divisional RASC
- 13th Infantry Brigade Company
- 15th Infantry Brigade Company
- 17th Infantry Brigade Company
- Divisional Company

### Divisional RAOC
- 5th Ordnance Field Park
- Mobile Laundry and Bath Unit

### Divisional REME
- 13th Infantry Brigade Workshop
- 15th Infantry Brigade Workshop
- 17th Infantry Brigade Workshop

### Royal Army Medical Corps
- 141st Field Ambulance
- 158th Field Ambulance
- 164th Field Ambulance
- 24th Field Hygiene Section

— **Commander of the 13th Brigade.**
Brigadier W.H. Lambert.
— **Commander of the 15th Brigade.**
Brigadier C. Huxley.
— **Commander of the 17th Brigade.**
Brigadier C.B. Fairbanks.

**Commander of the Division**
Major-General R.A. Hull (24.11.1944)

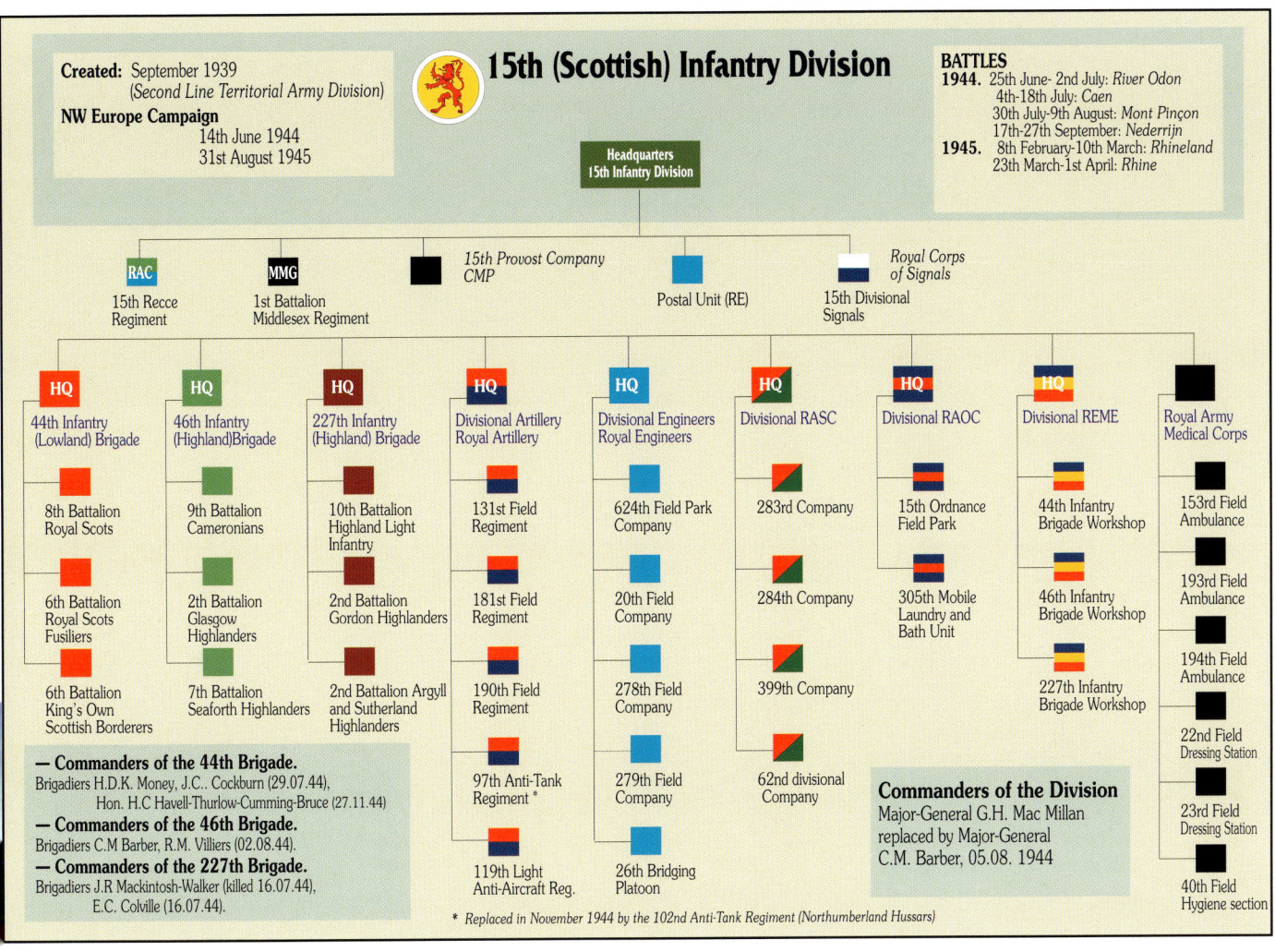

## 15th (Scottish) Infantry Division

**Created:** September 1939
*(Second Line Territorial Army Division)*

**NW Europe Campaign**
14th June 1944
31st August 1945

**BATTLES**
**1944.** 25th June- 2nd July: *River Odon*
4th-18th July: *Caen*
30th July-9th August: *Mont Pinçon*
17th-27th September: *Nederrijn*
**1945.** 8th February-10th March: *Rhineland*
23rd March-1st April: *Rhine*

**Headquarters 15th Infantry Division**

- 15th Recce Regiment (RAC)
- 1st Battalion Middlesex Regiment (MMG)
- 15th Provost Company CMP
- Postal Unit (RE)
- 15th Divisional Signals (Royal Corps of Signals)

### 44th Infantry (Lowland) Brigade
- 8th Battalion Royal Scots
- 6th Battalion Royal Scots Fusiliers
- 6th Battalion King's Own Scottish Borderers

### 46th Infantry (Highland) Brigade
- 9th Battalion Cameronians
- 2nd Battalion Glasgow Highlanders
- 7th Battalion Seaforth Highlanders

### 227th Infantry (Highland) Brigade
- 10th Battalion Highland Light Infantry
- 2nd Battalion Gordon Highlanders
- 2nd Battalion Argyll and Sutherland Highlanders

### Divisional Artillery Royal Artillery
- 131st Field Regiment
- 181st Field Regiment
- 190th Field Regiment
- 97th Anti-Tank Regiment *
- 119th Light Anti-Aircraft Reg.

### Divisional Engineers Royal Engineers
- 624th Field Park Company
- 20th Field Company
- 278th Field Company
- 279th Field Company
- 26th Bridging Platoon

### Divisional RASC
- 283rd Company
- 284th Company
- 399th Company
- 62nd divisional Company

### Divisional RAOC
- 15th Ordnance Field Park
- 305th Mobile Laundry and Bath Unit

### Divisional REME
- 44th Infantry Brigade Workshop
- 46th Infantry Brigade Workshop
- 227th Infantry Brigade Workshop

### Royal Army Medical Corps
- 153rd Field Ambulance
- 193rd Field Ambulance
- 194th Field Ambulance
- 22nd Field Dressing Station
- 23rd Field Dressing Station
- 40th Field Hygiene section

— **Commanders of the 44th Brigade.**
Brigadiers H.D.K. Money, J.C.. Cockburn (29.07.44),
Hon. H.C Havell-Thurlow-Cumming-Bruce (27.11.44)

— **Commanders of the 46th Brigade.**
Brigadiers C.M Barber, R.M. Villiers (02.08.44).

— **Commanders of the 227th Brigade.**
Brigadiers J.R Mackintosh-Walker (killed 16.07.44),
E.C. Colville (16.07.44).

**Commanders of the Division**
Major-General G.H. Mac Millan replaced by Major-General C.M. Barber, 05.08. 1944

* Replaced in November 1944 by the 102nd Anti-Tank Regiment (Northumberland Hussars)

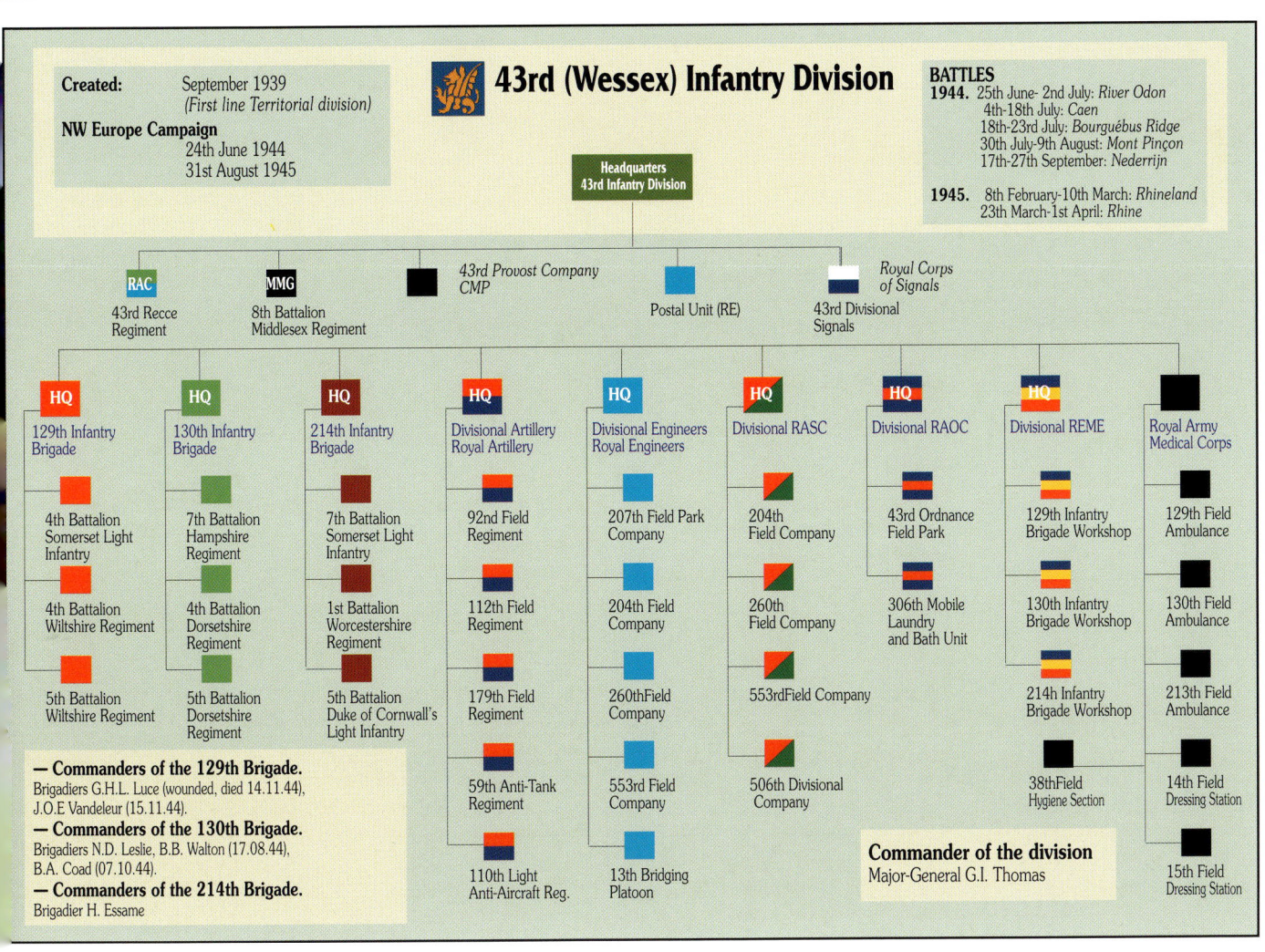

---

## 43rd (Wessex) Infantry Division

**Created:** September 1939
*(First line Territorial division)*

**NW Europe Campaign**
24th June 1944
31st August 1945

**BATTLES**
**1944.** 25th June- 2nd July: *River Odon*
4th-18th July: *Caen*
18th-23rd July: *Bourguébus Ridge*
30th July-9th August: *Mont Pinçon*
17th-27th September: *Nederrijn*
**1945.** 8th February-10th March: *Rhineland*
23rd March-1st April: *Rhine*

**Headquarters 43rd Infantry Division**

- 43rd Recce Regiment (RAC)
- 8th Battalion Middlesex Regiment (MMG)
- 43rd Provost Company CMP
- Postal Unit (RE)
- 43rd Divisional Signals (Royal Corps of Signals)

### 129th Infantry Brigade
- 4th Battalion Somerset Light Infantry
- 4th Battalion Wiltshire Regiment
- 5th Battalion Wiltshire Regiment

### 130th Infantry Brigade
- 7th Battalion Hampshire Regiment
- 4th Battalion Dorsetshire Regiment
- 5th Battalion Dorsetshire Regiment

### 214th Infantry Brigade
- 7th Battalion Somerset Light Infantry
- 1st Battalion Worcestershire Regiment
- 5th Battalion Duke of Cornwall's Light Infantry

### Divisional Artillery Royal Artillery
- 92nd Field Regiment
- 112th Field Regiment
- 179th Field Regiment
- 59th Anti-Tank Regiment
- 110th Light Anti-Aircraft Reg.

### Divisional Engineers Royal Engineers
- 207th Field Park Company
- 204th Field Company
- 260th Field Company
- 553rd Field Company
- 13th Bridging Platoon

### Divisional RASC
- 204th Field Company
- 260th Field Company
- 553rd Field Company
- 506th Divisional Company

### Divisional RAOC
- 43rd Ordnance Field Park
- 306th Mobile Laundry and Bath Unit

### Divisional REME
- 129th Infantry Brigade Workshop
- 130th Infantry Brigade Workshop
- 214th Infantry Brigade Workshop
- 38th Field Hygiene Section

### Royal Army Medical Corps
- 129th Field Ambulance
- 130th Field Ambulance
- 213th Field Ambulance
- 14th Field Dressing Station
- 15th Field Dressing Station

— **Commanders of the 129th Brigade.**
Brigadiers G.H.L. Luce (wounded, died 14.11.44),
J.O.E Vandeleur (15.11.44).

— **Commanders of the 130th Brigade.**
Brigadiers N.D. Leslie, B.B. Walton (17.08.44),
B.A. Coad (07.10.44).

— **Commanders of the 214th Brigade.**
Brigadier H. Essame.

**Commander of the division**
Major-General G.I. Thomas

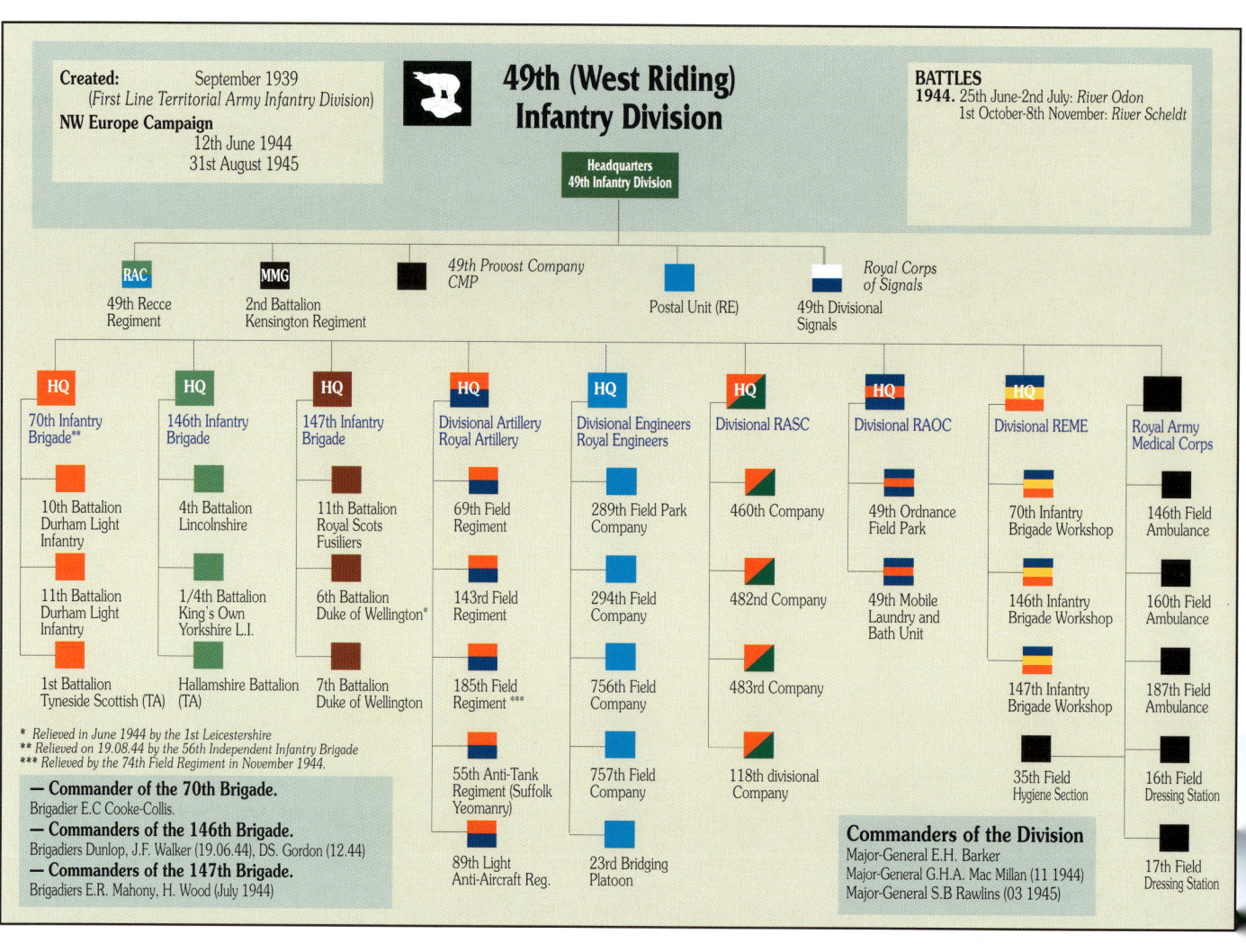

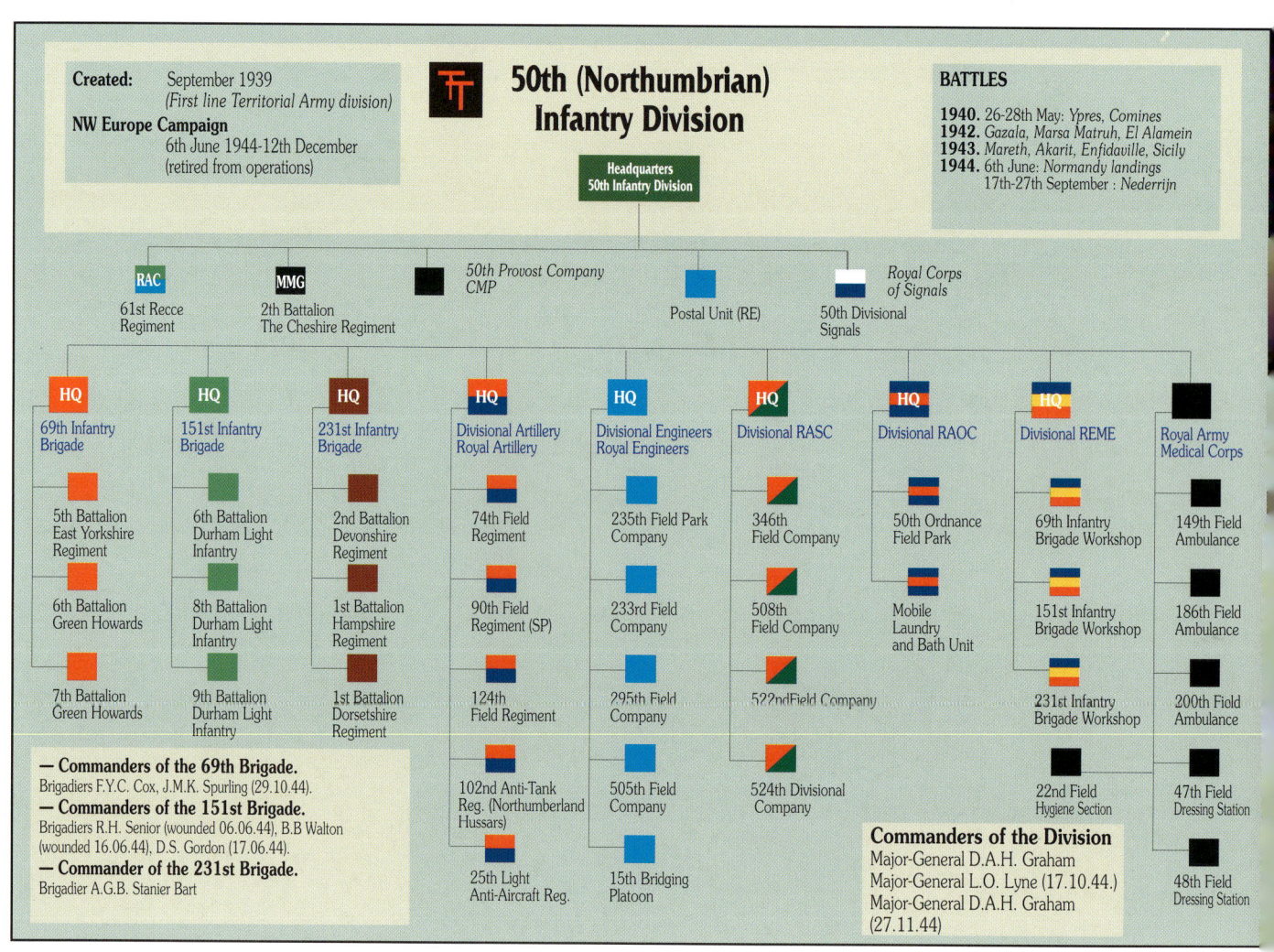

## 49th (West Riding) Infantry Division

**Created:** September 1939
*(First Line Territorial Army Infantry Division)*
**NW Europe Campaign**
12th June 1944
31st August 1945

**BATTLES**
**1944.** 25th June-2nd July: *River Odon*
1st October-8th November: *River Scheldt*

**Headquarters 49th Infantry Division**

- 49th Recce Regiment (RAC)
- 2nd Battalion Kensington Regiment (MMG)
- 49th Provost Company CMP
- Postal Unit (RE)
- 49th Divisional Signals (Royal Corps of Signals)

### 70th Infantry Brigade**
- 10th Battalion Durham Light Infantry
- 11th Battalion Durham Light Infantry
- 1st Battalion Tyneside Scottish (TA)

### 146th Infantry Brigade
- 4th Battalion Lincolnshire
- 1/4th Battalion King's Own Yorkshire L.I.
- Hallamshire Battalion (TA)

### 147th Infantry Brigade
- 11th Battalion Royal Scots Fusiliers
- 6th Battalion Duke of Wellington*
- 7th Battalion Duke of Wellington

### Divisional Artillery Royal Artillery
- 69th Field Regiment
- 143rd Field Regiment
- 185th Field Regiment ***
- 55th Anti-Tank Regiment (Suffolk Yeomanry)
- 89th Light Anti-Aircraft Reg.

### Divisional Engineers Royal Engineers
- 289th Field Park Company
- 294th Field Company
- 756th Field Company
- 757th Field Company
- 23rd Bridging Platoon

### Divisional RASC
- 460th Company
- 482nd Company
- 483rd Company
- 118th divisional Company

### Divisional RAOC
- 49th Ordnance Field Park
- 49th Mobile Laundry and Bath Unit

### Divisional REME
- 70th Infantry Brigade Workshop
- 146th Infantry Brigade Workshop
- 147th Infantry Brigade Workshop
- 35th Field Hygiene Section

### Royal Army Medical Corps
- 146th Field Ambulance
- 160th Field Ambulance
- 187th Field Ambulance
- 16th Field Dressing Station
- 17th Field Dressing Station

\* Relieved in June 1944 by the 1st Leicestershire
\** Relieved on 19.08.44 by the 56th Independent Infantry Brigade
\*** Relieved by the 74th Field Regiment in November 1944.

— **Commander of the 70th Brigade.**
Brigadier E.C Cooke-Collis.
— **Commanders of the 146th Brigade.**
Brigadiers Dunlop, J.F. Walker (19.06.44), D.S. Gordon (12.44)
— **Commanders of the 147th Brigade.**
Brigadiers E.R. Mahony, H. Wood (July 1944)

**Commanders of the Division**
Major-General E.H. Barker
Major-General G.H.A. Mac Millan (11 1944)
Major-General S.B Rawlins (03 1945)

---

## 50th (Northumbrian) Infantry Division

**Created:** September 1939
*(First line Territorial Army division)*
**NW Europe Campaign**
6th June 1944-12th December
*(retired from operations)*

**BATTLES**
**1940.** 26-28th May: *Ypres, Comines*
**1942.** *Gazala, Marsa Matruh, El Alamein*
**1943.** *Mareth, Akarit, Enfidaville, Sicily*
**1944.** 6th June: *Normandy landings*
17th-27th September : *Nederrijn*

**Headquarters 50th Infantry Division**

- 61st Recce Regiment (RAC)
- 2th Battalion The Cheshire Regiment (MMG)
- 50th Provost Company CMP
- Postal Unit (RE)
- 50th Divisional Signals (Royal Corps of Signals)

### 69th Infantry Brigade
- 5th Battalion East Yorkshire Regiment
- 6th Battalion Green Howards
- 7th Battalion Green Howards

### 151st Infantry Brigade
- 6th Battalion Durham Light Infantry
- 8th Battalion Durham Light Infantry
- 9th Battalion Durham Light Infantry

### 231st Infantry Brigade
- 2nd Battalion Devonshire Regiment
- 1st Battalion Hampshire Regiment
- 1st Battalion Dorsetshire Regiment

### Divisional Artillery Royal Artillery
- 74th Field Regiment
- 90th Field Regiment (SP)
- 124th Field Regiment
- 102nd Anti-Tank Reg. (Northumberland Hussars)
- 25th Light Anti-Aircraft Reg.

### Divisional Engineers Royal Engineers
- 235th Field Park Company
- 233rd Field Company
- 295th Field Company
- 505th Field Company
- 15th Bridging Platoon

### Divisional RASC
- 346th Field Company
- 508th Field Company
- 522nd Field Company
- 524th Divisional Company

### Divisional RAOC
- 50th Ordnance Field Park
- Mobile Laundry and Bath Unit

### Divisional REME
- 69th Infantry Brigade Workshop
- 151st Infantry Brigade Workshop
- 231st Infantry Brigade Workshop
- 22nd Field Hygiene Section

### Royal Army Medical Corps
- 149th Field Ambulance
- 186th Field Ambulance
- 200th Field Ambulance
- 47th Field Dressing Station
- 48th Field Dressing Station

— **Commanders of the 69th Brigade.**
Brigadiers F.Y.C. Cox, J.M.K. Spurling (29.10.44).
— **Commanders of the 151st Brigade.**
Brigadiers R.H. Senior (wounded 06.06.44), B.B Walton (wounded 16.06.44), D.S. Gordon (17.06.44).
— **Commander of the 231st Brigade.**
Brigadier A.G.B. Stanier Bart

**Commanders of the Division**
Major-General D.A.H. Graham
Major-General L.O. Lyne (17.10.44.)
Major-General D.A.H. Graham (27.11.44)

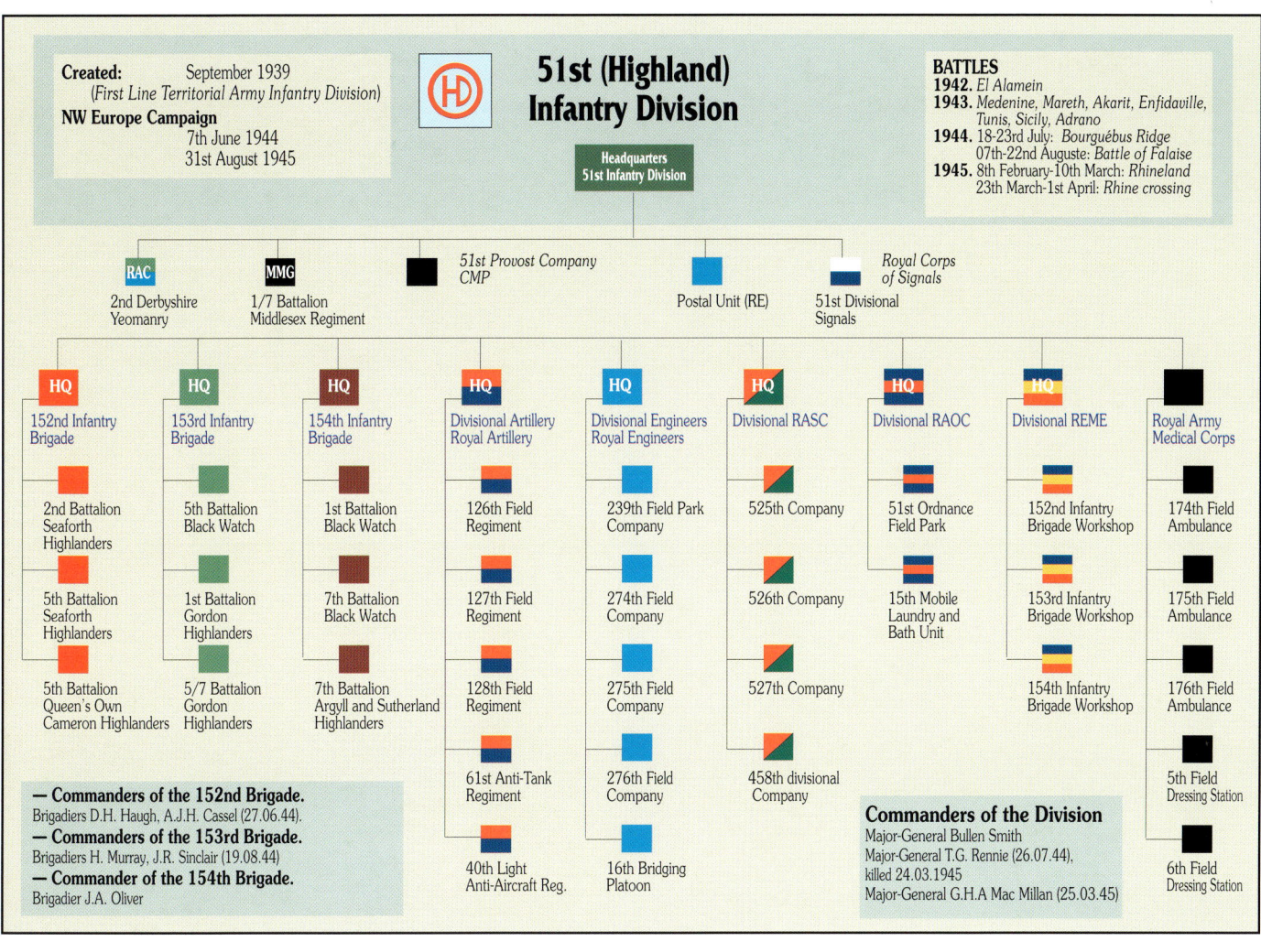

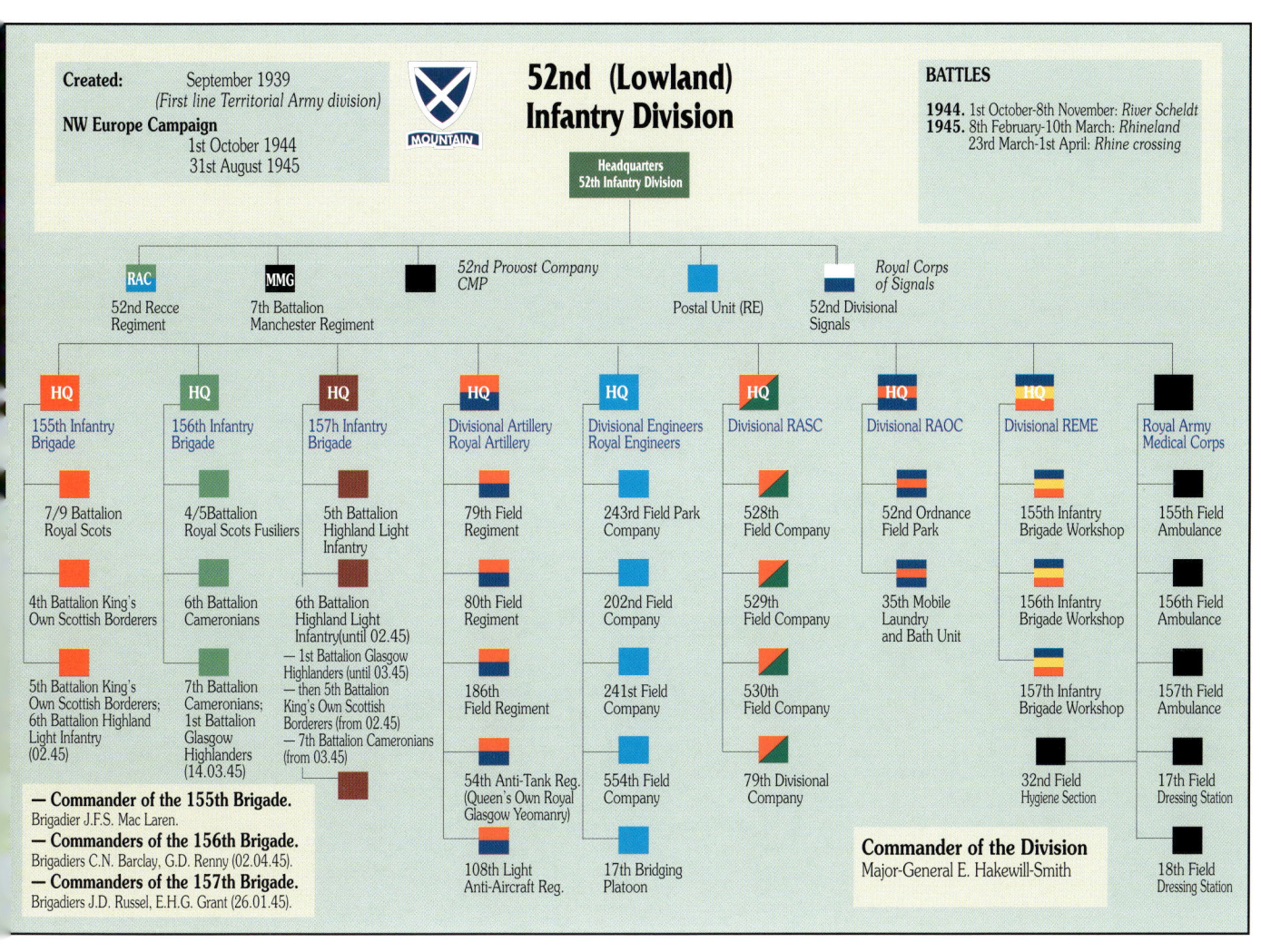

# 51st (Highland) Infantry Division

**Created:** September 1939
(First Line Territorial Army Infantry Division)
**NW Europe Campaign**
7th June 1944
31st August 1945

**BATTLES**
- **1942.** El Alamein
- **1943.** Medenine, Mareth, Akarit, Enfidaville, Tunis, Sicily, Adrano
- **1944.** 18-23rd July: Bourguébus Ridge
  07th-22nd Auguste: Battle of Falaise
- **1945.** 8th February-10th March: Rhineland
  23rd March-1st April: Rhine crossing

**Headquarters 51st Infantry Division**

- **RAC** — 2nd Derbyshire Yeomanry
- **MMG** — 1/7 Battalion Middlesex Regiment
- 51st Provost Company CMP
- Postal Unit (RE)
- Royal Corps of Signals — 51st Divisional Signals

### 152nd Infantry Brigade
- 2nd Battalion Seaforth Highlanders
- 5th Battalion Seaforth Highlanders
- 5th Battalion Queen's Own Cameron Highlanders

### 153rd Infantry Brigade
- 5th Battalion Black Watch
- 1st Battalion Gordon Highlanders
- 5/7 Battalion Gordon Highlanders

### 154th Infantry Brigade
- 1st Battalion Black Watch
- 7th Battalion Black Watch
- 7th Battalion Argyll and Sutherland Highlanders

### Divisional Artillery Royal Artillery
- 126th Field Regiment
- 127th Field Regiment
- 128th Field Regiment
- 61st Anti-Tank Regiment
- 40th Light Anti-Aircraft Reg.

### Divisional Engineers Royal Engineers
- 239th Field Park Company
- 274th Field Company
- 275th Field Company
- 276th Field Company
- 16th Bridging Platoon

### Divisional RASC
- 525th Company
- 526th Company
- 527th Company
- 458th divisional Company

### Divisional RAOC
- 51st Ordnance Field Park
- 15th Mobile Laundry and Bath Unit

### Divisional REME
- 152nd Infantry Brigade Workshop
- 153rd Infantry Brigade Workshop
- 154th Infantry Brigade Workshop

### Royal Army Medical Corps
- 174th Field Ambulance
- 175th Field Ambulance
- 176th Field Ambulance
- 5th Field Dressing Station
- 6th Field Dressing Station

— **Commanders of the 152nd Brigade.**
Brigadiers D.H. Haugh, A.J.H. Cassel (27.06.44).
— **Commanders of the 153rd Brigade.**
Brigadiers H. Murray, J.R. Sinclair (19.08.44)
— **Commander of the 154th Brigade.**
Brigadier J.A. Oliver

**Commanders of the Division**
Major-General Bullen Smith
Major-General T.G. Rennie (26.07.44), killed 24.03.1945
Major-General G.H.A Mac Millan (25.03.45)

---

# 52nd (Lowland) Infantry Division

**Created:** September 1939
(First line Territorial Army division)
**NW Europe Campaign**
1st October 1944
31st August 1945

**BATTLES**
- **1944.** 1st October-8th November: River Scheldt
- **1945.** 8th February-10th March: Rhineland
  23rd March-1st April: Rhine crossing

**Headquarters 52th Infantry Division**

- **RAC** — 52nd Recce Regiment
- **MMG** — 7th Battalion Manchester Regiment
- 52nd Provost Company CMP
- Postal Unit (RE)
- Royal Corps of Signals — 52nd Divisional Signals

### 155th Infantry Brigade
- 7/9 Battalion Royal Scots
- 4th Battalion King's Own Scottish Borderers
- 5th Battalion King's Own Scottish Borderers; 6th Battalion Highland Light Infantry (02.45)

### 156th Infantry Brigade
- 4/5 Battalion Royal Scots Fusiliers
- 6th Battalion Cameronians
- 7th Battalion Cameronians; 1st Battalion Glasgow Highlanders (14.03.45)

### 157h Infantry Brigade
- 5th Battalion Highland Light Infantry
- 6th Battalion Highland Light Infantry (until 02.45)
  — 1st Battalion Glasgow Highlanders (until 03.45)
  — then 5th Battalion King's Own Scottish Borderers (from 02.45)
  — 7th Battalion Cameronians (from 03.45)

### Divisional Artillery Royal Artillery
- 79th Field Regiment
- 80th Field Regiment
- 186th Field Regiment
- 54th Anti-Tank Reg. (Queen's Own Royal Glasgow Yeomanry)
- 108th Light Anti-Aircraft Reg.

### Divisional Engineers Royal Engineers
- 243rd Field Park Company
- 202nd Field Company
- 241st Field Company
- 554th Field Company
- 17th Bridging Platoon

### Divisional RASC
- 528th Field Company
- 529th Field Company
- 530th Field Company
- 79th Divisional Company

### Divisional RAOC
- 52nd Ordnance Field Park
- 35th Mobile Laundry and Bath Unit

### Divisional REME
- 155th Infantry Brigade Workshop
- 156th Infantry Brigade Workshop
- 157th Infantry Brigade Workshop
- 32nd Field Hygiene Section

### Royal Army Medical Corps
- 155th Field Ambulance
- 156th Field Ambulance
- 157th Field Ambulance
- 17th Field Dressing Station
- 18th Field Dressing Station

— **Commander of the 155th Brigade.**
Brigadier J.F.S. Mac Laren.
— **Commanders of the 156th Brigade.**
Brigadiers C.N. Barclay, G.D. Renny (02.04.45).
— **Commanders of the 157th Brigade.**
Brigadiers J.D. Russel, E.H.G. Grant (26.01.45).

**Commander of the Division**
Major-General E. Hakewill-Smith

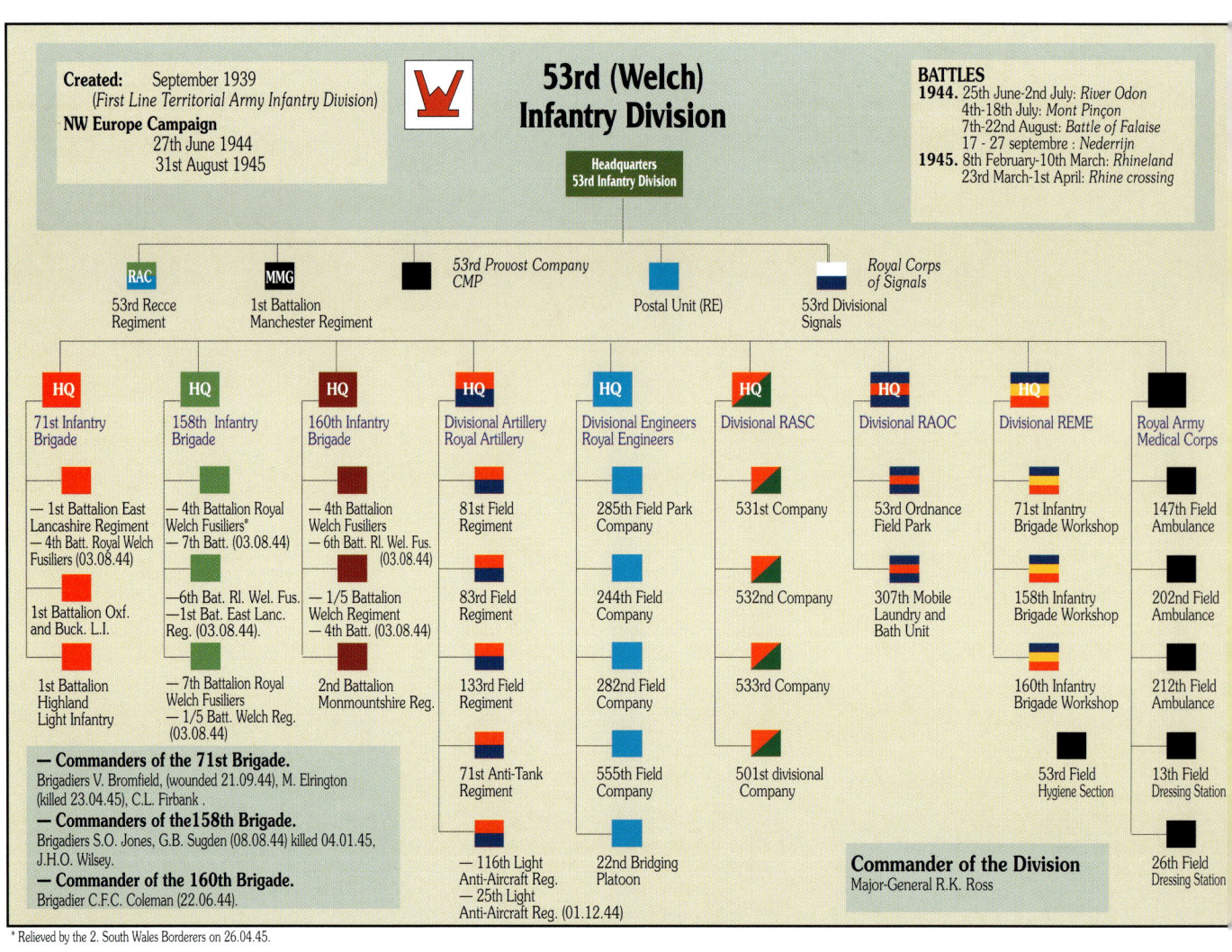

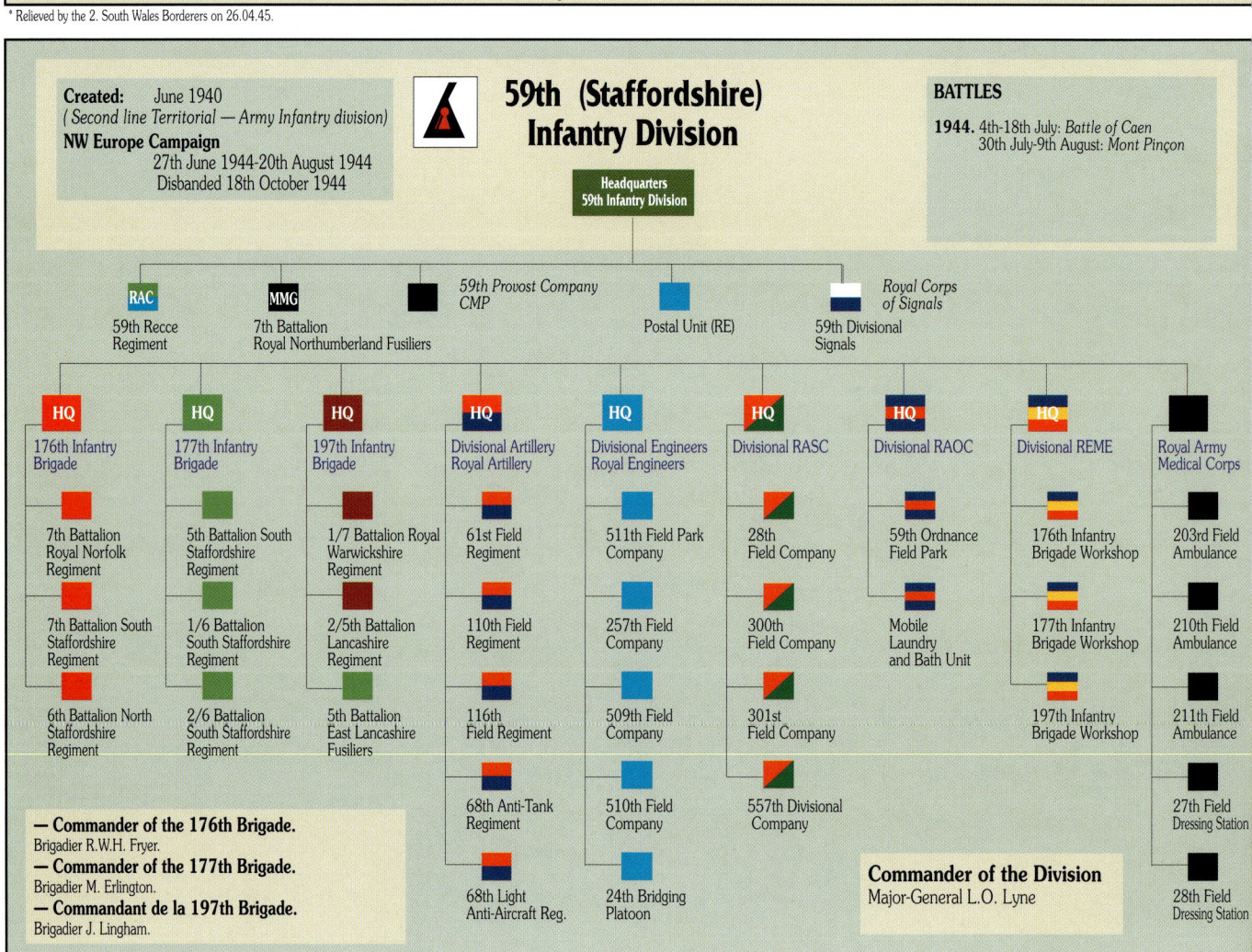

## 53rd (Welch) Infantry Division

**Created:** September 1939
(First Line Territorial Army Infantry Division)
**NW Europe Campaign**
27th June 1944
31st August 1945

**Headquarters 53rd Infantry Division**

**BATTLES**
**1944.** 25th June-2nd July: *River Odon*
4th-18th July: *Mont Pinçon*
7th-22nd August: *Battle of Falaise*
17 - 27 septembre : *Nederrijn*
**1945.** 8th February-10th March: *Rhineland*
23rd March-1st April: *Rhine crossing*

- **RAC** — 53rd Recce Regiment
- **MMG** — 1st Battalion Manchester Regiment
- 53rd Provost Company CMP
- Postal Unit (RE)
- *Royal Corps of Signals* — 53rd Divisional Signals

### 71st Infantry Brigade (HQ)
- 1st Battalion East Lancashire Regiment
- 4th Batt. Royal Welch Fusiliers (03.08.44)
- 1st Battalion Oxf. and Buck. L.I.
- 1st Battalion Highland Light Infantry

### 158th Infantry Brigade (HQ)
- 4th Battalion Royal Welch Fusiliers* — 7th Batt. (03.08.44)
- 6th Bat. Rl. Wel. Fus. — 1st Bat. East Lanc. Reg. (03.08.44).
- 7th Battalion Royal Welch Fusiliers — 1/5 Batt. Welch Reg. (03.08.44)

### 160th Infantry Brigade (HQ)
- 4th Battalion Welch Fusiliers — 6th Batt. Rl. Wel. Fus. (03.08.44)
- 1/5 Battalion Welch Regiment — 4th Batt. (03.08.44)
- 2nd Battalion Monmouthshire Reg.

### Divisional Artillery Royal Artillery (HQ)
- 81st Field Regiment
- 83rd Field Regiment
- 133rd Field Regiment
- 71st Anti-Tank Regiment
- 116th Light Anti-Aircraft Reg.
- 25th Light Anti-Aircraft Reg. (01.12.44)

### Divisional Engineers Royal Engineers (HQ)
- 285th Field Park Company
- 244th Field Company
- 282nd Field Company
- 555th Field Company
- 22nd Bridging Platoon

### Divisional RASC (HQ)
- 531st Company
- 532nd Company
- 533rd Company
- 501st divisional Company

### Divisional RAOC (HQ)
- 53rd Ordnance Field Park
- 307th Mobile Laundry and Bath Unit
- 53rd Field Hygiene Section

### Divisional REME (HQ)
- 71st Infantry Brigade Workshop
- 158th Infantry Brigade Workshop
- 160th Infantry Brigade Workshop

### Royal Army Medical Corps
- 147th Field Ambulance
- 202nd Field Ambulance
- 212th Field Ambulance
- 13th Field Dressing Station
- 26th Field Dressing Station

**Commander of the Division**
Major-General R.K. Ross

— **Commanders of the 71st Brigade.**
Brigadiers V. Bromfield, (wounded 21.09.44), M. Elrington (killed 23.04.45), C.L. Firbank.
— **Commanders of the 158th Brigade.**
Brigadiers S.O. Jones, G.B. Sugden (08.08.44) killed 04.01.45, J.H.O. Wilsey.
— **Commander of the 160th Brigade.**
Brigadier C.F.C. Coleman (22.06.44).

* Relieved by the 2. South Wales Borderers on 26.04.45.

---

## 59th (Staffordshire) Infantry Division

**Created:** June 1940
(Second line Territorial — Army Infantry division)
**NW Europe Campaign**
27th June 1944-20th August 1944
Disbanded 18th October 1944

**Headquarters 59th Infantry Division**

**BATTLES**
**1944.** 4th-18th July: *Battle of Caen*
30th July-9th August: *Mont Pinçon*

- **RAC** — 59th Recce Regiment
- **MMG** — 7th Battalion Royal Northumberland Fusiliers
- 59th Provost Company CMP
- Postal Unit (RE)
- *Royal Corps of Signals* — 59th Divisional Signals

### 176th Infantry Brigade (HQ)
- 7th Battalion Royal Norfolk Regiment
- 7th Battalion South Staffordshire Regiment
- 6th Battalion North Staffordshire Regiment

### 177th Infantry Brigade (HQ)
- 5th Battalion South Staffordshire Regiment
- 1/6 Battalion South Staffordshire Regiment
- 2/6 Battalion South Staffordshire Regiment

### 197th Infantry Brigade (HQ)
- 1/7 Battalion Royal Warwickshire Regiment
- 2/5 Battalion Lancashire Regiment
- 5th Battalion East Lancashire Fusiliers

### Divisional Artillery Royal Artillery (HQ)
- 61st Field Regiment
- 110th Field Regiment
- 116th Field Regiment
- 68th Anti-Tank Regiment
- 68th Light Anti-Aircraft Reg.

### Divisional Engineers Royal Engineers (HQ)
- 511th Field Park Company
- 257th Field Company
- 509th Field Company
- 510th Field Company
- 24th Bridging Platoon

### Divisional RASC (HQ)
- 28th Field Company
- 300th Field Company
- 301st Field Company
- 557th Divisional Company

### Divisional RAOC (HQ)
- 59th Ordnance Field Park
- Mobile Laundry and Bath Unit

### Divisional REME (HQ)
- 176th Infantry Brigade Workshop
- 177th Infantry Brigade Workshop
- 197th Infantry Brigade Workshop

### Royal Army Medical Corps
- 203rd Field Ambulance
- 210th Field Ambulance
- 211th Field Ambulance
- 27th Field Dressing Station
- 28th Field Dressing Station

**Commander of the Division**
Major-General L.O. Lyne

— **Commander of the 176th Brigade.**
Brigadier R.W.H. Fryer.
— **Commander of the 177th Brigade.**
Brigadier M. Erlington.
— **Commandant de la 197th Brigade.**
Brigadier J. Lingham.

18

# 4. The Armoured Divisions

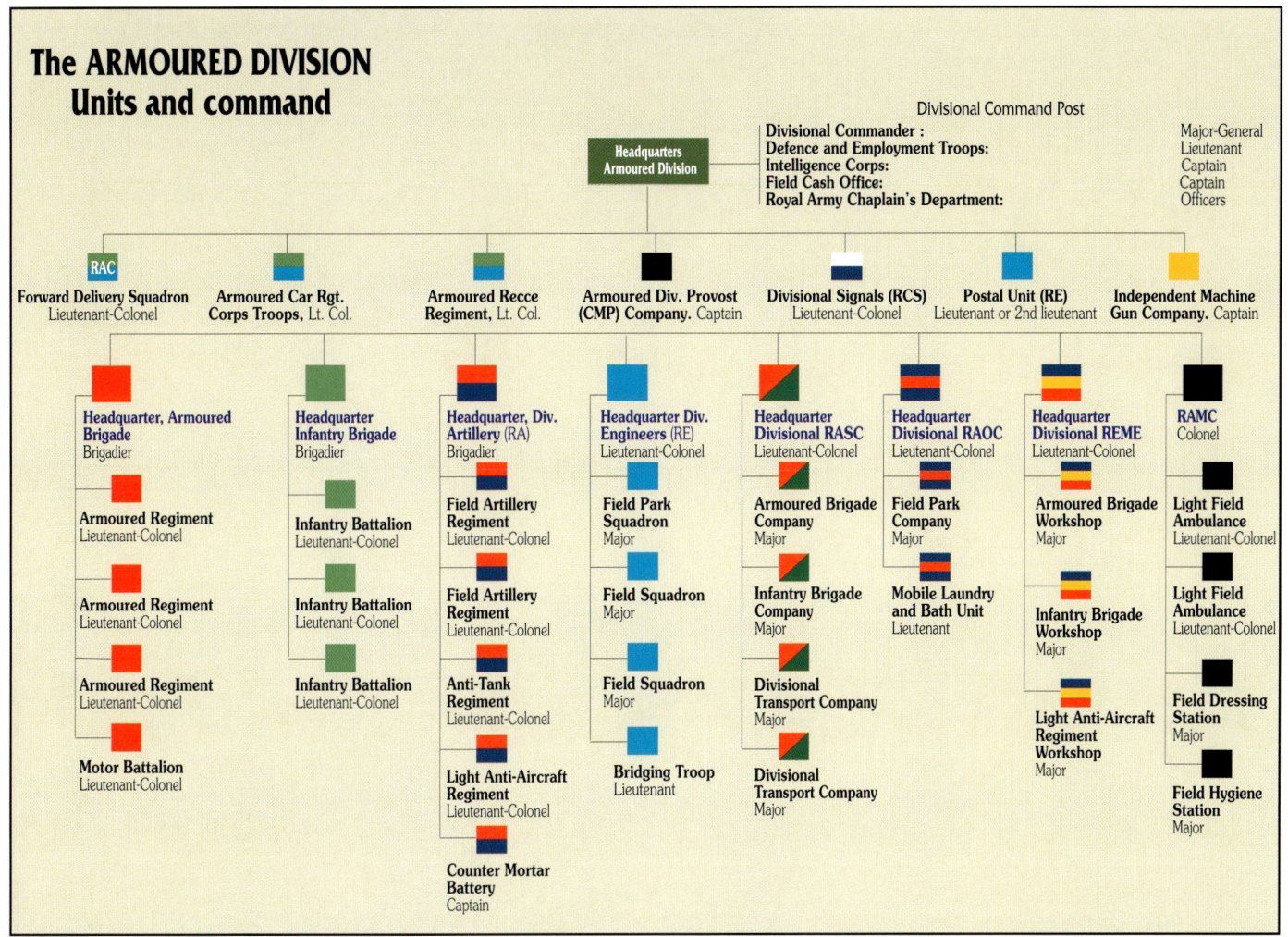

## ARMOURED DIVISION
### Armament and transport

Total division strength: **14 964 officers and men.**

### Armament

| | |
|---|---:|
| **Pistols, revolvers** | 2 324 |
| **Rifles** | 6 689 |
| **Sten guns** | 6 204 |
| **Bren guns** | 1 376 |
| **Vickers machine guns** | 22 |
| **2 in. mortars** | 132 |
| **3 in. mortars** | 24 |
| **4.2 in. mortars** | 4 |
| **PIATs** | 302 |
| **20mm AA cannon** | 87 |
| **40mm AA cannon** | 36 |
| **40mm AA cannon** (on tank) | 18 |
| **25 pounder gun** | 24 |
| **25 pounder self-propelled** | 24 |
| **6 pounder anti-tank gun** antichars | 30 |
| **17 pounder anti-tank gun** | 24 |
| **17 pounder anti-tank gun** (self-propelled) US - M10 | 24 |

### Vehicles and machines

| | |
|---|---:|
| **Motor-bikes** | 853 |
| **Miscellaneous light vehicles, Jeeps** | 390 |
| **Scout-Cars** | 87 |
| **Bren gun carriers, Half-Tracks** | 261 |
| **Ambulances** | 36 |
| **15 cwt Trucks** | 789 |
| **3 Ton Trucks.** | 1 309 |
| **Various tractors** | 130 |

### Vehicles (cont.)

| | |
|---|---:|
| **Various trailers** | 219 |
| **Armoured Command vehicles** | 19 |
| **Recovery vehicles** | 14 |
| **Ambulances** | 36 |

### TANKS

| | |
|---|---:|
| **Battle tanks** (*Cruisers*) [1] | 246 |
| **Anti-Aircraft tanks** | 27 |
| **Stuart light tanks** | 63 |
| **Forward observation tanks** | 27 |
| **Bridging tanks** | 3 |

### 1. Battle tanks, utilisation

**Cromwell tanks**
Used by the Armoured Reconnaissance Regiments of the Armoured Division and all the armoured regimenst of the *7th Armoured Division*.

**Sherman tanks**
Used by the armoured regiments of the Guards Armoured Division and the 11th Armoured Division.

**Sherman "Firefly" tanks**
In theory one Firefly per Troop, including the Armoured Regiments of the *7th Armoured Division*.

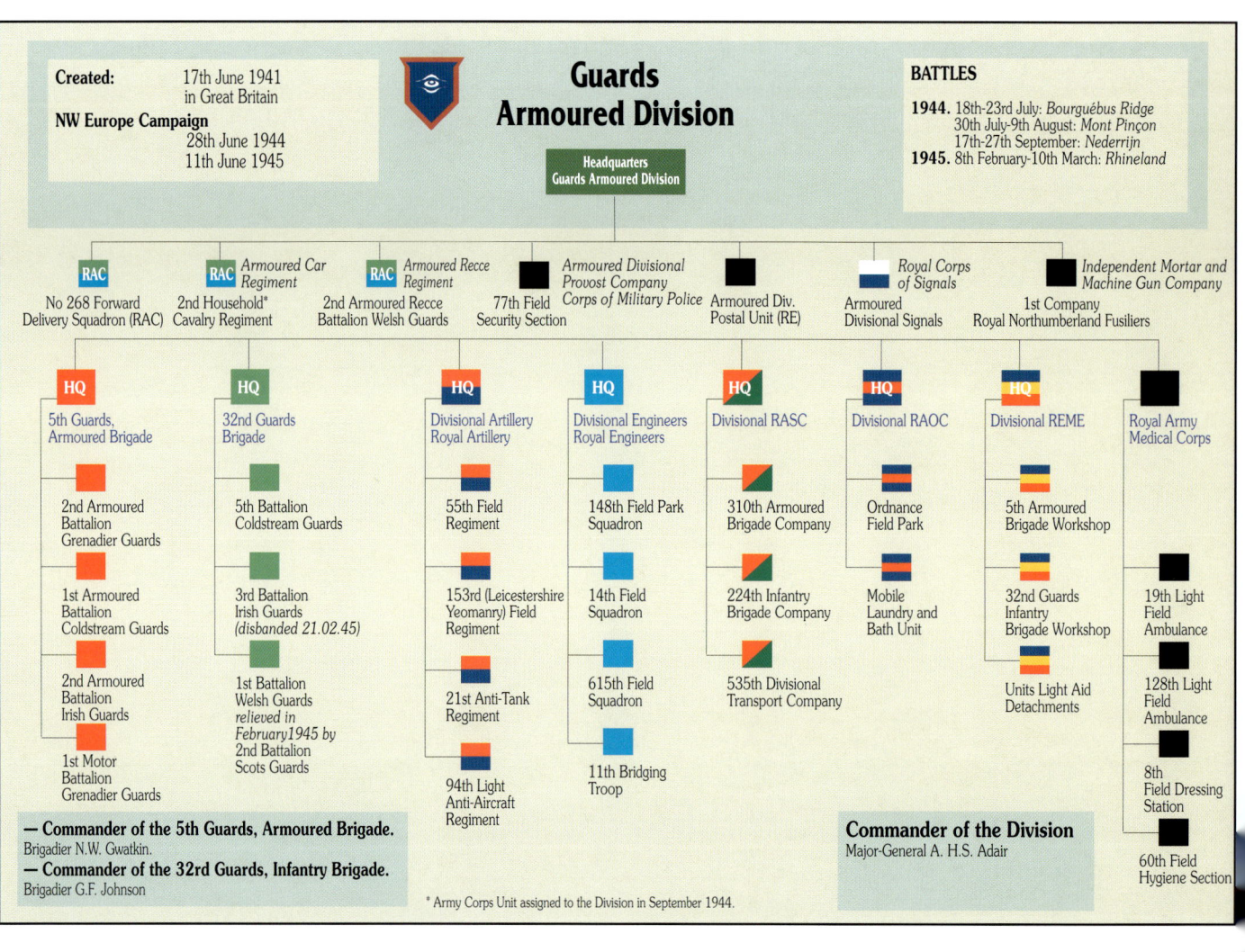

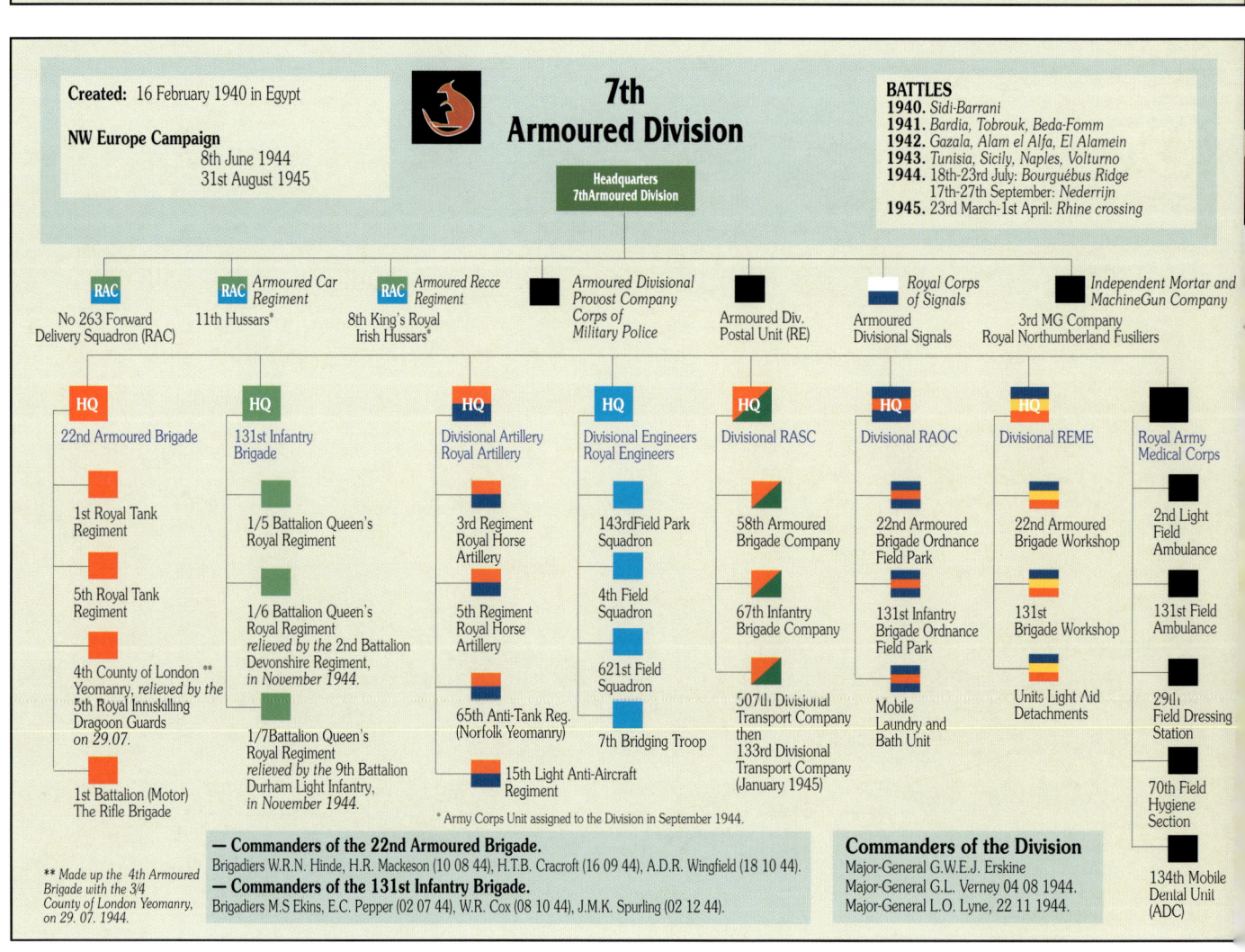

# Guards Armoured Division

**Created:** 17th June 1941 in Great Britain

**NW Europe Campaign**
28th June 1944
11th June 1945

**BATTLES**
**1944.** 18th-23rd July: *Bourguébus Ridge*
30th July-9th August: *Mont Pinçon*
17th-27th September: *Nederrijn*
**1945.** 8th February-10th March: *Rhineland*

**Headquarters Guards Armoured Division**

- **RAC** — No 268 Forward Delivery Squadron (RAC)
- **RAC** *Armoured Car Regiment* — 2nd Household* Cavalry Regiment
- **RAC** *Armoured Recce Regiment* — 2nd Armoured Recce Battalion Welsh Guards
- 77th Field Security Section
- *Armoured Divisional Provost Company Corps of Military Police*
- Armoured Div. Postal Unit (RE)
- *Royal Corps of Signals* — Armoured Divisional Signals
- *Independent Mortar and Machine Gun Company* — 1st Company Royal Northumberland Fusiliers

### 5th Guards, Armoured Brigade (HQ)
- 2nd Armoured Battalion Grenadier Guards
- 1st Armoured Battalion Coldstream Guards
- 2nd Armoured Battalion Irish Guards
- 1st Motor Battalion Grenadier Guards

### 32nd Guards Brigade (HQ)
- 5th Battalion Coldstream Guards
- 3rd Battalion Irish Guards *(disbanded 21.02.45)*
- 1st Battalion Welsh Guards *relieved in February 1945 by 2nd Battalion Scots Guards*

### Divisional Artillery Royal Artillery (HQ)
- 55th Field Regiment
- 153rd (Leicestershire Yeomanry) Field Regiment
- 21st Anti-Tank Regiment
- 94th Light Anti-Aircraft Regiment

### Divisional Engineers Royal Engineers (HQ)
- 148th Field Park Squadron
- 14th Field Squadron
- 615th Field Squadron
- 11th Bridging Troop

### Divisional RASC (HQ)
- 310th Armoured Brigade Company
- 224th Infantry Brigade Company
- 535th Divisional Transport Company

### Divisional RAOC (HQ)
- Ordnance Field Park
- Mobile Laundry and Bath Unit

### Divisional REME (HQ)
- 5th Armoured Brigade Workshop
- 32nd Guards Infantry Brigade Workshop
- Units Light Aid Detachments

### Royal Army Medical Corps
- 19th Light Field Ambulance
- 128th Light Field Ambulance
- 8th Field Dressing Station
- 60th Field Hygiene Section

— **Commander of the 5th Guards, Armoured Brigade.** Brigadier N.W. Gwatkin.
— **Commander of the 32nd Guards, Infantry Brigade.** Brigadier G.F. Johnson.

**Commander of the Division**
Major-General A. H.S. Adair

*Army Corps Unit assigned to the Division in September 1944.

---

# 7th Armoured Division

**Created:** 16 February 1940 in Egypt

**NW Europe Campaign**
8th June 1944
31st August 1945

**BATTLES**
**1940.** *Sidi-Barrani*
**1941.** *Bardia, Tobrouk, Beda-Fomm*
**1942.** *Gazala, Alam el Alfa, El Alamein*
**1943.** *Tunisia, Sicily, Naples, Volturno*
**1944.** 18th-23rd July: *Bourguébus Ridge*
17th-27th September: *Nederrijn*
**1945.** 23rd March-1st April: *Rhine crossing*

**Headquarters 7th Armoured Division**

- **RAC** — No 263 Forward Delivery Squadron (RAC)
- **RAC** *Armoured Car Regiment* — 11th Hussars*
- **RAC** *Armoured Recce Regiment* — 8th King's Royal Irish Hussars*
- *Armoured Divisional Provost Company Corps of Military Police*
- Armoured Div. Postal Unit (RE)
- *Royal Corps of Signals* — Armoured Divisional Signals
- *Independent Mortar and MachineGun Company* — 3rd MG Company Royal Northumberland Fusiliers

### 22nd Armoured Brigade (HQ)
- 1st Royal Tank Regiment
- 5th Royal Tank Regiment
- 4th County of London** Yeomanry, *relieved by the 5th Royal Inniskilling Dragoon Guards on 29.07.*
- 1st Battalion (Motor) The Rifle Brigade

### 131st Infantry Brigade (HQ)
- 1/5 Battalion Queen's Royal Regiment
- 1/6 Battalion Queen's Royal Regiment *relieved by the 2nd Battalion Devonshire Regiment, in November 1944.*
- 1/7 Battalion Queen's Royal Regiment *relieved by the 9th Battalion Durham Light Infantry, in November 1944.*

### Divisional Artillery Royal Artillery (HQ)
- 3rd Regiment Royal Horse Artillery
- 5th Regiment Royal Horse Artillery
- 65th Anti-Tank Reg. (Norfolk Yeomanry)
- 15th Light Anti-Aircraft Regiment

### Divisional Engineers Royal Engineers (HQ)
- 143rd Field Park Squadron
- 4th Field Squadron
- 621st Field Squadron
- 7th Bridging Troop

### Divisional RASC (HQ)
- 58th Armoured Brigade Company
- 67th Infantry Brigade Company
- 507th Divisional Transport Company then 133rd Divisional Transport Company (January 1945)

### Divisional RAOC (HQ)
- 22nd Armoured Brigade Ordnance Field Park
- 131st Infantry Brigade Ordnance Field Park
- Mobile Laundry and Bath Unit

### Divisional REME (HQ)
- 22nd Armoured Brigade Workshop
- 131st Brigade Workshop
- Units Light Aid Detachments

### Royal Army Medical Corps
- 2nd Light Field Ambulance
- 131st Field Ambulance
- 29th Field Dressing Station
- 70th Field Hygiene Section
- 134th Mobile Dental Unit (ADC)

** Made up the 4th Armoured Brigade with the 3/4 County of London Yeomanry, on 29.07.1944.

— **Commanders of the 22nd Armoured Brigade.** Brigadiers W.R.N. Hinde, H.R. Mackeson (10 08 44), H.T.B. Cracroft (16 09 44), A.D.R. Wingfield (18 10 44).
— **Commanders of the 131st Infantry Brigade.** Brigadiers M.S Ekins, E.C. Pepper (02 07 44), W.R. Cox (08 10 44), J.M.K. Spurling (02 12 44).

**Commanders of the Division**
Major-General G.W.E.J. Erskine
Major-General G.L. Verney 04 08 1944.
Major-General L.O. Lyne, 22 11 1944.

*Army Corps Unit assigned to the Division in September 1944.

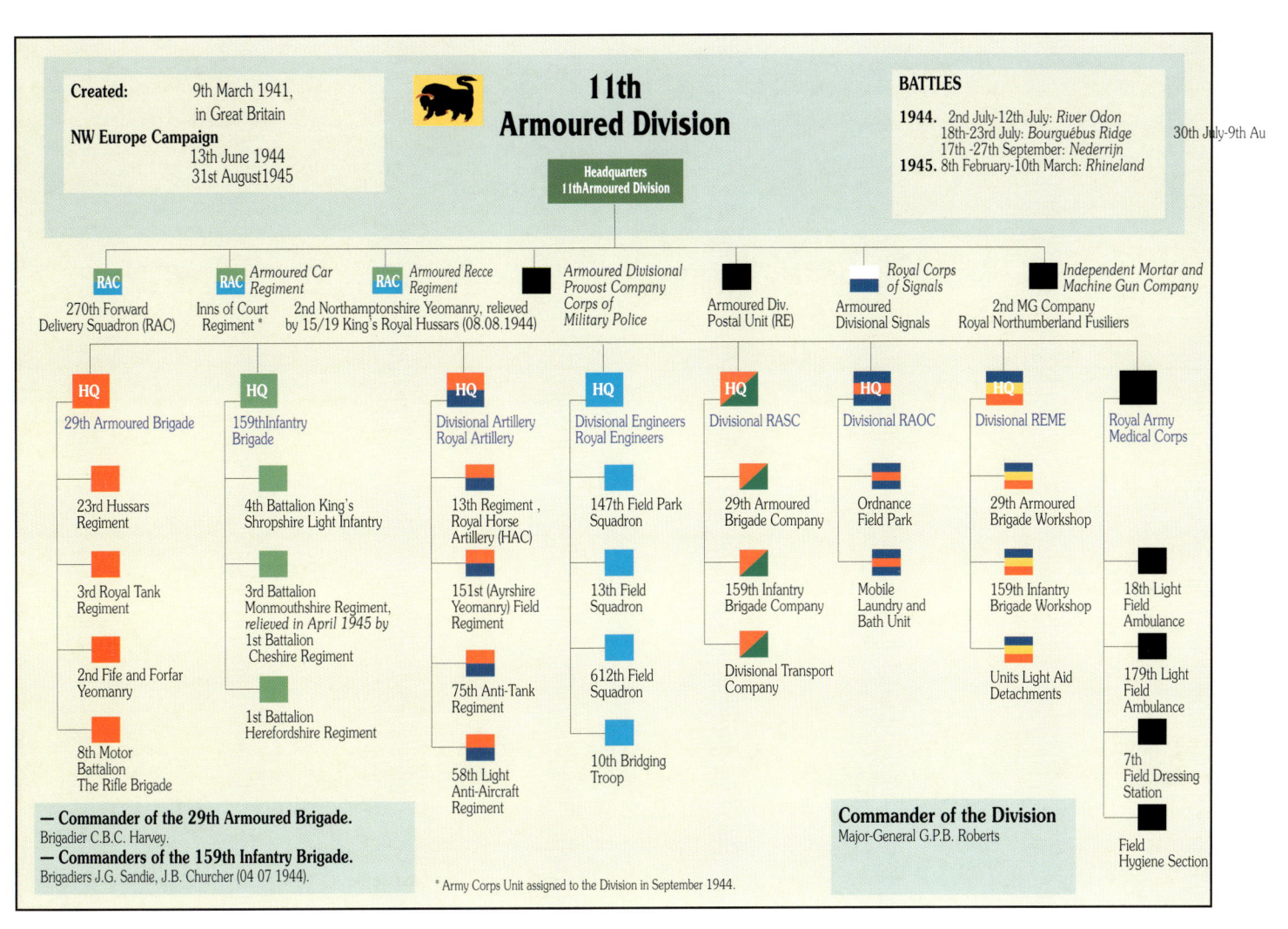

# 11th Armoured Division

**Created:** 9th March 1941, in Great Britain
**NW Europe Campaign** 13th June 1944 – 31st August 1945

**BATTLES**
**1944.** 2nd July-12th July: *River Odon*
18th-23rd July: *Bourguébus Ridge*  30th July-9th Au[g]
17th -27th September: *Nederrijn*
**1945.** 8th February-10th March: *Rhineland*

**Headquarters 11th Armoured Division**

- 270th Forward Delivery Squadron (RAC)
- *Armoured Car Regiment* — Inns of Court Regiment *
- *Armoured Recce Regiment* — 2nd Northamptonshire Yeomanry, relieved by 15/19 King's Royal Hussars (08.08.1944)
- Armoured Divisional Provost Company Corps of Military Police
- Armoured Div. Postal Unit (RE)
- *Royal Corps of Signals* — Armoured Divisional Signals
- *Independent Mortar and Machine Gun Company* — 2nd MG Company Royal Northumberland Fusiliers

**HQ 29th Armoured Brigade**
- 23rd Hussars Regiment
- 3rd Royal Tank Regiment
- 2nd Fife and Forfar Yeomanry
- 8th Motor Battalion The Rifle Brigade

**HQ 159th Infantry Brigade**
- 4th Battalion King's Shropshire Light Infantry
- 3rd Battalion Monmouthshire Regiment, *relieved in April 1945 by 1st Battalion Cheshire Regiment*
- 1st Battalion Herefordshire Regiment

**HQ Divisional Artillery Royal Artillery**
- 13th Regiment, Royal Horse Artillery (HAC)
- 151st (Ayrshire Yeomanry) Field Regiment
- 75th Anti-Tank Regiment
- 58th Light Anti-Aircraft Regiment

**HQ Divisional Engineers Royal Engineers**
- 147th Field Park Squadron
- 13th Field Squadron
- 612th Field Squadron
- 10th Bridging Troop

**HQ Divisional RASC**
- 29th Armoured Brigade Company
- 159th Infantry Brigade Company
- Divisional Transport Company

**HQ Divisional RAOC**
- Ordnance Field Park
- Mobile Laundry and Bath Unit

**HQ Divisional REME**
- 29th Armoured Brigade Workshop
- 159th Infantry Brigade Workshop
- Units Light Aid Detachments

**Royal Army Medical Corps**
- 18th Light Field Ambulance
- 179th Light Field Ambulance
- 7th Field Dressing Station
- Field Hygiene Section

— **Commander of the 29th Armoured Brigade.** Brigadier C.B.C. Harvey.
— **Commanders of the 159th Infantry Brigade.** Brigadiers J.G. Sandie, J.B. Churcher (04 07 1944).

**Commander of the Division** Major-General G.P.B. Roberts

* Army Corps Unit assigned to the Division in September 1944.

---

17th July 1944, three Sherman Flail tanks of the 79th Armoured Division moving towards Ecoville, near the Caen-Cabourg road. The unit insignia can be clearly distinguished painted on the left of the tool box. Although nearly all mines had been destroyed by the massive bombardment which preceded Operation Goodwood, these machines were still indispensible.
These three tanks belong to the 1st Lothians and Border Horse Yeomanry; See the organogram of the 79th Armoured Division on the next page.
*(IWM)*

# 5. 79th Armoured Division

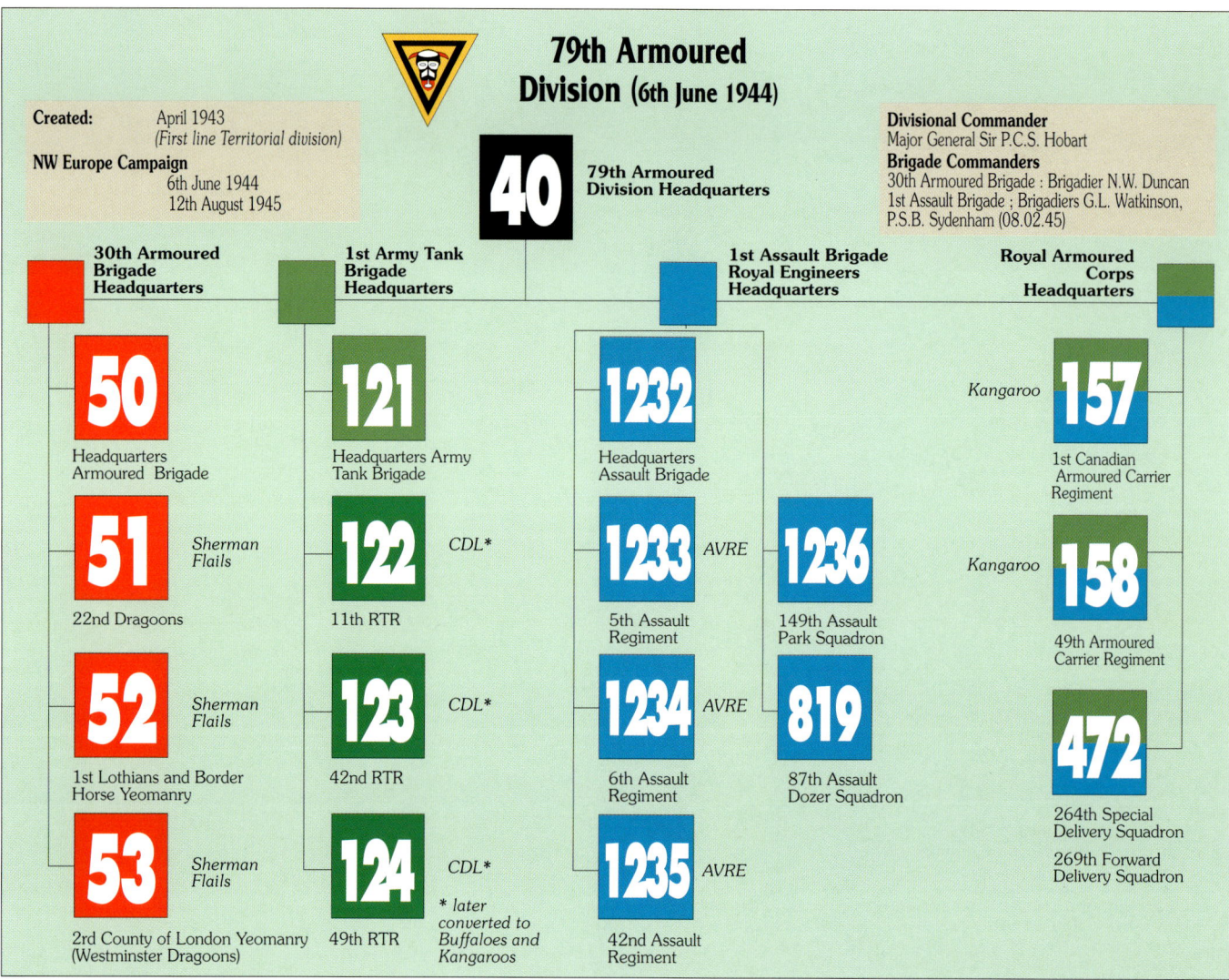

## The 79th Armoured Division

The 79th Armoured Division was not slated to be engaged as a division in its own right

Organised as a tactical formation, it had special machines intended to support the infantry and armoured divisions at its disposal.

During the NW Europe Campaign, the division was placed under the direct command of the 21st Army Group which spread its elements out according to the demands of the various operations.

Several modifications took place during the course of the campaign especially the disbanding of the 1st Tank Brigade in November 1944 and the incorporation of the 31st and 33rd Tank Brigades in November 1944 and January 1945.

The 79th Armoured Division didn't have its own infantry or artillery; the support units consisted of the following:

- **5 companies** from the Royal Corps of Signals
- **2 companies** from the Royal Army Service Corps
- **2 ambulances** from the Royal Army Medical Corps
- **4 companies** from the Royal Army Ordnance Corps pool
- **10 light workshops** from the Royal Electrical and Mechanical Engineers.

## Principal Material used by the 79th Armoured Division

| BASIC MATERIAL | NAME | CONVERSION |
|---|---|---|
| Sel-Propelled US M7 or **Ram** (Canada) | Kangaroo | Armament removed. Transformed into a personnel carrier |
| Churchill | Crocodile | Hatch machine gun replaced by flame thrower. |
| Sherman | Crab or Flail | Rotating drum mounted on the front equipped with chains caused mines to explode. |
| Churchill | AVRE (Armoured Vehicle Royal Engineers) d'obstacles. | — 75 mm replaced by 290 mm bomb-lauching mortar. — Carrying faggots for crossing obstacles — Carrying Bridging elements |
| Sherman | Duplex-Drive (DD) | Addition of folding canvas hull and two propellers to make it amphibian. |
| Grant | Canal Defence Light (CDL) | replacement of the turret by a powerfull search light for night fighting |
| LVT «Buffalo» (Landing Craft Vehicle) | | American made amphibious tracked vehicle used in Holland for crossing the Rhine |

# 6. The Airborne Divisions

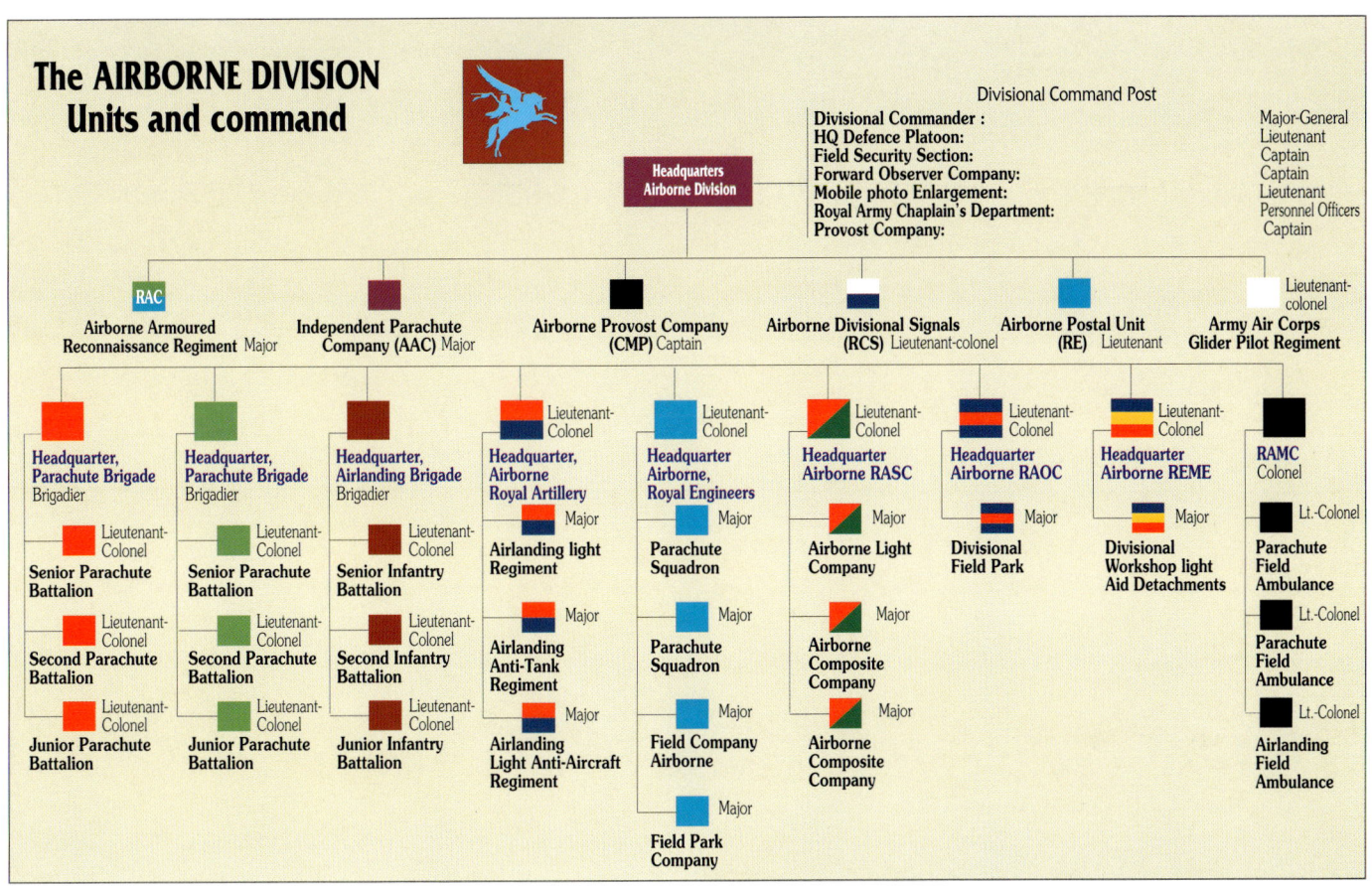

*Below*
5th June 1944. Parachutists ready to get into the planes that are going to drop them over Normandy in a few hours' time. *(IWM)*

## AIRBORNE DIVISION
### Armament and transport

Total division strength : **12 416 officers and men.**

### Armament

| | |
|---|---:|
| Pistols, revolvers | 2 942 |
| Rifles | 7 171 |
| Sten guns (Airborne) Mk V | 6 504 |
| Bren guns | 966 |
| Vickers machine guns | 46 |
| 2 in. mortars | 474 |
| 3 in. mortars | 56 |
| 4.2 in. mortars | 5 |
| PIATs | 392 |
| No 2 Flame throwers | 38 |
| 20mm AA cannon | 23 |
| 75mm Pack Howitzer (USA) | 27 |
| 6 pounder anti-tank gun | 84 |
| 17 pounder anti-tank guns | 16 |

### Vehicles and machines

| | |
|---|---:|
| Bicycles | 1 907 |
| Folding bicycles | 1 362 |
| Light motor-bikes | 529 |
| Motor-bikes (individual) | 704 |
| Miscellaneous light vehicles, Jeeps | 1 044 |
| Bren gun carriers | 25 |
| Ambulances | 24 |
| 15 cwt trucks | 129 |
| 3 Ton trucks | 438 |
| Various tractors | 26 |
| Various trailers | 935 |
| Trolleys (light infantry trailers) | 211 |

### Tanks (6th Airborne)

| | |
|---|---:|
| Light tanks *(Tetrarch)* replaced in July 1944 by **Cromwell cruisers tanks** | 11 |

## 1st Airborne Division

**Created:** November 1941
**NW Europe Campaign**
17th-29th September 1944
Destroyed at Arnhem, reformed in Great Britain, took part in the disarming of German soldiers in Norway, May 1945.

**BATTLES**
**1943.** North Africa, Sicily, Italy
**1944.** 17th-27th September: Arnhem

**Headquarters 1st Airborne Division**
- HQ Defence Platoon
- 1st Forward Observation Unit (RA)

*1st Airborne Armoured Recce Regiment*
1st Airlanding Reconnaissance Squadron (RAC)

*Army Air Corps*
21st Independent Parachute Company (Pathfinders),

89th Field Security Section (Intelligence Corps)
Divisional Provost (CMP) Company

*Airborne Divisional Signals*
1st Airborne Division Signals Element

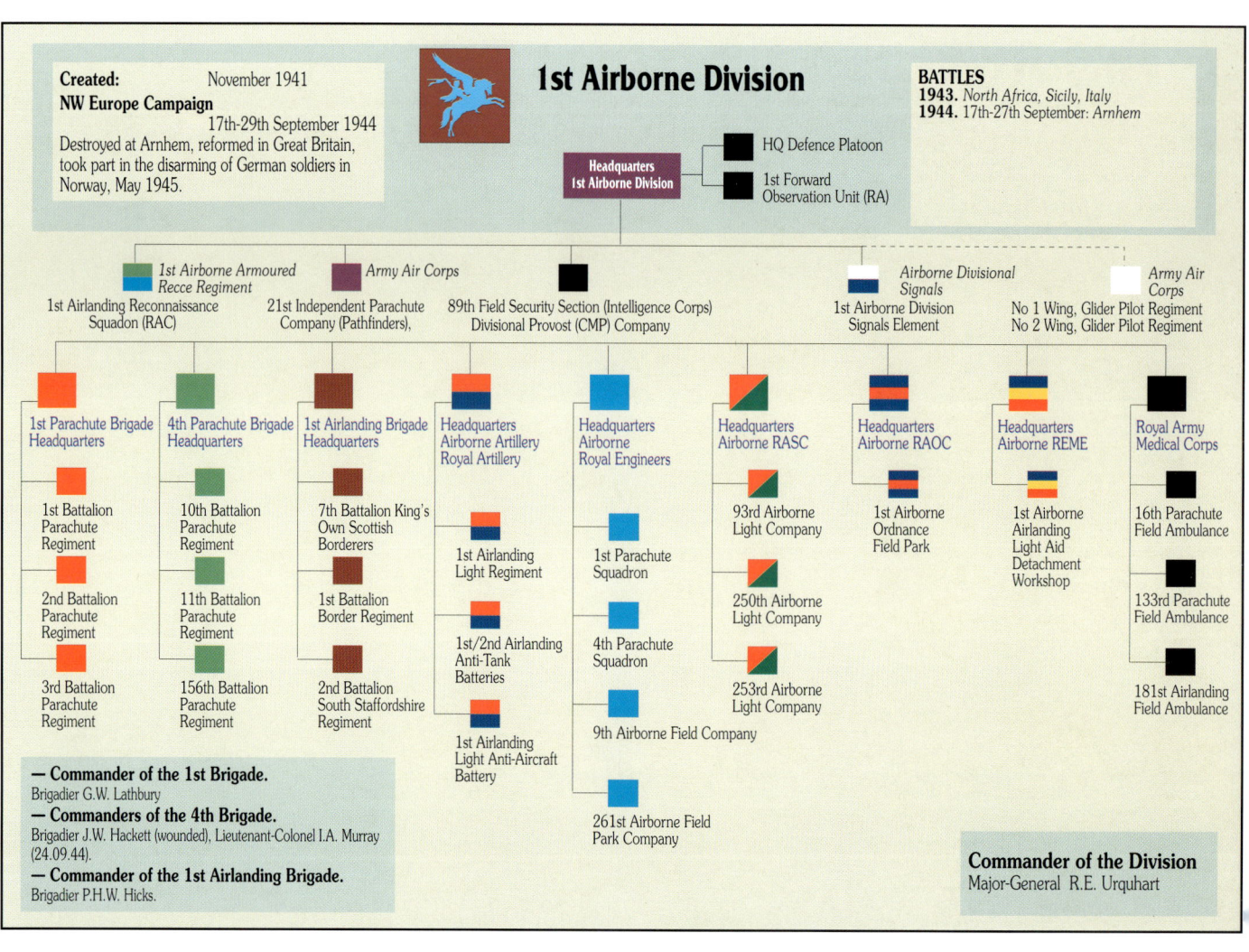

*Army Air Corps*
No 1 Wing, Glider Pilot Regiment
No 2 Wing, Glider Pilot Regiment

**1st Parachute Brigade Headquarters**
- 1st Battalion Parachute Regiment
- 2nd Battalion Parachute Regiment
- 3rd Battalion Parachute Regiment

**4th Parachute Brigade Headquarters**
- 10th Battalion Parachute Regiment
- 11th Battalion Parachute Regiment
- 156th Battalion Parachute Regiment

**1st Airlanding Brigade Headquarters**
- 7th Battalion King's Own Scottish Borderers
- 1st Battalion Border Regiment
- 2nd Battalion South Staffordshire Regiment

**Headquarters Airborne Artillery Royal Artillery**
- 1st Airlanding Light Regiment
- 1st/2nd Airlanding Anti-Tank Batteries
- 1st Airlanding Light Anti-Aircraft Battery

**Headquarters Airborne Royal Engineers**
- 1st Parachute Squadron
- 4th Parachute Squadron
- 9th Airborne Field Company
- 261st Airborne Field Park Company

**Headquarters Airborne RASC**
- 93rd Airborne Light Company
- 250th Airborne Light Company
- 253rd Airborne Light Company

**Headquarters Airborne RAOC**
- 1st Airborne Ordnance Field Park

**Headquarters Airborne REME**
- 1st Airborne Airlanding Light Aid Detachment Workshop

**Royal Army Medical Corps**
- 16th Parachute Field Ambulance
- 133rd Parachute Field Ambulance
- 181st Airlanding Field Ambulance

— **Commander of the 1st Brigade.**
Brigadier G.W. Lathbury
— **Commanders of the 4th Brigade.**
Brigadier J.W. Hackett (wounded), Lieutenant-Colonel I.A. Murray (24.09.44).
— **Commander of the 1st Airlanding Brigade.**
Brigadier P.H.W. Hicks.

**Commander of the Division**
Major-General R.E. Urquhart

---

## 6th Airborne Division

**Created:** 3rd May 1943
**NW Europe Campaign**
6 June-3rd September 1944
24th December 1944-24th February 1945
24th March-19th May 1945

**BATTLES**
**1944.** 6th June: Normandy Airlandings
**1945.** 23rd March-18th April: Rhine crossing

**Headquarters 6th Airborne Division**
- HQ Defence Platoon
- 2nd Forward Observation Unit (RA)

*Airborne Armoured Recce Regiment*
6th Airborne Regiment (RAC)

*Army Air Corps*
22nd Independent Parachute Company (Pathfinders),

317th Field Security Section (Intelligence Corps)
Divisional Provost (CMP) Company

6th Airborne Postal Unit (RE)

*Airborne Divisional Signals*
6th Airborne Division Signals Element

*Army Air Corps*
No 1 Wing, Glider Pilot Regiment
No 2 Wing, Glider Pilot Regiment

**3rd Parachute Brigade Headquarters**
- 8th Battalion Parachute Regiment
- 9th Battalion Parachute Regiment
- 1st Canadian Parachute Battalion

**5th Parachute Brigade Headquarters**
- 7th Battalion Parachute Regt. (Light Infantry)
- 12th Battalion Parachute Regt. (Yorkshire)
- 13th Battalion Parachute Regt. (Lancashire)

**6th Airlanding Brigade Headquarters**
- 12th Battalion Devonshire Regiment
- 2nd Battalion Oxf. and Buck. Light Infantry
- 1st Battalion Royal Ulster Rifles

**Headquarters Airborne Artillery Royal Artillery**
- 53rd (Worcestershire Yeomanry) Airlanding Light Regiment
- 2nd, 3rd, 4th Airlanding Anti-Tank Batteries
- 2nd Airlanding Light Anti-Aircraft Battery *

**Headquarters Airborne Royal Engineers**
- 3rd Parachute Squadron
- 591st Parachute Squadron
- 249th Airborne Field Company
- 286th Airborne Field Park Company

**Headquarters Airborne RASC**
- 716th Airborne Light Company
- 63rd Airborne Divisional Company
- 398th Airborne Divisional Company

**Headquarters Airborne RAOC**
- 6th Airborne Ordnance Field Park

**Headquarters Airborne REME**
- 6th Airborne Workshop Airborne Light Aid Detachment

**Royal Army Medical Corps**
- 224th Parachute Field Ambulance
- 225th Parachute Field Ambulance
- 195th Airlanding Field Ambulance

— **Commander of the 3rd Para Brigade.**
Brigadier S.J.L. Hill
— **Commander of the 5th Para Brigade.**
Brigadier J.H.N. Poett
— **Commanders of the 6th Airlanding Brigade.**
Brigadier Hon. H.K.M. Kinderley (wounded),
Brigadiers E.W.C. Flawell (15 06 44), R.H. Bellamy (19 01 45).

\* Became the 6th Airlanding Anti-tank battery in January 1945.

**Commanders of the Division**
Major-General R.N. Gale
Major-General E.L. Bols (08 12 44)

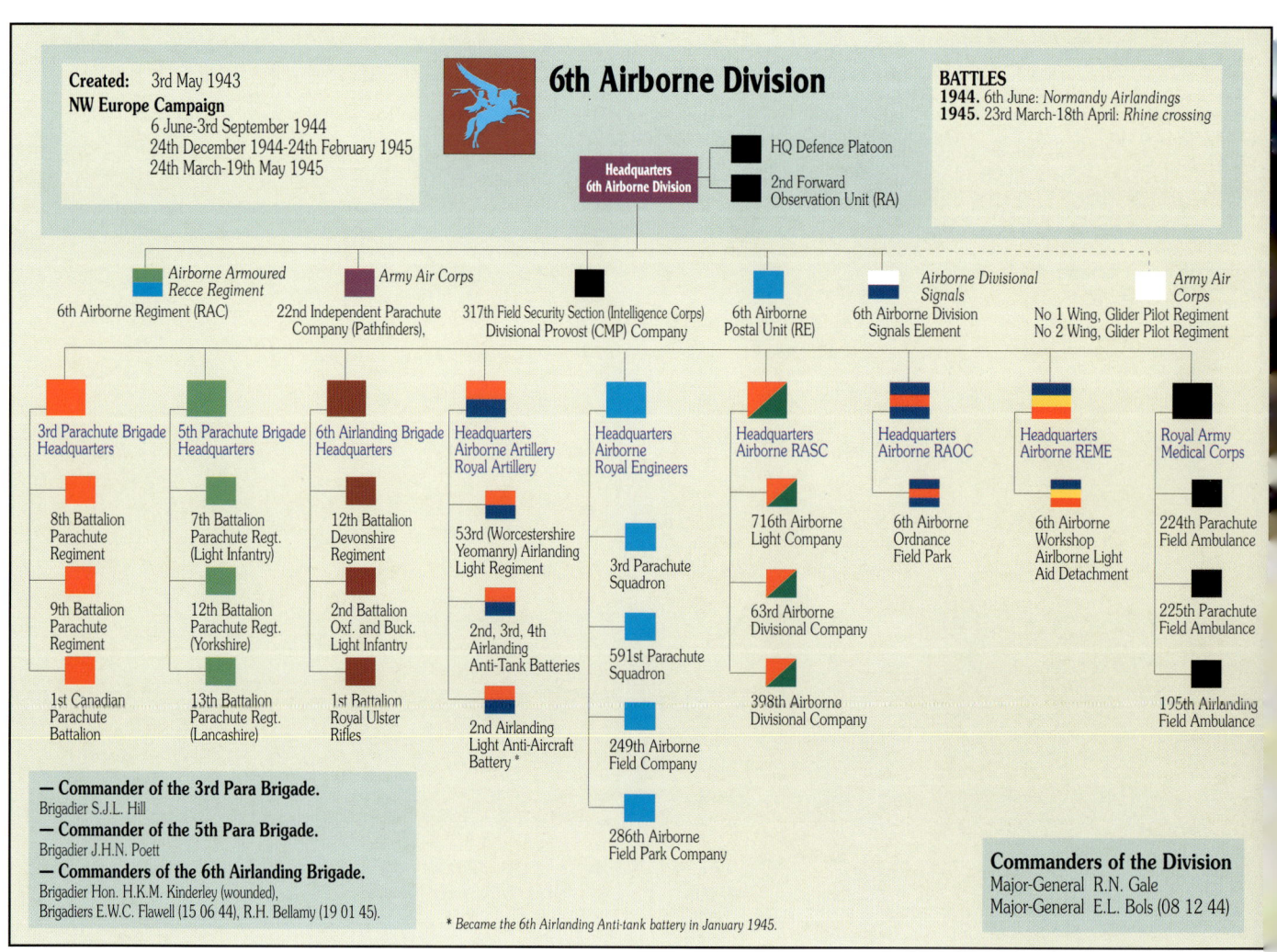

# 7. The Independent Armoured Brigades

## Armoured and Army Tank Brigades

Although they had undergone training permitting them to participate wholly in operations, these brigades were essentially general reserve units whose principal objective was to support infantry divisions.

They included three tank regiments - Churchills or Shermans - and light units from the services. These brigades were of the «A» type if they included a battalion of motorised infantry and of the «B» type if they did not include infantry.

As of January 1945, the Army Tank Brigades were called Armoured Brigades.

This succinct organogram of these formations is presented in the form of the tactical markings used at the time of their commitment in the campaign.

*Above.* **A Churchill of the 147th RAC, one of the three Armoured Battalions of the 34th Army Tank Brigade.** *(IWM)*

*Below.*
**17th July 1944 to the North-East of Caen, the crew of a Churchill of the 107 RAC (5. Battalion King's Own Regiment) loading ammunition into the tank.** *(IWM)*

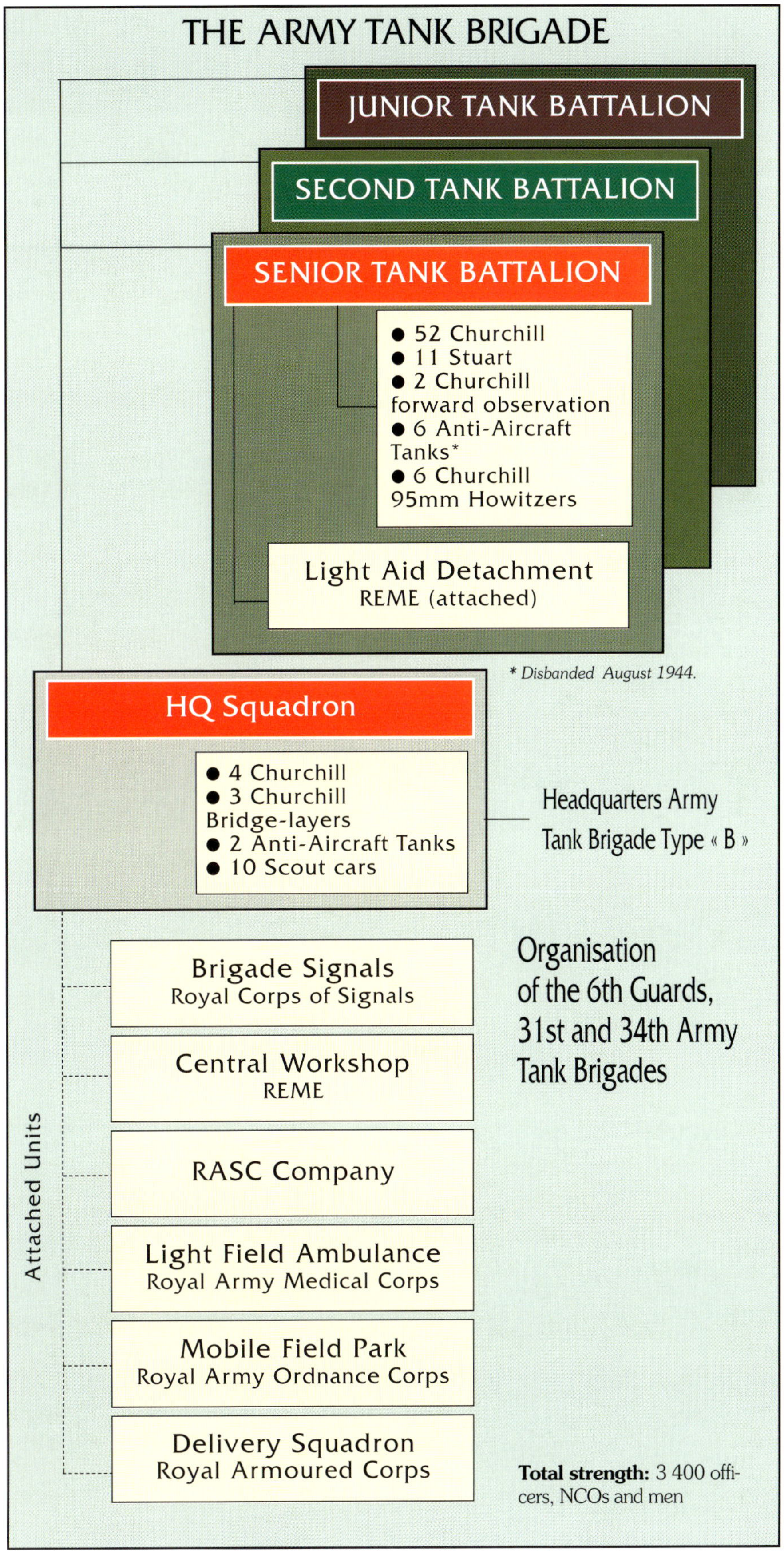

## THE ARMY TANK BRIGADE

**JUNIOR TANK BATTALION**

**SECOND TANK BATTALION**

**SENIOR TANK BATTALION**
- 52 Churchill
- 11 Stuart
- 2 Churchill forward observation
- 6 Anti-Aircraft Tanks*
- 6 Churchill 95mm Howitzers

Light Aid Detachment
REME (attached)

*\* Disbanded August 1944.*

**HQ Squadron**
- 4 Churchill
- 3 Churchill Bridge-layers
- 2 Anti-Aircraft Tanks
- 10 Scout cars

Headquarters Army Tank Brigade Type «B»

**Attached Units**

Brigade Signals
Royal Corps of Signals

Central Workshop
REME

RASC Company

Light Field Ambulance
Royal Army Medical Corps

Mobile Field Park
Royal Army Ordnance Corps

Delivery Squadron
Royal Armoured Corps

Organisation of the 6th Guards, 31st and 34th Army Tank Brigades

**Total strength:** 3 400 officers, NCOs and men

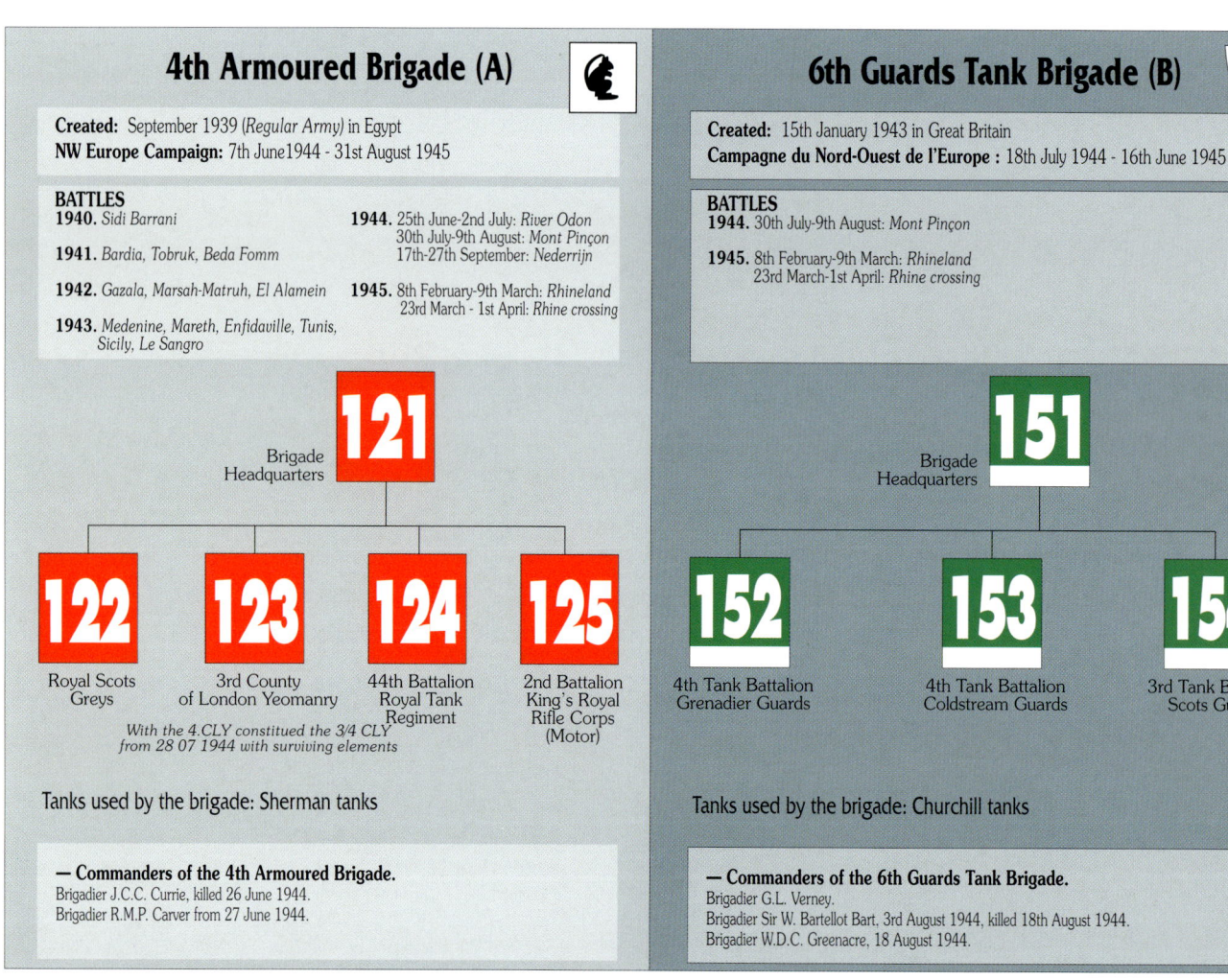

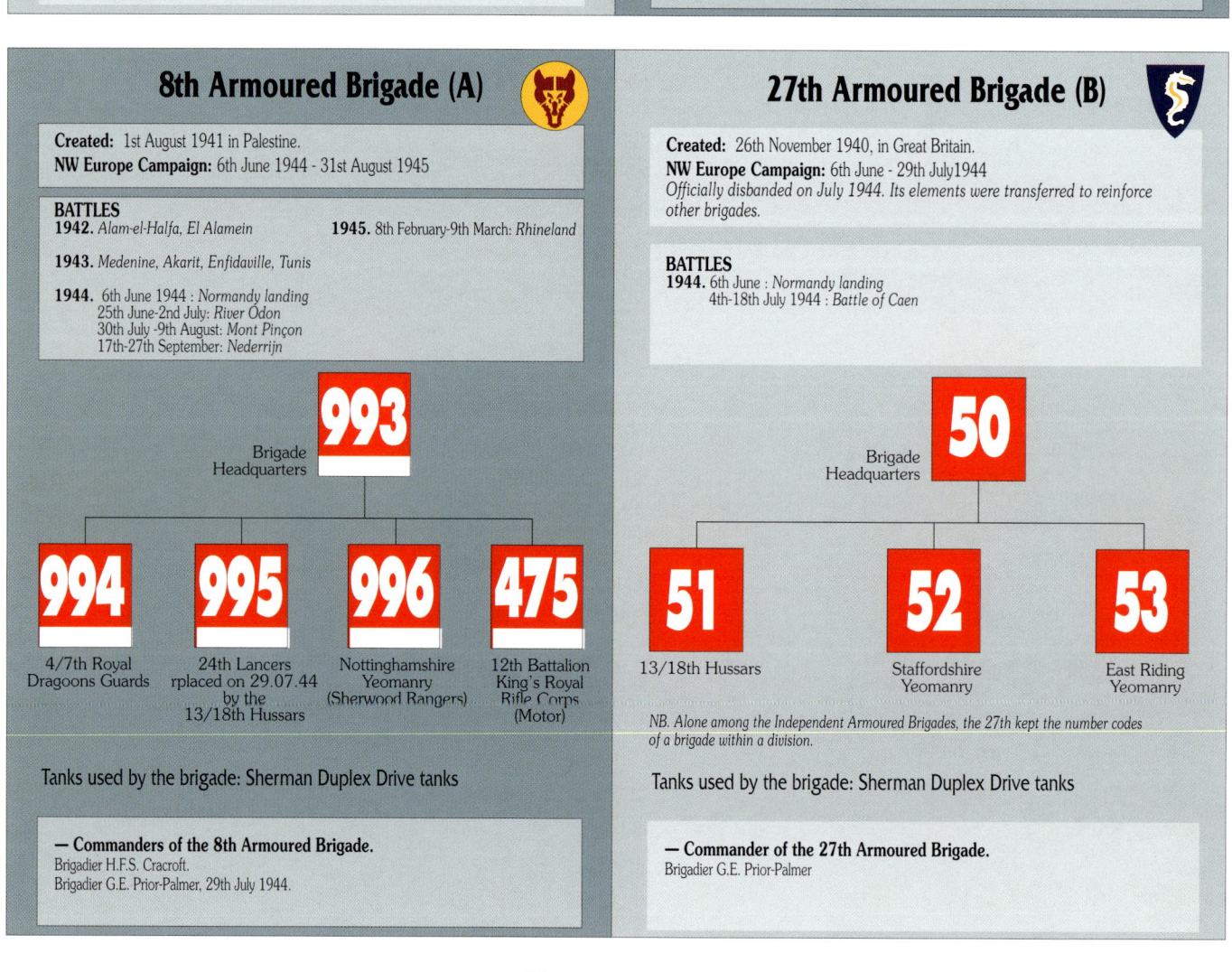

## 4th Armoured Brigade (A)

**Created:** September 1939 (*Regular Army*) in Egypt
**NW Europe Campaign:** 7th June 1944 - 31st August 1945

**BATTLES**
**1940.** *Sidi Barrani*
**1941.** *Bardia, Tobruk, Beda Fomm*
**1942.** *Gazala, Marsah-Matruh, El Alamein*
**1943.** *Medenine, Mareth, Enfidaville, Tunis, Sicily, Le Sangro*
**1944.** 25th June-2nd July: *River Odon*
30th July-9th August: *Mont Pinçon*
17th-27th September: *Nederrijn*
**1945.** 8th February-9th March: *Rhineland*
23rd March - 1st April: *Rhine crossing*

**121** Brigade Headquarters

- **122** Royal Scots Greys
- **123** 3rd County of London Yeomanry *With the 4.CLY constitued the 3/4 CLY from 28 07 1944 with surviving elements*
- **124** 44th Battalion Royal Tank Regiment
- **125** 2nd Battalion King's Royal Rifle Corps (Motor)

Tanks used by the brigade: Sherman tanks

— **Commanders of the 4th Armoured Brigade.**
Brigadier J.C.C. Currie, killed 26 June 1944.
Brigadier R.M.P. Carver from 27 June 1944.

## 6th Guards Tank Brigade (B)

**Created:** 15th January 1943 in Great Britain
**Campagne du Nord-Ouest de l'Europe :** 18th July 1944 - 16th June 1945

**BATTLES**
**1944.** 30th July-9th August: *Mont Pinçon*
**1945.** 8th February-9th March: *Rhineland*
23rd March-1st April: *Rhine crossing*

**151** Brigade Headquarters

- **152** 4th Tank Battalion Grenadier Guards
- **153** 4th Tank Battalion Coldstream Guards
- **154** 3rd Tank Battalion Scots Guards

Tanks used by the brigade: Churchill tanks

— **Commanders of the 6th Guards Tank Brigade.**
Brigadier G.L. Verney.
Brigadier Sir W. Bartellot Bart, 3rd August 1944, killed 18th August 1944.
Brigadier W.D.C. Greenacre, 18 August 1944.

## 8th Armoured Brigade (A)

**Created:** 1st August 1941 in Palestine.
**NW Europe Campaign:** 6th June 1944 - 31st August 1945

**BATTLES**
**1942.** *Alam-el-Halfa, El Alamein*
**1943.** *Medenine, Akarit, Enfidaville, Tunis*
**1944.** 6th June 1944 : *Normandy landing*
25th June-2nd July: *River Odon*
30th July -9th August: *Mont Pinçon*
17th-27th September: *Nederrijn*
**1945.** 8th February-9th March: *Rhineland*

**993** Brigade Headquarters

- **994** 4/7th Royal Dragoons Guards
- **995** 24th Lancers rplaced on 29.07.44 by the 13/18th Hussars
- **996** Nottinghamshire Yeomanry (Sherwood Rangers)
- **475** 12th Battalion King's Royal Rifle Corps (Motor)

Tanks used by the brigade: Sherman Duplex Drive tanks

— **Commanders of the 8th Armoured Brigade.**
Brigadier H.F.S. Cracroft.
Brigadier G.E. Prior-Palmer, 29th July 1944.

## 27th Armoured Brigade (B)

**Created:** 26th November 1940, in Great Britain.
**NW Europe Campaign:** 6th June - 29th July 1944
*Officially disbanded on July 1944. Its elements were transferred to reinforce other brigades.*

**BATTLES**
**1944.** 6th June : *Normandy landing*
4th-18th July 1944 : *Battle of Caen*

**50** Brigade Headquarters

- **51** 13/18th Hussars
- **52** Staffordshire Yeomanry
- **53** East Riding Yeomanry

*NB. Alone among the Independent Armoured Brigades, the 27th kept the number codes of a brigade within a division.*

Tanks used by the brigade: Sherman Duplex Drive tanks

— **Commander of the 27th Armoured Brigade.**
Brigadier G.E. Prior-Palmer

# 31st Army Tank Brigade (B)

**Created:** 15th January 1941 in Great Britain
**NW Europe Campaign:** 19th July 1944 - 31st August 1945

**BATTLES**
**1944.** 25th June-2nd July: *River Odon*
4th-18th July: *Battle of Caen*

Equipped with special machinery, the brigade was assignated to the 79th Armoured Division in September 1944.

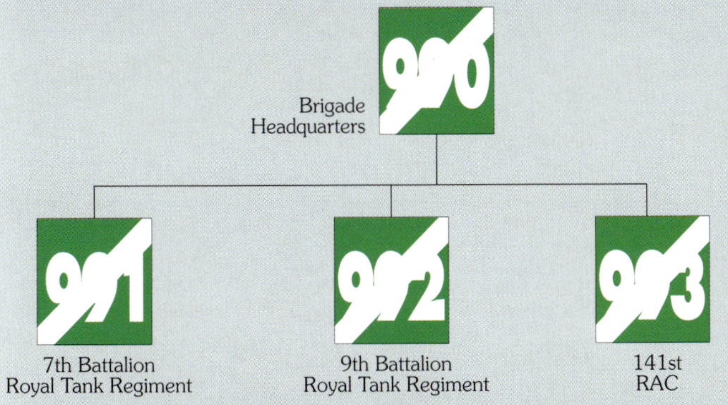

996
Brigade Headquarters
991
7th Battalion Royal Tank Regiment
992
9th Battalion Royal Tank Regiment
993
141st RAC


Tanks used by the brigade: Churchill tanks

**Composition of the brigade from 5th september 1944.**

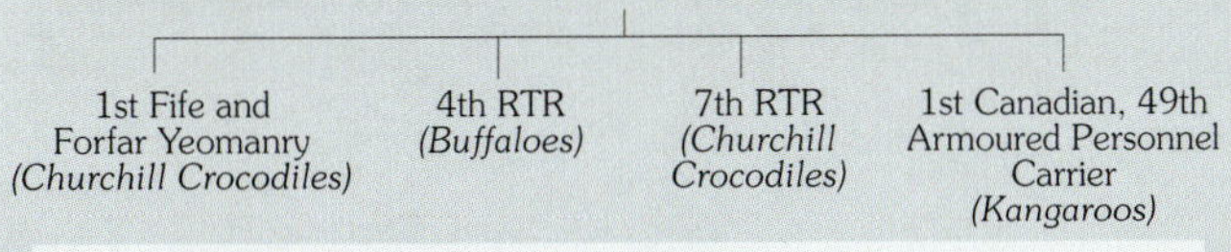

1st Fife and Forfar Yeomanry (Churchill Crocodiles)
4th RTR (Buffaloes)
7th RTR (Churchill Crocodiles)
1st Canadian, 49th Armoured Personnel Carrier (Kangaroos)


**— Commander of the 31st Armoured Brigade.**
Brigadier G.S. Knight.

# 33rd Armoured Brigade (B)

**Created:** 30th August 1941 in Great Britain.
**NW Europe Campaign:** 13th June 1944 - 21st August 1945

**BATTLES**
**1944.** 4th-18th July: *Battle of Caen*

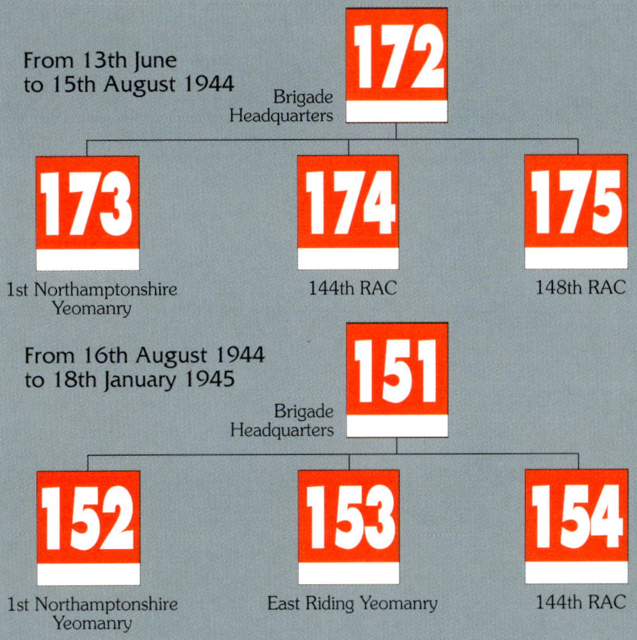

From 13th June to 15th August 1944
172
Brigade Headquarters
173
1st Northamptonshire Yeomanry
174
144th RAC
175
148th RAC
From 16th August 1944 to 18th January 1945
151
Brigade Headquarters
152
1st Northamptonshire Yeomanry
153
East Riding Yeomanry
154
144th RAC


Tanks used by the brigade: Sherman tanks, the Buffaloes and Kangaroos

**— Commander of the 33rd Armoured Brigade.**
Brigadier H.B. Scott.

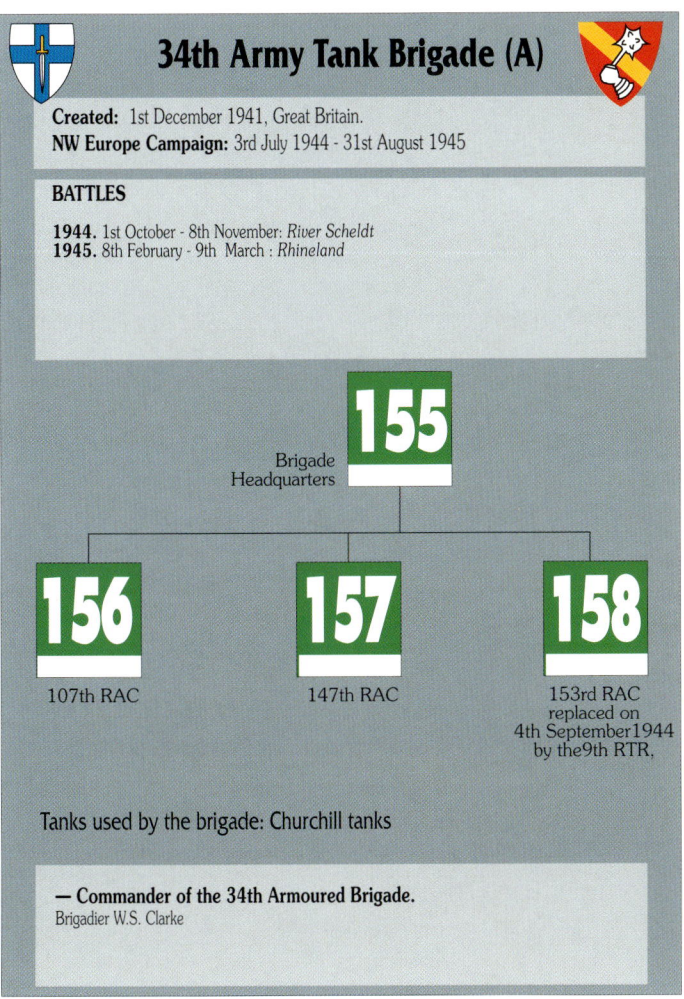

# 34th Army Tank Brigade (A)

**Created:** 1st December 1941, Great Britain.
**NW Europe Campaign:** 3rd July 1944 - 31st August 1945

**BATTLES**

**1944.** 1st October - 8th November: *River Scheldt*
**1945.** 8th February - 9th March : *Rhineland*

155
Brigade Headquarters
156
107th RAC
157
147th RAC
158
153rd RAC replaced on 4th September1944 by the9th RTR,


Tanks used by the brigade: Churchill tanks

**— Commander of the 34th Armoured Brigade.**
Brigadier W.S. Clarke

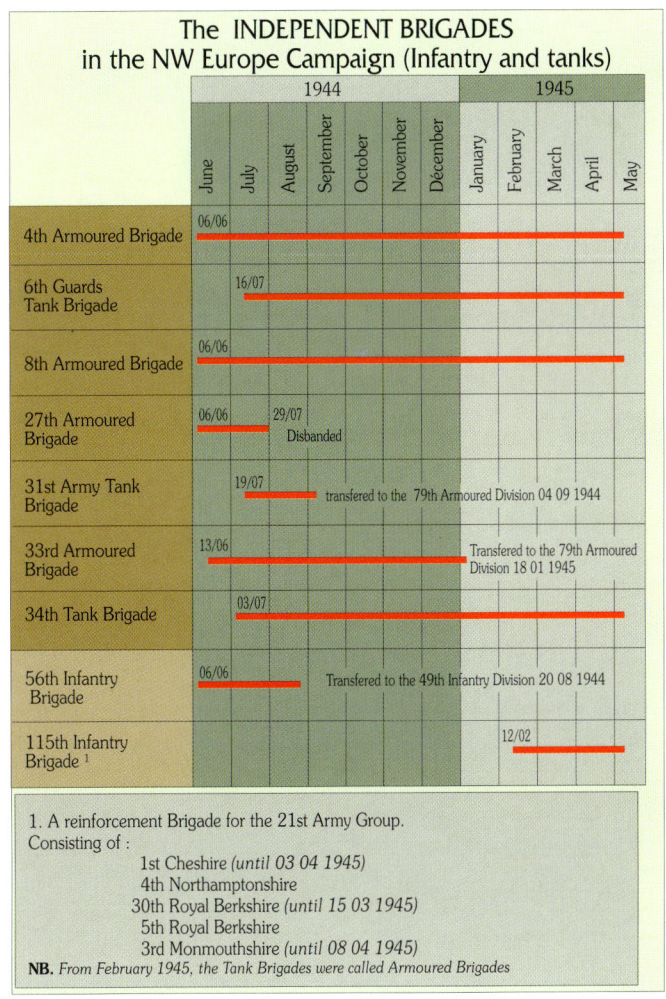

## The INDEPENDENT BRIGADES in the NW Europe Campaign (Infantry and tanks)

1944
1945
June
July
August
September
October
November
December
January
February
March
April
May
4th Armoured Brigade
06/06
6th Guards Tank Brigade
16/07
8th Armoured Brigade
06/06
27th Armoured Brigade
06/06
29/07
Disbanded
31st Army Tank Brigade
19/07
transfered to the 79th Armoured Division 04 09 1944
33rd Armoured Brigade
13/06
Transfered to the 79th Armoured Division 18 01 1945
34th Tank Brigade
03/07
56th Infantry Brigade
06/06
Transfered to the 49th Infantry Division 20 08 1944
115th Infantry Brigade [1]
12/02


1. A reinforcement Brigade for the 21st Army Group.
Consisting of :
1st Cheshire *(until 03 04 1945)*
4th Northamptonshire
30th Royal Berkshire *(until 15 03 1945)*
5th Royal Berkshire
3rd Monmouthshire *(until 08 04 1945)*

**NB.** *From February 1945, the Tank Brigades were called Armoured Brigades*

# CHAPTER 2 The ARMS and the SERVIVCES

## 1. The notion of the Regiment

The term regiment has two different meanings: it designates either the corps to which a unit belonged, or a tactical unit (a fighting unit). The artillery was gathered under the denomination Royal Regiment of Artillery. The denomination Regiment was kept for tradition's sake and was applied equally to tactical numbered units: 69th Field Regiment, 102nd Anti-Tank Regiment, etc.

Other units bore the name regiment: the Royal Tank Regiment, the Parachute Regiment. Here it was a question of designating the corps to which they belonged on the whole, since the tactical units were numbered.

In the Infantry, the word regiment had no tactical sense. With its traditional denomination, it had the function of a training centre, a depot and depository of traditions. The tactical units were the numbered battalions following their number within the regiment (see chapter on the Infantry)

The armoured units originating from the horse cavalry as well as the the Reconnaissance corps were tactical units: they bore the word regiment.

## 2. Royal Armoured Corps

The armoured corps was created in April 1939. It undertook the recruitment, training, personnel management and took part also in perfecting the material used.

### COMPOSITION

- **Armoured Regiments** from the former horse cavalry: Dragoons, Lancers, Hussars, Carabiniers.
- **Yeomanry** [1]: armoured regiments of the Territorial Army who adopted the name of their county; in peacetime, certain regiments made up the permanent Yeomanry (traditional professionalised units).
- **Royal Tank Regiment:** organised in tank battalions numbered from 1 to 12 for the Regular Army and 40 to 51 for the Territorial Army.
- **RAC tank regiments**, organised by the corps itself from 1941 and coming from converted Infantry Batta-

1. The name Yeomanry comes from Yeomen (volunteers) who, at the end of the 18th century, joined the army with their own steed. The majority of the Yeomanry was principally made up of landowners or tenants.

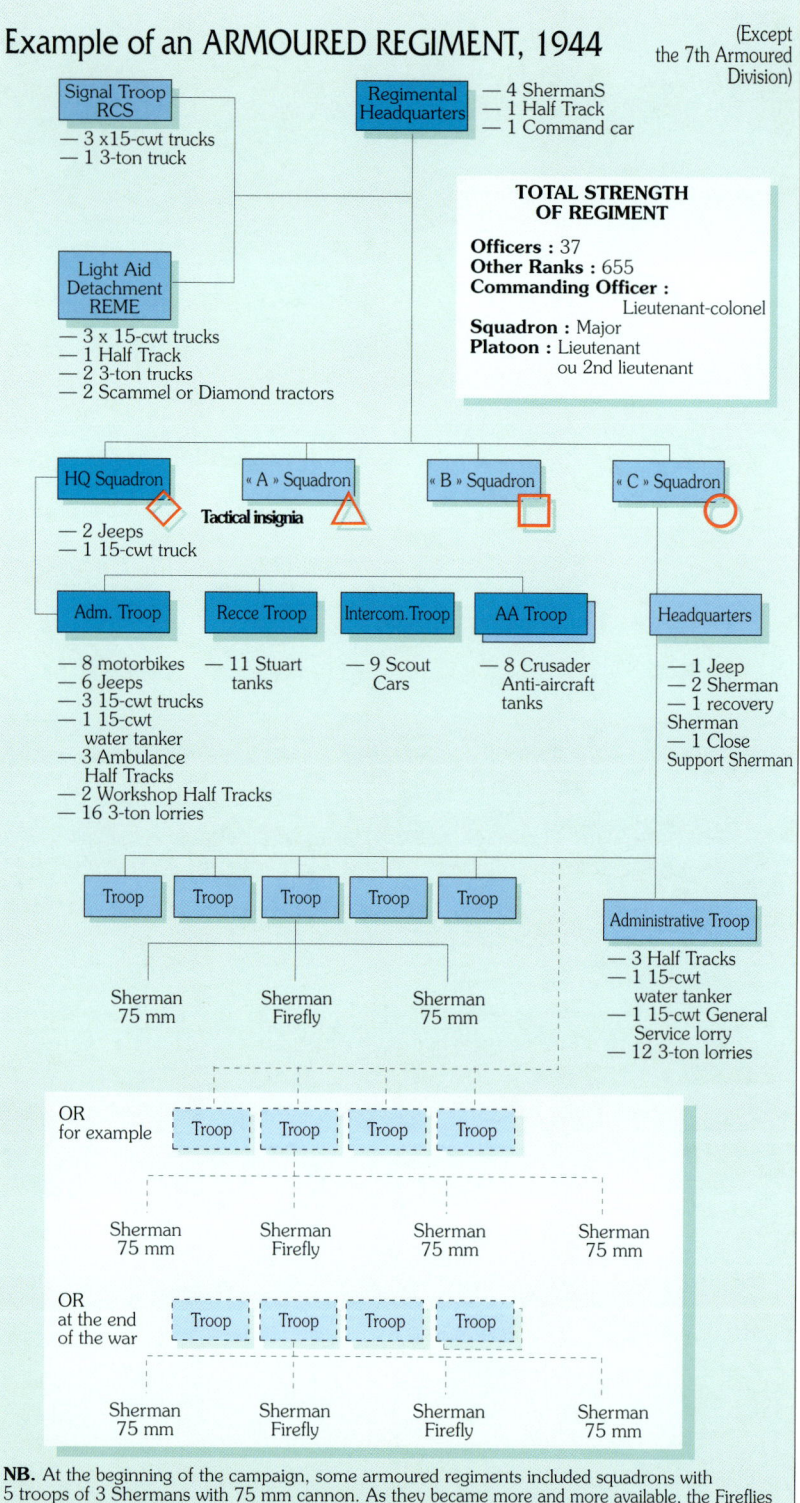

lions. Numbered in the series 107 - 163.

- **Armoured Delivery Squadrons:** personnel and equipment replacement, and convoying units.
- **General Headquarters, liaison regiments** (Phantom units): 850-man strong units equipped with light armour and powerful radio equipment.

Their mission was to keep the General Headquarters informed of the movements and the position of the Allied formations.

*Opposite right*
*Normandy 17th June 1944.*
*A Sherman Firefly Vc and a Cromwell of the Guards Armoured Division just crossing London Bridge, one of the bridges over the River Orne, between Caen and the sea.*
*(IWM)*

## ARMOURED CAR REGIMENT (RAC)
### (The Army Corps Reconnaissance unit)
#### combat vehicles

**44** — Code Number of Armoured Car Regiments

**Regimental Headquarters and Headquarters Squadron**
- 1 Daimler Scout Car
- 12 Humber Scout Cars
- 1 Daimler Armoured Car
- 3 Staghounds
- 1 Armoured Command Vehicle *
- 4 Humber Anti Aircraft *

Signal Platoon (RCS)

Light Aid Detachment (REME)

**D Squadron**
**C Squadron**
**B Squadron**
**A Squadron**
Squadron HQ
- 1 Daimler Scout Car
- 4 Staghounds
- 1 Daimler Armoured Car

**Heavy Troop**
- 1 Daimler Scout Car
- 2 AEC Armoured Cars 75mm

**Support Troop**
- 1 Daimler Scout Car
- 3 White Scouts Cars with 1 .2 in. Mortar

**1. Reconnaissance Troop** (2, 3, 4, 5)
- 2 Daimler Scout Cars
- 2 Daimler Armoured Cars

2nd Household Cavalry Regiment in July 1944 (from the Regimental History)
The types of machines varied from one regiment to another.

**Total strength.**
55 officers
778 other ranks.

*\* The Anti-Aircraft troops were disbanded in August 1944.*

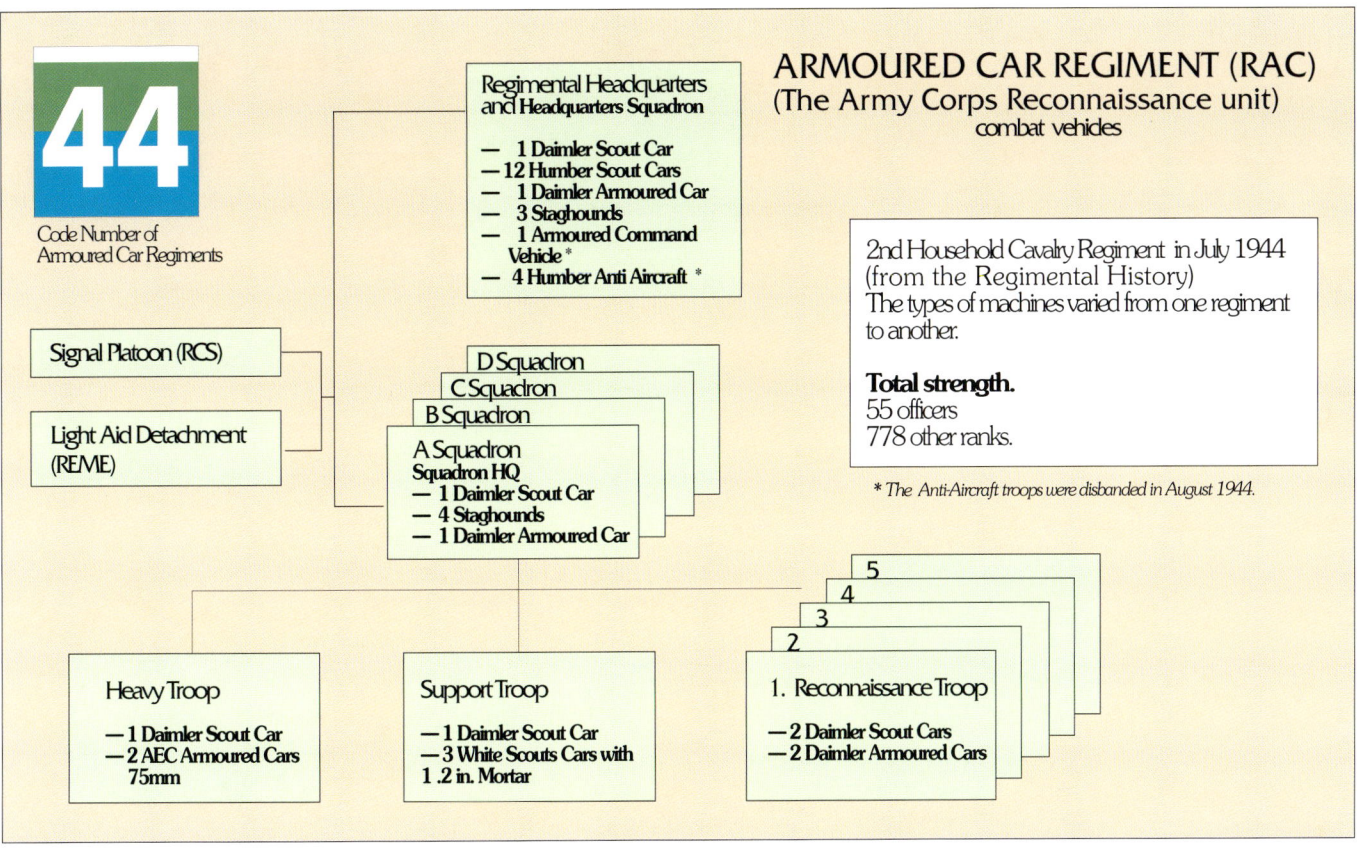

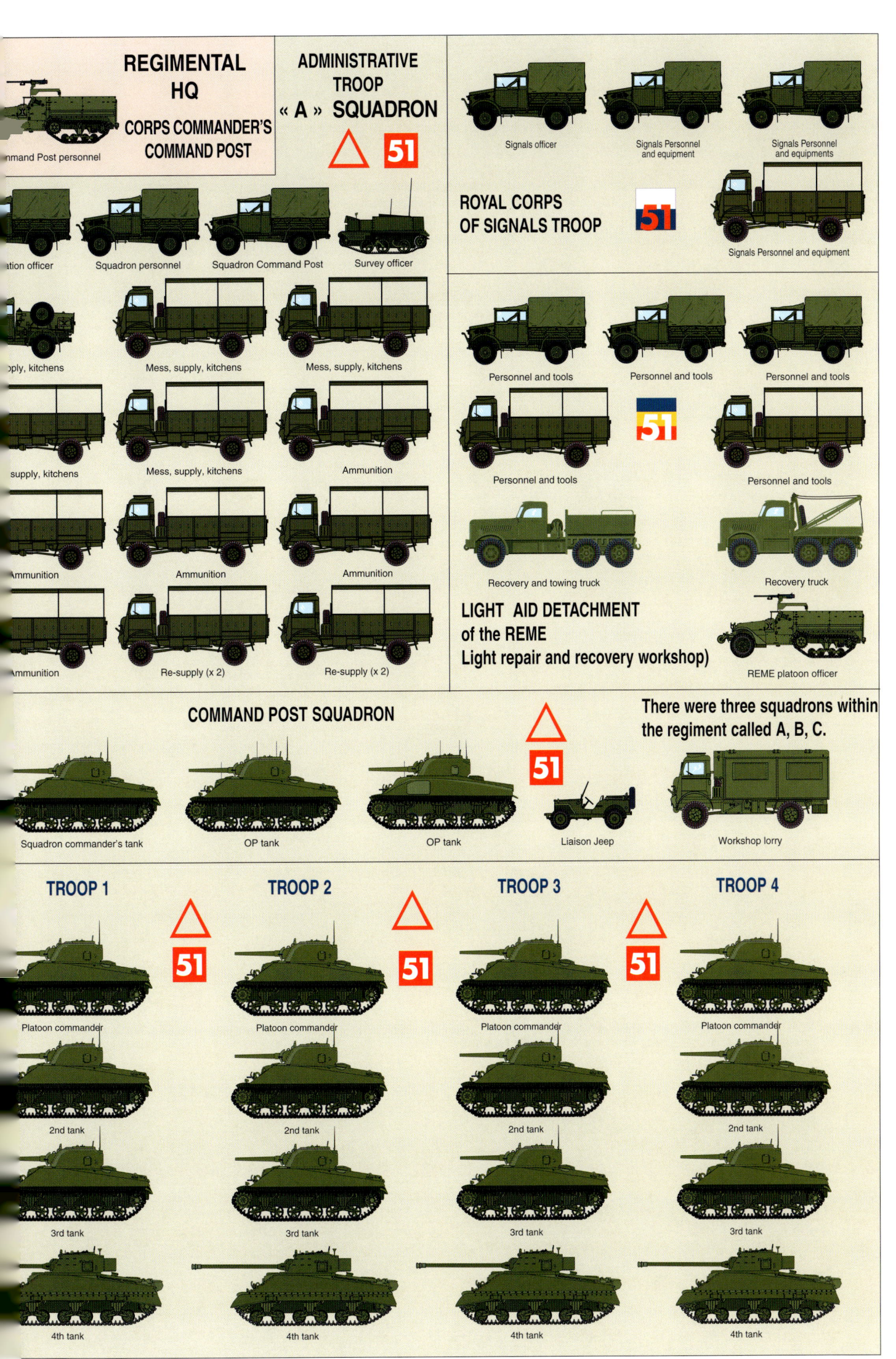

# 3. The Royal Regiment of Artillery

A single corps which recruited, trained and instructed in the use of the various means of this arm. All the units were numbered and kept the traditional name of the regiment

Composition:

**1.- Regiments from the Regular or from the Territorial Army.**

**2.- Regiments coming from the former mounted cavalry of the Territorial Army** (Yeomanry), transfered to the Royal Artillery. Traditionally they kept their original name at the same time as having a number. Example : 153rd (Leicestershire Yeomanry) Field Regiment, Royal Artillery, T.A.

**3.- Regiments of the Royal Horse Artillery tranfered to the Armoured Divisions** of which certain batteries preserved the traditions of the Honourable Artillery Company.

**4.- Regiments coming from converted infantry battalions.**

**5.- Counter Mortar Batteries.** Groups for detecting mortars by radar or sonar. They were incorporated into the divisions from July 1944.

**6.- Searchlight batteries.** Searchlight units attached to general reserve Anti-Aircraft Regiments.

**7.- Air Observation Post Squadrons.** Light aircraft squadrons used for observation and artillery spotting, attached to the Army or to Army Corps.

The pilots and the observers belonged to the Royal Artillery, whereas the aircraft and the ground staff were the responsibility of the RAF.

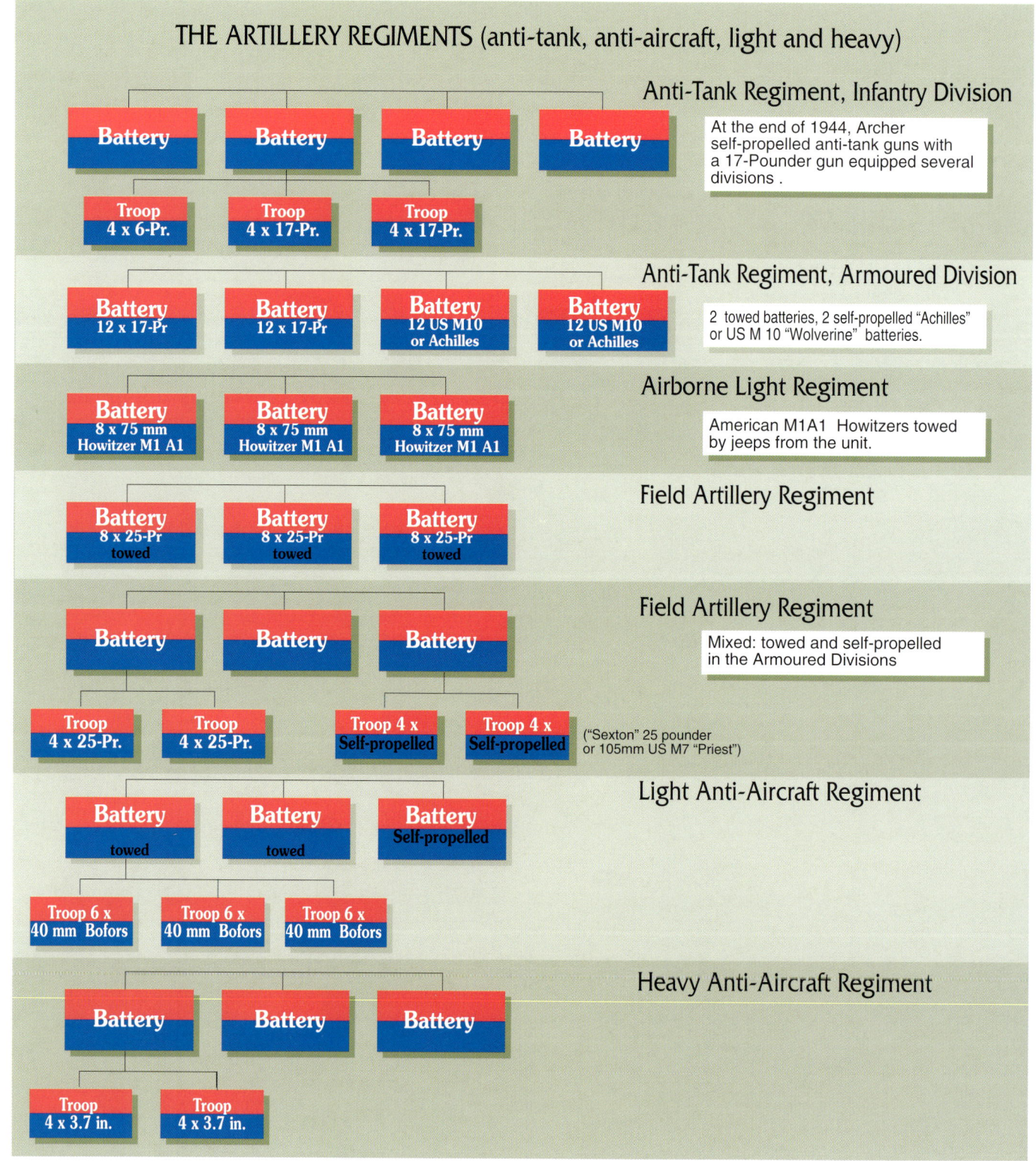

# The Field Artillery Regiment

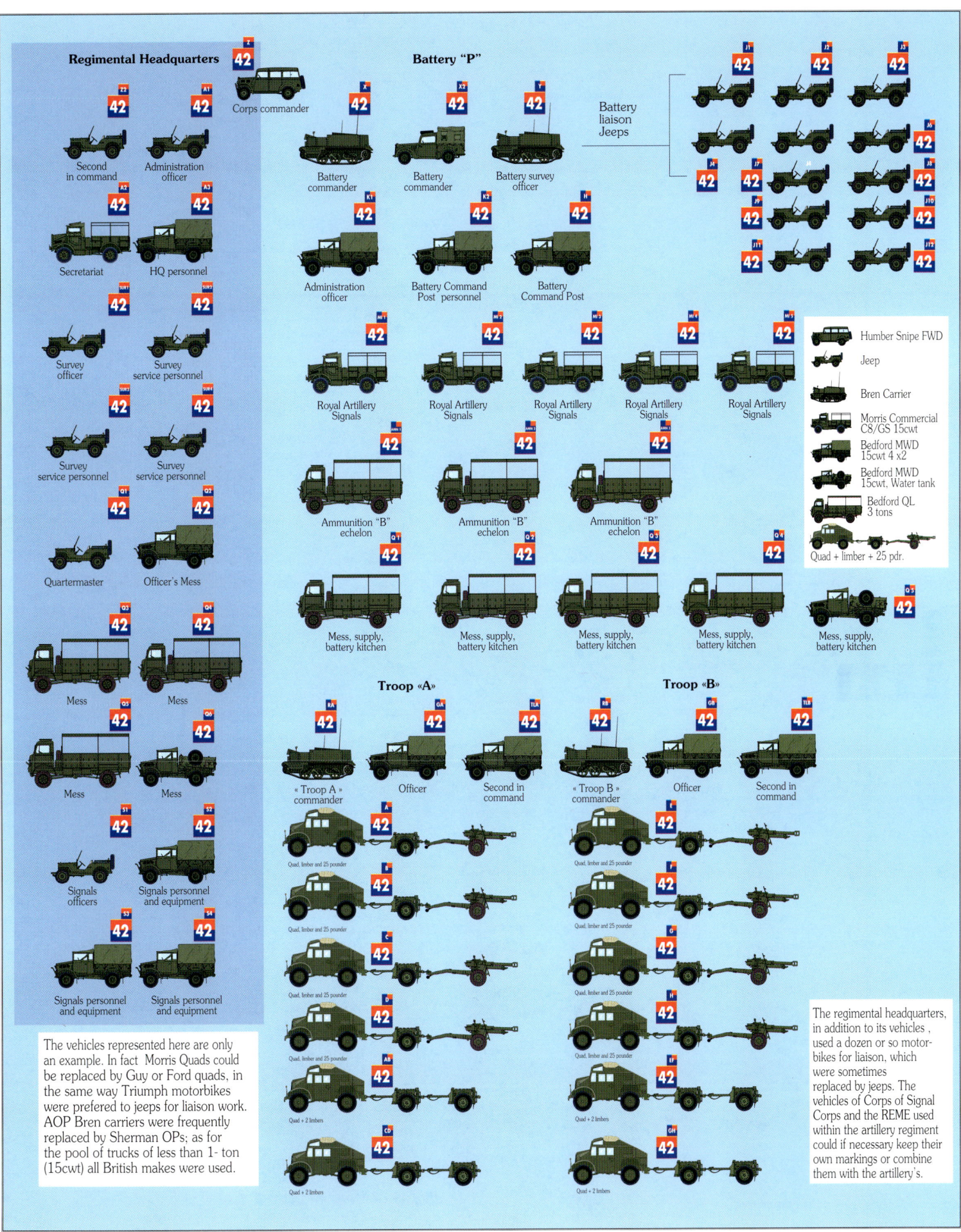

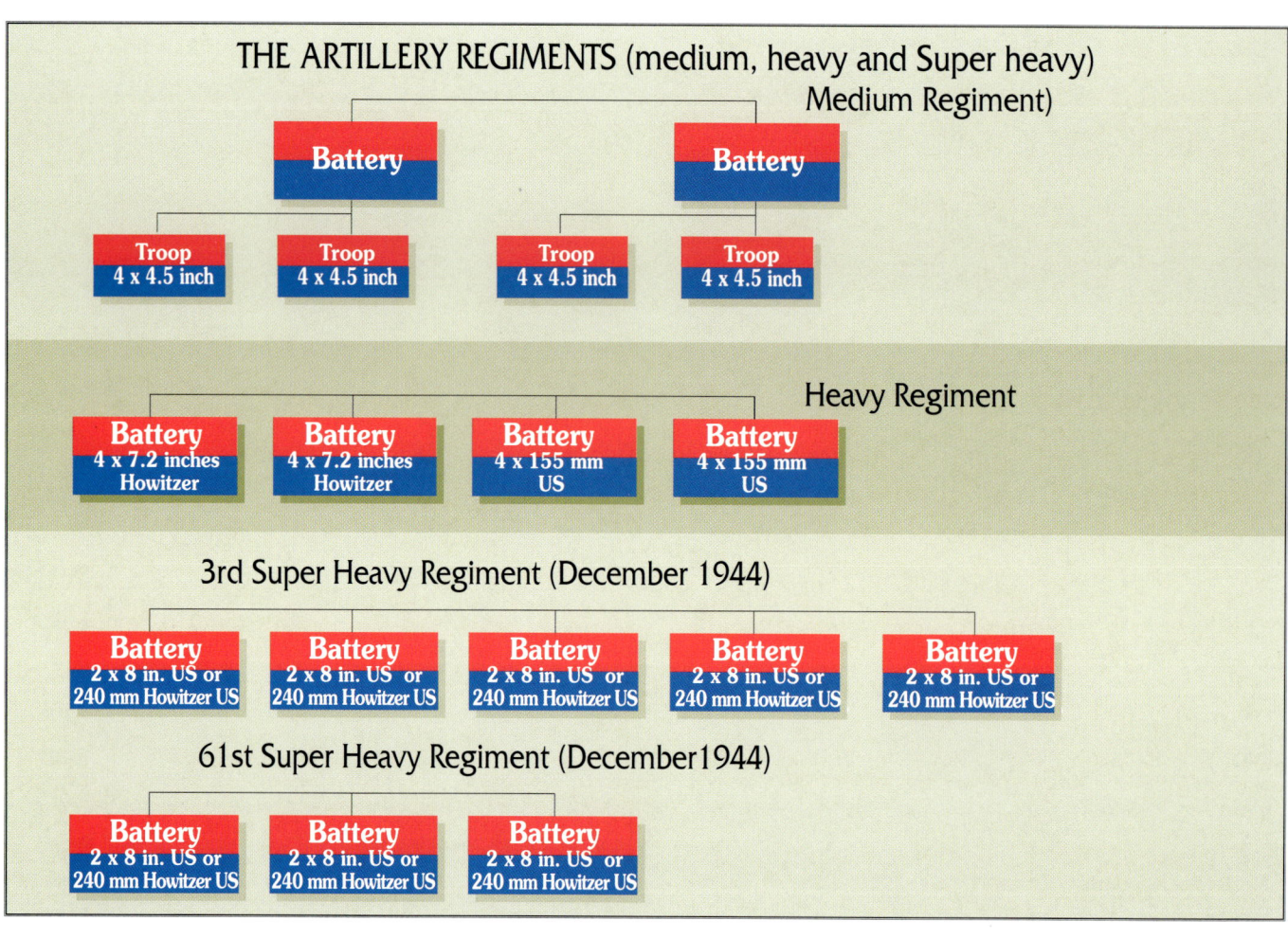

## THE ARTILLERY REGIMENTS (medium, heavy and Super heavy)

### Medium Regiment

- Battery
  - Troop 4 x 4.5 inch
  - Troop 4 x 4.5 inch
- Battery
  - Troop 4 x 4.5 inch
  - Troop 4 x 4.5 inch

### Heavy Regiment

- Battery 4 x 7.2 inches Howitzer
- Battery 4 x 7.2 inches Howitzer
- Battery 4 x 155 mm US
- Battery 4 x 155 mm US

### 3rd Super Heavy Regiment (December 1944)

- Battery 2 x 8 in. US or 240 mm Howitzer US (×5)

### 61st Super Heavy Regiment (December 1944)

- Battery 2 x 8 in. US or 240 mm Howitzer US (×3)

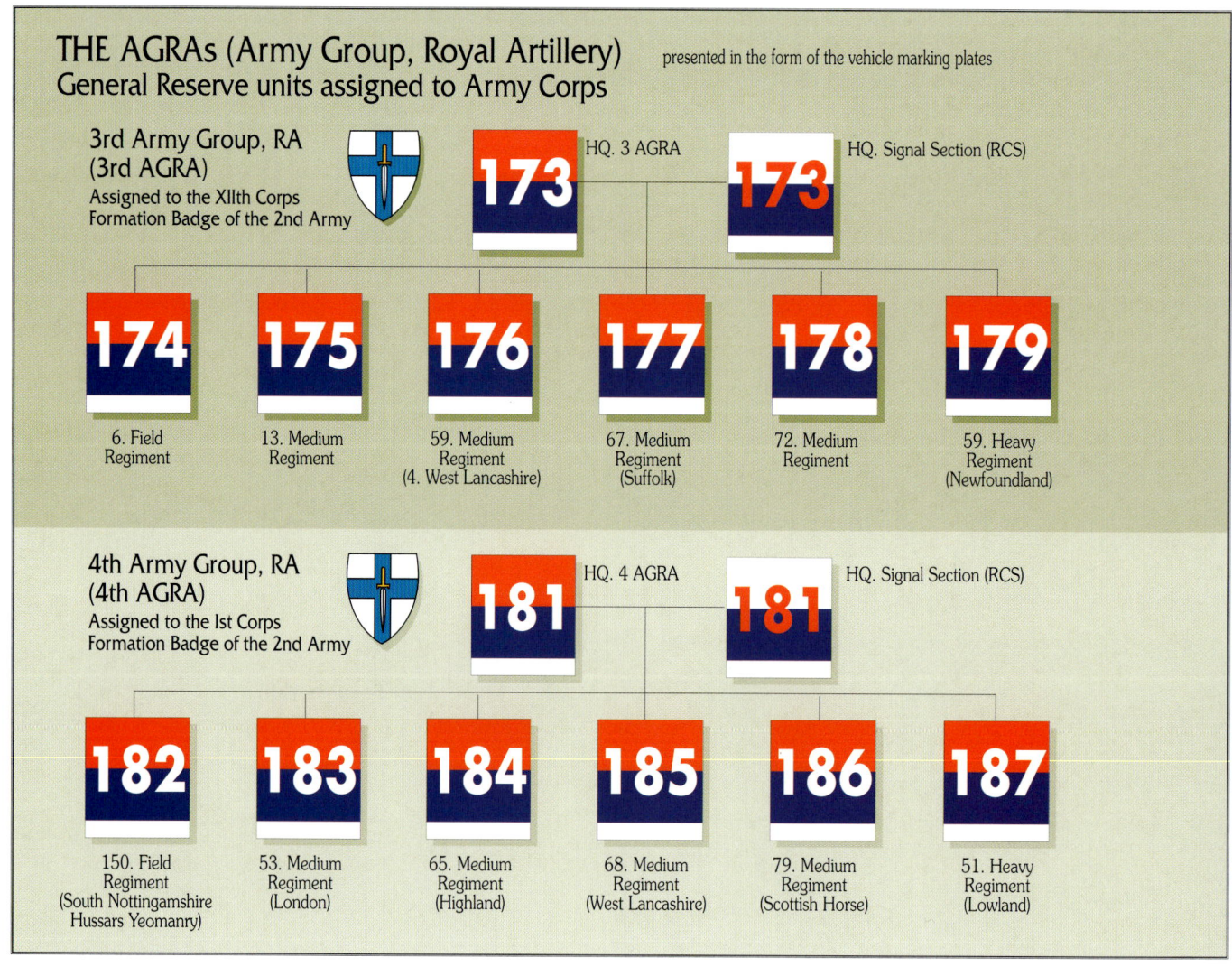

## THE AGRAs (Army Group, Royal Artillery)
### General Reserve units assigned to Army Corps
*presented in the form of the vehicle marking plates*

**3rd Army Group, RA (3rd AGRA)**
Assigned to the XIIth Corps
Formation Badge of the 2nd Army

- 173 — HQ. 3 AGRA
- 173 — HQ. Signal Section (RCS)

| 174 | 175 | 176 | 177 | 178 | 179 |
|---|---|---|---|---|---|
| 6. Field Regiment | 13. Medium Regiment | 59. Medium Regiment (4. West Lancashire) | 67. Medium Regiment (Suffolk) | 72. Medium Regiment | 59. Heavy Regiment (Newfoundland) |

**4th Army Group, RA (4th AGRA)**
Assigned to the Ist Corps
Formation Badge of the 2nd Army

- 181 — HQ. 4 AGRA
- 181 — HQ. Signal Section (RCS)

| 182 | 183 | 184 | 185 | 186 | 187 |
|---|---|---|---|---|---|
| 150. Field Regiment (South Nottinghamshire Hussars Yeomanry) | 53. Medium Regiment (London) | 65. Medium Regiment (Highland) | 68. Medium Regiment (West Lancashire) | 79. Medium Regiment (Scottish Horse) | 51. Heavy Regiment (Lowland) |

*Opposite*
**A 25-pounder battery of a Field Artillery Regiment in action during the Normandy campaign in July 1944.**
*(IWM)*

## Classifying units

**Field Artillery Regiments**
Field artillery forming the divisions' direct artillery support

**Medium regiments**
Medium calibre artillery assigned to the corps and assembled within the Army Groups, Royal Artillery (AGRA) including five or six regiments each.

**Heavy and super heavy Regiments**
The heavy artillery of the Army general reserve.

**Anti-Tank Regiments**
Anti-tank defence including the towed batteries and the self-propelled anti tank guns

**Anti-Aircraft Regiments**
Gathered together the Light AA Regiments in the divisions and the Heavy AA Regiments assigned to the Army Corps or to the Army.

**Survey Regiments**
Survey and observation units.

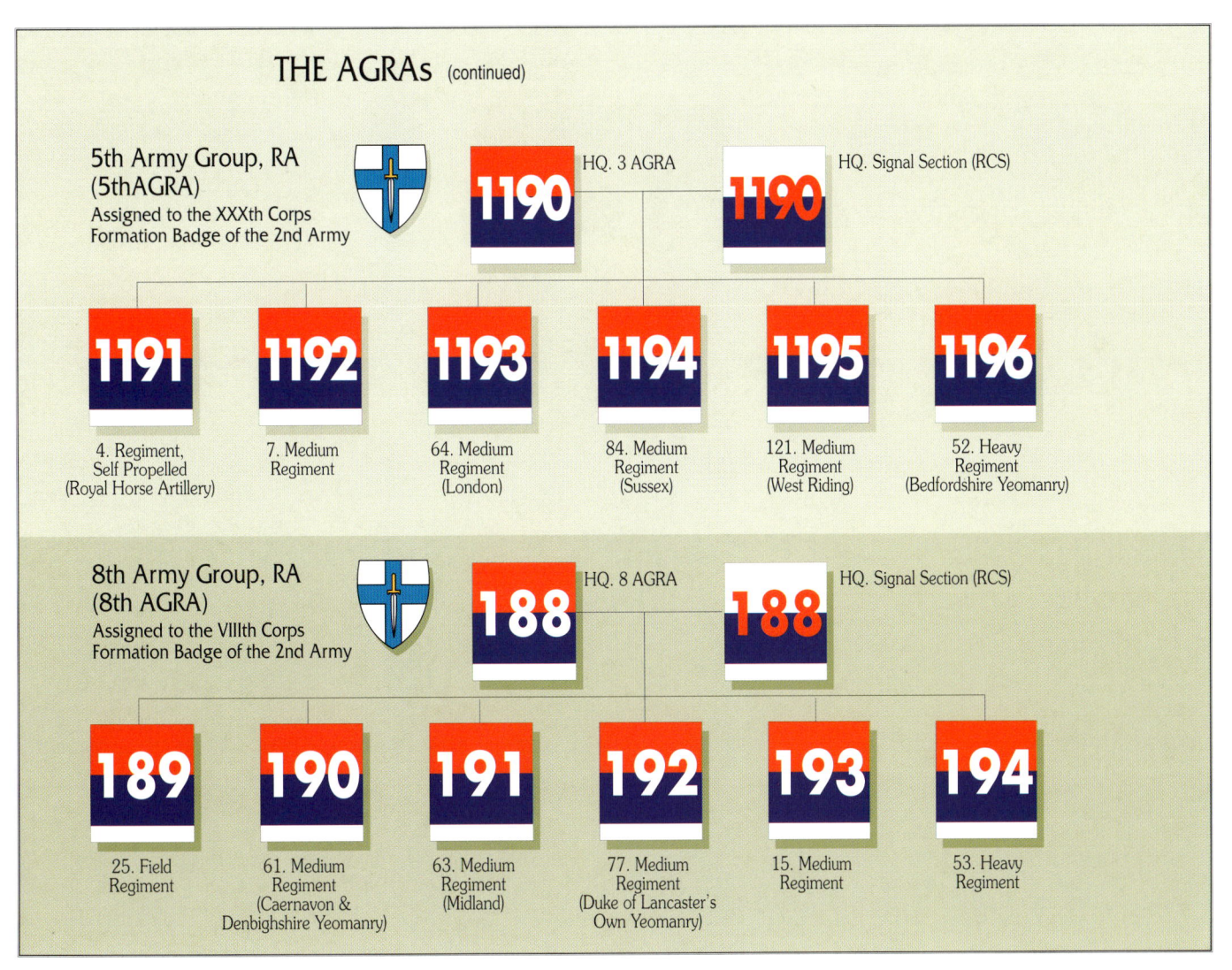

---

## THE AGRAs (continued)

**5th Army Group, RA (5thAGRA)**
Assigned to the XXXth Corps
Formation Badge of the 2nd Army

- HQ. 3 AGRA — 1190
- HQ. Signal Section (RCS) — 1190

- 1191 — 4. Regiment, Self Propelled (Royal Horse Artillery)
- 1192 — 7. Medium Regiment
- 1193 — 64. Medium Regiment (London)
- 1194 — 84. Medium Regiment (Sussex)
- 1195 — 121. Medium Regiment (West Riding)
- 1196 — 52. Heavy Regiment (Bedfordshire Yeomanry)

**8th Army Group, RA (8th AGRA)**
Assigned to the VIIIth Corps
Formation Badge of the 2nd Army

- HQ. 8 AGRA — 188
- HQ. Signal Section (RCS) — 188

- 189 — 25. Field Regiment
- 190 — 61. Medium Regiment (Caernavon & Denbighshire Yeomanry)
- 191 — 63. Medium Regiment (Midland)
- 192 — 77. Medium Regiment (Duke of Lancaster's Own Yeomanry)
- 193 — 15. Medium Regiment
- 194 — 53. Heavy Regiment

## 4. Royal Engineers

**The Engineers supported the assault troops and carried out work on the battlefield and in the rear.**

The Field Companies (squadrons in the Armoured and Airborne Divisions) worked at divisional level with a strength of 7 officers and 250 men.

The Field Park Company included a magazine workshop, various earth-moving machines which included bulldozers and specialised equipment.

The Bridging Platoon had equipment enabling it to construct a Bailey bridge with a 25m bay and 40 tonnes maximum weight at its disposal. The large bridging operations were undertaken by the Sappers of the army corps or of the army.

The Royal Engineers used regiments equipped with special armour, using converted Churchill and Sherman tanks. They were called Armoured Vehicles, Royal Engineers (AVRE);

Finally, water supply and postal deliveries were carried out by specialised units of the Royal Engineers.

### The "R" Force

The "R" Force was an inter-arm unit attached directly to the headquarters of the 21st Army Group and placed under the orders of the Royal Engineers.

At the time of the Normandy battles, certain units fulfilled a deception role, and bore the insignia of the 76th Infantry Division.

*Above*
**Normandy, 18th July 1944. A Cromwell tank of the 7th Armoured Division crossing the Orne on a Bailey bridge which had been christened "York". It was a single level, double trellis bridge, using boats to support the junction in the middle.**
*(IWM)*

*Opposite left*
**Cloth insignia of "R" Force**

*Below*
**A tracked Caterpillar tractor D8 of the Royal Engineers extracts one of the Royal Engineers' diesel locomotives from an LCT.**
*(IWM)*

## The BAILEY BRIDGE

It was made up of metal elements assembled with pins and nuts and bolts.

Depending on the junctions, the Bailey Bridge could be built with or without intermediate support, or on floating supports (boats).

It could take a weight of up to 70 tonnes, this depending on the number of levels and supports put in place.

It took a Bridging Platoon of 40 men 2 to 3 hours to erect a 24 metre span, 40 tonne bridge without supports. Interrupted bridging sections could be constructed across water by supporting Bailey Bridge elements on pontoons.

Movement was effected by means of a small motor boat or by guidelines from the shores.

*Opposite right*
**The different types of Bailey bridge, trellis and stages from an instruction Manual in French.**
*(DR)*

*Above.*
**Carried by 6 men with metal carrying bars**
*(DR)*

*Above and left*
**One of the Bailey Bridge panels and handling methods used by the sappers of the Royal Engineers**
*(DR)*

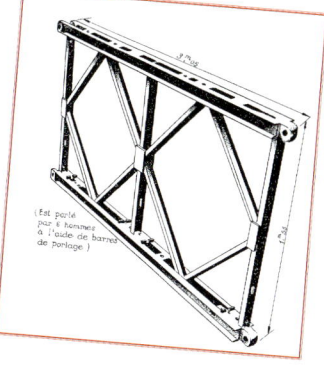

*Below*
**Wood and canvas folding boat. Capacity:**
**One Infantry section and two sappers**
**Mobility: oars, hauling or outboard motors**
**Land transport: RASC lorries.**
**Operation: under the responsibility of the Royal Engineers.**
*(DR)*

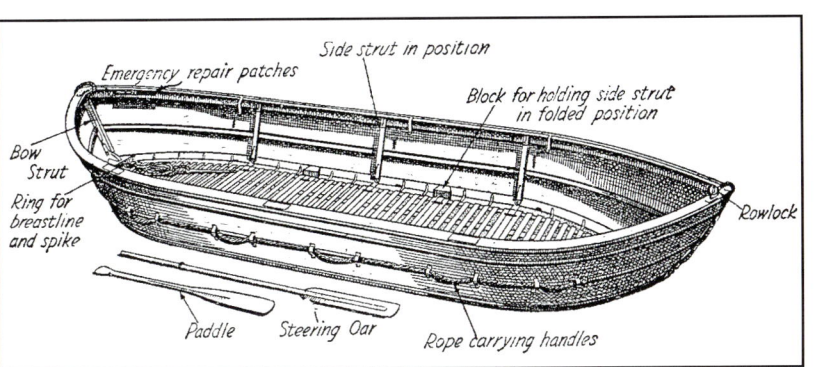

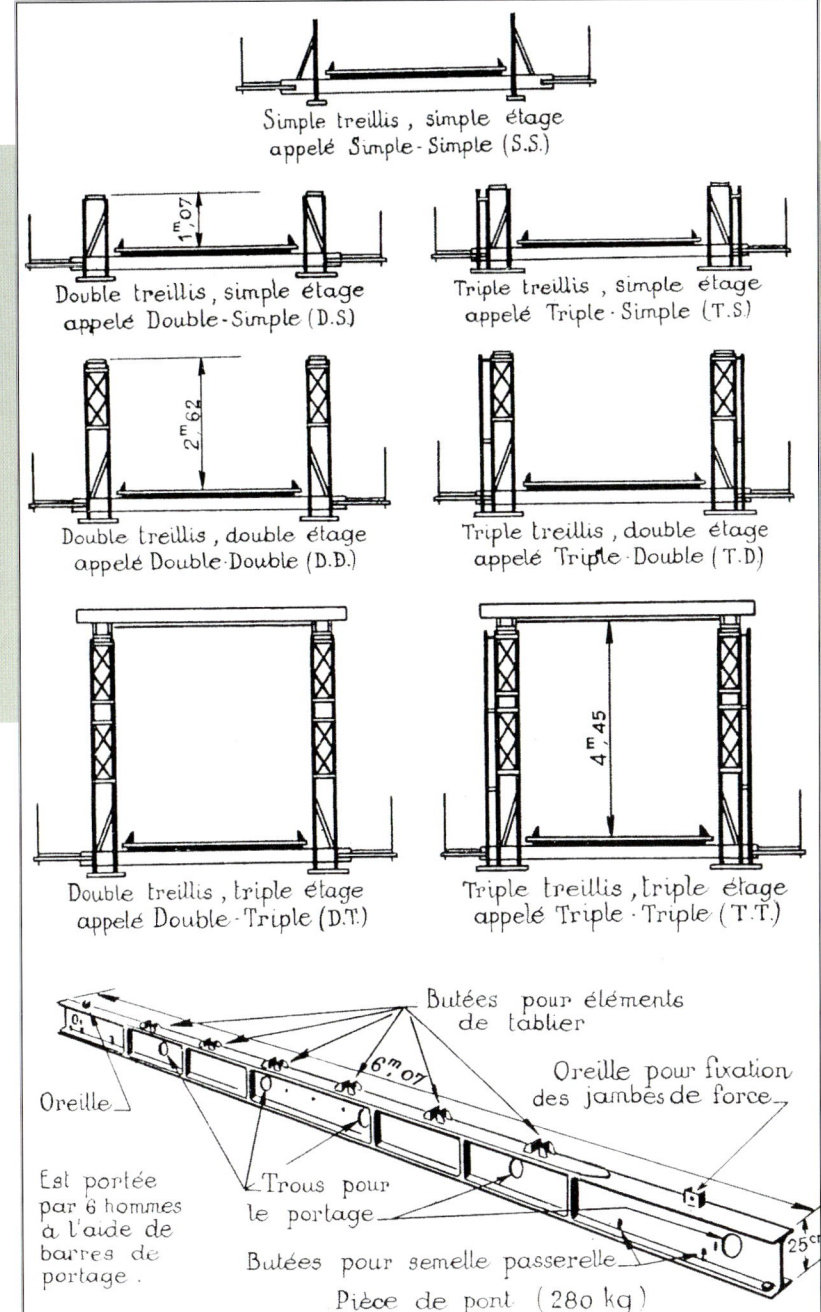

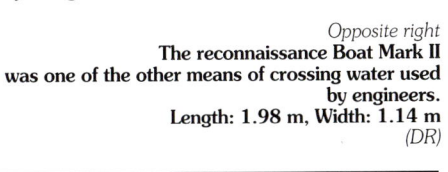

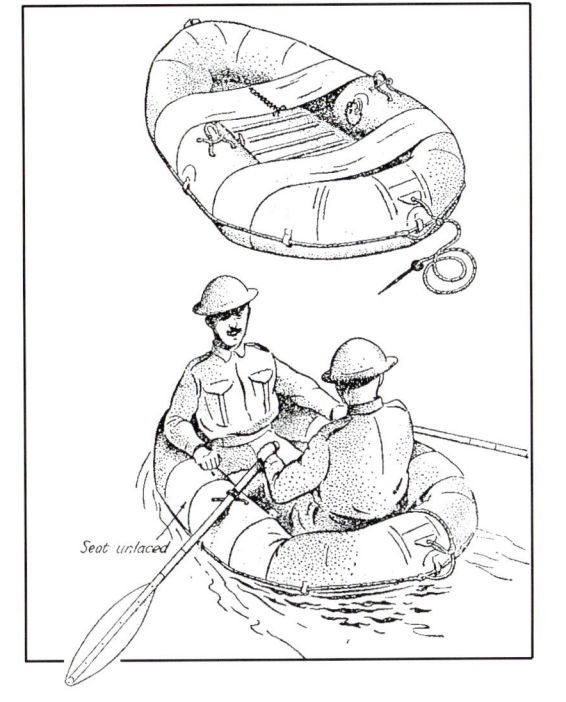

*Opposite right*
**The reconnaissance Boat Mark II was one of the other means of crossing water used by engineers.**
**Length: 1.98 m, Width: 1.14 m**
*(DR)*

37

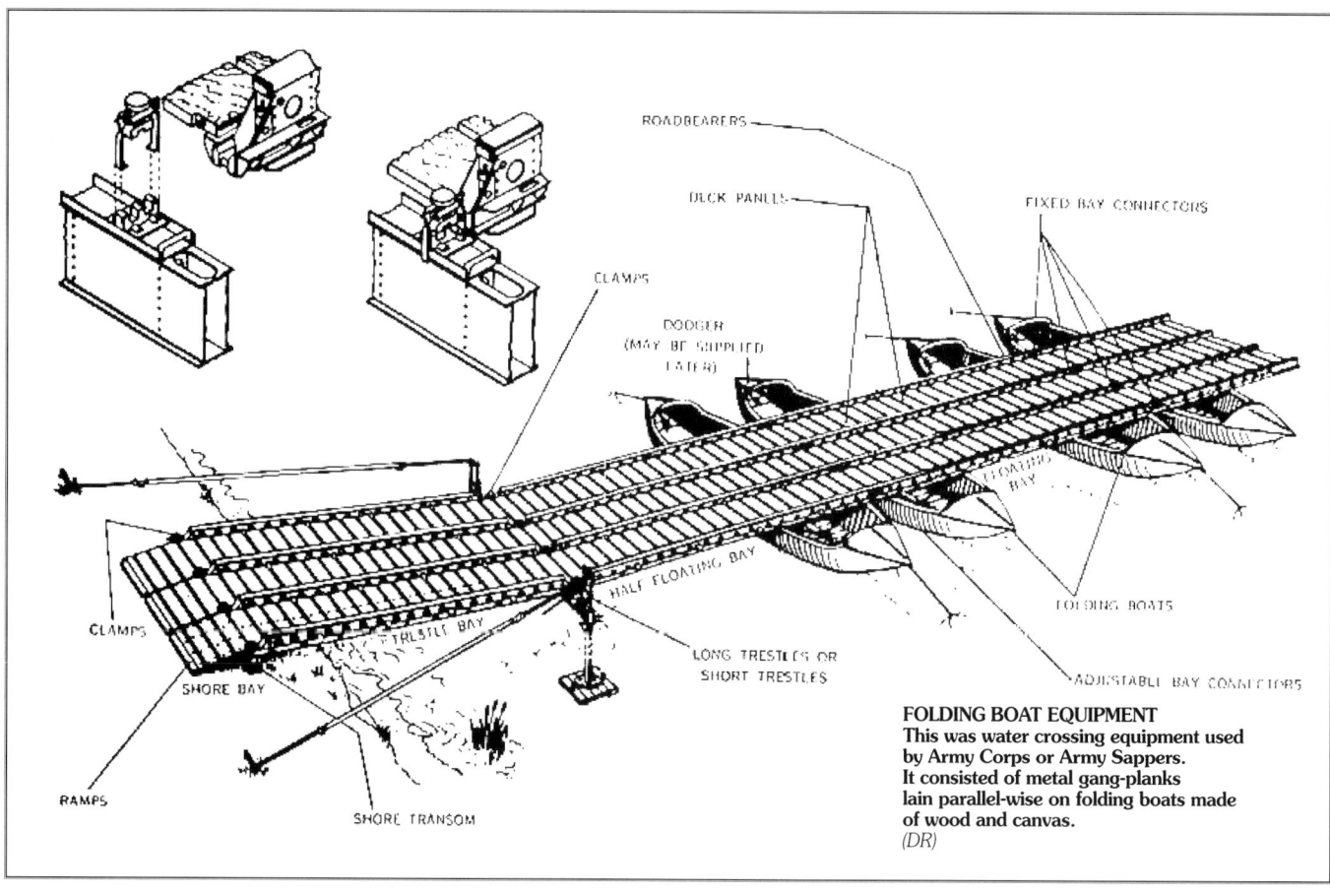

**FOLDING BOAT EQUIPMENT**
This was water crossing equipment used by Army Corps or Army Sappers. It consisted of metal gang-planks lain parallel-wise on folding boats made of wood and canvas.
*(DR)*

*Previous page, top.*
**Belgium, October 1944.** A 30-cwt lorry crossing a triple trellis single stage Bailey Bridge set up by the Bridging Platoon of the 49th "West Riding" Infantry Division.
*(IWM)*

*Above left*
**Normandy, June 1944.** A Caterpillar D6 Bulldozer on a beach. These machines had many uses on the beaches as well as behind the front-line: clearing away, towing, opening up roads, etc.
*(Private collection)*

*Above right*
An armoured Caterpillar D7 bulldozer equipped with a Hyser D7N winch at the rear in the middle of a clearing up operation.
*(IWM)*

*Opposite right.*
This shot taken at Mesnil-Patry, near Bretteville l'Orgueuilleuse, shows various machines at work, Caterpillar D6, excavator and tip-lorry. *(IWM)*

*Below*
**Steam Locomotive of the Royal Engineers of the WD Austerity Class 2-8-0.**
*(Musée des Chemins de Fer, France)*

39

# 5. The Royal Corps of Signals*

The units of the signals arm were present at all levels of the command structure.

They used all communication means: radio, telephones, teletypewriter, and liaison personnel. At division level, the Royal Corps of Signals had a strength of about 28 officers and 700 NCOs spread around in three companies (called Squadrons in the Armoured Divisions).

One company was assignated to divisional headquarters, one to the artillery, the third allocating its elements in each brigade command post. RCS personnel were detached to practically all the other arms and services.

## RCS vehicles

The main means of transport for the RCS were:
— Truck, 15 cwt, 4 x 2 Wireless, House Type, Morris C4 Mk III.
— Truck, 15 cwt, 4 x 2 Wireless, light Warning Type A, Ford WOT 2H.
— Truck, 15cwt, 4 x 2 Wireless, GS, FFR, Bedford MWR, Nos 19 or 21 Radio sets.
— Lorry, 3 ton, 4 x 4, Bedford QLR Wireless.

---

* See also Chapter 10, Vol. 1, page 128 "Signalisation, surveying, optics, signals".

# 6. Infantry

## The Regiment.

Under the command of a colonel, the infantry regiment did not have a fighting unit function. It existed as an administrative centre, for training, depot and as the keeper of the traditions of the unit.

The regiment took its name either from a defined area (Dorsetshire, Northamptonshire, etc) or from the local aristocracy or from the Royal Family (Duke of Wellington's, King's Own).

There were two subdivisions within infantry regiments.

— **the Fusiliers.** An honorary title symbolised by the flaming grenade worn on the cap badge.

— **the Light Infantry and the Rifles.** These were regiments which carried on the traditions of the light infantry companies which, during the 18th century, carried out the reconnaissance for the main body of the Army and signalled their presence by sounding their horns. This instrument was still present on their cap badges, with the exception of the Royal Ulster Rifles.

The distinctive colours of the Rifles were black and dark green, black and scarlet for the KRRC.

The designation King's Royal Rifle Corps or Rifle Brigade did not imply any particular tactical organisation, the battalion remained the basic fighting unit.

## The Battalions

These were commanded by a lieutenant-colonel, the battalions were units making up a whole. They constituted the infantry fighting elements, including the airborne part.

## INFANTRY BATTALION TOOLS
(excluding tools supplied with vehicles and machines)

| | |
|---|---|
| Mine Bars | 13 |
| Saws | 15 |
| Chainsaws | 4 |
| Axes | 37 |
| Sledgehammers | 12 |
| Pickaxes | 160 |
| Bill-hooks | 8 |
| Spades | 198 |
| Shovels | 2 |
| Machettes | 56 |
| Folding wire-cutters | 57 |
| Sand bags | 800 |

*Field Engineering (Army Council Instruction war Office, 5th February 1944)*

## INFANTRY BATTALION
### War Strength (36 officers, 809 men, total 845 men)

| | Battalion Headquarters | Headquarter Company — Headquarters | Headquarter Company — Signal Platoon | Headquarter Company — Administrative Platoon | Support Company — Headquarters | Support Company — 3 in Mortar Platoon | Support Company — Carrier Platoon | Support Company — Anti-Tank Platoon | Support Company — Pioneer Platoon | 4 Rifle Companies (A,B,C,D) — Headquarters | 4 Rifle Companies — Platoon x 3 |
|---|---|---|---|---|---|---|---|---|---|---|---|
| Battalion Commander Lieutenant colonel | 1 | | | | | | | | | | |
| Second in Command Major | 1 | | | | | | | | | | |
| Major ou Captain | | 1 | | | 1 | | | | | 1 | |
| Adjutants (Captain) [1] | 1 | | | | | | | | | | |
| Captains | | | | | | | 1 | 1 | 1 | | |
| Subalterns [2] | 1 | | 1 | 1 | | 1 | 1 | 1 | 1 | | 1 |
| Quartermaster [3] | | | | 1 | | | | | | | |
| **Total Officers** | 4 | 1 | 1 | 2 | 1 | 1 | 2 | 2 | 1 | 2 | 1 |
| Warrant Officers and Other Ranks | 45 [4] | 5 | 35 | 51 | 8 | 41 | 60 | 51 | 21 | 14 [5] | 36 |
| **Total** | 49 | 6 | 36 | 53 | 9 | 42 | 62 | 53 | 22 | 16 | 37 |

**Personnel attached 1 Chaplain (Royal Army Chaplain Department)**

| | | | | | | | | | | | |
|---|---|---|---|---|---|---|---|---|---|---|---|
| Medical officer (Royal Army Medical Corps) | 1 | | | | | | | | | | |
| Armourers and car mechanics (REME) | | | | | 3 | | 1 | 1 | 2 | | |
| Cobbler (Royal Army Ordnance Corps) | | | | | 1 | | | | | | |
| Cooks (Army Catering Corps) | | | | | 15 | | | | | | |

Base and reinforcement personnel: 1 Captain, 6 subalterns, 175 Warrant Officers and men
Scottish- and Irish- recruited Battalions (except Royal Ulster Rifles) : 5 pipers including 1 Sergeant

---

1. Office personnel commander and Second in command
2. Lieutenants or Second Lieutenants
3. Detail Officer
4. including 20 stretcher-bearers
5. including 2 sharpshooters

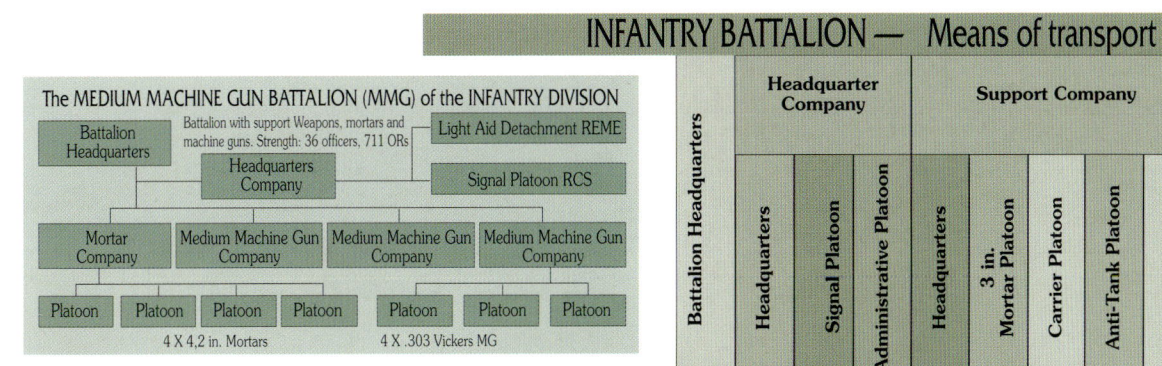

### The MEDIUM MACHINE GUN BATTALION (MMG) of the INFANTRY DIVISION

Battalion with support Weapons, mortars and machine guns. Strength: 36 officers, 711 ORs

- Battalion Headquarters
- Headquarters Company
- Light Aid Detachment REME
- Signal Platoon RCS
- Mortar Company — Platoon (4 X 4,2 in. Mortars)
- Medium Machine Gun Company — Platoon
- Medium Machine Gun Company — Platoon
- Medium Machine Gun Company — Platoon (4 X .303 Vickers MG)

## INFANTRY BATTALION — Means of transport

| | Battalion Headquarters | Headquarters | Signal Platoon | Administrative Platoon | Headquarters | 3 in. Mortar Platoon | Carrier Platoon | Anti-Tank Platoon | Pioneer Platoon | Headquarters x 4 | Platoon x 3 each | TOTAL INFANTRY BATTALION |
|---|---|---|---|---|---|---|---|---|---|---|---|---|
| Bicyclets | 6 | | 3 | | | | | | | 3 | 1 | 33 |
| Motorbikes solo | 5 | | 4 | 2 | | 3 | 7 | | 5 | | | 26 |
| Jeep | 2 | | 1 | 1 | 1 | | | | 3 | 1 | | 12 +1* |
| 15 cwt 4 x 2 trucks General Service | 2 | 1 | 2 | 1 | 1 | 3 | 2 | 2 | 2 | 3 | | 28 |
| 15 cwt 4 x 2 truck Office | 1 | | | | | | | | | | | 1 |
| 15 cwt 4 x 2 truck 900-litre tanker | | | | 1 | | | | | | | | 1 |
| 15 cwt 4 x 4 truck Personnel | 1 | | 1 | | | | | | | | | 2 |
| 3-ton 4 x 4 truck General service | | | | 13 | | | | | 1 | | | 14 |
| Bren gun Carriers Loyd | | | | | | | | 12 | | | | 12 |
| Bren gun Carriers Universal | 1 | | | | | | 13 | 1 | 1 | | | 19 |
| Bren gun Carriers Universal 3-in mortar | | | | | | 7 | | | | | | 7 |
| Trailers 10cwt general service | | | | 1 | | | | | 2 | | | 3 |
| Trailers 15 cwt 800 litre- water tanker | | | | 1 | | | | | | | | 1 |

*Chaplain

### INDEPENDENT MEDIUM MACHINE GUN COMPANY

A unit always taken from an Infantry Battalion, entirely in the case of an Infantry Division, at company level in the case of Armoured Division.

- Company Headquarters
- Mortar Platoon (4 X 4,2 in. Mortars)
- Machine Gun Platoon (4 X .303 Vickers MG)
- Machine Gun Platoon
- Machine Gun Platoon
- Flamethrower Platoon (6 "Wasp" Carriers)

## INFANTRY BATTALION — Weapons

| | Battalion Headquarters | Headquarters | Signal Platoon | Administrative Platoon | Headquarters | 3 inc. Mortar Platoon | Carrier Platoon | Anti-Tank Platoon | Pioneer Platoon | Headquarters x 4 | Platoon x 3 each | TOTAL INFANTRY BATTALION |
|---|---|---|---|---|---|---|---|---|---|---|---|---|
| .380 revolver | 4 | 1 | 1 | 1 | 1 | 1 | 2 | 2 | 1 | 2 | 1 | 34 |
| Sten Gun | 1 | 1 | | 1 | 1 | | | | | 1 | 4 | 32 |
| No4 Rifle | 44 | 4 | 35 | 32 | 7 | 41 | 60 | 51 | 21 | 13 | 29 | 695 |
| Bren Gun | 1 | | | 3 | | 2 | 9 | 6 | 2 | 1 | 3 | 63 |
| 2 in. Mortar | | | | | | | | | | 1 | 1 | 26 |
| 3 in. Mortar | | | | | | 6 | | | | | | 6 |
| PIAT | | | | 3 | | 4 | | 4 | | 3 | | 23 |
| 6 pounder Anti-Tank gun | | | | | | | | 6 | | | | 6 |

*Above.*
**An infantryman of the 3rd Infantry Division in position behind a little wall, on the morning of 18th July 1944 in Normandy, during Operation Goodwood.** *(IWM)*

Each regiment provided a certain number of battalions which made up afterwards (though they were more often than not split up) the composition of the Infantry Brigades whether these were in divisions or not.

It is therefore possible to notice identical insignia (cap badges, titles) worn by men fighting on different fronts.

Apart from the infantry battalions, Infantry support units were made up of:

Medium Machine gun Battalions in the Infantry Divisions, Medium machine gun Companies in the Armoured divisions.

# THE BRITISH INFANTRY SEC[TION]

## RIFLE GROUP

**Section Commander (Corporal)** — **Rifle No 1** — **Rifle No 2** — **Rifle No 3**

Sten Mk III

SMLE No4 MkI*

SMLE No4 MkI*

SMLE No4 MkI*

SMLE No4 MkI*

SMLE No4 M[kI*]

- 5 Sten gun magazines
- 160 9mm cartridges
- 2 No36 Mills Bomb

- 10 magazine clips
- 2 Bren gun magazines
- 1 No36 Mills Bomb

- 10 magazine clips
- 2 Bren gun magazines
- 1 No36 Mills Bomb

- 10 magazine clips
- 2 Bren gun magazines
- 1 No36 Mills Bomb

- 10 magazine clips
- 2 Bren gun magazines
- 1 No36 Mills Bomb

1 tool (spade)) — 1 tool (spade) — 1 tool (spade) — 1 tool (pick-a[xe])

The Corporal-Section commander was assisted by a deputy (Lance-Corporal, second in command) who was also the commander of the Bren group. Who carried which tool was at random, except for the machette which was for the Lance-corporal second in command. This fighting unit was concentrated around the light Machine Gun and each member of the group, except the section commander, carried several spare magazines. Ammunition was seven hundred .303 cartridges in 25 magazines.

# N, 1944-1945

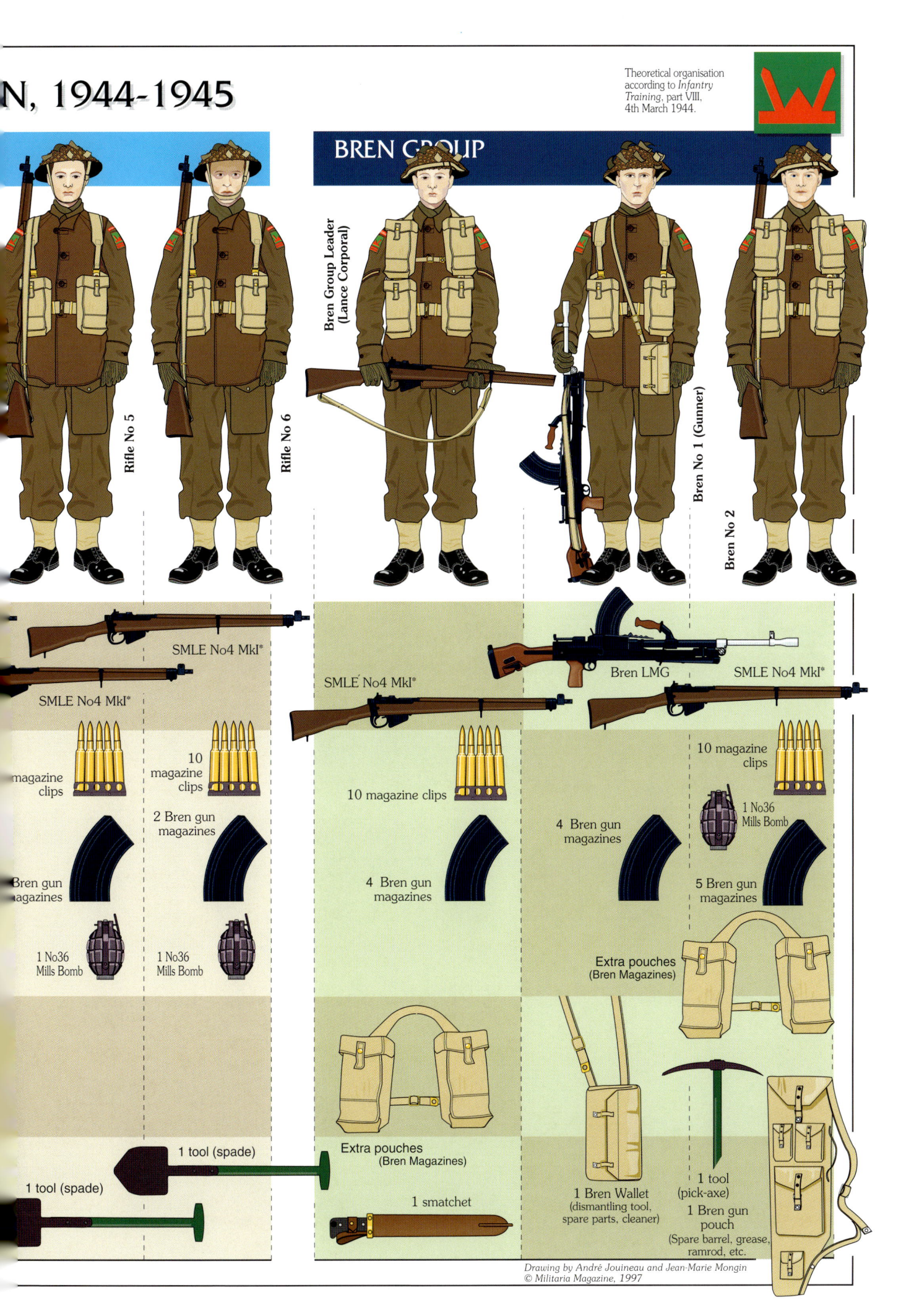

**BREN GROUP**

Theoretical organisation according to *Infantry Training*, part VIII, 4th March 1944.

Rifle No 5 — Rifle No 6 — Bren Group Leader (Lance Corporal) — Bren No 1 (Gunner) — Bren No 2

SMLE No4 MkI* — SMLE No4 MkI* — SMLE No4 MkI* — Bren LMG — SMLE No4 MkI*

10 magazine clips — 10 magazine clips — 10 magazine clips — 4 Bren gun magazines — 10 magazine clips

Bren gun magazines — 2 Bren gun magazines — 4 Bren gun magazines — — 1 No36 Mills Bomb

1 No36 Mills Bomb — 1 No36 Mills Bomb — — — 5 Bren gun magazines

Extra pouches (Bren Magazines)

1 smatchet

1 Bren Wallet (dismantling tool, spare parts, cleaner)

1 tool (pick-axe)

1 Bren gun pouch (Spare barrel, grease, ramrod, etc.)

1 tool (spade) — 1 tool (spade)

*Drawing by André Jouineau and Jean-Marie Mongin*
© *Militaria Magazine, 1997*

43

# The Motor Battalion of the Armoured Brigade

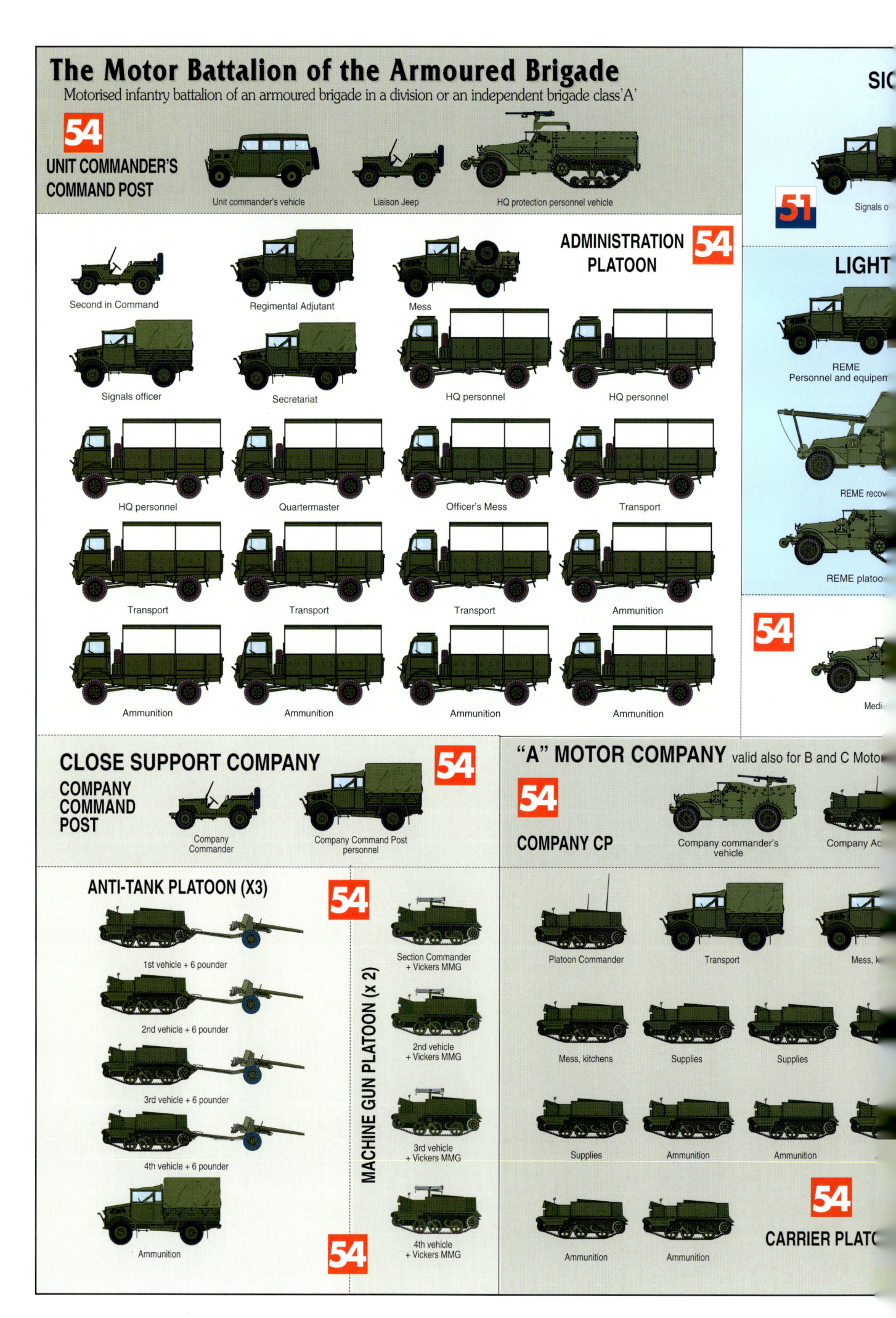

Motorised infantry battalion of an armoured brigade in a division or an independent brigade class 'A'

## 54 UNIT COMMANDER'S COMMAND POST

- Unit commander's vehicle
- Liaison Jeep
- HQ protection personnel vehicle

## ADMINISTRATION PLATOON 54

- Second in Command
- Regimental Adjutant
- Mess
- Signals officer
- Secretariat
- HQ personnel
- HQ personnel
- HQ personnel
- Quartermaster
- Officer's Mess
- Transport
- Transport
- Transport
- Transport
- Ammunition
- Ammunition
- Ammunition
- Ammunition
- Ammunition

## CLOSE SUPPORT COMPANY 54

### COMPANY COMMAND POST
- Company Commander
- Company Command Post personnel

### ANTI-TANK PLATOON (X3) 54
- 1st vehicle + 6 pounder
- 2nd vehicle + 6 pounder
- 3rd vehicle + 6 pounder
- 4th vehicle + 6 pounder
- Ammunition

### MACHINE GUN PLATOON (x 2) 54
- Section Commander + Vickers MMG
- 2nd vehicle + Vickers MMG
- 3rd vehicle + Vickers MMG
- 4th vehicle + Vickers MMG

## "A" MOTOR COMPANY valid also for B and C Motor... 54

### COMPANY CP
- Company commander's vehicle
- Company A...
- Platoon Commander
- Transport
- Mess, k...
- Mess, kitchens
- Supplies
- Supplies
- Supplies
- Ammunition
- Ammunition
- Ammunition
- Ammunition

## CARRIER PLATO... 54

---

44

## CORPS PLATOON

- Signals personnel and equipment
- Signals personnel and equipment

## DETACHMENT (REME)

- REME Personnel and equipement
- REME Personnel and equipement
- REME workshop lorry

- Medical evacuation

- Company personnel
- Company secretariat
- Company Command Post
- Company Command Post personnel

**PLATOON 1**
- Platoon commander's vehicle
- 2nd vehicle
- 3rd vehicle
- 4th vehicle

**PLATOON 2**
- Platoon commander's vehicle
- 2nd vehicle
- 3rd vehicle
- 4th vehicle

**PLATOON 3**
- Platoon commander's vehicle
- 2nd vehicle
- 3rd vehicle
- 4th vehicle

*Above*
Bren gun carrier from the 1st Motor Battalion (white number 54 on a red square) Grenadier Guards of the Guards Armoured Division (the insignia is an eye on the front left mudguard) crossing the Orne during Operation *Goodwood*. (IWM)

45

*Above.*
**Rifle Battalions.**
Here the 7th Cameronians (Scottish Rifles) parade by marching at the double, carrying their weapons in their right hand.
The band is composed of bugles and drums.
*(IWM)*

### COMPANY HEADQUARTER (platoon command)

| | | | | | |
|---|---|---|---|---|---|
| Officers | Major | 1 | .38 revolver | 2 |
| | Captain, Second in Command | 1 | Sten gun | 1 |
| WO/OR | Company Sergeant Major (CSM) | 1 | No 4 Rifle | 13 |
| | Company Quartermaster Sergeant (CQMS) | 1 | Bren gun | 1 |
| | Secretary | 1 | Piat | 3 |
| | Corporal (driver, car mechanic) | 1 | 2 in.Mortar (signalisation) | 1 |
| | Corporal (Mess) | 1 | | |
| | Privates (supply) | 1 | Bicycle | 3 |
| | Laison staff | 3 | Jeep | 1 |
| | cook, butcher | 1 | 15-cwt Truck GS | 3 |
| | Orderies, batmen | 4 | Universal Carrier | 1 |
| | Total | 16 | radio sets SET 18 and SET 38 | |

## COMBAT COMPANY

### 3rd INFANTRY PLATOON
### 2nd INFANTRY PLATOON
### 1st INFANTRY PLATOON

| Platoon Command Post | No 4 Rifle | Cartridges | Sten gun | Mag. | Cart. | Bren gun | Mag. | Cart. | 2-in. Mortar | explosive shells | Smoke bombs | Hand grenades | Misc. |
|---|---|---|---|---|---|---|---|---|---|---|---|---|---|
| Platoon Commander 1st or 2nd Lieut. | | | | | | | | | | | | | .38 revolver |
| Platoon Sergeant | 1 | 50 | | | | | | | | | | 4 | |
| Lance Corporal (Mortar) | 1 | 50 | | | | | | | | 3 | 9 | | |
| Mortar, No1 | | | 1 | 5 | 160 | | | | 1 | 3 | 3 | | |
| Mortar, No2 | 1 | 50 | | | | | | | | 6 | 6 | | |
| Liaison (runner) | 1 | 50 | | | | | | | | | | 2 | |
| Orderly | 1 | 50 | | | | | | | | | | | Radio set¹ |
| **Three sections of fusiliers each** | | | | | | | | | | | | | |
| Corporal, section commander | | | 1 | 5 | 160 | | | | | | | 2 | |
| No 1 Rifle | 1 | 50 | | | | 2 | 56 + 50 | | | | | 1 | |
| No 2 Rifle | 1 | 50 | | | | 2 | 56 + 50 | | | | | 1 | 6 grenades with the command post and 10 grenades per sectiion of the 36, 69 and 77 type.s and types 74 and 75 according to circumstances. |
| No 3 Rifle | 1 | 50 | | | | 2 | 56 + 50 | | | | | 1 | |
| No 4 Rifle | 1 | 50 | | | | 2 | 56 + 50 | | | | | 1 | |
| No 5 Rifle | 1 | 50 | | | | 2 | 56 + 50 | | | | | 1 | |
| No 6 Rifle | 1 | 50 | | | | 2 | 56 + 50 | | | | | 1 | |
| **Bren Group** | | | | | | | | | | | | | |
| Lance Corporal | 1 | 50 | | | | 4 | 112 | | | | | | |
| Gunner | | | | | | 1 | 4 | 112 | | | | | |
| Loader | 1 | 50 | | | | 5 | 140 | | | | | 2 | |

(1) Radio sets SET 18 and SET 38

# 7. Reconnaissance Corps

Created in January 1941. Although having its own organisation and individual insignia, this corps became a sub-division of the Royal Armoured Corps in January 1944. It made up the reconnaissance regiments of the Infantry Divisions exclusively, the numbering being that of the division to which it belonged.

(Except for the 51st (Highland) Infantry Division which had a reconnaissance Regiment originating from the Cavalry, the 2nd Derbyshire Yeomanry)

*Below.*
**September 1944. A convoy of the 15th Reconnaissance Regiment [15th (Scottish) Infantry Division] moving towards the Belgian border.**
*(IWM)*

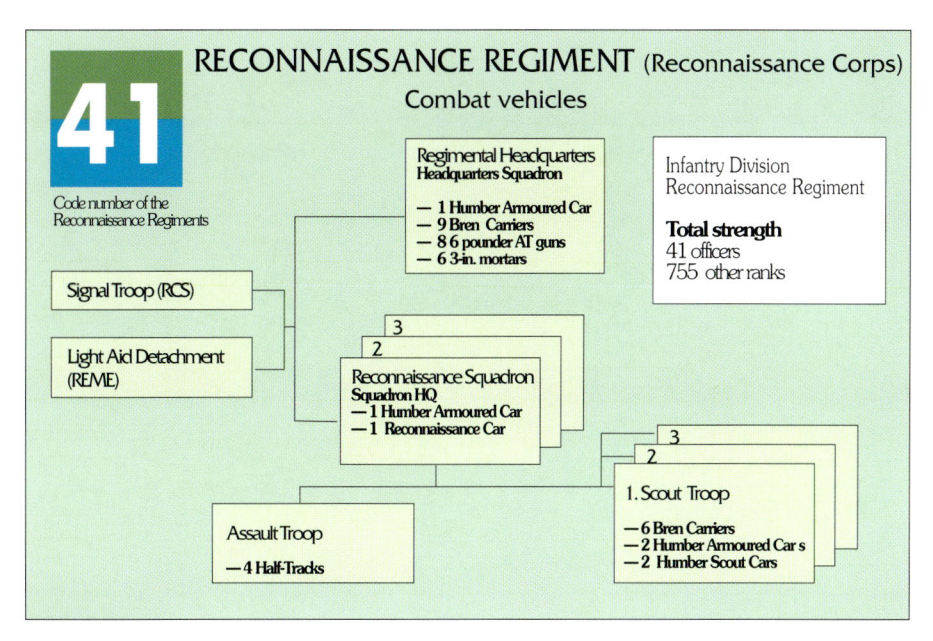

## RECONNAISSANCE REGIMENT (Reconnaissance Corps)
### Combat vehicles

**41** — Code number of the Reconnaissance Regiments

**Regimental Headquarters / Headquarters Squadron**
- 1 Humber Armoured Car
- 9 Bren Carriers
- 8 6 pounder AT guns
- 6 3-in. mortars

**Infantry Division Reconnaissance Regiment**

**Total strength**
41 officers
755 other ranks

- Signal Troop (RCS)
- Light Aid Detachment (REME)

**Reconnaissance Squadron** (×3)
Squadron HQ
- 1 Humber Armoured Car
- 1 Reconnaissance Car

**1. Scout Troop** (×3)
- 6 Bren Carriers
- 2 Humber Armoured Cars
- 2 Humber Scout Cars

**Assault Troop**
- 4 Half-Tracks

# 8. Army Air Corps

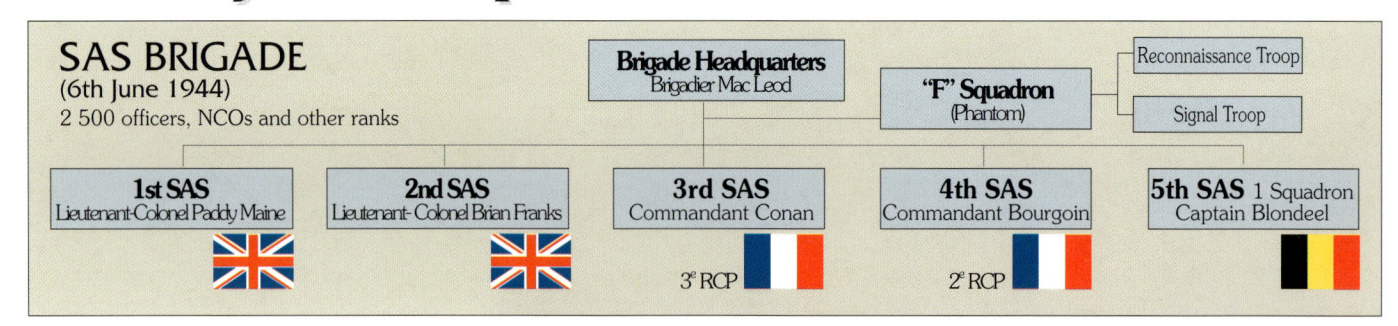

**SAS BRIGADE** (6th June 1944)
2 500 officers, NCOs and other ranks

- Brigade Headquarters: Brigadier Mac Leod
- "F" Squadron (Phantom)
  - Reconnaissance Troop
  - Signal Troop
- 1st SAS — Lieutenant-Colonel Paddy Maine 🇬🇧
- 2nd SAS — Lieutenant-Colonel Brian Franks 🇬🇧
- 3rd SAS — Commandant Conan 🇫🇷 3ᵉ RCP
- 4th SAS — Commandant Bourgoin 🇫🇷 2ᵉ RCP
- 5th SAS — 1 Squadron Captain Blondeel 🇧🇪

The Air Corps of the Army was created in February 1942 and consisted of:
- **the Glider Pilot Regiment** (1942), pilots and co-pilots of gliders.
- **the Parachute regiment** (1942) parachute battalions
- **the Special Air Service** (17th November 1941). Parachute units integrated into the Army Air Corps in January 1944.
- **the Independent Parachute Companies** (Pathfinders). Parachute companies for lighting and marking out.

## Special Air Service Regiment

This was a brigade organised within the Army Air Corps in January 1944. It was made up of 5 basic units of which 4 form a light battalion of about 450 officers, NCOs and men and operating most often as isolated units.

Most missions were behind enemy communication lines: sabotage, information, support for resistance movements.

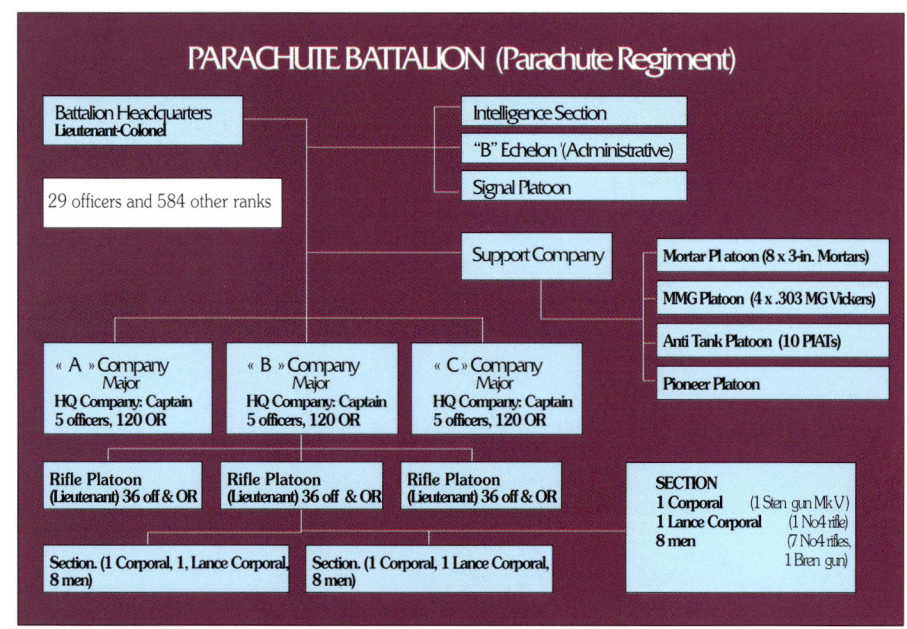

### PARACHUTE BATTALION (Parachute Regiment)

- Battalion Headquarters Lieutenant-Colonel — 29 officers and 584 other ranks
  - Intelligence Section
  - "B" Echelon (Administrative)
  - Signal Platoon
  - Support Company
    - Mortar Platoon (8 x 3-in. Mortars)
    - MMG Platoon (4 x .303 MG Vickers)
    - Anti Tank Platoon (10 PIATs)
    - Pioneer Platoon
  - "A" Company Major — HQ Company: Captain — 5 officers, 120 OR
  - "B" Company Major — HQ Company: Captain — 5 officers, 120 OR
  - "C" Company Major — HQ Company: Captain — 5 officers, 120 OR
    - Rifle Platoon (Lieutenant) 36 off & OR
      - Section. (1 Corporal, 1 Lance Corporal, 8 men)
    - Rifle Platoon (Lieutenant) 36 off & OR
      - Section. (1 Corporal, 1 Lance Corporal, 8 men)
    - Rifle Platoon (Lieutenant) 36 off & OR
  - **SECTION**
    - 1 Corporal (1 Sten gun Mk V)
    - 1 Lance Corporal (1 No4 rifle)
    - 8 men (7 No4 rifles, 1 Bren gun)

# 9. Royal Army Chaplain's Department

A corps of military chaplains, all of whom had officer rank.

It included the chaplains of Christian Churches: Anglican, Catholic and other denominations as well as Jewish.

The chaplains were present in all large units.

*Right.*
**Rev. J. Gwinnett, Padre of the Airborne Forces (9th Parachute Battalion) completed the training course for the Parachute Regiment, whose wings he wears.**
*(IWM)*

*Far Right.*
**A convoy of RASC Chevrolet trucks returning empty after having re-supplied a unit fighting near Caen in July 1944.**
*(IWM)*

# 10. Royal Army Service Corps

A transport and supply service organised in numbered companies.

## The functions of the RASC

Supplying units with food, fuel, ammunition and miscellaneous equipment (except weapons, vehicles and machines) from depots established by the Service at brigade, division, army corps or army level.

It had also to ensure transport for men and material to units which did not have their own means of transport.

## The RASC Companies

— **Transport Section** including 5 groups of 6 trucks plus 3 in reserve.

— **General services**, supplying personnel for handling, liaison work and road control.

— **Repair sections** carrying out first or second level repairs on service vehicles.

— **Ambulance companies** detached from the Royal Army Medical Corps

— **Loading companies**, stowage and dropping of equipment dispatched by plane.

*Left*
**Normandy 16th July 1944.**
A Sergeant medical orderly of the 4th Royal Welsh Fusiliers (53rd Infantry Division) checking the contents of the Regimental Pannier. The assistant of the Medical Officer (RAMC) detached to the battalion was either an NCO having followed the First Aid Medical Orderly's course as here, or a officer cadet, a doctor from the RAMC.
*(IWM)*

*Below.*
**Evacuation Tags.**
This was tied to dead bodies or to those who had lost consciousness. Completed by an officer or a medical orderly, it had to mention the date, the hour of discovery of the body, apparent lesions and eventually whether a tourniquet had been applied or a shot of morphine given.
*(IWM)*

*Next page, bottom left*
**Installing a Dental Corps field dentistry.**
*(IWM)*

# 11. The Royal Army Medical Corps

The Medical Corps principal function was to keep numbers up in the front-line, in effect preparing and maintaining health conditions and prophylaxy; attending to the sick, evacuation and care for the wounded, clearing up the battlefield and cantonments, documentation and information to the families.

## Services attached to the RAMC

— **Army Dental Corps** (ADC) ensured dental care to units by means of specially transformed vehicles

— **Queen Alexandra Imperial Military Nursing Service** (QAIMNS) Military Nurses' Corps created by Queen Alexandra in 1902.

— **Quakers.**
Conscientious objectors affected to the RAMC as orderlies or stretcher-bearers.

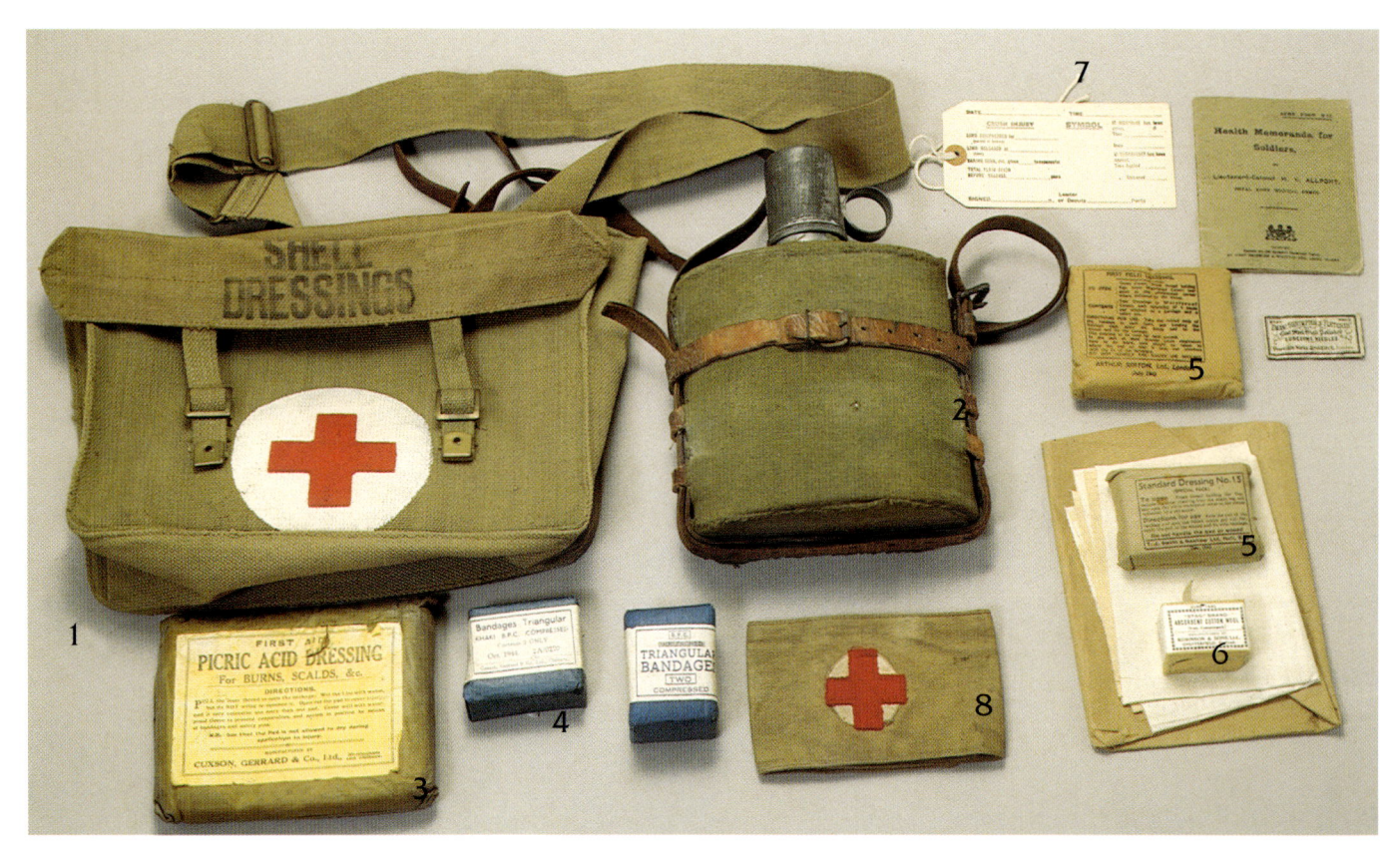

*Above.*
**Equipment necessary for Medical Orderlies.**
1. Bag
2. Flask
3. Bandages for burns.
4. Bandages and compresses
5. Individual Plasters
6. Albuplast, Hydrophilic cotton
7. Evacuation Tag (filled in by the Medical officer)
8. Armband

*Opposite right*
**Emergency anaesthetics**
1. Glass phial of chloroform in a cotton bag. Breaking the bag enables the drug to be inhaled by the victim.
2. An injectable dose of morphine given to combat units. The evacuation teams had to indicate that the victim had had a shot by tying the tag to the uniform or some part of his individual equipment.

*Below right*
**Armbands worn by RAMC and ADC personnel**
1. Model defined as under the international convention of the Red Cross in Geneva.
2. Variant for distribution.

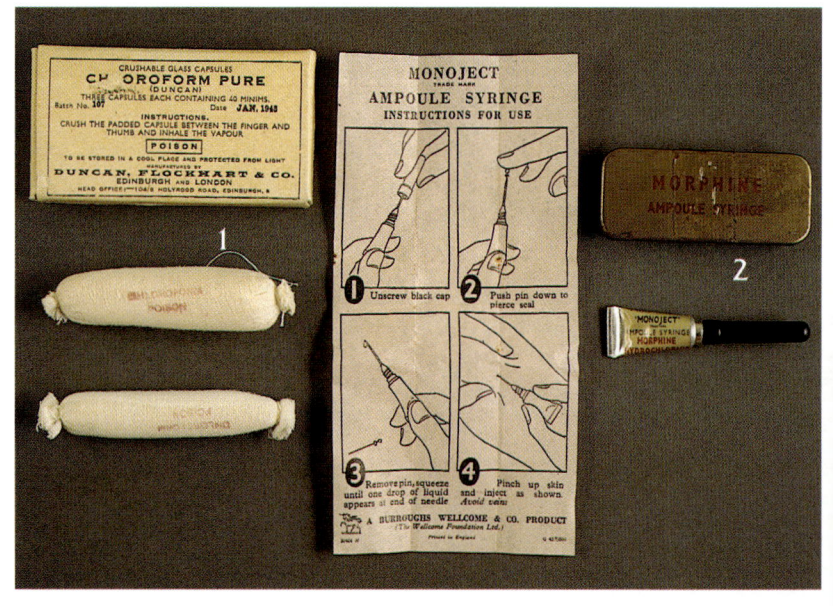

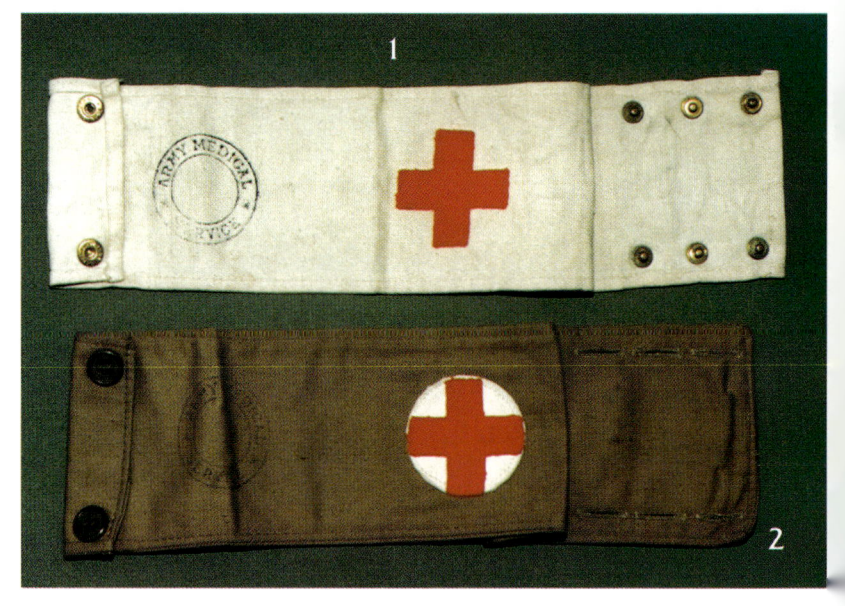

50

## Ambulance Heavy 4x2 Bedford M1

**SPECIFICATIONS**
**Engine:** 6 cylinder petrol, 72 hp
**Transmisssion:** 4 speed gearbox + reverse
**Capacity:** 4 stretcher cases or 10 sitting wounded.
**Range:** 180 kilometres
**Other model:** Austin K 2 - Y

*Opposite right.
Standard stretcher
and medical
orderly
of the evacuation /
collection units.
A folding model
of stretcher
was supplied
mainly
to the airborne
troops.
(Reconstruction)*

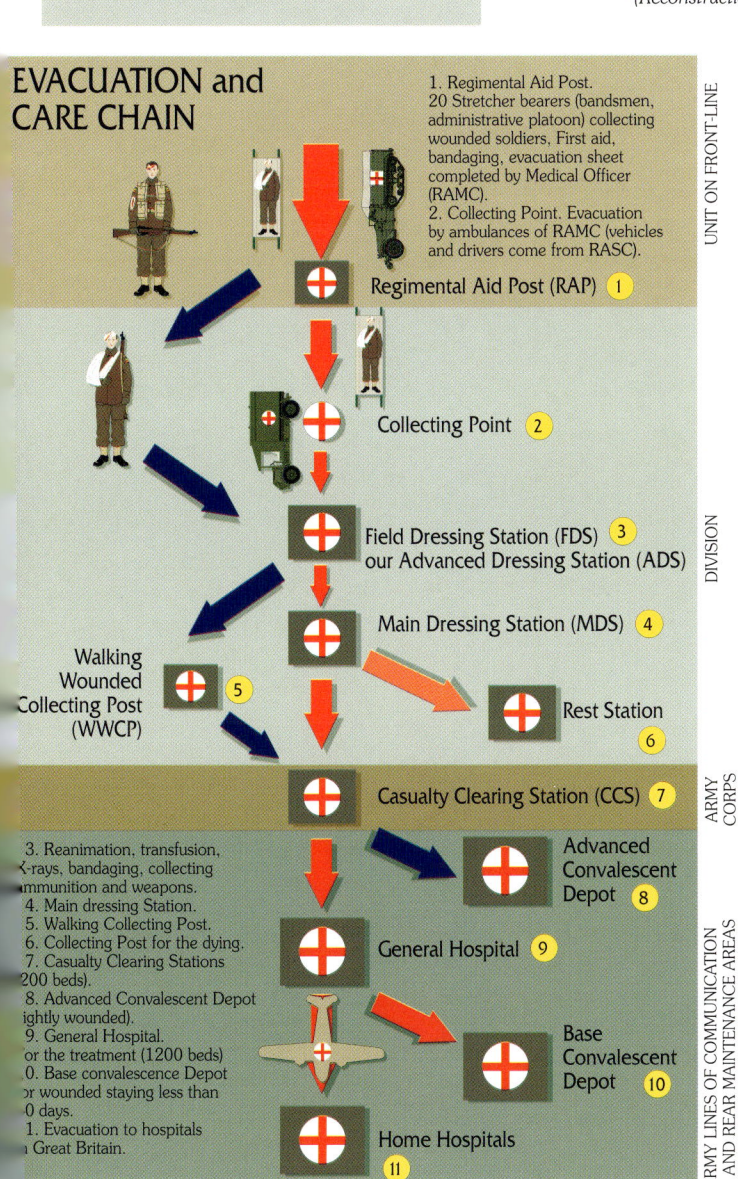

## EVACUATION and CARE CHAIN

1. Regimental Aid Post.
20 Stretcher bearers (bandsmen, administrative platoon) collecting wounded soldiers, First aid, bandaging, evacuation sheet completed by Medical Officer (RAMC).
2. Collecting Point. Evacuation by ambulances of RAMC (vehicles and drivers come from RASC).

UNIT ON FRONT-LINE

- Regimental Aid Post (RAP) 1
- Collecting Point 2
- Field Dressing Station (FDS) 3 our Advanced Dressing Station (ADS)
- Main Dressing Station (MDS) 4
- Walking Wounded Collecting Post (WWCP) 5
- Rest Station 6
- Casualty Clearing Station (CCS) 7

DIVISION

- Advanced Convalescent Depot 8
- General Hospital 9
- Base Convalescent Depot 10
- Home Hospitals 11

ARMY CORPS

ARMY LINES OF COMMUNICATION AND REAR MAINTENANCE AREAS

3. Reanimation, transfusion, X-rays, bandaging, collecting ammunition and weapons.
4. Main dressing Station.
5. Walking Collecting Post.
6. Collecting Post for the dying.
7. Casualty Clearing Stations (200 beds).
8. Advanced Convalescent Depot (lightly wounded).
9. General Hospital.
 or the treatment (1200 beds)
10. Base convalescence Depot
 or wounded staying less than
 0 days.
11. Evacuation to hospitals
 n Great Britain.

51

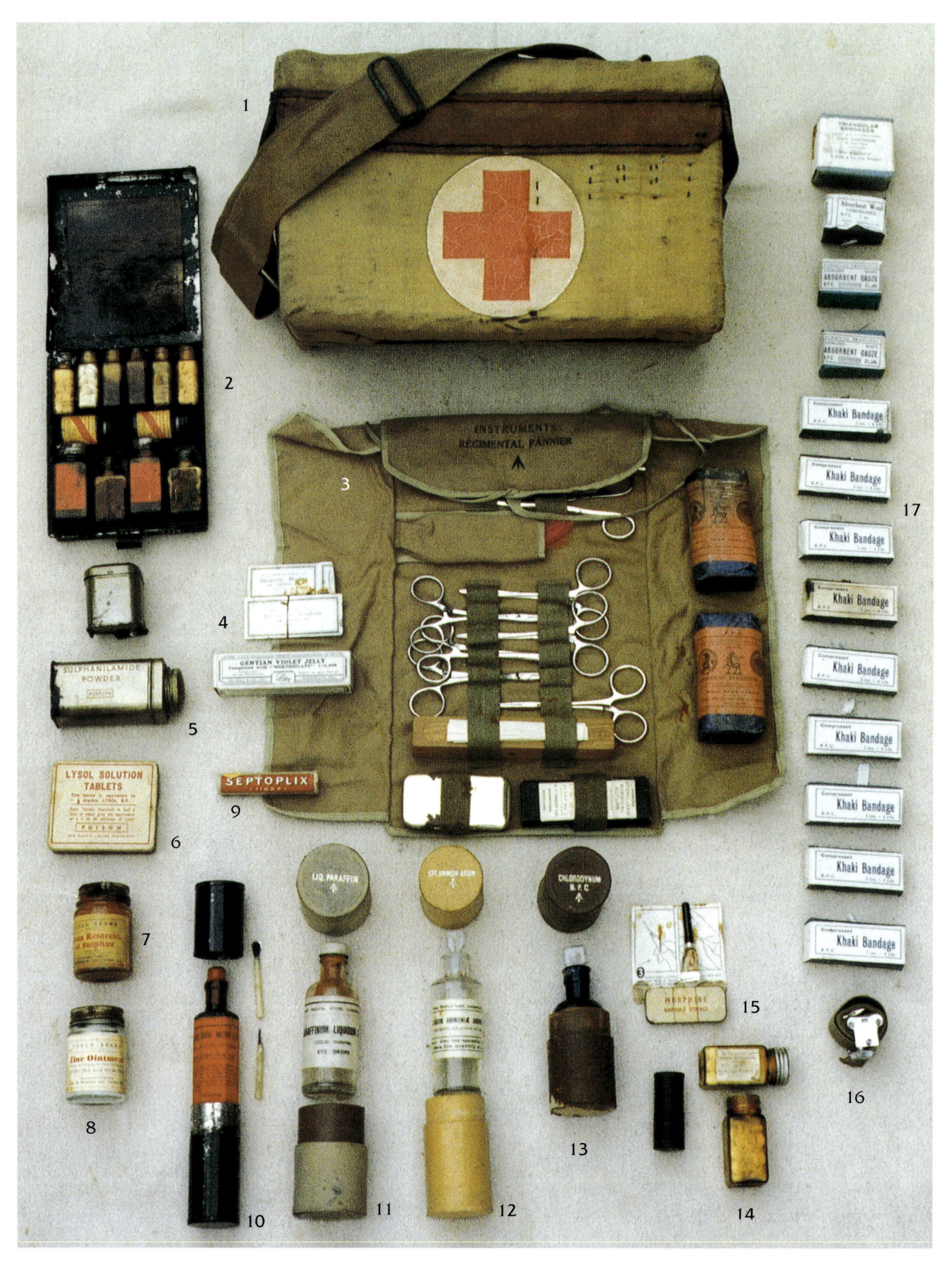

## Regimental Pannier

**Medical and surgical instrument kit for emergency and first aid available in each infantry battalion.**
1. Container. A wicker basket covered in canvas
2. Metal box containing: Anti-tetanus serum, anti-cathar (salts for regaining consciousness) Mercury chloride (purgative), bi-carbonate of soda (digestion), disinfectants (to be drunk in water), cough drops
3. Small surgery bag
4. Antiseptic (gentian violet)
5. Sulfamides
6. Disinfecting tablets for sterilising instruments
7. Antiseptic cream
8. Zinc oxide scarring cream
9. Septoflix. Sulfamide anti septic powder.
10. Tincture of iodine
11. Collyre (for eye burns)
12. Ammoniac liquor
13. Powerful analgesic
14. Aspirine
15. Injection of morphine
16. Tourniquet
17. Bandages and compresses

# 12. Royal Army Ordnance Corps

This was a service ensuring the storage and supply of armament, ammunition, vehicles, armoured vehicles, signals apparatus, clothing certain engineering machines and medical equipment.

Each division or independent brigade had an RAOC pool gathering together immediately available supplies, re-supplying being done in depots stationed at the rear. Moreover the RAOC provided cinema entertainment for the troops. Whether supplied by an arsenal or by a civilian contractor, all supplies for the Army had to be controlled by a commission of civil servants from the War Office and officers from the Royal Army Ordnance Corps.

## Mobile Laundry and bath units

Provision of laundry and shower-bath units was carried out by the RAOC. Each division had an element of this type ensuring the washing or the exchanging of clothes and providing, normally, two weekly baths or showers per man.

*Opposite right*
Sappers of the 154th Field Park Company (code number 48 on the jacket sleeve .divisional engineering units of the 3rd Infantry division, exchanging and leaving clothes at the Mobile laundry and Bath unit of the RAOC of their division.

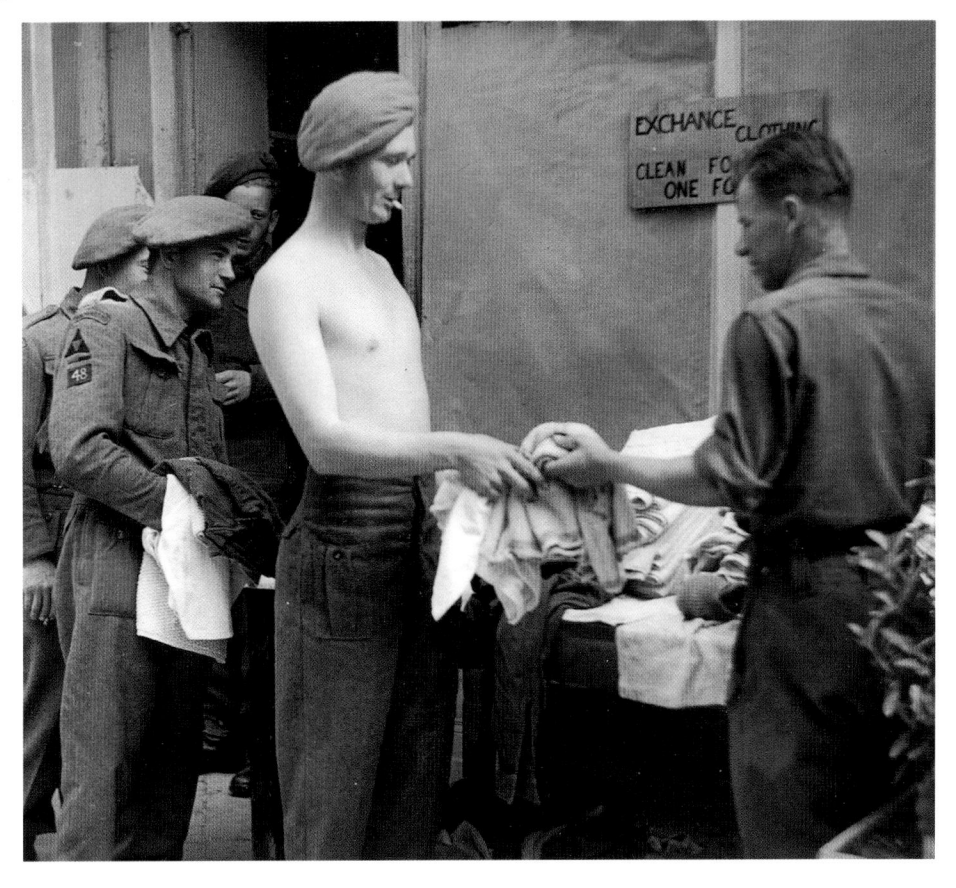

# 13. Royal Electrical and Mechanical Engineers

Created in 1942 this corps ensured the maintenance, repairs and modifications of all the electrical and mechanical material of the Army as well as the recovery of allied or enemy material in the field.

In each division there was a central repair workshop and light workshops (Light Aid Detachments) were spread through the different units.

## Classification of Repairs.

**First level.** Adjustment, replacing of individual spare parts.
**Second level.** Replacement of larger parts or whole units.
**Third level.** Repair, maintenance of units that could not be carried out in the field installations.
**Fourth level.** Repairs needing heavy equipment.

The first and the second levels were carried out at divisional or brigade level, the third and fourth at workshops in bases at the rear.

# 14. Royal Army Pay Corps

This was a service ensuring the financial management of the Army and the paying of the troops, carried out by treasury officers of the Royal Army Pay Corps detached to the units.

# 15. Royal Army Veterinary Corps

Operating at first as individuals, the veterinary surgeons ensured the health - particularly anti-rabies - of the dogs used by the Corps of Military Police (VP) and certain sections of the Royal Engineers where after training, they were used for mine detecting. As the campaign progressed, the presence of thousands of horses left behind by the German Army necessitated the presence of a veterinary hospital in France.

After sorting out and medical care the animals were, for a large part, handed over to French or Belgian farmers. A few left over were used in the port of Antwerp by the services of the 21st Army Group (Horsed) Transport units of the RASC.

# 16. Army Educational Corps

Personnel of the AEC provided theoretical lessons in schools and military academies.

Within the large formations, they carried out the functions of interpreter, giving perfection lessons, refresher courses and foreign language courses.

In the field mobile libraries provided books, notably bilingual dictionaries for lending or sale. The Corps published and circulated information newpapers for the soldiers.

AEC officers could also re-inforce headquarters by ensuring the operational watch.

*Next page below.*
**The front and back pages of the Second Army Newspaper published by the Educational Corps for soldiers in the field; this edition is dated 18th June 1944, midday.**

# 17. Corps of Military Police

Organised into companies or platoons, the Military Police units were present in all the big formations at the front and at the rear.

Their main functions were orientation, marking out of routes (setting up signposts), directing road traffic, controlling prisoners of war, controlling civilians moving around or living in the military area, controlling the behaviour and the military passes of military personnel in the garrison or on leave.

The Military Police wore a khaki cloth cap with a red band for the above missions. An arm insignia in the shape of a lozenge and dark blue in colour with the letters TC (traffic Control) was worn by the sections affected to road traffic control.

## CMP, Vulnerable Points.

The Corps of Military Police, Vulnerable Points was created in 1941 and ensured the the surveillance of strategic positions: depots, radio stations, works of art, etc. The men wore the khaki cloth cap with the blue headpiece and the blue and red lozenge sleeve insignia, bearing the letters VP (Vulnerable Points).

At the end of 1944 and in 1945 battalions made up from the FFIF (French Forces of the Interior), affected to the 21st Army Group, ensured a part of the tasks encumbing to the Corps of Military Police, Vulnerable points.

*Opposite left*
**Normandy, July 1944. A Corps of Military Police Sergeant performing traffic duties.**
*(IWM)*

# 18. The Military Provost Staff Corps

This was the court of military justice composed of judges and lawyers giving verdicts on crimes and offences committed in the war zone.

Its staff was responsible for guarding prisons and internment camps.

# 19. The Pioneer Corps

The Pioneer Corps supplied companies of workers to different units at the front and at the rear.

These units depended on the army or the lines of communication and maintenance zones.

They reinforced:
— the Royal Engineers for road construction, buildings pipelines, etc.
— the Royal Army Service Corps for handling
— the Royal Army Medical Corps for installing hospitals and carrying stretchers.

The Pioneer Corps could employ civilian personnel.

# 20. Intelligence Corps

Created in 1940, this service's purpose was gathering information, counter-espionnage, and evaluating the order of battle and the condition of enemy forces. Military security was also the resposibility of the Intelligence Corps.

In the field, Field Security Sections attached to a division or placed directly under the orders of the army or the army corps were made up of an officer (Field Security Officer) and fifteen or so NCOs who spoke several languages fluently.

# 21. The Army Catering Corps

Created in 1941, the Army Catering Corps had to train and provide cooks for the messes, canteens and field kitchens.

The ACC included apart from the instructors, technical advice officers, management officers, chief-cooks, cooks, bakers, butchers, etc.

An officer (a major or a captain) was assigned at divisional level and a Lieutenant or a Second lieutenant to all units of more than 1,000 men.

Battalions and regiments included personnel from the ACC ensuring the kitchen service, supplies of food being carried out by the Royal Army Service Corps.

# 22. The Army Physical Training Corps

Physical training instructor corps created in 1941. Its personnel were spread through the training centres and the large formations.

# 23. The General Service Corps or General List

The General service Corps gathered all personnel not assigned to a unit and who were present at the depots or training centres

# 24. The Auxiliary Territorial Service

This consisted of auxiliary women volunteers listed for four years or for the duration of the hostilities.

From 1941 the ATS were placed directly under the administration and jurisdiction of the field army where they replaced men in a lot of functions: signals, secretariat, drivers, etc.

At the end of 1944, the ATS serving anti-aircraft guns within the Anti-Aircraft Command were assignedto the anti-aircraft defence of the port of Antwerp.

*Above.*
**Auxiliary Territorial Service cap**

*Inset .*
**Cap Badge and Title of ATS.**
*(DR)*

# 25. Army Commandos

Made up of volunteers coming from various units in the Army, the Army Commandos were incorporated into the brigades of the Royal Marines.

On the 6th of June 1944, the following units took part:

— **No 3 Commando,**
Lieutenant-Colonel Peter Young

— **No 4 Commando,**
Lieutenant-Colonel R. W. D. Dawson

— **No 5 Commando,**
Lieutenant-Colonel Derek Mills-Robert.

*Below*
**An exposition organised by the RAOC showing the diverse equipment and weapons used by the Commandos.**
*(IWM)*

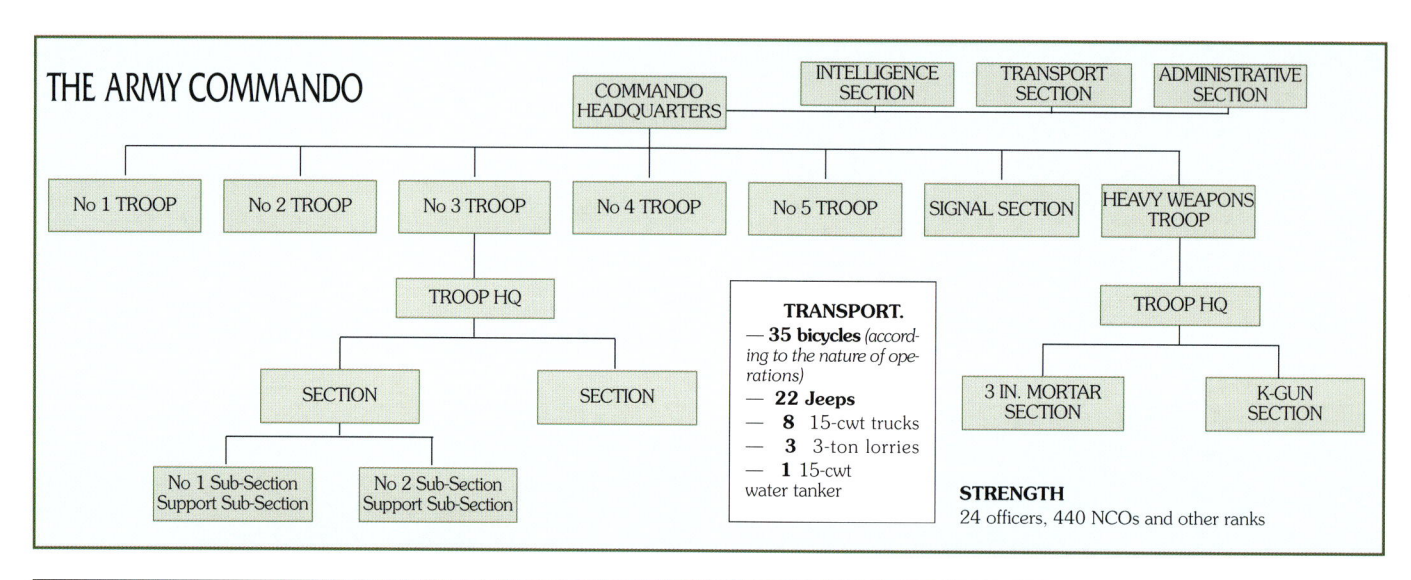

### THE ARMY COMMANDO

- COMMANDO HEADQUARTERS
  - INTELLIGENCE SECTION
  - TRANSPORT SECTION
  - ADMINISTRATIVE SECTION
  - No 1 TROOP
  - No 2 TROOP
  - No 3 TROOP
    - TROOP HQ
      - SECTION
        - No 1 Sub-Section / Support Sub-Section
        - No 2 Sub-Section / Support Sub-Section
      - SECTION
  - No 4 TROOP
  - No 5 TROOP
  - SIGNAL SECTION
  - HEAVY WEAPONS TROOP
    - TROOP HQ
      - 3 IN. MORTAR SECTION
      - K-GUN SECTION

**TRANSPORT.**
— **35 bicycles** *(according to the nature of operations)*
— **22** Jeeps
— **8** 15-cwt trucks
— **3** 3-ton lorries
— **1** 15-cwt water tanker

**STRENGTH**
24 officers, 440 NCOs and other ranks

## TROOP HEADQUARTERS

| | | |
|---|---|---|
| Captain | Colt pistol | binoculars, Very pistol, Map-case, compass |
| Lieutenant | No4 Rifle | Very pistol |
| Troop Sergeant-Major | No4 Rifle | Very pistol |
| Lance Corporal Medical Orderly | No4 Rifle | First Aid kit |
| Runner | No4 Rifle | Radio set W SET 38 |
| | 1 PIAT per Troop | |

### SECTION
Commanded by a Lieutenant armed with a No.4 Rifle and a Very pistol.

### SECTION
Commanded by a Lieutenant armed with a No.4 Rifle and a Very pistol.

### No2 ASSAULT SUB SECTION
Like No.1 but with an extra supply of 18 kg of explosives among the Rifle Group.

### No1 ASSAULT SUB SECTION

| | | | | |
|---|---|---|---|---|
| **RIFLE GROUP** | Sergeant | Thompson SMG 2 hand grenades | 5 SMG magazines | Map-case |
| | Corporal | Thompson MG 2 hand grenades | 5 SMG magazines | Toggle Rope Wire-cutters |
| | No 1,2,3,4,5 Riflemen | No 4 Rifle 2 hand grenades | 50 cartridges 2 Bren gun magazines | Togle Rope, 3 pick-axes 2 Tools |
| **BREN GROUP** | Corporal | No 4 Rifle | 50 cartridges 4 Bren gun magazines | Pick-axe |
| | No 1 Bren | Bren gun | 4 Bren gun magazines | Pick-axe |
| | No 2 Bren | No 4 Rifle | 50 cartridges 4 Bren gun magazines | Tool kit + 1 spare barrel |
| | No 3 Bren | No 4 Rifle | 50 cartridges 4 Bren gun magazines | Tools |

### THE SUPPORT SUB-SECTION

| | | | | |
|---|---|---|---|---|
| **MORTAR GROUP** | Corporal | Thompson SMG 2 hand grenades | 5 SMG magazines | Binoculars Compass |
| | Lance Corporal | No 4 Rifle | 50 cartridges 12 explosive and smoke bombs | |
| | No 1 Mortarman | 2-in. Mortar Colt Pistol | 3 pistol magazines 6 explosive and smoke bombs | |
| | No 2 Mortarman | No 4 Rifle | 50 cartridges 12 explosive and smoke bombs | |
| **SNIPER** | Sniper | No 4T rifle or No 1 Mk III with telescopic lensessight | 50 cartridges 2 Bren gun magazines | Binoculars |

*Ouistreham, 6th June 1944. A Fusilier from French Troop (No.4 Army Commando) welcomed by the inhabitants of the town (IWM)*

*Opposite from top to bottom*
**Typical organisation of an Army Commando Troop. This unit has a strength of 60 men, officers, NCOs and men.**

*Below.* **Commando Insignia.**

**A Support sub section sniper (see opposite left.** *(Reconstruction)*

# 26. Beach Groups

These were independent groups of about four to five thousand men assigned to each of the landing beaches in the British sector on 6th June 1944.

They were placed under the orders of the assault division; one or two Beach groups with one in reserve followed immediately on the heels of the first elements ashore.

Each Beach group included units from the Royal Engineers, Royal Army service Corps, Corps of Military Police, Royal Army Medical Corps as well as other specialist units from the REME and the Corps of Signals.

An infantry battalion having undergone a special training course was affected to the Beach groups as well as units from the Royal Navy and the Royal Air Force.

## Functions

— **Setting up and preparation** of beach exits.
— **Traffic control** for unloading units.
— **Unloading and storage** of various material, supplies and ammunition.
— **Setting up of Emergency First Aid Posts**
— **Neutralisation of enemy strongpoints** left behind after the passage of the first assault waves.

(from *Beach Organisation and Maintenance, Combined Operations,* part 2, March 1944)

*Opposite left*
The Breach at Hermenville, 6th june 1944. The Beach Groups were composed of men from different arms an services. These motorcyclists of the CMP are wearing their particular sleeve insignia. On the helmet (steel helmet, dispatch riders) is painted the white band of the Beach groups. Under this band is also painted a second blue band with the letters MP painted red on the front of the helmet. These MPs are wearing boots done up with laces and and buckles reserved for motorcyclists. The trousers are standard battledress.
(IWM)

*Below*
8th June 1944 on Queen beach (Sword) Beach Group personnel land.
(IWM)

## Helmet Markings for the Beach Groups

- **PBM** — Principal Beach Master
- **BMR** — Beach Master
- **ABM** — Assistant Beach Master
- **MLO** — Military Landing Officer
- **AMLO** — Assistant Military Landing Officer
- **BGPC** — Beach Group Commander and Second in Command
- **BCC** — Beach Company Commander and Second in Command
- **CEO** — Casualty Evacuation Officer (RAMC)
- Beach Group Personnel

## Depot Signposts

### ROYAL ARMY SERVICE CORPS
- Food
- Fuel, Lubricants
- General Magazines

### ROYAL ARMY ORDNANCE CORPS
- Vehicles and machines
- Spares
- Clothing
- Forward Depot

### ROYAL ENGINEERS
- Machinery
- Harbour unloading point
- Material for Road and Railway
- Drinking Water

- Veterinary Surgeon
- Royal Navy
- Printing
- Royal Air Force
- Medical Supplies
- CA — Civil Affairs
- Mess or Canteens

## Beach Signposting ("Charlie Sector")

**Daytime:** Rectangular signs on the left and on the right 3.6 m x 1.20m
Central signposts 1.08m x 1.08m
**Night-time:** luminous beacons.

RED BEACH — Left Boundary / Centre (C) / Right Boundary — DAY / NIGHT

WHITE BEACH — Left Boundary / Centre (C) / Right Boundary — DAY / NIGHT

GREEN BEACH — Left Boundary / Centre (C) / Right Boundary — DAY / NIGHT

# 27. Navy, Army & Air Force Institutes (NAAFI)

A cooperative service of the army, managed by personnel from the three services and under the resposibility of a civilian officer responsible to the Treasury.

The NAAFI, equipped with mobile shops, installed under tents or in requisitioned buildings provided many products at a reduced price for the soldiers: cigarettes, sweets, toiletries and stationery, etc.

After the Normandy landings, the service adopted the name EFI (Expeditionary Forces Institutes). It was placed under the command of the 21st Army Group.

*Left.*
**NAAFI cap badge.**

*Opposite right and below*
**Some period publications for products available at NAAFI shops.**
*(DR)*

# 28. Lines of Communications and Rear Maintenance areas

Placed under the command of a Major-General and responsible to the Army Group, the lines of communications and rear maintenance areas ensured the management of the zones immediately behind the front-line area.

## Main Functions

- **Reception of personnel, material and supplies of all kinds.**

— **Moving these ressources forward to the front.**

— **Hospitalisation and evacuation of the wounded and sick.**

—- **Evacuation of materials for returning**

— **Storage of material and supplies reserves.**

It had its own means in arms and services units; the rear maintenance area also ensured:

— **Setting up road or rail,** water or air communications

— **the maintenance of military installations**

— **Recovery of material**

— **Guarding and convoying of POWs**

— **Exploitation of local resources** (industries, supplies, forests, civilian labour, requisitionable civilian bulidings.)

# 29. Graves Registration Units

The Graves registration service was attached to the rear maintenance areas and ensured the regrouping of the bodies of the killed and the making up of registers enabling the graves to be situated.

Whatever the rank or social position, it was prescribed that all dead were to remain on the soil where they had fallen, or eventually be regrouped in a regional cemetery.

In the field each unit was responsible for burying its dead and for the respecting the procedure permitting the tomb to be localised and the victim identified. The family was generally informed by an officer or the chaplain.

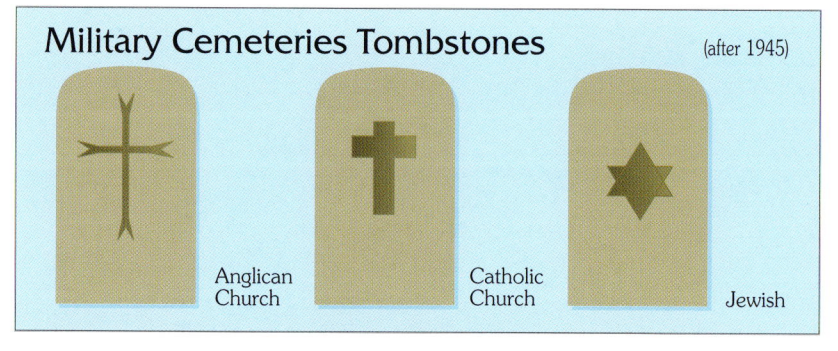

**Military Cemeteries Tombstones** (after 1945)

Anglican Church | Catholic Church | Jewish

# 30. Army Film and Photography Units & War Correspondents

These were units of photographers responsible to the department of Public Relations of the War Office.

In the field, the AFPU personnel and the war correspondents were administratively attached to the Royal Army Service Corps.

*Left.*
**AFPU personnel sleeve insignia.**

*Opposite right*
**1. Zeiss Ikon super Ikanta 532/16-6x9 Camera bearing the arrow of the War Department (purchases obtained through Spain during the hostilities).
2. The epaulette loop of a War Correspondent' accredited to the Command.
3. Correspondent's hat badge.**

60

# RECAPITULATION of CORPS and UNITS PRESENT in the ORDER of BATTLE in 1944-1945 (ALL FRONTS INCLUDED)

THIS LIST WAS ESTABLISHED ACCORDING TO THE ORDER OF PRECEDENCE : THE LIST

**Notes on the infantry regiments**
**A.** The numbering indicates seniority. Numbers missing represent units disbanded after WWI.
**B.** Names in italics are those of Territorial Army Battalions having preserved their old name for tradition's sake. Each of these names follows the number of its original regiment.

**Example:**
*Tyneside Scottish* is the Territorial battalion of the Black Watch.
Within the Infantry brigades, and in the order of precedence, these units are always placed after the units of the list.
**C. Reminder**
*Cambridgeshire*: Territorial Battalions of the Suffolk Regiment disbanded in 1942
*Highland Regiment*: Depot unit disbanded in 1943
*Lowland Regiment*: Depot unit disbanded in 1943
*Tower Hamlets Rifles*: Battalion of the Rifle Brigade disbanded in 1941.

Life Guards
(1st Household Cavalry Regiment)
Royal Horse Guards
(2nd Household Cavalry Regiment)

## ROYAL ARMOURED CORPS

### DRAGOON GUARDS

1st King's Dragoon Guards
Queen's Bay —2nd Dragoons Guards
3rd Carabiniers — Prince of Wales Dragoon Guards
4/7 Royal Dragoon Guards
5th Royal Inniskilling Dragoon Guards

### CAVALRY OF LINE

Royal Dragoons — 1st Dragoons
Royal Scots Greys — 2nd Dragoons
3rd King's Own Hussars
4th Queen's Own Hussars
7th Queen's Own Hussars
8th King's Royal Irish Hussars
9th Queen's Royal Lancers
10th Royal Hussars — Prince of Wales Own
11th Royal Hussars — Prince Albert Own
12th Royal Lancers — Prince of Wales
13/18th Royal Hussars ( Queen Mary Own)
14/20th King's Hussars
15/19th Lancers
17/21st Lancers
22nd Dragoons
23rd Hussars
24th Lancers
25th Dragoons
27th Lancers

**Royal Tank Regiment**

### SPECIAL RESERVE

North Irish Horse

### YEOMANRY

Royal Wiltshire Yeomanry
Warwickshire Yeomanry
Nottinghamshire Yeomanry — Sherwood Rangers
Staffordshire Yeomanry — Queen's Own Royal Regiment
1st Derbyshire Yeomanry
2nd Derbyshire Yeomanry
1st Lothians and Border Horse
2nd Lothians and Border Horse
1st Fife and Forfar Yeomanry
2nd Fife and Forfar Yeomanry
Westminster Dragoons — 2nd County of London Yeomanry
3rd County of London Yeomanry — Sharpshooters
4th County of London Yeomanry — Sharpshooters
1st Northamptonshire Yeomanry
2nd Northamptonshire Yeomanry
East Riding (of Yorkshire) Yeomanry
Inns of Court Regiment
Lovat Scouts

**Infantry Battalions converted to the RAC**

**Royal Regiment of Artillery**
Royal Horse Artillery

Honourable Artillery Company

**Corps of Royal Engineers**

**Royal Corps of Signals**

### FOOT GUARDS

Grenadier Guards
Coldstream Guards
Scots Guards
Irish Guards
Welsh Guards

### INFANTRY

1. Royal Scots — Royal Regiment
2. Queen's Royal Regiment — West Surrey
3. Buffs — Royal East Kent Regiment
4. King's Own Royal Regiment — Lancaster
5. Royal Northumberland Fusiliers
6. Royal Warwickshire Regiment
7. Royal Fusiliers — City of London
8. King's Regiment — Liverpool
    *8th Irish Battalion, King's Regiment*
9. Royal Norfolk Regiment
10. Lincolnshire Regiment
11. Devonshire Regiment
12. Suffolk Regiment
13. Somerset Light Infantry — Prince Albert's
14. West Yorkshire Regiment — Prince of Wales Own
15. East Yorkshire Regiment — Duke of York Own
16. Bedfordshire and Hertfordshire Regiment
    *Hertfordshire Regiment, Bedfordshire and Hertfordshire Regiment*
17. Leicestershire Regiment
19. Green Howards — Alexandra, Princess of Wales Yorkshire Regiment
20. Lancashire Fusiliers
21. Royal Scots Fusiliers
22. Cheshire Regiment
23. Royal Welch Fusiliers
24. South Wales Borderers
    *Monmouthshire Regiment*
    *Brecknockshire Battalion, South Wales Borderers*
25. King's Own Scottish Borderers
26. Cameronians — Scottish Rifles
27. Royal Inniskilling Fusiliers
28. Gloucestershire Regiment
29. Worcestershire Regiment
30. East Lancashire Regiment
31. East Surrey Regiment
32. Duke of Cornwall Light Infantry
33. Duke of Wellington Regiment - West Riding
34. Border Regiment
35. Royal Sussex Regiment
37. Hampshire Regiment
    *11th Battalion, Island of Jersey, Hampshire Regiment*
38. South Staffordshire Regiment
39. Dorsetshire Regiment
40. South Lancashire Regiment — Prince of Wales Volunteers
41. Welch Regiment
42. Black Watch — Royal Highland Regiment
    *Tyneside Scottish, Black Watch*
43. Oxfordshire and Buckinghamshire Light Infantry
    *1st, 2nd Buckinghamshire Battalions, Oxs and Bucks Light Infantry*
44. Essex Regiment
45. Sherwood Foresters — Nottinghamshire & Derbyshire Regiments
47. Loyal Regiment — North Lancashire
48. Northamptonshire Regiment
49. Royal Berkshire Regiment — Princess Charlotte of Wales
50. Queen's Own Royal west Kent Regiment
51. King's Own Yorkshire Light Infantry
53. King's Shropshire Light Infantry
    *Herefordshire Regiment, KSLI*
57. Middlesex Regiment — Duke of Cambridge Own
    *Kensington Regiment, Middlesex Regiment*
60. King's Royal Rifle Corps
    *The Rangers, Queen's Westminster, KRRC*
62. Wiltshire Regiment — Duke of Edinburgh's
63. Manchester
64. North Staffordshire Regiment — Prince of Wales
    *4th Hallamshire Battalion, York and Lancaster Regiment*
68. DURHAM LIGHT INFANTRY
    *6th Battalion, Durham Light Infantry*
71. Highland Light Infantry — City of Glasgow
    *Glasgow Highlanders, HLI*
72. Seaforth Highlanders — Ross-Shire Buffs, Duke of Albany's
    *5th Battalion (Caithness and Sutherland) Seaforth Higlanders*
75. Gordon Highlanders
    *London Scottish, Gordon Highlanders*
79. Queen's Own Cameron Highlanders
83. Royal Ulster Rifles
    *London Irish Rifles, Royal Ulster Rifles*
87. Royal Irish Fusiliers — Princess Victoria's
91. Argyll and Sutherland Highlanders — Princess Louise's
Rifle Brigade — Prince Consort Own

**Reconnaissance Corps**

**Army Air Corps**
Glider Pilot Regiment
Parachute Regiment
Special Air Service Regiment

## SERVICES

**Royal Army Chaplains' Department**
**Royal Army Service Corps**
**Royal Army Medical Corps**
**Royal Army Ordnance Corps**
**Royal Electrical and Mechanical Engineers**
**Royal Army Pay Corps**
**Royal Army Veterinary Corps**
**Army Educational Corps**
**Army Dental Corps**
**Corps of Military Police**
**Military Provost Staff Corps**
**Pioneer Corps**
**Intelligence Corps**
**Army Catering Corps**
**Army Physical Training Corps**
**General Service Corps**
**Queen Alexandra's Imperial Military Nursing Service**
**Auxiliary Territorial Service**

## UNLISTED

Army Commandos (attached to the Royal Marines)

# CHAPTER 3 SMALL ARMS and EXPLOSIV

# 1. Knives
## Bayonets, knives and Daggers

*Right.*
1. Smatchet. Large combat Knife. Blade length 27.5cms
2. Bayonet No. 4 Mk II; fits on to the No4 Mk I* Rifle and the Sten machine pistol Mk V Blade length : 20cms.
2a. Scabbard and frog.
3. Jack knife with marlin spike
4. Fairbairn dagger (made by Wilkinson) supplied to Commandos and Army Air Corps units. Blade length: 17.7 cms
4a. Leather metal-reinforced scabbard
5. Instruction booklet for hand to hand fighting.

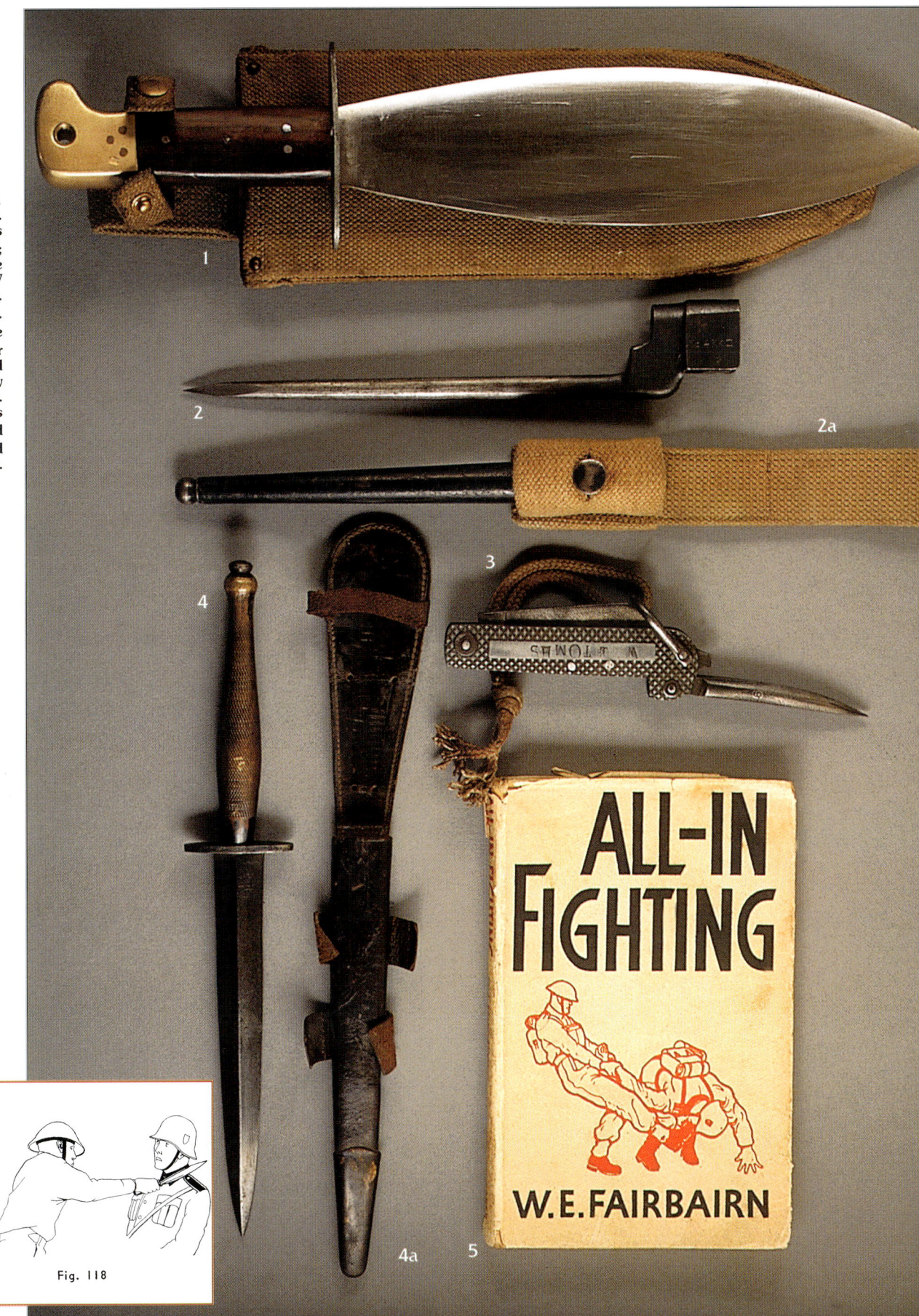

*Below*
**Illustrations from the Booklet *All-in Fighting* presenting different ways of striking with the Smatchet.**
(DR)

Fig. 116    Fig. 118

# Enfield revolver No2 Mark I *

# 2. Hand Guns

**American Automatic Pistol Colt .45 M1911 A1.**

**American Automatic Pistol Colt .45 M1911.**

# Automatic Pistol Colt .45 M1911 and M1911 A1

# Browning FN - Inglis No2 Mark I*

## Pistol, revolver No2 MK I*

**Calibre:** .38 (9 mm)
**Weight:** 0,780 Kg
**Length:** 264 mm
**Practical range** 30 m
**Initial velocity:** 185 m/s
**Magazine:** 6 cartridges in the cylinder
**Mechanism:** double action only. Empty shells extracted by tipping the barrel and the cylinder
**Makers:** Albion Motors, Enfield R.S.A.F.
**Provided to:** Machine crews, officers, miscellaneous personnel not equipped with a rifle, machine pistol or sten (except airborne troops).
From 1942 progressively replaced the Webley Mk IV

## Browning FN-Inglis No2 MK I*

**Calibre :** 9 mm
**Weight:** 1,060 kg with magazine
**Practical range:** 50 m
**Initial Velocity:** 400 m/s
**Magazine:** 13 cartridges magazine
**Ammunition:** 9 mm Parabellum (identical to the Sten and certain German guns)
**Makers:** Inglis, Canada
**Provided to:** Certain units of the Army Air Corps and the Commandos

*Opposite*
1. Type RAC Holster for Mk I* revolver (Pattern 42 RAC pistol case)
2. Pouch for 2 Colt or Inglis magazines
3. Standard holsters for revolvers and pistols (Pattern 37 pistol case)
4. Pouch for 12 revolver cartridges attached to the holster by two horizontal hooks.

## Automatic Pistol Colt .45, 1911 A 1

American-made weapon
**Calibre :** .45 (11,43 mm)
**Weight with full magazine:** 1.255 kg
**Length:** 216 mm
**Practical range:** 30 m
**Initial Velocity:** 260 m/s
**Magazine:** 7 cartridge magazine
**Provided to:** Commandos (Royal Marines and Army), Army Air Corps

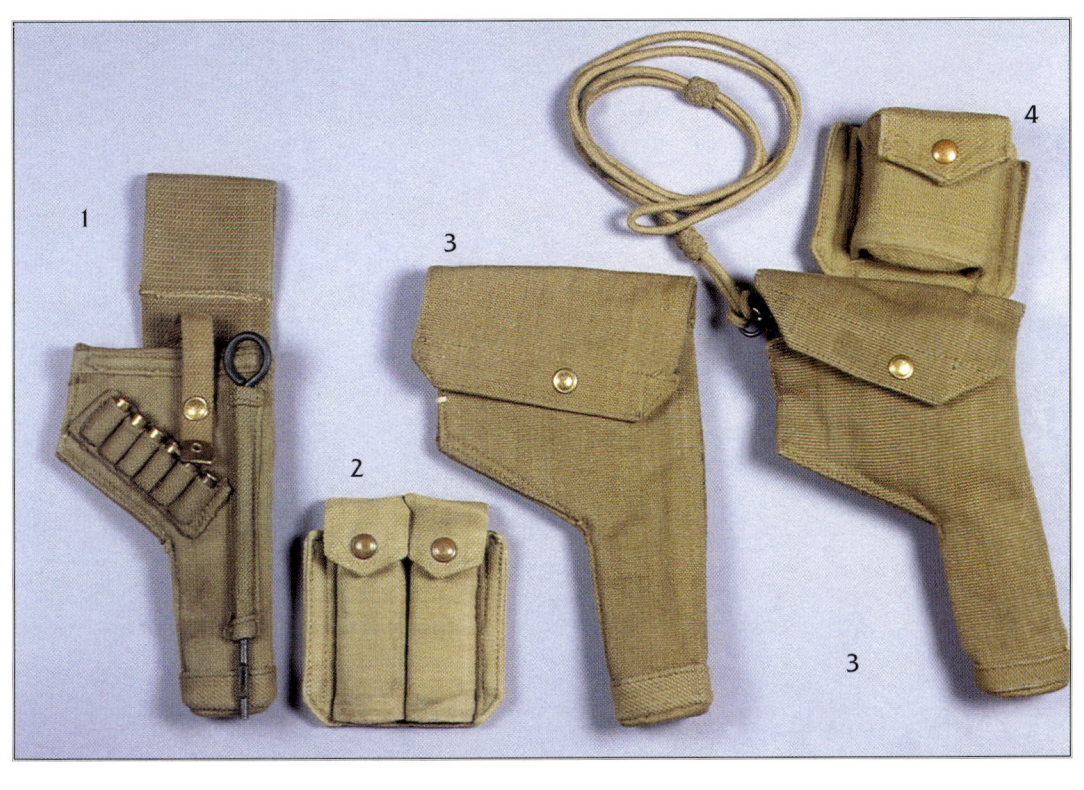

# 3. The No4 Mark I* Rifle

*Above.*
**The British infantry No4 Mk 1* .303 calibre Rifle with its bayonet, 5-round clip. The pull-through and the brass oiler were contained in the butt.**

*Left.*
**Normandy, 26th June 1944. An infantryman of the 6th RSF (15th Scottish Infantry Division) waiting for the assault signal to be given. The bayonet is fixed onto the No.4 Mk.1* Rifle.**
(IWM)

This was the standard rifle of the British Army and was put into service in 1942.
**Calibre:** .303 (7.7mm)
**Weight:** 4 kg
**Length:** 1,130 m
**Range:** 1 800 m
**Practical range:** 270 m

**Initial velocity:** 745 m/s
**Mechanism:** Bolt action. Manual
**Magazine:** 10 cartridges
**Sights:**
simplified folding backsight with two eyeholes: bayyle ranges of 270 m and 1 800 m.
**Makers from 1942 to 1945**

- Royal Ordnance Factory Fazarkeley
- R.O.F. Maltby
- B.S.A. Shirley
- SAL/CAL Long Branch, Canada (by order of the War Office
- Savage Arms Co, USA ( as part of the military aid plan)

*Below left*
1. .303 (7.7mm) Cartridge for No.1, No.4 Bren Gun, Vickers Machine guns and K-Guns. Length: 7.7 cms, weight: 30gms, initial velocity 745 m/s
2. 5 cartridge Magazine Clip for rifles No.1 and No.4.

*Below right*
American leather M 1907 sling for the sniper's rifle.
(DR)

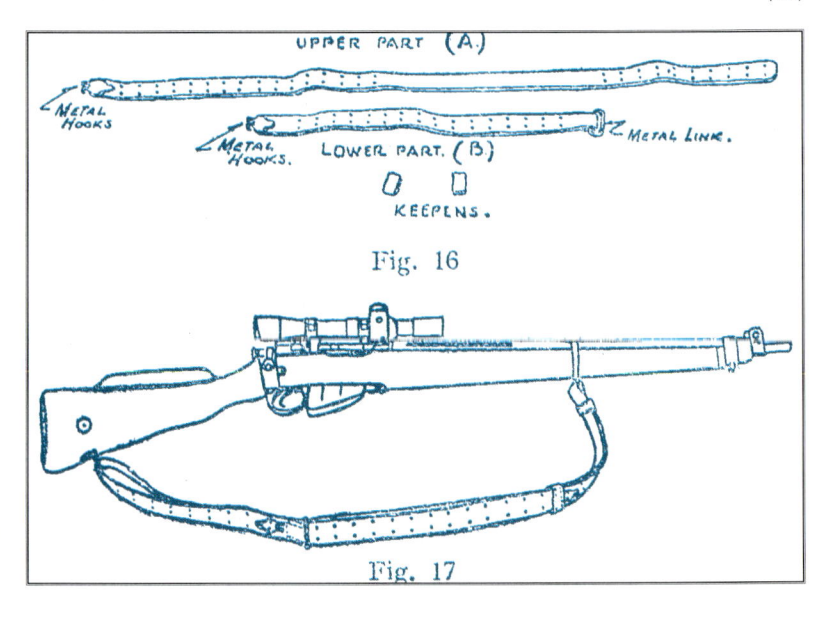

Fig. 16

Fig. 17

## Sniper Rifle accessories

1. No.4 (T) Rifle with No 32 Mk I Telescope
2. Breech cover
3. Protective valise made out of thick felt given out to the parachute units
4. Basic pouch and bandoleer with 5 pouches each holding 2 clips of 5 cartridges. Supplied with 50 .303 SAA cartridges plus
5 tracer bullets (red point)
2 No.36 or 77 grenades
5 armour piercing bullets (black point)
1 telescope with carrying case.

## Sniper's equipment

1 pair of No. 2 MkII binoculars with case
1 compass with case
1 watch
1 camouflage net and if necessary a Denison smock.

*Above right.* **Normandy 6th June 1944; Snipers of the Army Commandos, armed with the No.1 MkIII SMLE rifle. The adjustable backsight made this more accurate than the the No.4 Rifle.** *(IWM)*

*Opposite.* **Three step arm-movement to position the American leather sling for sharpshooting.** *(DR)*

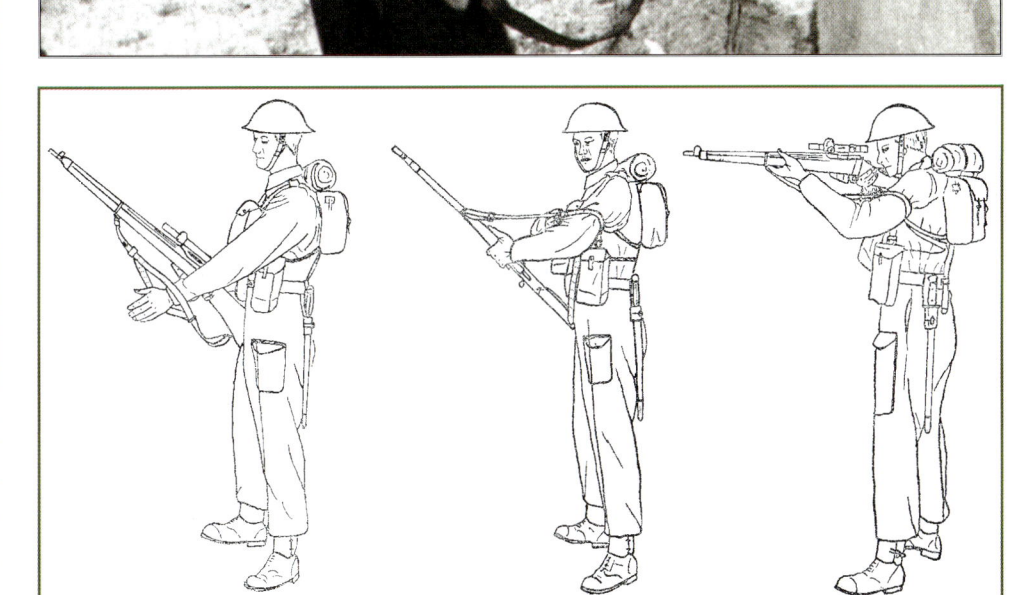

# 4. The US M1 and M1 A1 Carbines

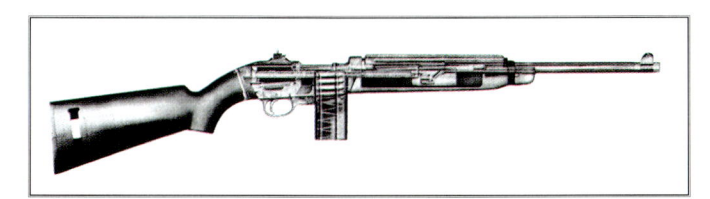

American-made weapon
**Calibre:** .30 (7.62mm)
**Weight M1:** 2.480 Kg
**Weight M1 A1:** 2.790 Kg
**Length:** 0.905 m

**Length with folded butt (M1 A1):** 0.650 m
**Mechanism:** Gas operated.
**Single shot.** Automatic reloading

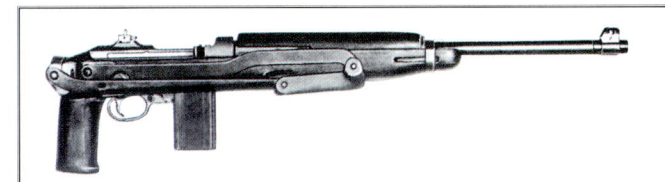

**Magazine:** 15 round magazine
**Range:** 1 270m
**Practical range:** 200 m
**Initial velocity:** 590 m/s
**Provided to:** certain airborne units.

# 5. Machine Carbines

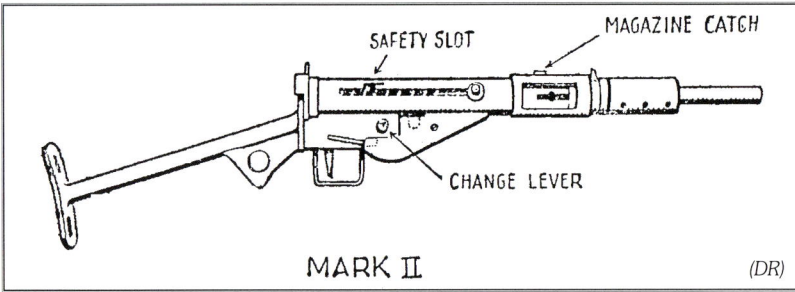

## The Sten Gun and it accessories
*Above*
1. Web sling
2. Sten Mk II with skeleton butt
3. Packet of 9 mm Parabellum cartridges
4. Magazine
5. Sten Mk V for Airborne Troops. A lug at the end of the barrel enables the Mk II bayonet to be fixed.
6. Bayonet frog with pouch for the simplified magazine loader.
7. Sten gun magazine carrier (Airborne troops).

# Sten Machine Carbine

*Above and below.*
**Sten Mk II with straight tubular butt.**
**Sten Mk III.**

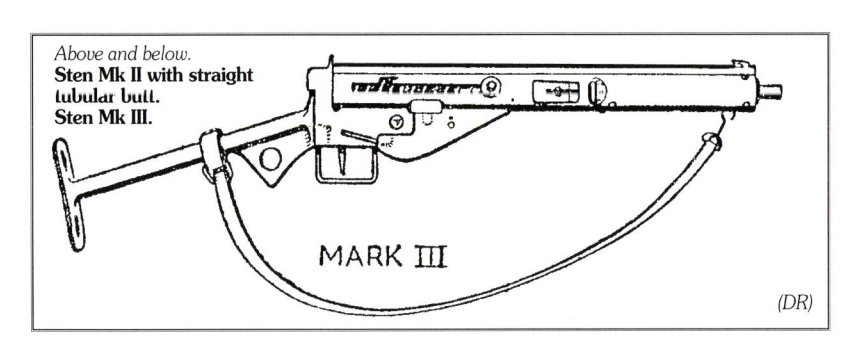

Sten gun magazine loader.

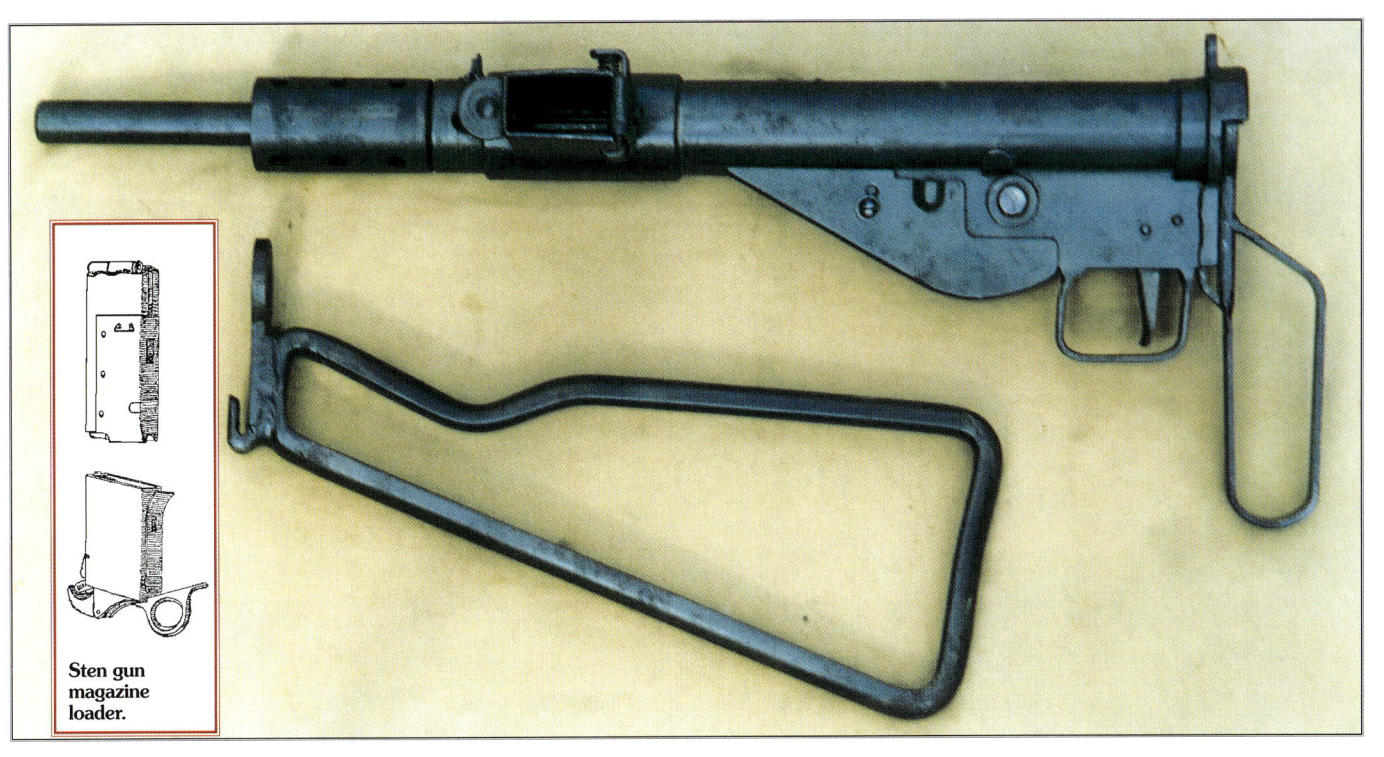

## Sten Machine Carbine

**Calibre:** 9 mm ( 9 mm Parabellum cartridge)
**Weight with loaded magazine:** from 3.650 kg to 4,5 kg
**Length:** 0,762 m
**Initial Velocity:** 365 m/s
**Rate of Fire:** 550 shots a minute
**Practical range:** 100 m
**Magazine straight:** 32-cartridge magazine
**Mechanism:** breech unlocked /breech block single or multiple shot
**Provided to:** Corporal, (Section leaders, infantry, including Airborne. No.1 server of 2-in mortar, RCS, CMP liaison personnel...1 Sten gun was supplied to each Sherman, Cromwell and Churchill tank.

*Above.*
**Sten Machine carbine, here with an adaptable pistol grip, usable with all Sten models. The skeleton butt is dismantled.**

*Below.* **The main parts of the Sten gun.**
*(From an instruction Manual in French).*

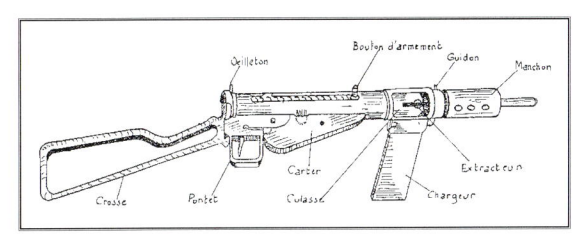

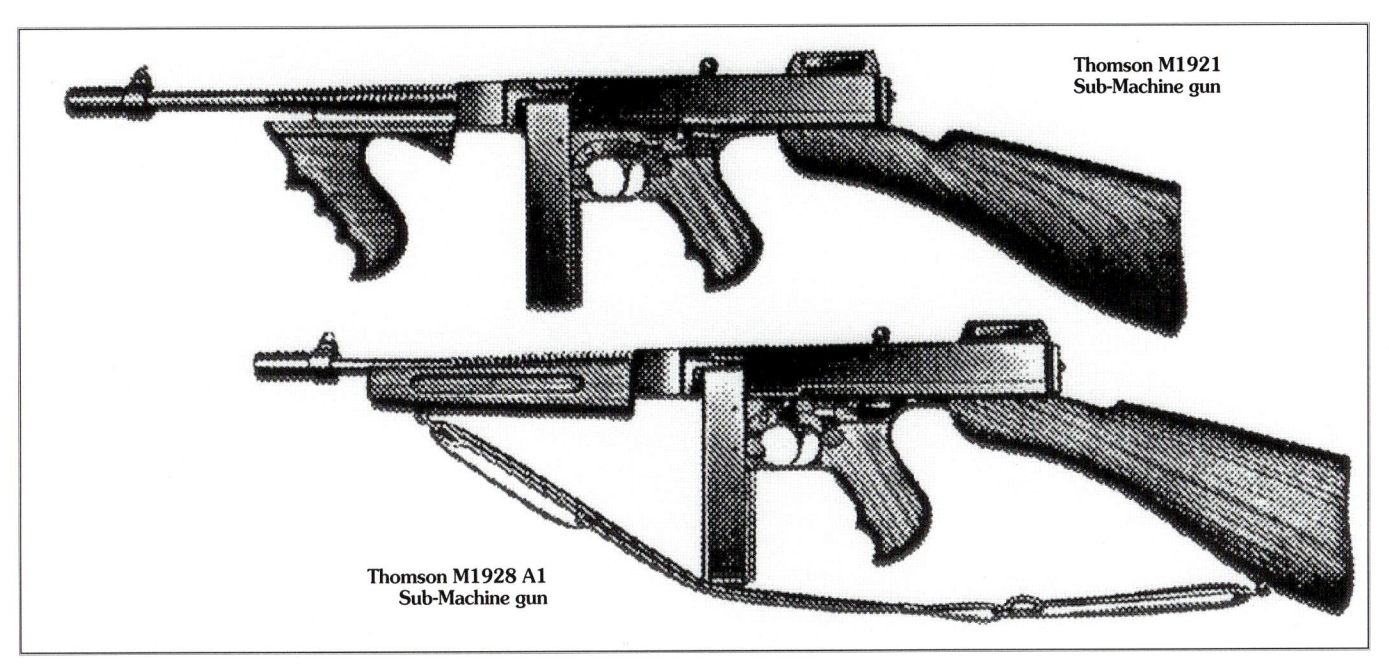

Thomson M1921 Sub-Machine gun

Thomson M1928 A1 Sub-Machine gun

# Thomson M1921 & M1928 A1 Sub-Machine Gun

American-made weapon
**Calibre:** .45 (11.43mm)
**Weight:** 4.42 kg without magazine
**Length:** 0.838 m with compensator
**Rate of fire:** 550 rounds a minute

**Practical range:** 100 m
**Initial Velocity:** 500 m
**Magazine :** Straight 20-round magazine
**Mechanism:** breech unlocked, single or multiple shot

**Provided to:** statutory for the Army Commandos and the Royal marines.

In the other units it was progressively replaced by the Sten gun after 1942.

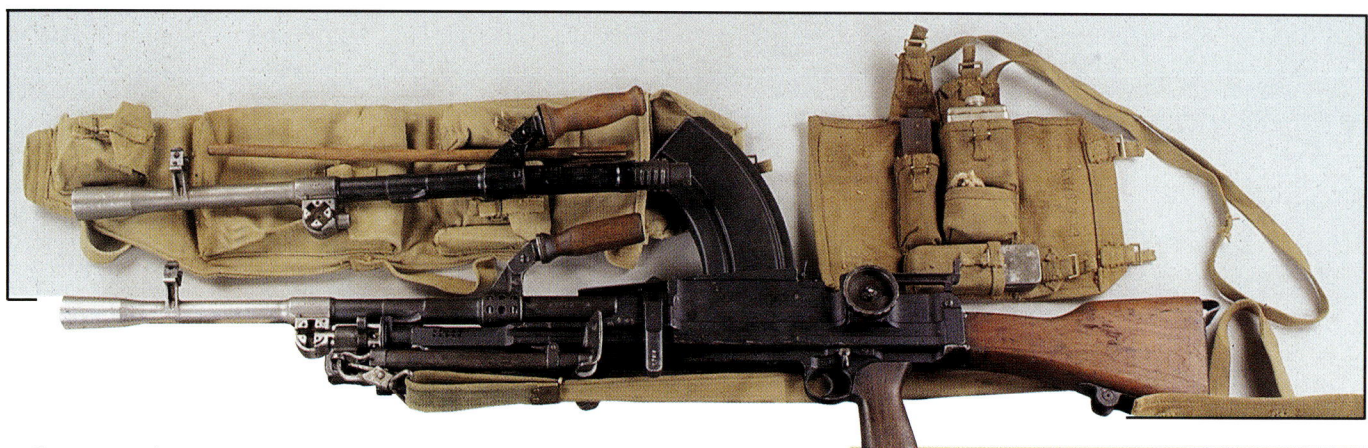

# 6. The Bren Light Machine gun

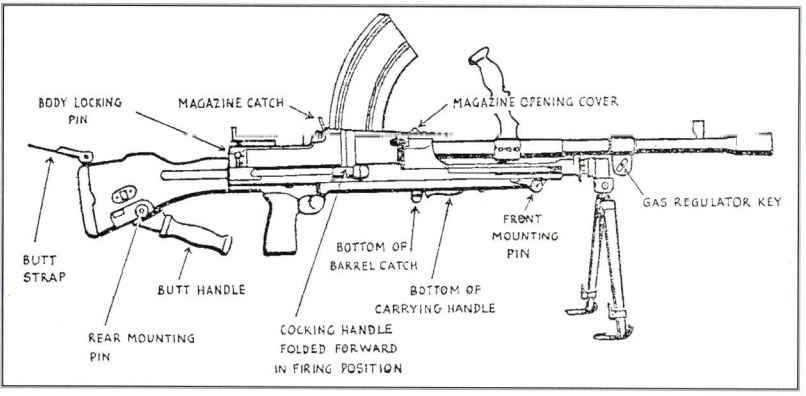

## The Bren Light Machine Gun Mk I

**Calibre:** .303 (7.7 mm)
**Weight:** 10,500 kg
**Length:** 1.15 m
**Range:** 1 500 m
**Practical range:** 600 m
**Mechanism:** gas oerated
**RATE OF FIRE**
**single shot:** 40 shots per minute
**burst:** 650 shots per minute .
**Initial velocity:** 745 m/s
**Magazine:** 30-round magazine box (28 practical load)

**Makers from 1939 to 1945**
- Royal Small Arms Factory, Enfield,
- Monotype Group
- Inglis Canada (on orders from the War Office)

**NB.** During the course of 1943, a simplified version was put into service with in particular a straight loading lever instead of a folding one and the suppression of the backsight drum. A model with a shortened barrel (MkIII) was made after May 1944.

**Use:** Infantry Section weapon for neutralisatiion fire (see distribution in the Infantry Battalion chapter) It was also used in the majority of front-line units.

*Left.*
Holland, October 1944.This Bren gun No1 from the 6th KOSB, 15th (Scottish) Infantry Division, 44th Infantry Brigade is on his way to the front. He is also carrying a slarge shovel.

*Top.*
the Bren Light machine Gun and its accessories.

*Left.*
Plates taken from English and French instruction manuals of the period. *(DR)*

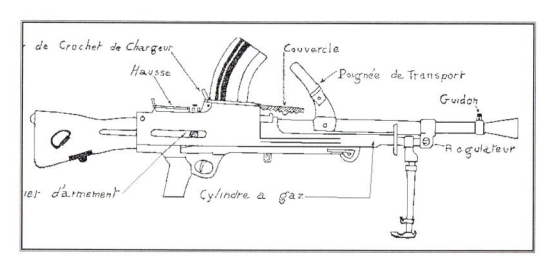

*Above.*
**Canvas carrier for 4 Bren gun magazines.**

*Right.*
1. Case with spare barrel, spare parts, cleaning rod and small tools
2. Bren Gun ammunition cases for transport by Vehicles. They each contained 12 magazines.

*Below*
A. Accessory and cleaning kit for the Bren group No2
1. Tool for regulating the gas cylinder
2. Oiler
3. Cloth
4. Spare parts box
5. Clip extractor
6. Pull through
B. Additional pouches for 2 magazines each (these were not specific to the Bren Gun and could hold grenades, 2-in mortar bombs or other ammunition).

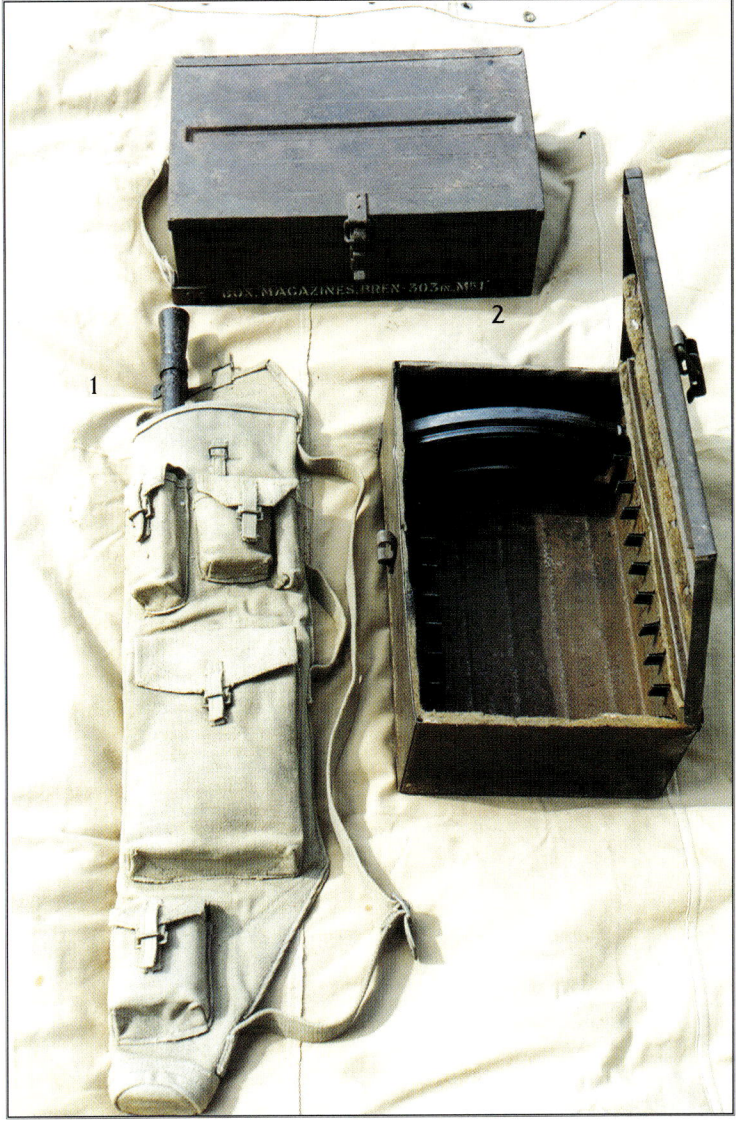

71

# 7. The "K" Gun

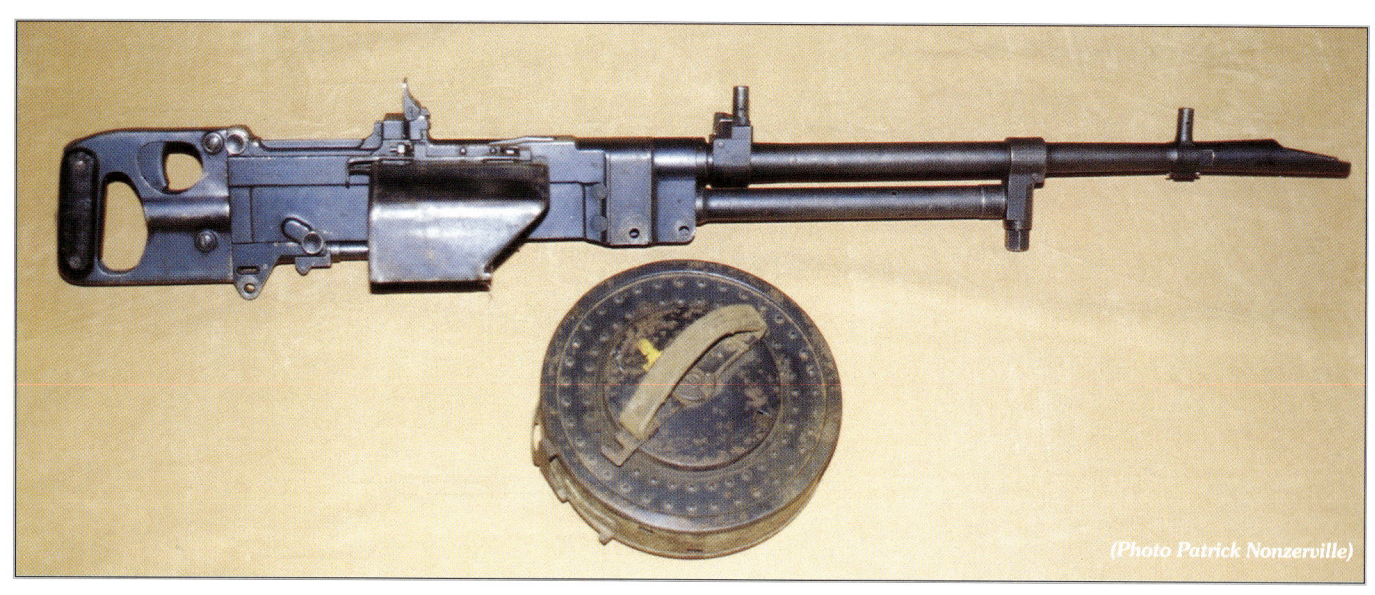

## Aircraft Machine Gun, Class K
## (K-Gun, Vickers, Gas operated)

*(Photo Patrick Nonzerville)*

Aviation type machine gun
**Makers:** Vickers Armstrong Ltd
**Calibre:** .303 (7.7 mm)
**Weight:** 8.900 Kg
**Length:** 1.016 m
**Range:** 1 500 m
**Practical range:** 500 m
**Rate of fire:** 950 rounds a minute
**Magazine:** 96 cartridge drum type magazine
**Mechanism:** gas operated
**Use:** replaced the .303 Vickers Machine gun in certain units
- **with bipod:** Heavy Troops Royal Marines, Army Commandos
- **on a jeep** ( mounted singly or in pairs): Special Air Service

*Opposite left*
Normandy, 6th June 1944, Riva Bella.
Smiling, a "K" gunner server advancing with his unit of the Army Commandos which have just landed on the French coast. Each man is carrying 2 magazines for the "K" gun in pouches fixed to their belts and held up by braces.
(DR)

*Below*
Magazine pouches for the Vickers "K" gun.

# 8. The Infantry support Machine guns

## .303 Inch. Machine Gun, Vickers

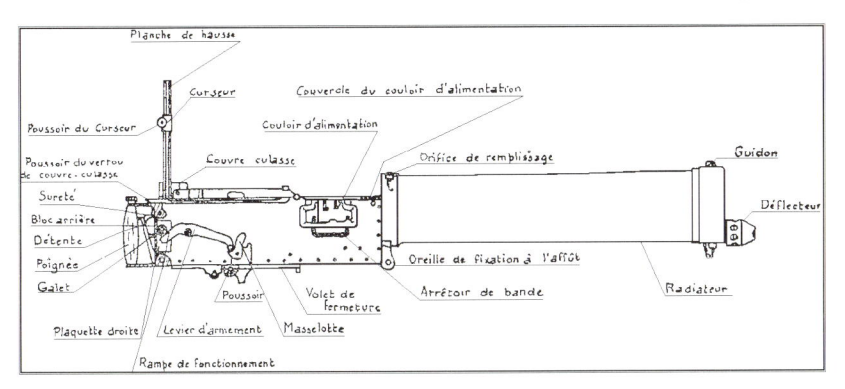

*Above*
Machine Gunners of the 2 Battalion,
the Middlesex Regiment (Support Machine Gun Battalion
of the 3rd Infantry Division) training.
The cooling sleeve of the Vickers machine gun
is covered with its protective skeath. The cooling system
pipe is fixed at the end.
*(IWM)*

*Opposite left*
The .303 Vickers machine gun and its principal parts
explained in an instruction manual in French.
*(DR, from an instruction Manual in French).)*

**Calibre :** .303 (7.7 mm)
**Total weight ready for action:** 42.5 kg
**Range:** 4 500 m
**Practical range:** 800 m
**Sustained Trajectory:**
man standing at 600 m
**Mechanism:** short recoil of the barrel, water cooled.
**Rate of fire:** 500 rounds per minute

**Ammunition:** cylindrical and conical cartridges in a rolled sleeve/case. Bullet cased in nickelsilver, lead-core.
**Packaging:** Supplied in wooden cases containing 2 metal boxes each containing one 250 round soft canvas belt
**Crew:** 3 men:
**1 lance-corporal gunner,** carried the tripod
**1 loader,** carried the gun, the accessory bag, the condensator pipe
**1 ammunition bearer,** carried two 250 cartridges case and a jerrycan of water
**Use:** Support weapon supplied to Mortar and Machine Gun Battalions of the Infantry Divisions (36 of them transported by Universal carriers) as well as in the Independent MMG Companies of the Armoured Divisions (12 items).

# 9. Vehicle Mounted Machine guns

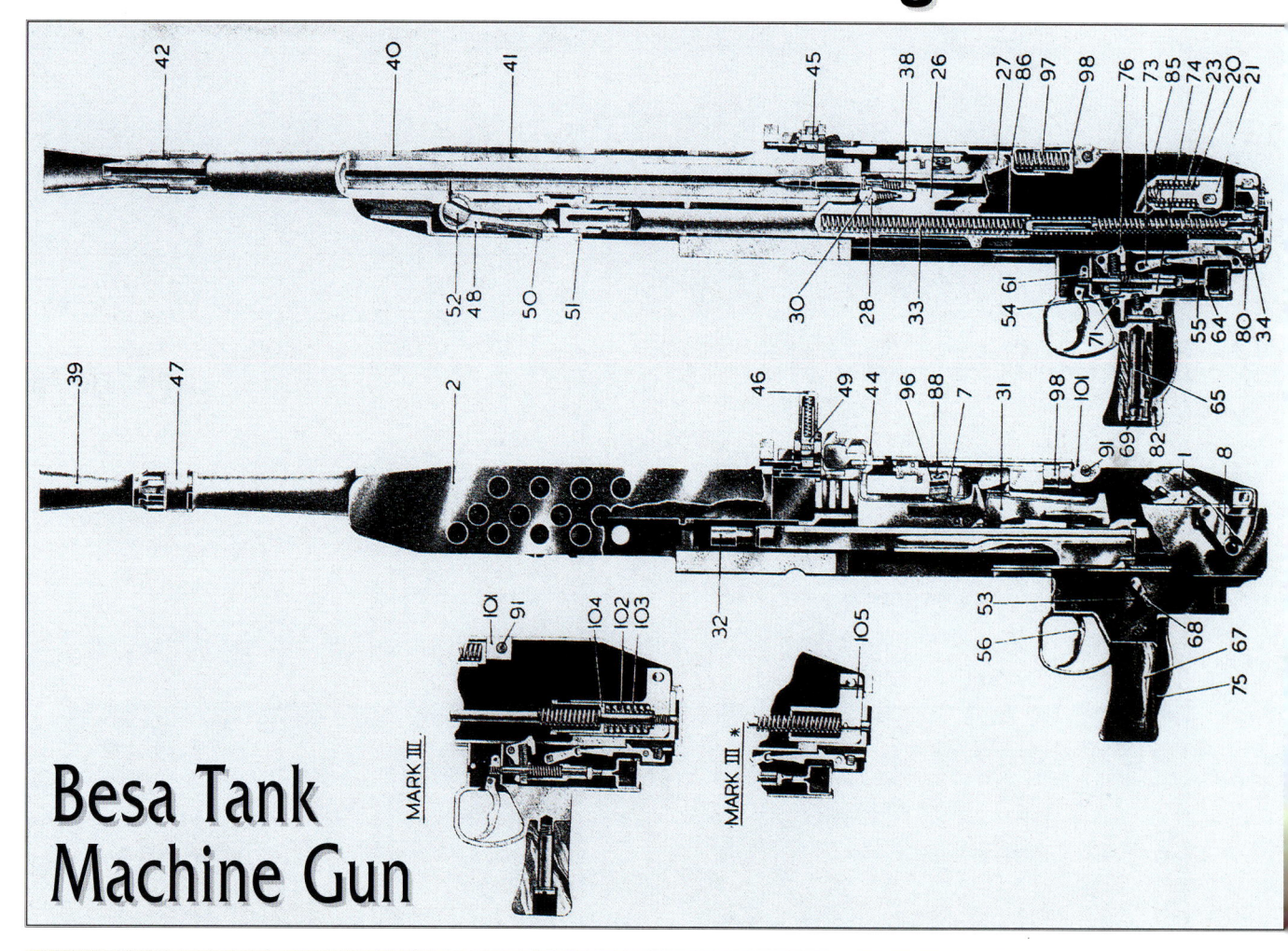

## Besa Tank Machine Gun

Czech-designed machine gun built under licence by B.S.A.
**Calibre:** 7.62 mm (cartridge identical to the German 7.62 mm)
**Weight:** 22 kg
**Length:** 1.10 m
**Rate of fire:** 450-750 rounds per minute
**Magazine:** metal or cotton belt with 225 rounds
**Mechanism:** gas operated
**Use:** secondary armament for tanks and armoured cars of British origin.

## American Machine guns

supplied under the terms of the Allied aid plan and mounted on vehicles.

### Browning, caliber .30, Machine Gun
**Calibre:** 7.62 mm
**Weight without mounting:** 13.75 kgs
**Rate of fire:** 450 rounds/minute
**Range:** 2 200 m
**Practical range:** 800 m
**Magazine:** Cartridges mounted on re-usable cotton canvas belt
**Mechanism:** Breech block, short barrel recoil

*Above*
**Browning, Caliber .30 Machine Gun.** *(DR)*

### Browning, caliber .50, Heavy Machine Gun
**Calibre:** 12.7 mm
**Weight without mounting:** 38 kg
**Rate of fire:** 500 rounds/minute
**Range:** 2 600 m
**Practical range:** 1 200 m
**Magazine:** cartridges on a belt made up of expendable metal links
**Mechanism:** gas operated, recoiling barrel.

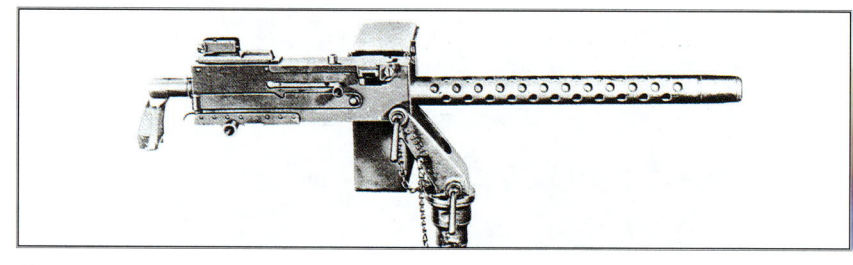

*Below.* **Browning, Caliber .50 Machine Gun.** *(DR)*

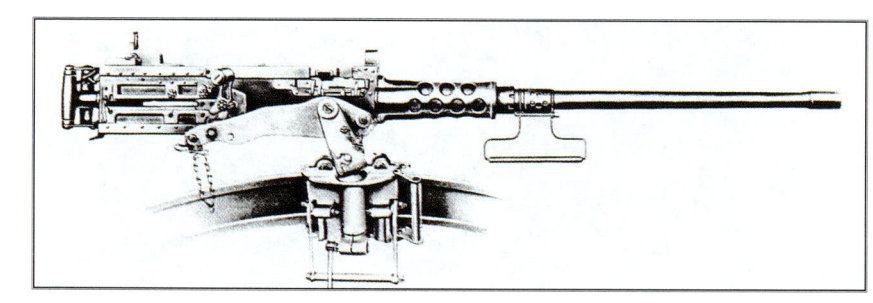

# 10. The PIAT (Projector Infantry Anti-tank)

**ANTI-TANK BOMB LAUNCHER**
**Weight:** 16 kg
**Length:** 0.95 m
**Practical range**
- Anti-tank: 100 m
- Houses, bunkers: 350m

**Rate of fire:** 5 - 6 rounds / minute

**Projectile:** weight: 1.130 kg . Green rocket, red crosses on the body of the charge. Penetrated the armour of all tanks then in service

**Mechanism:** the rocket was propelled by the action of the gases acting on the projectile and the hammer which rearmed automatically.

**Use:** see use with the Infantry battalion. The PIAT was also in use with the majority of other front-line unit.

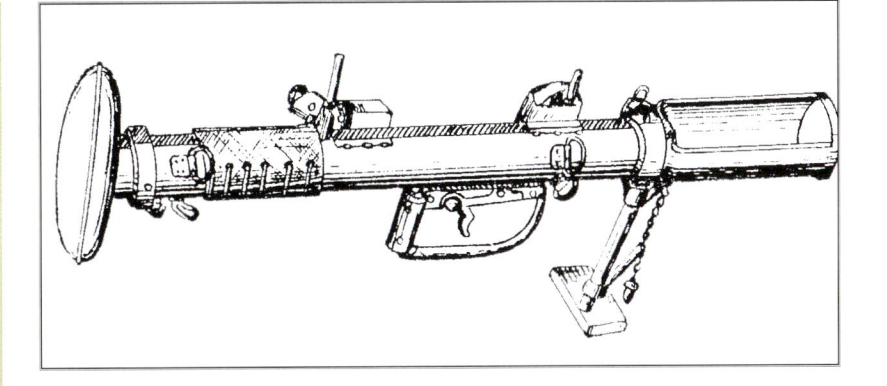

*Opposite.*
**The assembled weapon ready for action (above)**
**The PIAT rocket projectile (below).**

# 11. The Mortars

## The 2-inch Mortar

*Above.*
**Holland,
October 1944.
3rd Monmouthshire
Fusiliers
(11th Armoured
Division) firing
with 2-in. Mortar.**
*(IWM)*

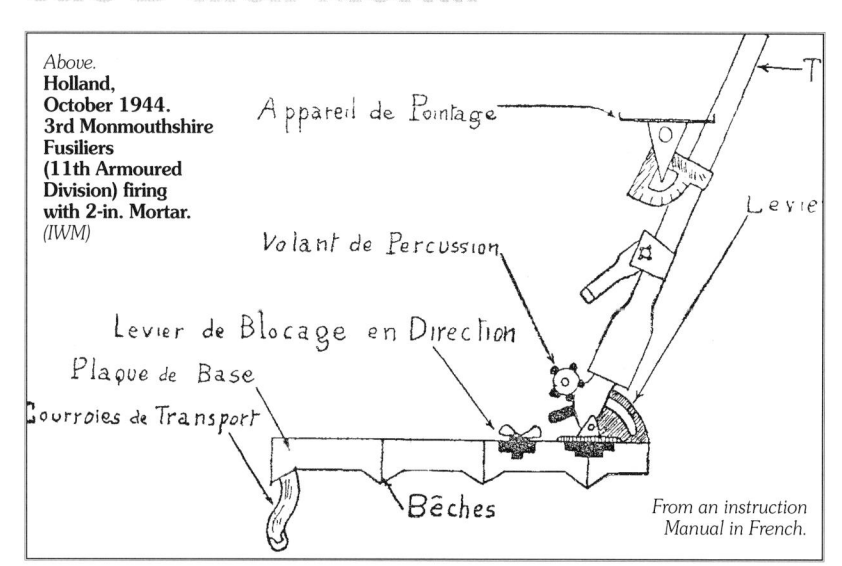

*From an instruction Manual in French.*

### The 2-inch Mortar

**Caliber:** 2 - inch (50.8 mm)
**Weight:** 10.65 kgs
**Practical range:** 450m
**Rate of fire:** normally 4 rounds / minute
**PROJECTILE**
**Explosive:** weight: 1.130 kg . Brown, red and green band
**Smoke:** weight: **0.9 k**g, green red band. Gave off two minute's worth of smoke screen on average 50 metres
**Crew:** Two men. The gunner, an NCO, carried the weapon, the mortar No2 carried the ammunition.
**Use:** close support of the Infantry platoon (see table page 41)

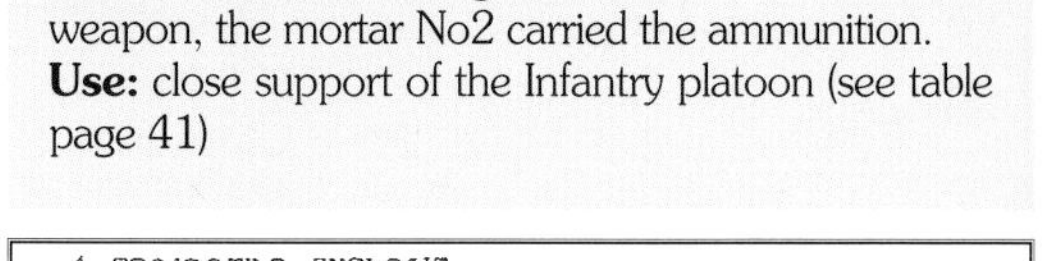

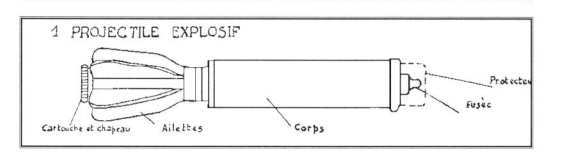

# The 3-inch Mortar

### The 3-inch Mortar

**Calibre**: 76.2mm
**Total weight:** 60 Kg
**Practical range:** from 115 m to 2 500 m depending on the charge
**Rate of fire:** 5 round per minute
**Projectile weight:** 4.5 Kg
**Piece divided into 3 loads:** tube, tripod, base-plate.
**Crew:** 3
**Transportation:** Universal carrier
**Use:** Support weapon in service with *Infantry Battalions* and *Motor Battalions* (Mortar Platoon).

# The 4.2-inch Mortar

### The 4.2-inch Mortar

**Caliber:** 106.7mm
**Total Weight:** ready for action: 213 kgs
**Practical range:** from 1 000 m to 3 750 m depending on the charge.
**Rate of fire:** 8-10 rounds per minute
**Projectile weight:** 8.9 kgs
**Crew:** 4 (crew commander: lance corporal and three gunners)
**Piece divided into three loads:** tube, tripod, base-plate.
**Transportation:** Loyd tracked carrier with trailer.
**Use:** Support weapon in service with the Mortar and Machine Guns Battalions of the Infantry Divisions (16 mortars) as well as in the Independent MMG Companies of the Armoured divisions (4 mortars).

*Opposite right*
**A 4.2 inch mortar crewed by men of the 2nd Middlesex Regiment.**
*(IWM)*

*Below.* **The Loyd Mortar carrier and its trailer.**

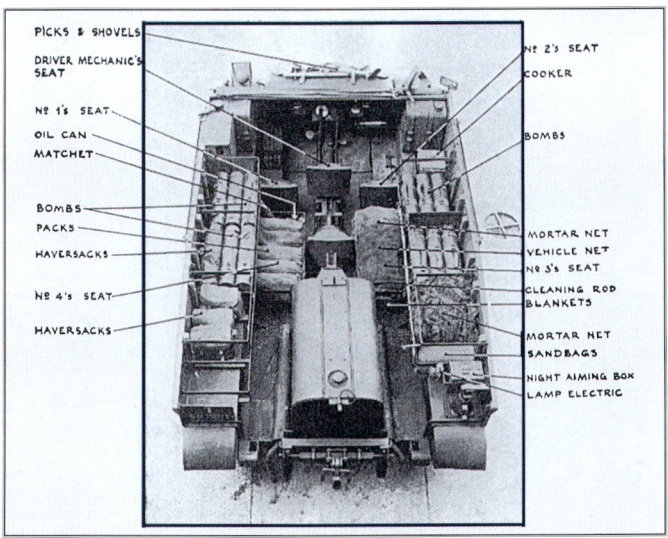

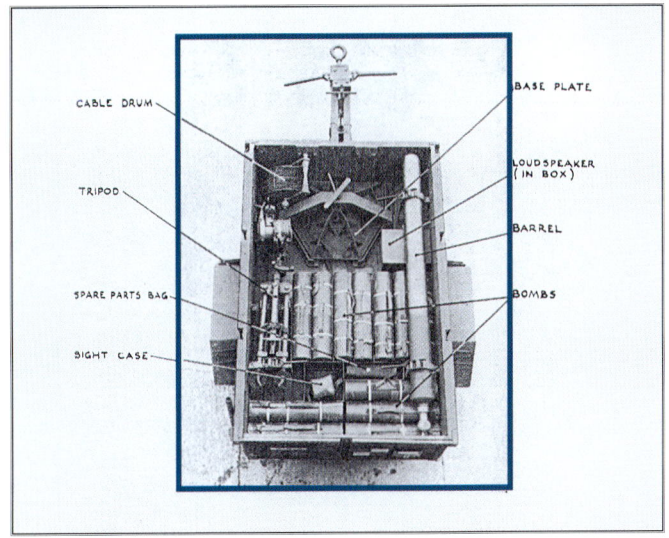

77

# 12. Flame throwers

## Flame Throwers

### 1. Ack Pack
Portable on a man's back
**Total weight**: 22 Kg
**Volume of inflammable liquid:** 18.6 l
**Range:** 45 m
**Operation:**
fired by .303 cartridges
**Time of each blast:** 2 seconds, repeatable ten times.

### 2. Wasp

Flame thrower mounted on a Universal tracked carrier-
**Total weight**: 727 Kg
**Volume of inflammable liquid:** 358 l
**Range:** 100 m
**Operation:** electric ignition.
**Time of each blast**: 2 seconds
**Use:** depending on availability: Medium Machine Gun Company in the Armoured Division.

*Opposite.*
**The Ack-Pack operated by an infantryman of the 1st KOSB (3rd Infantry Division) during an exercise in Britain.**
*(IWM)*

# 13. Various grenades, explosives and mines

*Right.*
1. Hawkins Anti-Tank Mine, set off by being run over
2. Clam magnetic mine against all vehicles
3. Smoke Grenade
4. Depression igniter
5. Pliers to set mines
6. Grenade 82 (plastic charge)
7. Mills No.36 Defensive Grenade
8. Mills No.69 Defensive Grenade
9. Phosphorus grenade No. 73
10. Tube of primary explosives
11. Cone of primary explosives
12. Plastic and 808, available also in rolls
13. Delayed action ignition pencils
14. Box of detonators
15. Bickford cord and cigarettes for ignition

*Above*
1. No 36 defensive grenade
2. No 82 "Gammon' grenade. A ball of plastic (explosive in the form of malleable putty) weighing about 1 kg contained iside a canvas skirt. After unscrewing the top of the plastic, the user threw the grenade primed by means of a cord weighted with lead which unrolled automatically. The detonator set off the charge upon contact with an obstacle

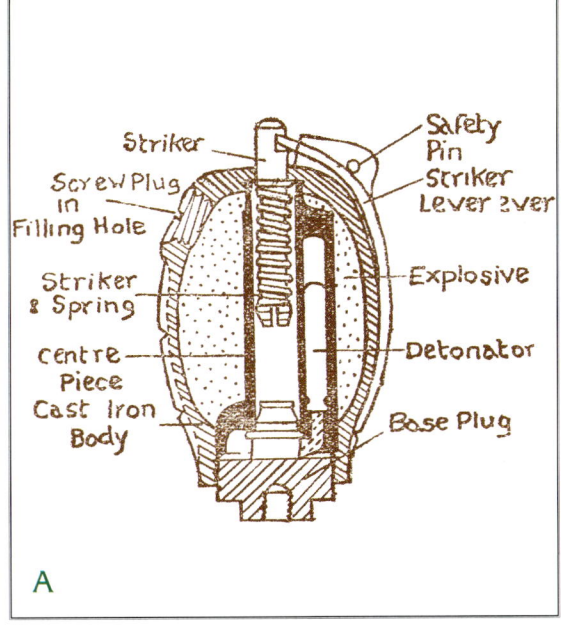

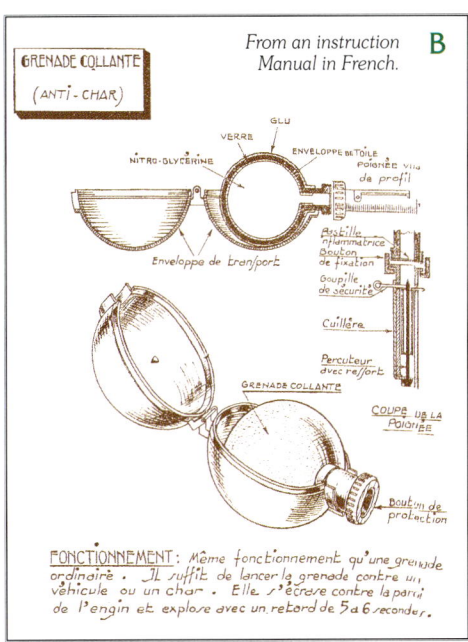

# Grenades

*Opposite from left to right and from top to bottom*

A. No.36 grenade. Defensive fragmentation grenade (thrower under shelter). Weight: 0.68 kg; fuse length 4 seconds.

B. Stunt grenade. Anti-tank grenade

C. No.69 Offensive grenade with Bakelite casing, weight: 0.35 kg

D. No 77. Smoke grenade, weight: 0.34 kg

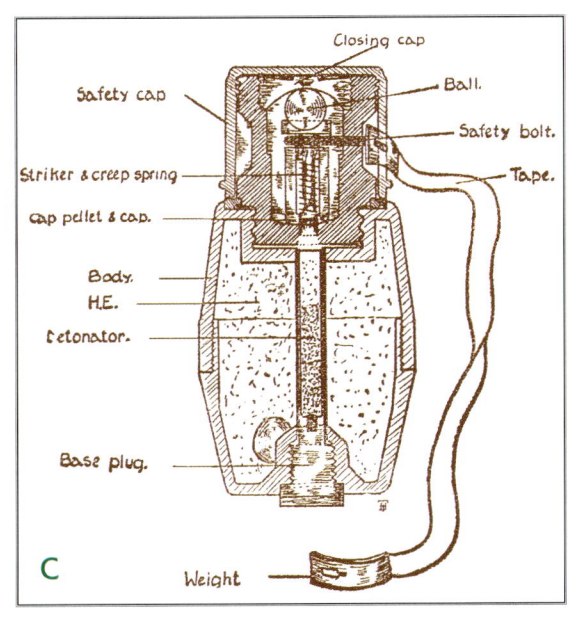

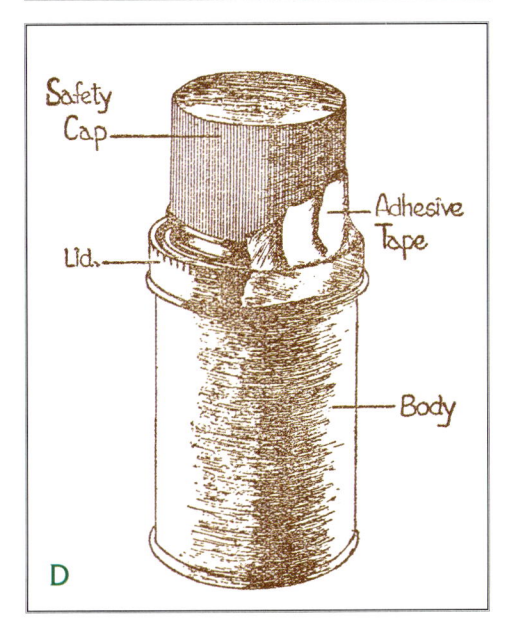

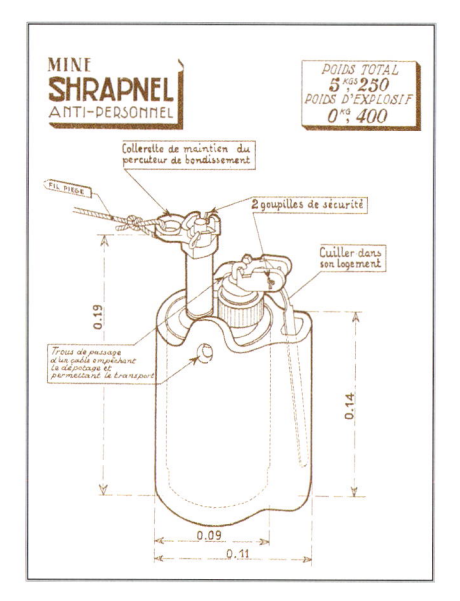

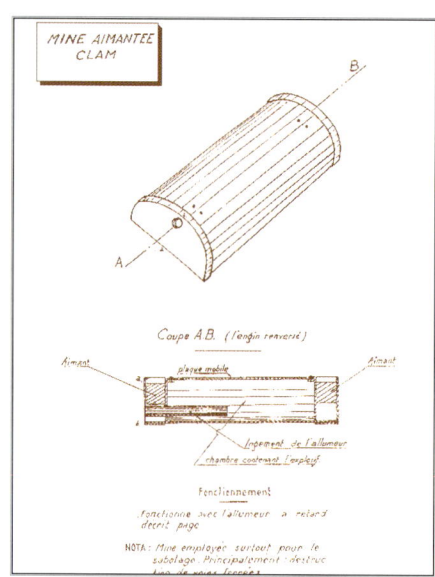

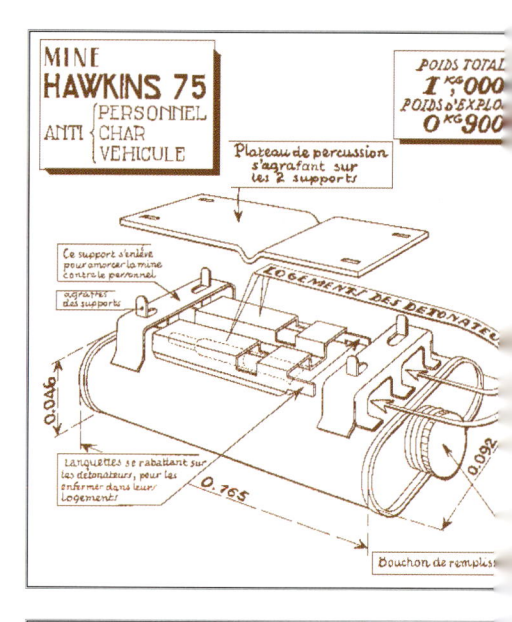

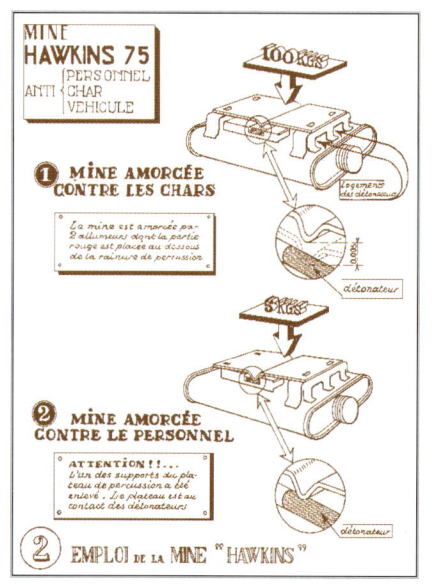

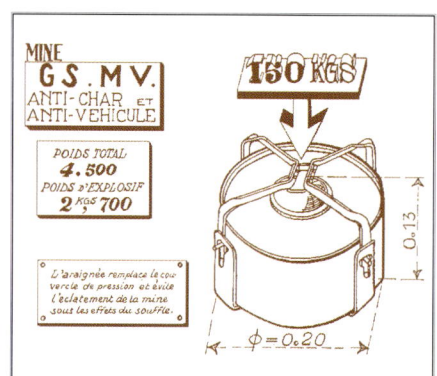

# Anti-personnel and anti-tank mines

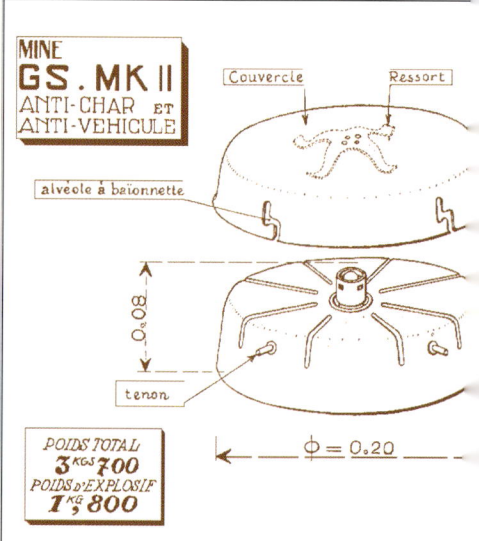

*These drawings come from an instruction Manual in French.*

Normandy, July 1944. The easiest way of clearing a minefield after it had been detected by the minesweeping teams was still the Sherman «Flail» tanks of the 79th Armoured Division.
*(IWM)*

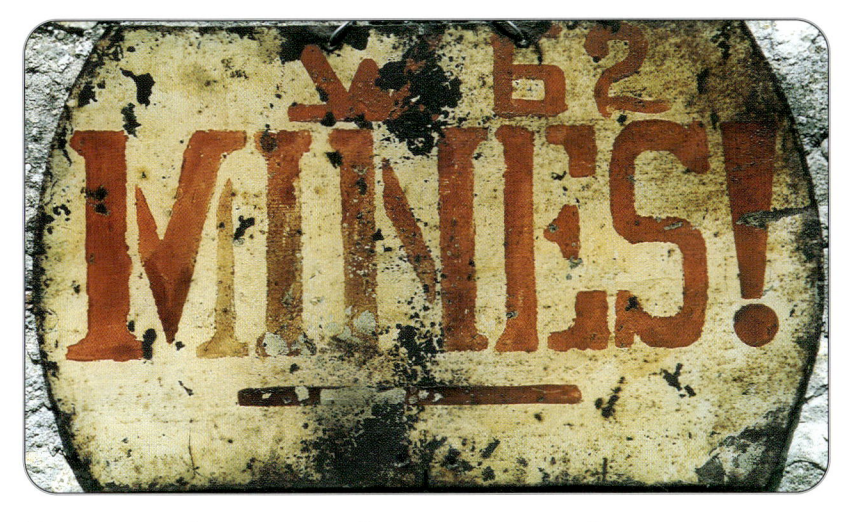

# Detecting and preventing

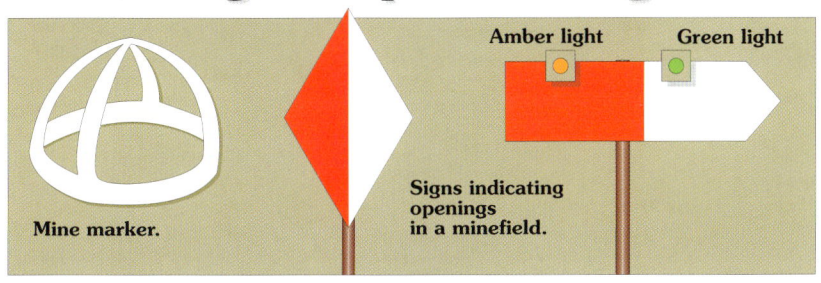

*Above*
"Danger Mines" warning sign placed by the Pioneer Platoon of the 7th Battalion, Royal Welch Fusiliers before 3rd August 1944. The sign was cut out from the bottom of a 200-litre barrel. This type of sign was always done in red paint on a white background.

**Mine marker.**

**Signs indicating openings in a minefield.** (Amber light / Green light)

**No.4 Light Mine Detector**
How it worked:
Held about 10 cms above the ground, the detecor-plate created a magnetic field. When this met a metallic object, a impulse was created, and by means of the amplifier, made a sound in the headphones of the operator.
Detection capacity:
"Teller" mine: 50 cms
"S" mine: 30 cms
ZZ-42 Igniter: 10 cms
Supplied to Field Companies, Royal Engineers, Pioneer Corps, Pioneer Battalions of the Infantry Divisions.

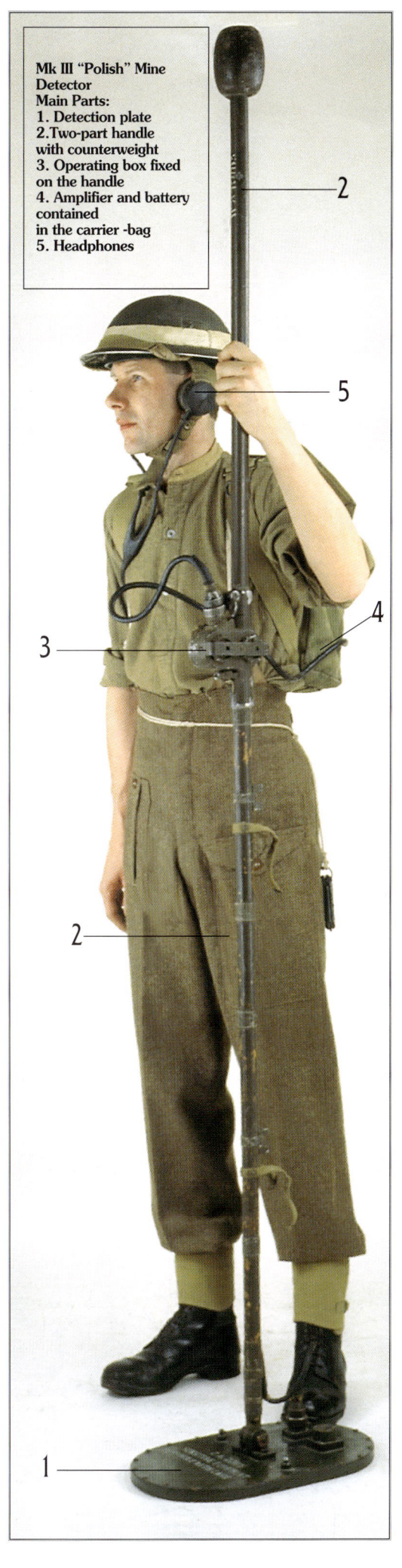

**Mk III "Polish" Mine Detector**
Main Parts:
1. Detection plate
2. Two-part handle with counterweight
3. Operating box fixed on the handle
4. Amplifier and battery contained in the carrier-bag
5. Headphones

81

Normandy, July 1944. Sherman tank moving up to the front. The markings (code and unit badge) are reversed in relation to regulations.
*(IWM)*

# CHAPTER 4   ARMOURED VEHICLES

### Universal Carrier
**SPECIFICATIONS**
**Total weight ready for action:** 4,285 kg
**Total length:** 3.97 m
**Width:** 2.13 m. **Height:** 1.54 m
**Engine:** Ford V8 85hp.
**Transmission:** 4 forward and 1 reverse gears
**Fuel tank:** 90 litres
**Min. armour plating:** 7.5 mm.
**Max. armour plating:** 12 mm
**Crew:** 2 - 4 men depending on task

**USE**
Multiple use: reconnaissance, liaison, forward observation (see "Supply" in Infantry Battalion chapter)

The **"Wasp" Universal Carrier** was equipped with a flame thrower, supplied theoretically to support units (MMG)

*Above*
This Universal Carrier of the Staffordshire Yeomanry HQ Squadron has been equipped with higher steel plate sides to stop water overflowing during amphibious operatins. A .50 machine gun has replaced the usual Bren gun.
*(IWM)*

# 1. Personnel Carriers

### Loyd Carrier
**SPECIFICATION**
**Total Weight ready for action:** 4,050 kg
**Total length:** 4.14 m
**Width:** 1,42 m
**Engine:** Ford V8 85hp.
**Transmission:** 4 forward and 1 reverse gears
**Max. Speed:** 48 km/h
**Fuel tank:** 90 litres
**Min. armour plating:** 6 mm
**Crew:** depending on task

**USE**
Towing the 6-Pr. anti-tank gun. Carrying the 4.2 in. mortar.
*Note.* This machine can be equipped with a canvas hood supported by removable hoops. A special trailer enables 4.2 mortar shells to be transported.

*Above left.* Universal Carrier of the 9th Cameronians, 15th (Scottish) Infantry Division moving through the Normandy fields, loaded with the classic impedimenta of a fighting vehicle.

*Below.* A Kangaroo APCon a Ram Chassis of the 79th Armoured Division transporting infantrymen of the 43rd (Wessex) Infantry Division during the advance on Bremen in 1945.

*Above.* Loyd Carrier of the 43rd (Wessex) Infantry Division in Normandy, July 1944. This machine was attached to the MG battalion of the division: the 8th Battalion, Middlesex Regiment and is towing a trailer containing 4.2 inch mortar shells.

### Armoured Personnel Carrier « Kangaroo »

A Canadian "Ram" tank with turret removed for transporting 8 men.
**Crew:** 2 (one vehicle commander, one driver)
**Other versions**: Sherman tank without turret (10 infantrymen)
US M7 Self-propelled gun (12 men) after removal of the 105 mm howitzer (*Unfrocked Priest*)

**USE**
Machines gathered within the 79th Armoured Division and aassigned as needs arose to various units.

## Landing Vehicle Tracked (LVT) "Buffalo" IV
Amphibious machine propelled by its tracks in the water

### SPECIFICATIONS
**Total Weight ready for action:** 16,800 kgs
**Total length:** 7.83 m
**Width:** 3.25 m
**Height:** 2.43 m
**Engine:** Continental air-cooled 250 hp 7 cylinder radial
**Transmission:** 4-speed gearbox, 1 reverse
**Min. armour plating:** 6 mm
**Crew:** 5
**Armament:** one .50 (12.7 mm) MG, one .30 (7.62 mm) MG, one Polsten Oerlikon 20 mm cannon
**Load:** 3 800 kgs : 30 men or 1 jeep, or 1 Universal Carrier, or 1 scout car, or 1 6-pounder.

### USE
Waterborne landings, river crossings. First supplied to the 5th Assault Regiment, Royal Engineers in September 1944.
**Other versions:** Buffalo I and II with engine at the rear and without loading ramp.

*Above.* **A Buffalo of the 79th Armoured Division before crossing the Rhine on 24th March 1945. The Polsten Oerlikon 20 mm cannon equipping the British LVT can be clearly seen.** *(IWM)*

*Right.* **The Buffalo IV. Another 79th Armoured Division LVT unloading a Universal Carrier from an infantry on the right bank of the Rhine, Operation Plunder.** *(IWM)*

*Below.* **A Half-Track Personnel Carrier of an infantry battalion, the 8th Rifle Brigade, destroyed during the hard fighting in Normandy.** *(IWM)*

## Half-Tracked Personnel Carrier M5 - M9

### SPECIFICATIONS
**Maker:** International Harvester
**Total Weight ready for action:** 8,500 kg
**Total length:** 6.13 m
**Width:** 2.20 m
**Height including MG ring mount:** 2.32 m
**Engine:** International Harvester 143 hp 6 cylinder petrol.
**Transmission:** 4 speed gearbox + 1 reverse; 1 auxiliary reduction box for front axle.
**Max. Speed:** 70 km/h
**Fuel tank:** 230 litres
**Range:** 320 kilometres
**Min. armour plating:** 6.4 mm; 12.7 for the plate protecting the windshield
**Armament:** according to model: one .30 MG (M5 - M9); one .30MG and one .50 (M5 A1 - M9 A1).
**Load:** M5: 13 men; M9: 10 men

### USE
Motor Battalions, Armoured Regiments, various units of the Royal Engineers, Royal Artillery, Royal Army Medical Corps.
*Note.* M5 A1 - M9 A1 designated HTs equipped with the ring mount for the AA MG.

# 2. Command Vehicles

## Armoured Command Vehicle 4 x 4 Mk I

**SPECIFICATIONS**
**Maker:** AEC
**Total weight ready for action:** 10,500 kg
**Total length:** 6 m
**Width:** 2.20 m
**Height:** 2.40 m
**Engine:** AEC 6-cylinder diesel, 95 hp
**Transmission:** 4 forward and 1 reverse gears
**Max. armour plating:** 12 mm
**Radio equipment:** 1 No.9 set, 1 No.14 set, 1 set for transceiving coded messages
**Crew:** 1 driver, 2 radio operators, 4 officers

**USE**
Command vehicle supplied to armoured units.

# 3. Reconnaissance Vehicles

## Daimler "Dingo" Scout Car

**SPECIFICATIONS**
**Total weight ready for action:** 3,000 kg
**Total length:** 3.17 m
**Width:** 1.71 m
**Height:** 1.50 m
**Engine:** Daimler 6-cylinder, 60hp.
**Transmission:** 5-speed gearbox with inverser
**Max. road speed:** 55mph
**Range:** 320 kilometres
**Min. Max. armour plating:** 30 mm
**Armament:** 1 Bren gun
**Crew:** 2 men

**USE**
Reconnaissance, liaison

## Humber Scout Car

**SPECIFICATIONS**
**Total weight ready for action:** 3,390 kg
**Total length:** 3.83 m
**Width:** 1.89 m
**Height:** 2.12 m
**Engine:** Rootes 6-cylinder, 87 hp
**Transmission:** 4 speed gearbox with inverser
**Max. road speed:** 55 mph
**Range:** 320 kilomètres
**Min. Max. armour plating:** 14 mm
**Armament:** 1 or 2 Bren guns
**Crew:** three

**USE**
Reconnaissance, liaison.

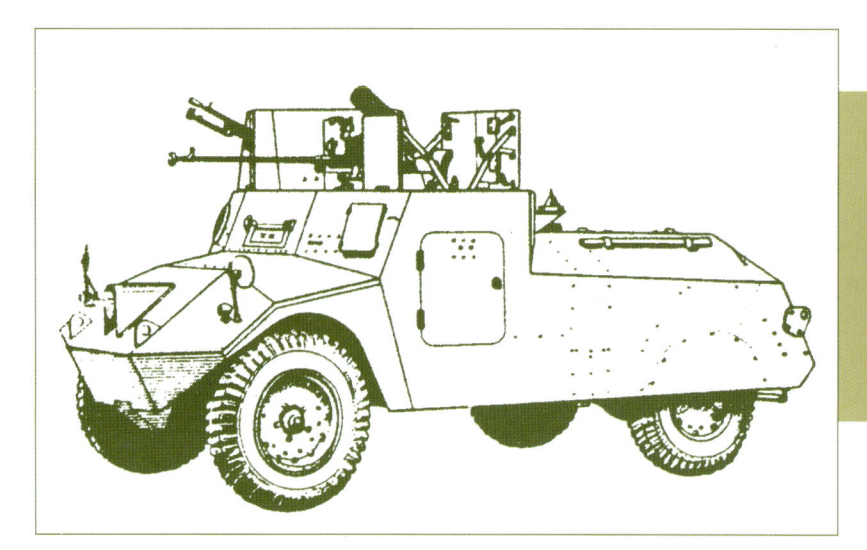

### Morris Light Reconnaissance Car Mk II
**SPECIFICATIONS**
**Total weight ready for action:** 3,700 kg
**Total length:** 4.05 m
**Width:** 2.03 m
**Height:** 1.88 m
**Engine:** Morris, 4-cylinder, 70 hp petrol
**Transmission:** 4 forward and one reverse gears, and one tranfer box
**Max. road ppeed:** 50 mph
**Range:** 250 kilometres
**Max. armour plating:** 14 mm
**Armament:** 1 14 mm anti-tank gun, 1 Bren gun
**Crew:** 3

**USE**
Infantry reconnaissance regiments (Reconnaissance Corps)

### Daimler Mark I Armoured Car
**SPECIFICATIONS**
**Total weight ready for action:** 7 600 kg
**Total length:** 3.90 m
**Width:** 2.40 m
**Height:** 2.20 m
**Engine:** Daimler 6-cylinder, 95 hp
**Transmission:** 5 speed gearbox with inverser (there was a second driving seat at the rear of the vehicle)
**Max. road ppeed:** 50 mph
**Range:** 320 kilometres
**Max. armour plating:** 16 mm
**Armament:** 1 2-pounder (40 mm)*, 1 BESA co-axial machine gun
**Crew:** 3

**USE**
Armoured car regiments, Infantry reconnaissance regiments (Reconnaissance Corps)
* *An adaptable lining enabled the barrel to be lengthened and so increase the initial velocity.*

### Armoured Car Humber Mark IV*
**SPECIFICATIONS**
**Total weight ready for action:** 6,500 kg
**Total length:** 4.50 m
**Width:** 2.15 m
**Height:** 2.35 m
**Engine:** Rootes 6-cylinder, 90 hp
**Transmission:** four forward and one reverse gears
**Max. speed:** 45 mph
**Range:** 400 kilometres
**Max. armour plating:** 15 mm
**Armament:** one 37mm gun, 1 BESA co-axial machine gun
**Crew:** 3

**USE**
Infantry reconnaissance regiments (Reconnaissance Corps)
**Other versions:** Humber Anti-Aircraft Mk.I, equipped with 4 BESA 7.92 mm machine guns in a turret

*Left.*
**A Humber Mk. IV Armoured car.**
*(IWM)*

*Above.*
A T 17 E1 «Staghound» Armoured car of an Armoured car regiment.
Another model, the T 17 E2 with a Frazer Nash turret equipped with two .50 AA machine guns, is used by the Anti-Aircraft Troops of the Armoured car regiments.
(DR)

## T17 E1 "Staghound" Armoured Car
### SPECIFICATIONS
**Total weight ready for action:** 14,500 kg
**Total length:** 5.40 m
**Width:** 2.65 m
**Height:** 2.40 m
**Engine:** two 97 hp (each) GMC 270
**Transmission:** Hydramatic
**Max. road speed:** 60 mph
**Range:** 400 kilomètres
**Max. armour plating:** 32 mm
**Armament:** one 37 mm gun, three .30 MGs (one co-axial, one in the front, one anti-aircraft fixed outside
**Crew:** 4

### USE
Armoured Car Regiments

**Other versions:** T 17 E2 With a Frazer Nash turret equipped with two .50 AA machine guns, used by the Anti-Aircraft Troops of the Armoured car regiments

## AEC Mark II, III Armoured Cars
### SPECIFICATIONS
**Total weight ready for action:** 12,900 kg
**Total length:** 5.61 m
**Width:** 2.70 m
**Height:** 2.69 m
**Engine:** AEC 6-cylinder, 158 hp diesel
**Transmission:** 4 forward and one reverse and one transfer box
**Max. road speed:** 38 mph
**Range:** 400 kilometres
**Max. armour plating:** 30 mm
**Armament:** (AEC Mk.II) one 6-pounder, (AEC Mk.III) one 75 mm gun, one BESA co-axial MG
**Crew:** 4

### USE
Armoured car regiments, Heavy Troops

## White M3 A1 (truck 1-ton Personnel Armoured Scout Car)
### SPECIFICATIONS
**Total weight ready for action:** 5 900 kg
**Total length:** 5,62 m. **Width** 2,03 m. **Height:** 2,11 m
**Engine:** one Hercules JXD, 6-cylinder, 110 hp petrol
**Transmission:** 4 forward and one reverse gears (two engine differentials), one transfer box
**Max. road speed:** 50 mph
**Fuel tank:** 233 litres     **Range:** 400 km
**Max. armour plating:** 12.7 mm on the front, 6.35 mm on the sides
**Crew:** depending on use, maximum 8 men

### USE
Command, reconnaissance, artillery observation

# 4. Light tanks

## M22 "Locust" Airborne Light Tank

### SPECIFICATIONS
**Total weight ready for action:** 7 380 kg
**Total length:** 3,95 m. **Width:** 2,25 m. **Heigth:** 1,80 m
**Engine:** Lycoming 0-435T, flat - 6, 162 hp air-cooled petrol
**Transmission:** Marmon-Herringon Synchromesh 4F1R, four forward one reverse
**Max. road speed:** 35 mph   **Range:** 180 kilomètres
**Armour plating:** 9 - 25 mm
**Armament:** one 37 mm gun (5 shells), one .30 mg (2 500 rounds)
**Crew:** 3 (two in the turret)

### USE
Used for training. In March 1945, 12 Locusts, of the 6th Airborne and transported by Hamilcar glider, were used in the crossing of the Rhine (Operation *Varsity*)

## "Tetrarch" Light Tank MK VII

### SPECIFICATION
**Total weight ready for action:** 7,000 kg
**Total length :** 2.70 m.
**Width:** 4.35 m.
**Height:** 2.20 m
**Engine:** Meadows MAT flat-12, 165 hp petrol
**Transmission:** 5 forward and one reverse gears
**Max. road speed:** 40 mph
**Tank capacity:** 171 litres
**Armour plating:** 4 - 14 mm
**Armament:** one 2 pounder (50 shells), one BESA co-axial machine gun (2 025 rounds)
**Crew:** 3 (2 in the turret)

### USE
Air-transportable by Hamilcar glider.
Used by Armored Reconnaissance Regiment of the 6th Airborne, 6th June 1944.
During the Normandy campaign and after the 6th June 1944, the Tetrarch was replaced by the Cromwell in the 6th Airborne.

## M3 A3 "Stuart" (*Honey*) Light Tank

### SPECIFICATION
**Total weight ready for action:** 13,300 kg
**Total length:** 4.52 m.
**Width:** 2.52 m
**Height:** 2.64 m
**Engine:** 7-cylinder aircraft-type air-cooled radial
**Transmission:** 5 forward and one reverse gears
**Max. road speed:** 30 mph
**Range:** 160 km
**Armour plating:** 12.7 mm - 38.1 mm
**Armament:** one 37 mm gun (138 rounds), three .30 machine guns (9 000 rounds)
**Crew:** 4
**Communications:** SCR 508, 528, 538, US set or Set 19

### USE
Recconaissance troops of the Armoured regiments. With the turret dismantled, it was used as a forward observation vehicle.

*Right*
**An M5 A1 of the Scots Greys belonging to a mixed column of the 4th Armoured Brigade, entering Wismar on 2nd May 1945. The differences with the M3 A3 can be clearly seen on this three-quarter front photograph.** (IWM)

## M5 A1 Light Tank

The majority of American light tank supplies was made up of the M3 A3. Delivered in limited quantities, the M5 A1 differed from the M3 A3 on the following points: two V-8 Cadillac engines, needing a modification of the rear ( heightened instead of being flat; transmission was by means of a Hydramatic automatic gearbox: modification of the front hull.). Note: In 1945 some units received the M24 Chaffee for trials, especially the 8th King's Royal Irish Hussars.

# 5. Medium Tanks

*Left.*
**A Cromwell IV** of the Headquarters of the 11th Armoured Division in Normandy. *(IWM)*

*Below.*
**A Cromwell VIII** equipped with the large 95 mm howitzer for infantry support. *(IWM)*

*Bottom.*
**A Cromwell Armoured Recovery Vehicle** of the 11th Armoured Division towing a Panzer IV taken the 6th July 1944 a little before the battle for Caen. *(IWM)*

*Page 90, top.*
**A Centaur IV** of the Royal Marine Armoured Support Regiment. The differences between the Centaur IV and the ordinary Cromwell are: the 95 mm howitzer and the compass scale painted on the turret. It is powered by a Liberty and not a Rolls-Royce Meteor engine. *(IWM)*

*Page 90 bottom.* **A Challenger**, a lengthened Cromwell with a longer 17-pounder barrel in a modified turret of the Armoured Recce regiment (2nd Northamptonshire Yeomanry) of the 11th Armoured Division. *(IWM)*

## Cromwell IV Cruiser Tank

### SPECIFICATION
**Total weight ready for action:** 28 000 kg
**Total length:** 6,55 m
**Width:** 3,04 m
**Height:** 2,50 m
**Engine:** Rolls-Royce Meteor, V-12, 600 hp
**Transmission :** 5 forward and one reverse gears
**Max. road speed:** 40 mph
**Armour plating:** 8 mm - 76 mm
**Armament:** one 75 mm gun (64 rounds) whose penetration is 68 mm of armour plating at 30° at 500 metres. Two BESA machine guns, one co-axial, one mounted in front of the assistant driver (4 950 rounds)
**Communications:** one Set No.19
**Crew:** 5 (three in the turret)

### USE
Armoured reconnaissance Regiments and all the Armoured regiments of the 7th Armoured Division.

### OTHER VERSIONS
**Cromwell VI:** close support 95 mm-Howitzer
**Cromwell VII:** 75 mm gun welded hull, front armour plating of 101 mm
**Cromwell VIII:** 95 mm Howitzer, welded hull, front armour plating of 101 mm
**Cromwell OP :** (Observation post) Forward artillery observation tank equipped with a mock cannon and extra radio equipment
**Cromwell Armoured recovery vehicle:** Turretless, adapted for recovery and towing (winch, hoist, etc)

89

## Centaur IV 🇬🇧

### SPECIFICATIONS
**Total weight ready for action :** 28 600 kg
**Total length :** 6,25 m
**Width:** 2,97 m. **Height:** 2,90 m
**Engine:** Liberty V-12, 395 hp
**Transmission:** 5 forward and one reverse gears
**Max. road speed:** 27 mph
**Armour plating:** 20 - 76 mm
**Armament:** 95 mm Howitzer (51 rounds), one BESA co-axial machine gun
**Communications:** one Set No.19, one telephone mounted on the outside of the turret, enabling an observer to give the tank commander target coordinates, the scale marked on the turret corresponding to the regulation compass grid.
**Crew:** 5, 3 in the turret

### USE
**Use:** Infantry (Royal Marines) close support tank, 80 produced

### OTHER VERSIONS
**Centaur Observation post**
**Centaur Armoured recovery vehicle**
**Centaur Dozer:** turretless tank with a bulldozer blade mounted on the front.

Setting the Centaur's gun by the observer on the outside

*Above.*
**This drawing shows an observer on the outside setting the Centaur's gun by using the compass scale painted on the turret and the outside telephone placed on the rear of the tank.**

## Challenger 🇬🇧

A enlarged turret fitted with a 17-pounder on a lengthened Cromwell chassis (6 wheels instead of 5).

### SPECIFICATION
**Total weight ready for action:** 32,500 kgs
**Total length:** 7.00 m
**Width:** 3.05 m.
**Height:** 2.72 m
**Mechanical elements identical to the Cromwell**
**Armament:** one 17-pounder
**Crew:** 5

### USE
Destined for use with the Armoured Regiments or the Armoured Reconnaissance Regiments equipped with Cromwells and not yet having received the "Firefly".

## Comet. Cruiser Tank

### SPECIFICATIONS
**Total weight ready for action:** 35 000 kg
**Total length:** 7,65 m
**Width:** 3,04 m. **Height:** 2,70 m
**Engine:** Rolls Royce Meteor MkIII, V-12, 600 hp, petrol
**Transmission:** 5 forward and one reverse gears
**Max. road speed:** 30 mph
**Fuel tank:** 440 litres
**Range:** 200 kms
**Amour plating:** 14 - 101 mm
**Armament:** one 77 mm gun with a real calibre of 76.2 mm (61 rounds), two BESA machine guns, one co-axial, the other mounted in front of the assistant driver, on the left (5 173 rounds), one Bren gun (600 rounds)
**Crew:** 5, three in the turret

### USE
Delivered for training in December 1944 to the Armoured regiments of the 11th Armoured Division. In operation effectively from March 1945, replacing the M4 Sherman.

*Above.* A Sherman III ( M4 A2) of the 11th Armoured Division transporting a platoon of infantry from the 3rd DI. The extra radio antenna indicates that it is probably a command tank. *(IWM)*

## M4 "Sherman' Cruiser Tank
(see table opposite)

### SPECIFICATIONS
**Total weight ready for action:** 31 500 kg
**Total length:** 5,90 m (sauf M4 A4 : 6,06 m)
**Width:** 2,62 m. **Height:** 2,67 m
**Engine:** depending on version
**Transmission:** 5 forward and one reverse gears
**Max. road speed:** 26 mph
**Range:** 160 kms
**Armour plating (Hull):** 51 mm front, 38 mm sides
**Armour plating (Turret):** 76.2 mm front, 51 mm sides
**Armament:** one 75 mm gun (98 rounds) with a penetration capability of 70 mm armour plating at 30° at 500 metres. One .50 machine gun mounted externally; two .30 (6 750 rounds), one co-axial and one served by the assistant driver.
**Crew:** 5, three in the turret
**Communications:** SCR 506 or 508 (a British adaptation of the 19 set)

### USE
Armoured Regiments. **Sherman Observation post:** Forward observation tank equipping certain Royal Artillery regiments. The gun is a dummy and the turret was re-equipped with a map table and extra equipment.

### THE M4 SHERMAN VERSIONS DELIVERED BY THE USA

| AMERICAN NAME | BRITISH NAME | GUN CALIBRE | ENGINE | NUMBERS DELIVERED |
|---|---|---|---|---|
| M4[1] | Sherman I | 75 mm | aviation type 9-cylinder radial petrol | 2,096 |
| M4 A1[2] | Sherman II | 75 mm | ditto | 942 |
| M4 A2[1] | Sherman III | 75 mm | Two coupled 6-cylinder diesel | 5,041 |
| M4 A4[1] | Sherman V | 75 mm | five coupled 6-cylinder petrol | 7,163[3] |
| M4 105 Howitzer[1] | Sherman IB | 105 mm | Aviation type 9-cylinder radial petrol | 593 |
| M4 A1[2] 76,2 mm | Sherman II A | 76,2 mm | ditto | 1,330 |

1. Welded Hull. 2. cast hull
3. The base for the "Firefly" conversion; Hull length 6.05 metres
Only a dozen each of the M4 A3 and M4 A2 76 mm were delivered for trials.

A Sherman VC «Firefly» of the 13/18th Hussars (27th Armoured Brigade) accompanied by infantrymen of the 3rd Infantry Division during Operation Goodwood. *(IWM)*

## Sherman "Firefly"

(see page 95 for units using the Firefly)

### SPECIFICATIONS

A British modification of the American M4. The M4 A4 (**Sherman V** which became **VC**) was principally used in these modifcations.

**Principal modifications:**
75 mm gun replaced by the 17 pounder (76.2) with therefore:
— rebalancing of the turret and displacing the radio set 19 to an outside box, at the back of the turret.
— addition of a hatch above the loader's post.
— removal of the position of second driver's post replaced by shell stowage space

**Ammunition:** 78 rounds of 17 pounds shells.

### USE

Depending on availability (transformations were carried out after March 1944). This tank was destined for the Armoured regiments: 1 Firefly per Cromwell or 75 mm Sherman Troop. Up till the end of the war 60 Fireflies were used.

## Sherman M4 A2 Duplex Drive

### SPECIFICATIONS

*See specification for standard M4 on the previous page.*
— A water-tight canvas skirt allowing the tank to be suspended in water and to wade over a short distance during landing operations
— Motion is provided by propellers which were activated when the tank went into the water.
— When it reached the beach, the skirt was pulled in and the tank could use its armament.

*Opposite right and below*
**The Sherman Beach Armoured Recovery vehicle (BARV)** seen from three-quarters front on a factory photograph...and almost from the same angle, in the middle of working on the Normandy beaches, towing a Bedford/Scammell OXC tractor.
*(Bovington & IWM)*

*Centre.*
**A Sherman "Crab" or "Flail" of the 79th Armoured Division in Normandy.**
*(IWM)*

*Bottom from left to right.*
**An ARV Sherman, turretless and an ARV MkII Sherman with turret and false cannon.**
*(IWM)*

## Beach Armoured Recovery Vehicle (BARV)

### SPECIFICATIONS

*See specification of M4 on page 92*

— turretless Sherman equipped with water-tight superstructure and a towing system.

— used on beaches for towing vehicles and machines.

— used by the Royal and Electrical and Mechanical Engineers.

## Sherman "Crab" or "Flail"

— At the front of the tank there was a rotating drum upon which chains were mounted which hit the ground, thereby exploding mines.

— Boxes on the sides of the hull let out chalk powder. This fell to the ground indicating the way which had been cleared of explosives.

— used by the Royal Engineers.

## Sherman Armoured Recovery Vehicle (ARV)

A breakdown recovery vehicle equipped with hoist and winch used by the REME *(below left)*.

## Sherman Armoured Recovery Vehicle Mk II

This has a dummy cannon mounted *(below right)*.

## M3 "Grant" Canal Defence Light (CDL)

### SPECIFICATIONS

A tank equipped with a powerful searchlight fed by a generator. During night operations, it was used to light up objectives and routes. Used by the 79th Armoured Division. The M3 CDL was used during the crossings of the Rhine and the Elbe

*Below.*
**Shermans I or III (Sherman M4 or M4 A2) of a British regiment ready to go. They have taken aboard infantrymen of the 3rd Infantry Division which they are to accompany, a few moments before the beginning of Operation Goodwood.**
*(IWM)*

## ARMOUR USED BY THE LARGE UNITS AT THE TIME OF THEIR FIRST COMMITMENT

| UNITS | SHERMAN | FIREFLY | CROMWELL | CHALLENGER | CHURCHILL |
|---|---|---|---|---|---|
| 4th Armoured Brigade | ■ | | | | |
| 6th Guards Tank Brigade | | | | | ■ |
| 8th Armoured Brigade | ■ | | | | |
| 27th Armoured Brigade | ■ | | | | |
| 31st Tank Brigade | | | | | ■ |
| 33rd Armoured Brigade | ■ | | | | |
| 34th Tank Brigade | | | | | ■ |
| Guards Armoured Division | | | 1 | 1 | |
| 7th Armoured Division | | | ■ | | |
| 11th Armoured Division | 4 | | 2 | 2 | |
| 79th Armoured Division | 3 | | | | 3 |

Summary of the different models of medium and heavy tanks in use in the units at the moment of their commitment

**Notes**
1. 2nd Welsh Guards
2. 2nd Northamptonshire Yeomanry 15/19th Hussars from 1.08.1944
3. Tanks converted for special uses
4. In March 1945, Shermans of the 11th Armoured Division were replaced by Comets.

95

# 6. Infantry tanks

## Churchill Infantry Tank 🇬🇧
(see table following page)

### SPECIFICATIONS
**Total weight ready for action:** 40 000 kg
**Total length:** 7,32 m
**Width:** 3,40 m. **Height:** 2,40 m
**Engine:** Bedford, flat-12, 350 hp
**Transmission:** 4 forward and one reverse gears
**Max. Road Speed:** 17 mph
**Range:** 150 km
**Armament:** depending on version (see table page 97). one BESA co-axial machine gun. One BESA machine gun mounted in front of the second driver
**Crew:** 5, three in the turret
**Communications:** Set No. 19 or 38

### USE
Infantry support tank (see table page 94). Depending on availability, machines equipped with the 6 pounder had this replaced by the 75 mm cannon during the campaign.

*Above.*
**A Churchill Mk V of the 7th Royal Tank Regiment (31st Armoured Brigade) accompanying infantrymen of the 15th Scottish Infantry Division on the 28th June 1944, during Operation Epsom.**
*(IWM)*

## CHURCHILL TANK VERSIONS

| Type | Gun/cal. + No of shells | Turret | Armour Max. Thickness | Lateral evacuation hatch |
|---|---|---|---|---|
| Mk III | 6 pounder 84 shells | Welded | 102 mm | Square |
| Mk IV | 6 pounder 84 shells | Cast | 102 mm | Square |
| Mk V | 95 mm (Howitzer) 47 shells | Cast | 102 mm | Square |
| Mk VI | 75 mm 84 shells | Cast | 102 mm | Square |
| Mk VII | 75 mm 84 shells | Composite | 152 mm | Round |
| Mk VIII | 95 mm (Howitzer) 47 shells | Composite | 152 mm | Round |

## Churchill V Close Support
(see characteristics above)

A Churchill V equipped with a 95 mm howitzer used in the Army Tank Brigades (5 Independent Brigades) as an infantry close support tank.

*Right.*
**An ARV Churchill of the REME armed with BESA machine guns. In the background an interesting version of the "Ram II" observation post can be seen.** *(IWM)*

## Churchill ARV
(see characteristics above)

— A turretless Churchill equipped with a hoist and first echelon breakdown recovery material. There were two BESA machine guns for close defence.
— This material was used by the REME

## The 79th Armour

**1. Churchill Small Box Girder (SBG)**
With its turret, this Mk IV Churchill transported and put into operation an articulated bridge enabling 9.10 metres to be crossed

**2 and 3. Churchill Bridge layer**
Turretless tank equipped with material to put a metallic gangway.
Equipped the Royal Armoured Corps which were equipped with Churchills

**4. Crocodile Churchill**
A flame thrower replaced the hull machine gun.
An armoured two-wheeled trailer transported the inflammable liquid;
**Practical flame-thrower range:** 185 metres.
**Volume of the trailer:** 908 litres

## n's Special Churchills

— **Breakdown Churchill** used by the REME and was not specific to the 79th Armoured Division. Equipped units using Churchills

— **Churchill Fascine-carrier**, using bundles of wood to fill in anti-tank ditches, used by the Royal Engineers

— **Churchill "Petard" Tank**, replacement of the turret gun by a 290 mm mortar.

**Projectile weight:** 18 kgs.

**Maximum range:** 250 metres.

**Practical range:** 80 metres.

**Loading:** from the outside using the front machine gunner's hatch.

**Used** for the destruction of fortifications by the Royal Engineers.

**THE 79TH ARMOURED DIVISION'S SPECIAL CHURCHILLS - THE "FUNNIES"**

1. Churchill Small box girder, first version, used for crossing gaps of not more than 9.10 metres.
2. Churchill bridge layer. Can also cross 4.8 m-walls
3. Churchill folding small box girder easier to use than than the single piece version
4. Crocodile Churchill and its trailer
5. Churchill Armoured Recovery Vehicle
6. Fascine Churchill for crossing ditches
7. Churchill "Petard" tank

# CHAPTER 5 THE ARTILLERY

# 1. Anti-tank Artillery

*(IWM)*

## 6-Pounder Anti-Tank Gun
### SPECIFICATIONS
**Calibre:** 57 mm
**Total weight:** 1 200 kg
**Projectile weight:** 2,84 kg
**Average range:** 1 000 m
**Initial velocity:** 825 m/s
**Penetration capability:** 83 mm at 500 m at 30° elevation (APCBP projectile)
**Rate of Fire:** 15 rounds a minute maximum
**Set-up time:** a few seconds without spreading the trails
**Gun carriage:** split trail type
**Transport:** towed by Bren gun carrier or by jeep (Airborne)
**Crew:** 4-5 men

### USE
Anti-Tank platoons, Infantry Battalions, Anti-tank regiments (RA), Infantry and Airborne Divisions

*Previous page.*
A 6 pounder gun set up in the streets of Caen, 10th July 1944, by the men of the Anti-tank platoon of the 1st King's Own Scottish Borderers. *(IWM)*

*Left.* A 17 pounder anti-tank gun and its crew on 27th June 1944 near Tilly-sur-Seulles. *(IWM)*

## 17-Pounder Anti-Tank Gun
### SPECIFICATION
**Calibre:** 76.2 mm
**Total weight:** 2 000 kg
**Projectile weight:** 7,65 kg
**Practical range:**
— 900 m on a moving target;
— 1,400 m on a stationary target
**Initial velocity:**
— (with ordinary charge) 997 metres / sec.
— (with special charge) 1 200 metres / sec.
**Penetration capability:** 180 mm at 90 metres at 30° angle of attack (APDS projectile)
**Rate of Fire:**
— (practical) 10 shots a minute
— (Maximum) 20 shots / min.
**Set-up time:** a few seconds without preading the trails
**Transport:** towed by a Morris C8 or Guy Quad Ant
**Crew:** 5-6 men

### USE
Anti-Tank Regiments (Royal Artillery)

## "Wolverine" M10, M10 A1 Tank Destroyer
### SPECIFICATIONS
**Total Weight ready for action :** 25,854 kg
**Total length :** 5.95 m.
**Width:** 3.04 m.
**Height:** 2.49 m
**Engine:**
— 2 coupled 6-cylinder General motors diesel for the M10
— 1 Ford V8 petrol for the M10 A1
**Transmission:** five forward and one reverse gears
**Armament:** one 76.2 mm gun (56 rounds). One .50. machine gun in the turret (300 rounds)
**Penetration:** 90 mm at 900 metres with 30° angle of attack
**Armour plating:** 12. mm - 50.8 mm
**Fuel tank:** 567 l (**M10**); 726 l (**M10 A1**)
**Range:** 320 km (**M10**); 250 km (**M10 A1**)
**Max. road speed:** 25 mph
**Crew:** 5 men
### USE
Anti-Tank Regiments (Royal Artillery)

*Above.* **Normandy, 6th June 1944. A tank destroyer M10 Wolverine supporting the 3rd Infantry Division.** *(IWM)*

*Below.* **An Achilles and its impressive 17 pounder, a few moments before its commitment in the Battle of the Odon River.** *(IWM)*

## "Achilles" Tank Destroyer
British modification of the American Tank destroyer M10.
**Main Transformations:**
Replacement of the 76.2 mm gun by a 17 pounder with a barrel counterweight on the muzzle. This mounting meant also modifying the turret mask

### USE
Anti-Tank Regiments (Royal Artillery)

## "Archer" 17-pounder Self Propelled Anti-Tank Gun
### SPECIFICATIONS
A 17 pounder mounted in a casemate on the chassis of a Valentine tank. The gun faces backwards so the tank must position itself facing the rear.
**Total weight ready for action:** 15 000 kg
**Engine:** GMC 165 hp M10 Diesel
**Max. road speed:** 16 mph
**Armament:** one 17 pounder (39 rounds)
**Penetration:** 90 mm at 900 metres at 30° angle of attack
**Armour plating:** 60 mm maximum
**Crew:** 4

### USE
Anti-Tank Regiments (Royal Artillery), Put into service at the end of 1944, one troop per battery in the Infantry Divisions.

*Opposite left.*
**An Archer and its gun in the casemate, mounted on the chassis of the Valentine Infantry tank Mark IX or X. Because of its rearward firing gun, the crew had to use particular tactics for setting the gun up when ambushing. In spite of this inconvenience, the Archer turned out to be a formidable weapon during the few months of its career.** *(DR)*

# 2. Field Artillery

### 25. Pounder, Field Gun Howitzer
**SPECIFICATION**
**Calibre:** 87.63 mm
**Total weight:** 1 800 kg
**Projectile weight:** 11.25 kgs (explosive)
**Maximum range:** 12,000 m
**Rate of Fire:** 5 rounds per minute (normal)
**Set-up time:** 1 to 2 minutes
**Gun carriage:** single trail
**Transport:**
drawn by Morris C8 or a Guy Quad Ant
**Crew:** 6
**USE**
Field Regiments (Royal Artillery)

*Left.*
**A 25 pounder artillery piece from one of the three Field Artillery Regiments (69th, 143rd or 185th Field Artillery Regiments) of the 49th (West Riding Infantry Division, during the attack on Caen, 8th July 1944.**
*(IWM)*

*Right.*
This view of a Sexton mounted on a Ram chassis allows one to differentiate it from its American partner the M7: the 25 pounder and its muzzle brake of the later versions, right handed driving post, no cupola.
*(DR)*

*Below.*
A Sexton going through Ecouché at the end of the battle of Normandy at the moment when the Falaise pocket had just been closed. For road running, the crew have put on the muzzle cover.
*(IWM)*

### "Sexton" 25-Pounder Tracked Self Propelled Gun
**SPECIFICATIONS**
**Weight ready for action:** 25 650 kg
**Engine:** aviation-type, 7-cylinder radial 400 hp, petrol
**Carriage:** Self-propelled based on the chassis of a Canadian Ram tank.
**Armament:**
— One 25-Pounder gun (see above for characteristics) 112 shells
— Two Bren guns (1 500 rounds)
**Crew:** 6 men
**USE**
Field Artillery Regiments (Royal Artillery) of Armoured Divisions

## M7 "Priest" Self Propelled Gun
### SPECIFICATIONS
**Total weight ready for action:** 22 000 kg
**Total length:** 6,46 m.
**Width:** 3,02 m.
**Height:** 2,74 m
**Engine:** Aviation-type, 9-cylinder radial, air-cooled, 400 hp petrol
**Armament:** one 105 mm howitzer (57 shells), one .50 machine gun in the turret (300 rounds)
**Projectile weight (shell):** 14 kg
**Maximum range:** 10,100 m (charge No7)
**Rate of Fire:** 4 shots / min
**Set up time:** 2 mins
**Crew:** 7

### USE
Field Artillery regiments - Self-propelled (Royal Artillery)
*Note.* At the end of August 1944, the vehicles of the seven Field regiments equipped with the M7 were gradually replaced, changing the 105 mm howitzer for the British 25 pounder.

*Above.*
The M7 Priest called thus by its users because of the peculiar shape of the the turret recalling the preacher's pulpit in church.
*(DR)*

*Left.*
The M 7 self-propelled gun with its 105 mm howitzer of a Field artillery Regiment, set up and perfectly camouflaged.
*(IWM)*

*Opposite page top.*
A Medium Artillery Regiment battery in the Normandy bocage, 13th June 1944. The quick way the battery has been set up, with neither special preparation, nor camouflage shows how harsh the fighting was in these first days of the campaign. Radio vehicles of the Royal Corps of Signals, attached to the Royal Artillery batteries can be seen in the background. *(IWM)*

*Opposite page bottom.*
A 5.5 inch gun drawn by its AEC Matador tractor passing through a Norman vilage. It belongs to the 68th (4th West Lancashire) Medium Artillery regiment, 4th Army Group Royal Artillery (AGRA), attached to the 1st Corps, 2nd Army.
*(IWM)*

# 3. Medium and Heavy Artillery

### 4.5 Inch Gun, Mark I
**SPECIFICATION**
**Calibre:** 114.3 mm. **Projectile weight.** 25 kgs (explosive)
**Total weight:** 7.200 kg
**Max. range:** 18,000 m
**Rate of Fire:** 2 rounds per minute. **Set-up time:** 3 minutes
**Gun carriage:** split trail
**Transport:** towed by an AEC Matador 4 x 4 tractor
**USE**
Medium Regiments (Royal Artillery), army general reserve.
*Note.* Was gradually replaced by the 5.5 during 1944-45.

### 5.5 Inch Gun
**SPECIFICATION**
**Calibre:** 139.7 mm. **Projectile weight:** 36 kgs (standard)
**Total weight:** 5,800 kg
**Max. range:** 14,500m (normal charge)
**Rate of Fire:** 2 - 5 rounds / min. **Set-up time:** 3 mins
**Gun carriage:** identical to the 4.5 inch
**Transport:** towed by an AEC Matador 4 x 4 tractor
**Crew:** 10 men
**USE**
Medium Regiments (Royal Artillery), army general reserve.

## 155 mm Gun, M1 A1 🇺🇸

### SPECIFICATIONS
**Calibre:** 155 mm.
**Total weight:** 13,500 kg
**Projectile weight:** 43.700 kg
**Max.range:** 23,000 m
**Rate of Fire:** 1 - 3 rounds / min
**Set-up time:** 30 mins
**Gun carriage:** split trail
**Transport:** drawn by Scammel or US Mack tractors
**Crew:** 14 men

### USE
Heavy Regiments (Royal Artillery), army general reserve.

*Above.*
**A 155 mm A1 M1 battery.** *(IWM)*

*Right.*
12th July 1944, artillerymen of the 410th battery, 52nd Heavy Artillery Regiment (4th AGRA) setting up their 155 mm Long Tom, of US origin.
*(IWM)*

## 7.2 inch Howitzer Mark I-V
### SPECIFICATIONS
**Calibre:** 182.8 mm.
**Total weight:** 10 500 kg
**Projectile weight:** 91,5 kg
**Max. range:** 16 000 m
**Rate of Fire:** 1 round / min
**Gun carriage:** Single trail arm
**Transport:** drawn by Scammel or Diamond tractors
**Crew:** 14

### USE
Heavy Regiments (Royal Artillery), army general reserve.

*Note.*
A version with an extended barrel, mounted on an M1 carriage, was put into service at the end of 1944 under the name of **7.2 inch Howitzer, Mk VI.**
**Weight:** 13,250 kg
**Max. range:** 18,000 m

*Above.*
Loading the 7.2 artillery piece by men of one of the 21st Corps AGRAs. The angle of the barrel suggests a medium range. *(IWM)*

*Right.*
Firing. The Artillerymen of the Heavy Artillery Brigade open fire from a distance by means of a lanyard. Behind the wheels are chocks placed there to reduce part of the recoil which would push the cannon far from its initial position, making the gunners go through the aiming procedure all over again. *(IWM)*

*Below right.*
The 303 mm cannon ( 8 inch) M1 on an M2 carriage; the ensemble barrel and breech - block are here in position for transport.
*(DR)*

*Below.*
The M2 gun carriage ready to be towed by a Scammel or Diamond tractor. *(DR)*

*Bottom.*
The 8 inch cannon set up.
*(DR)*

## M1 8 inch Gun
### SPECIFICATIONS
**Calibre:** 203 mm.
**Total weight:** 46,600 kg
**Projectile weight:** 108 kg
**Range:**
— 27,250 m (normal charge)
— 32,584 m (super charge)
**Rate of Fire:** 2 to 3 shots a minute
**Set-up time:** 1 to 2 hours
**Gun carriage:** split trail
**Transport:** drawn in two loads: the barrel and the carriage, by a Scammel or American M6 tractor
**Crew:** 14 men

### USE
Super Heavy Regiments (Royal Artillery), army general reserve.

*Above.*
**An M1 240mm gun set up. This shot was taken on the 27th January 1945. Setting the battery up took at least 2 hours with the help of a 20-ton crane. These pieces equipping the Super Heavy Regiments bombarded enemy positions from a distance. There were two Super Heavy Regiments, one in the 9th Army Group Royal Artillery (the 3rd) and the other, even though it was British, was detached to the 2nd Canadian Army Group, RA (the 61st). The 9th AGRA was not attached to a specific corps.**
*(IWM)*

## M1 240 mm Gun

### SPECIFICATIONS

**Calibre:** 240mm.
**Total weight:** 44,500 kgs (29,373 kgs when set up)
**Projectile weight:** 163.44 kg
**Maximum range:** 22,850 m
**Rate of Fire:** 2 shots in 3 minutes
**Set-up time:** 1 to 2 hours
**Gun carriage:** split trail
**Transport:** drawn in two loads: the barrel and the carriage by a Scammel or American M6 tractor

### USE

Super Heavy Regiments (Royal Artillery), army general reserve.

# 4. The Airborne Artillery

## M1 A1 75 mm Howitzer, Carriage M8

### SPECIFICATIONS

**Calibre:** 75mm.
**Total weight:** 600 kg
**Projectile weight:** 6.67 kg
**Maximum range:** 8,500 m
**Rate of fire:** 6 rounds/min
**Set-up time:** 3 minutes
**Gun carriage:** articulated single trail
**Transport:** towed by Bren Gun Carrier or Jeep

### USE

Equipped Field airborne artillery units (Airborne Light Regiments, Royal Artillery)

*Note.*
This howitzer could be transported in seven separate air-dropped loads or in one piece by Horsa Glider.

*Opposite right.*
**A 75 mm Pack Howitzer served by airborne artillerymen at Arnhem in September 1944.**
*(IWM)*

108

# 5. Anti-Aircraft Artillery

### Polsten Oerlikon Light Anti-Aircraft Gun
**SPECIFICATIONS**
**Calibre:** 20mm.
**Total weight:** 550 kg
**Ammunition:** Tracer, explosive, incendiary and armour piercing shells
**Loading:** boxes of 60 rounds
**Rate of Fire:** 460 rounds / minute
**Initial velocity:** 810 m/seconde
**Average range:** 1 000 mètres
**Gun carriage:** two wheel carriage
**USE**
In the Light Anti-Aircraft Regiments (Royal Artillery), Anti-Aircraft Sections of various units.

*Above.*
**21st March 1945, crossing the Rhine in Germany (Operation Varsity).**
*(Tank Museum, Bovington)*

*Right.*
A Centaur AA Mk II. The twin 20 mm Polsten Oerlikon guns were mounted in a special turret mounted on a Centaur IV chassis and equipped the Anti-Aircraft troops of the Armoured Regiments (six tanks) as well as the Headquarters of the armoured brigade (two tanks).
*(IWM)*

*Below.*
A MkIII AA Crusader equipped with twin 20mm Polsten Oerlikon guns. The Mk III was used mainly during the 1944-45 campaigns and was retired at the end of the conflict. This AA Crusader of the 27th armoured Brigade with the Sea-Horse insignia, belonged to the Staffordshire Yeomanry (number code white 52 on a red square), one of the tank regiments of the brigade. This shot was taken just a few days after the fall of Caen. The anti-aircraft tanks in the armoured regiments numbered six and formed one of the four troops of the regimental headquarters. Well before the end of the campaign in Normandy, the crews of these tanks - which no longer had any utility - were used to make up number losses in the tank squadrons. *(IWM)*

## Bofors 40 mm Mark III

**SPECIFICATIONS**
**Calibre:** 40 mm.
**Ammunition:** complete cartridge with explosive, tracer, self-destroying or armour piercing shells
**Total weight:** 2.120 kg
**Loading:** 4-round magazine
**Initial velocity:** 850 m/seconde
**Practical range:** 1 500 m direct firing
**Set-up time:** direct firing 2 mins; indirect firing: 30 mins
**Rate of Fire:** 120 rounds / minute (burst) or single shot
**Gun carriage:** on two sets of removable wheels with collapsible side trails
**Transport:**
— towed by 4 x 4 Bedford QL
— on a Crusader tank chassis with an armoured gun shield
— on a Morris lorry
**Crew:** 8

**USE**
Light Anti-Aircraft Regiments (Royal Artillery)

*Note.* The 40 mm Bofors gradually replaced the 20 mm Oerlikon batteries.

*Above.* **The 40 mm Bofors gun on its carriage. The two sets of wheels have been removed, and the two side trails unfolded. In this position, the gun was perfectly stable; this increased the efficiency of anti-aircraft firing. Note on the left the artileryman holding a 4 round magazine clip typical of this gun.** *(Tank Museum)*

*Opposite right.* **A 40 mm Bofors cannon mounted in a casemate on the chassis of a Crusader tank. This was called the Crusader A/A. Operational from 1943, 215 were built. the last versions, with a simplified casemate and a canvas hood were mainly mounted on the chassis of a Crusader Mk III.** *(IWM)*

*Opposite page top.* **A 3.7 in gun of a Heavy Anti-Aircraft Regiment, used here as an artillery piece to the south of Condé-sur-Noireau in Normandy, 15th August 1944.** *(IWM)*

*Below.* **The 40 mm Bofors cannon mounted on a Morris C9B lorry. This vehicle belonged to the 119th Light Anti-Aircraft Regiment of the 15th (Scottish) Infantry Division.** *(IWM)*

## Self Propelled Bofors Vehicle

**SPECIFICATIONS**
A 40 mm Bofors gun mounted on a Morris C9B lorry chassis.
**Calibre:** 40 mm.
**Total weight:** 6 000 kgs
**Ammunition:** (transported in the lorry): 120 shells
**Crew:** 4

**USE**
Light Anti-Aircraft Regiments (Royal Artillery)

*Below*
**This sketch shows the 40 mm Bofors cannon mounted on the Morris C9B. The tube protruding from the end of the lorry is the spare barrel of the gun.**

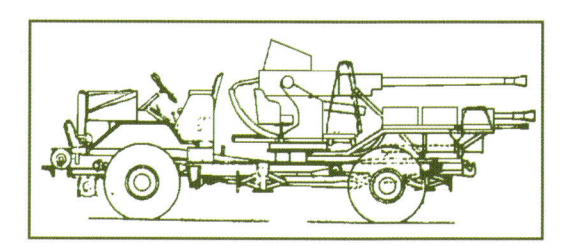

## 3.7 Inches Anti-Aircraft Gun

### SPECIFICATION
**Calibre:** 94 mm.
**Total weight:** 9 245 kg
**Projectile weight:** 12,5 kg
**Initial velocity:** 780 m/seconde
**Maximum range:**
**anti-aircraft :** 10 000m
**on groundtargets:** 18 000m
**Rate of Fire:**
— Manual loading : 10 shots / min
— Automatic loading : 25 shots / min.
**Gun carriage:** four folding trails, transported on two removable axles
**Transport:** towed

### USE
Heavy Anti-Aircraft Regiments (Royal Artillery), army general reserve.

## THE ARTILLERY IN LARGE FORMATIONS

| GUNS | Infantry Divisions | Armoured Divisions | Airborne Division | Army Corps | Army |
|---|---|---|---|---|---|
| 6 pounder Anti Tank | ■ | ■ | ■ | | |
| 17 pounder Anti Tank | ■ | ■ | | | |
| M10 Wolverine | 1 | 1 | | 1 | |
| M10 Achilles | | 1 | | 1 | |
| 17 pounder Archer | 2 | | | | |
| 25 pounder towed | ■ | | | ■ | ■ |
| 25 pounder Sexton | 1 | 1 | | | |
| M7 105 mm Priest | 1 | 1 | | | |
| 4.5 inches | | | | ■ | ■ |
| 5.5 inches | | | | ■ | ■ |
| 155 mm | | | | | ■ |
| 7.2 inches | | | | | ■ |
| 8 inches | | | | | ■ |
| 240 mm | | | | | ■ |
| 75mm Howitzer | | | ■ | | |
| Polsten Oerlikon towed | ■ | | ■ | | |
| Polsten Oerlikon (tank mounted) | | ■ | | | |
| 40mm Bofors towed | ■ | | | ■ | |
| 40mm Bofors (tank mounted) | | ■ | | | |
| 40mm Bofors (lorry mounted) | | | | | |
| 3.7 inch AA | | | | | ■ |

Summary of the different artillery pieces used in the formations at the time of their commitment on the front.

Note.
1. Assault Division on 6th June 1944
2. October 1944

# 6. Artillery Tractors

## 4 x 4 Field Artillery Tractor
### (Morris Commercial C-8)
**SPECIFICATIONS**
**Total weight ready for action:** 4,700 kgs without gun or limber
**Total length:** 4,50 m.
**Width:** 2,20 m.
**Height:** 2,25 m
**Engine:** Morris 4-cylinder, 3.5 litres petrol
**Transmission:** 4 forward and one reverse gears
**Fuel tank:** 135 l
**Crew:** 6 men (commander, driver, 4 men)

**USE**
Field Artillery Regiments (towed the 25-pounder). Anti-Tank Regiments (towed the 17-pounder)
**Other versions:** Morris C-8 Mk III appeared in 1944. Bodywork entirely of canvas, two side doors, trapezoid instead of rounded wheel arches.

## 4 x 4 Medium Artillery Tractor
### (AEC Matador)
**SPECIFICATIONS**
**Total weight ready for action:** 11 500kg
**Total length:** 6,50 m.
**Width:** 2,50 m.
**Height:** 3,30 m
**Engine:** AEC 6-cylinder, 7.8 litres, 95 hp diesel
**Transmission:** 4 forward and one reverse gears and an auxiliary box.
**Fuel tank:** 180 l

**USE**
Medium Artillery Regiments (towed the 4.5 or 5.5 inch gun)

*Note.* There was also a petrol-engined version

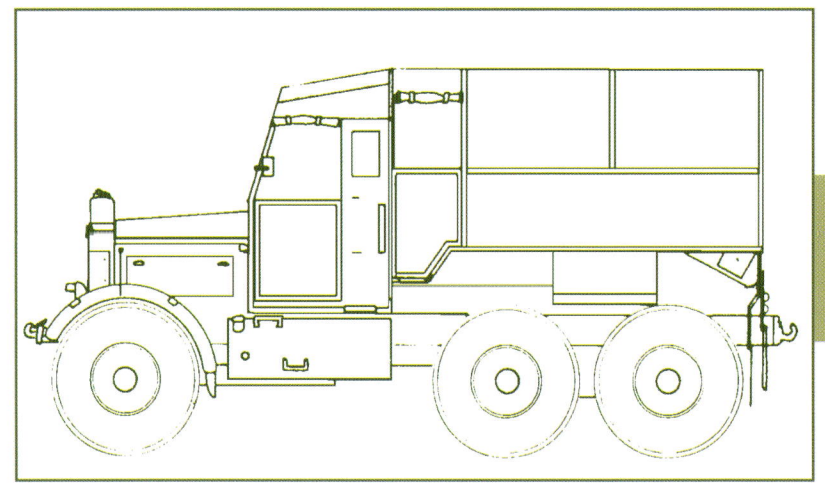

## 6 x 4 Gun Tractor
### (Scammel TRMU)
**SPECIFICATION**
**Total weight ready for action:** 10 000kg
**Engine:** Gardner 6 lw (diesel), 6-cylinder, 8.4 litres
**Transmission:** 6 forward and one reverse gears, and an auxiliary box
**Fuel Tank:** 245 l

**USE**
Heavy Artillery Regiments

*Note.* There was also a recovery version and a tank transporter tractor version with a modified cabin.

## Horsa Glider Mark I

**Makers:** Airspeed Ltd
**Total all-up weight:** 6 975 kg
**Length:** 20,43 m.
**Wingspan:** 26,43 m.
**Crew:** 2 (Pilot and Co-pilot of the Glider Pilot Regiment)
**Load:** depending on missions. For example:
— 29 - 32 men
— 1 jeep and 1 trailer
— 1 anti-tank 6-pounder with 1 jeep and three men

**Tugs:** C-47(Dakota), Albermarle, Stirling, Halifax
*Note.* Put into service during the campaign, the MkII was equipped with a forward opening front (the cockpit) permitting faster unloading.

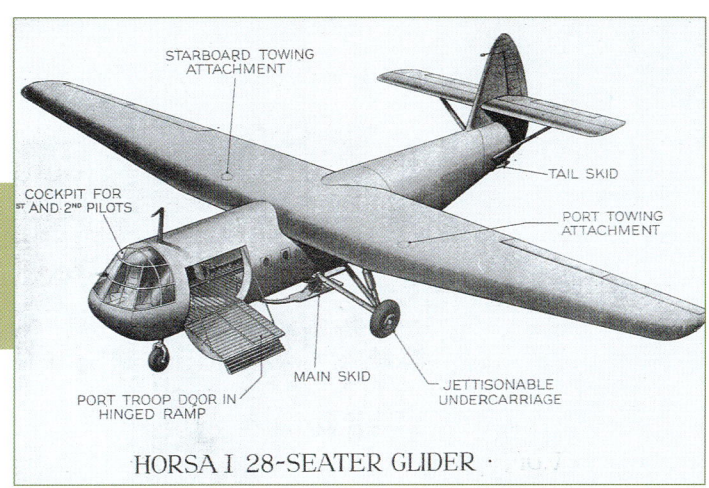

HORSA I 28-SEATER GLIDER

## Hamilcar I Glider

**Makers:** General Aircraft Ltd
**Total all-up weight:** 16 200 kg
**Length:** 20,75 m. **Wingspan:** 33,52 m.
**Crew:** 2 (Pilot and Co-pilot of the Glider Pilot Regiment)
**Load:** (according to missions)
— 1 Tetrarch light tank
— 1 25-pounder with its tractor
— 2 Universal Carriers
— 2 Dingo scout cars
— 1 17 pounder with its Loyd tractor
**Numbers built:** 412
**Tugs:** Lancaster, Stirling or Halifax
**Special characteristics:** a system of jacks enabled the undercarriage to be lowered to facilitate access.

# 7. The Aircraft of the Army Air Corps

## Air Observation Post, Auster Mark III

### SPECIFICATION
**Makers:** British Taylorcraft
**Total take-off weight:** 839 kg
**Length:** 6,83 m.
**Wingspan:** 10,97 m
**Height:** 2,44 m
**Engine:** 100 hp De Havilland Gipsy Major
**Crew:** 2, pilot and observer

### USE
Liaison and observation aircraft put into service by the RAF with crews from the Royal Artillery or Army Air Corps pilots.

# CHAPTER 6 TRANSPORT

A selection of the principal means used by front-line units

### BSA Standard Bicycle
**SPECIFICATIONS**
**Tyres:** 28 x 1 3/4
**Brakes:** actioned by rods, and ball and socket joints.

An advertisement for Firestone tyres which appeared in the *News Chronicle* of 30th August 1944.

# 1. Bicycles and Motorbikes

### Airborne Folding Bicycle
**How to operate the Folding Bicycle**
1. **Ready for use** (a rack can be installed over the front wheel)
2. **Folding.**
Two joints equipped with butterfly bolts (**A**) enabled the bike to be folded along a vertical axis. By the use of a special lever (**B**) the handlebars could be undone rapidly and placed parrallel to the frame. On certain models the pedal axle could be folded through 90° flush with the frame.
3. **Ready for transport.**
The folded parts were fixed to each other with straps. The bicycle could be parachuted by itself or with the parachutist in the same way as the kit bag.

*Note.*
This type of bicycle also equipped the Army and the Royal Marines.

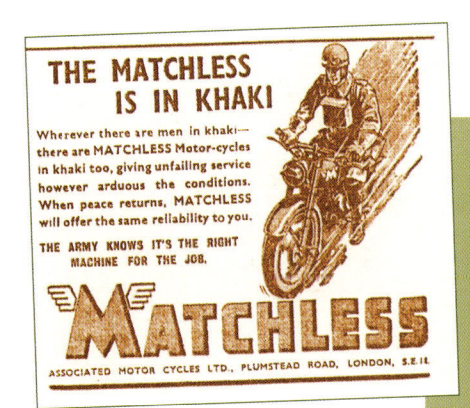

*Right.*
**A parachutist of the 6th Airborne presenting his Royal Enfield Lightweight WD RE.**
*(IWM)*

### Royal Enfield WD RE Lightweight Motorcycle
**SPECIFICATIONS**
**Total all-up weight:** 65 kg
**Engine:** single cylinder 125 cc
**Gearbox:** 3 speed, manual selector
**Max.Road Speed:** 40 mph

**USE**
Airborne troops, various units.

*Above*
**An advertisement for Matchless liaison bicycles which appeared in the *News Chronicle* of 30th August 1944.**

114

## Model W NG Ariel Motorcycle

**SPECIFICATIONS**
**Total all-up weight:** 170 kg
**Engine:** single cylinder 346 cc
**Gearbox:** 4-speed, foot pedal
**Tank:** 10 litres
**Max. road speed:** 70 mph one rider only

**USE**
liaison, direction

## Model 3 SW Triumph Motorcycle

**SPECIFICATIONS**
**Total all-up weight :** 150 kg
**Engine:** single cylinder 342 cc
**Gearbox:** 4-speed, foot pedal
**Tank:** 12 litres
**Max. road speed:** 60 mph one rider only

**USE**
Liaison, direction
**Other models of the same type:**
BSA, Royal Enfield, Matchless, Velocette.

## Model M 20 (B) BSA Motorcycle

**SPECIFICATIONS**
**Total all-up weight:** 180 kg
**Engine:** single cylinder 496 cc
**Gearbox:** 4-speed, foot pedal
**Tank:** 16 litres
**Max. road speed:** 60 mph one rider only
**USE**
Liaison, direction. **Other models of the same type:** Norton 16h

*Right.* **At Tinchebray on 17th August 1944, a meeting between American and British MPs. The BSA is ridden by two men from the Corps of Military Police, of the Headquarters of an Infantry Division (number 79 painted on a black background on the bike's fuel tank).** *(IWM)*

*Below.* **Parachutists of the 6th Airborne assembling the handlebars of a Welbike, a few moments after landing.** *(IWM)*

## Welbike Lightweight Motorcycle

**SPECIFICATIONS**
**Total all-up weight:** 38 kg
**Engine:** Two-stroke single cylinder 97 cc
**Tank:** 7 litres
**Range:** 145 km
**Max. road speed:** 30 mph
**Special characteristics:** saddle and handlebars could be dismantled to enable the bicycle to be fitted into a dropping container
**USE**
Airborne troops, Commandos, various units according to the type of operations.

# 2. Light Vehicles

The British Army had been entirely motorised since 1939 and had been using a considerable number of vehicles of all types, which were mainly military adaptations of existing civilian models. There were also some adaptations which were destined to ensure a minimum of standardisation, particularly for the main parts.
Within each category, usually defined by the load the vehicle could carry, there were often several models coming from different manufacturers, some of which were North-American. At the end of 1944, there was a special effort to ensure that front-line units had a maximum of 4WD vehicles, two-wheel drive vehicles being relegated to the rear.

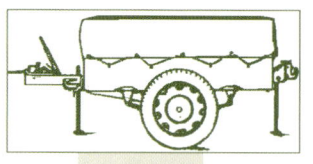

### Light Cargo Trailer
British made light cargo trailer for american Jeep.
**SPECIFICATION**
**Payload:** 500 kg
**Total laden weight:** 760 kg
**Length with shaft and hook:** 2,70 m.
**Track width:** 1,30 m

Made entirely of metal, with a canvas hood. A hook enabled another trailer to be towed.

*Bottom.* **A Jeep modified to carry three stretchers, two above on the frame and one on the bonnet.** *(IWM)*

### 4WD 5-Cwt Car "Jeep"
**SPECIFICATIONS**
**Total weight ready for action:** 1 475 kg
**Total length:** 3,36 m.
**Width:** 1,58 m.
**Height with hood:** 1,77 m
**Engine:** 4-cylinder, 60hp, 2.2 litres petrol
**Transmission:**
— 3 forward and one reverse
— 1 transfer drive box
**Fuel tank:** 56.8 l
**Range:** 450 kms on road
**Max. Speed:** 90 km/h

**USE**
All reconnaissance missions, liaison, command. Adapted for transporting stretchers.

*Below*
Piled into this jeep and its lightweight British-made trailer, these paratroops set off for their objective. The jeep here is modified for transport in a Horsa: the mudguards have been cut flush with the longerons and the side handles have been dismantled. *(IWM)*

*Left.*
**A jeep on its parachuting platform.**
*(Patrick Nonzerville Collection).*

*Bottom left.*
**France July 1944. A Jeep of the 1st SAS, armed with two twin Vickers K Guns.**
*(Collection JBY)*

*Below, top to bottom.*
**Germany, April 1945. Several types of jeeps used by the SAS. Note the armour-plating on the front of the vehicle protecting the radiator.**
*(Photo Jean-Pierre)*

## 4WD 5-Cwt Car "Jeep" "Special Air Service Regiment"

(Mechanical details are the same as for the ordinary vehicle described on the previous page)

**These are the principal modifications that were carried out by the workshops of the REME:**

— Addition of two extra petrol tanks, one above the rear right wheel, the other under the passenger seat, meaning a change in the positioning of the exhaust pipe.
— The spare tyre placed on the bonnet, and in its place a stores rack
— system to dismantle the steering wheel
— Instead of the windshield, two shields with half-moon-shaped bullet-proof glass screens (October 1944)
— On certain vehicles, an armoured radiator guard was mounted

**Armament:**
This varied according to the versions
— 2 twin Vickers K guns, one pair mounted in the front, the other in the rear.
— one American .50 calibre machine gun in the front and a pair of Vickers K guns at the rear.

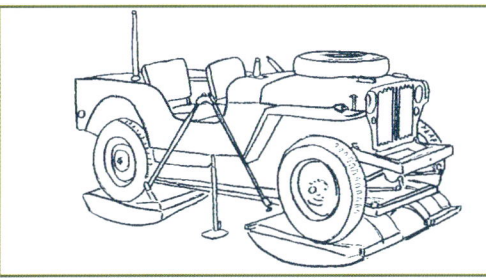

117

### 4WD Humber FWD Heavy Utility

**SPECIFICATIONS**
**Total weight ready for action:** 2 700 kg
**Total length:** 4,30 m.
**Width:** 1,88 m.
**Height:** 1,95 m
**Engine:** Humber 6-cylinder, 4.8 litre, petrol
**Transmission:**
4 forward and one reverse gears, one transfer drive box.
**Fuel tank:** 72 l
**Crew:** 1 driver, 5 passengers.

**USE**
Command and liaison vehicle. There was a transport version equipped for the transport of baggage.

*Tank Museum, Bovington*

# 3. Light Trucks

Photographs © IWM and Tank Museum, Bovington

### GS 4 x 2 15-cwt Truck

For model presented: Bedford MWD
**SPECIFICATIONS**
**Payload:** 750 kg
**Total weight ready for action:** 2 132 kg
**Total length:** 4,38 m.
**Width:** 1,98 m.
**Height:** 2.29 m with hood
**Engine:** Bedford OHV, 6-cylinder 73 hp petrol
**Transmission:** 4 forward and one reverse gears
**Fuel tank:** 90 litres

**USE**
General purpose truck. There was also a tanker version (900 litres) and a radio vehicle version
**Other models:** Morris Commercial, Fordson

# 4. Medium Trucks

### 4 x 2 30-Cwt Bedford OXD

**SPECIFICATION**
**Payload:** 1 500 kg
**Total weight ready for action:** 2 132 kg
**Total length:** 4,38 m.
**Width:** 1,98 m.
**Height:** 2.29 m with hood
**Engine:** 6 cylinder, 72 hp, 3.5 litre, petrol
**Transmission:** 4 forward and one reverse gears
**Fuel tank:** 90 litres

**USE**
General purpose medium truck
**Other 4 x 2 model:** Austin, Commer, Ford
**Other 4 x 4 models:** Ford, Chevrolet (Canada)

## 4 x 2 3-Ton Bedford OYD Truck

**SPECIFICATION**
**Payload:** 1 500 kg
**Total weight ready for action:** 2 132 kg
**Total length:** 4,38 m.
**Width:** 1,98 m.
**Height:** 2.29m with hood
**Engine:** 6 cylinder, 72 hp, 3.5 litre, petrol
**Transmission:** 4 forward and one reverse gears
**Fuel tank:** 120 litres

**USE**
General purpose truck
**Other models:** Austin, Commer
*Note.* There was also a a water bowser version with 3 600 litre-tanker.

# 5. Heavy Trucks

## 4 x 4 3-ton Lorry

**SPECIFICATION**
Bedford QL
**Engine:** Bedford 6-cylinder 3.5 litre petrol
**Transmission:** 4 forward and one reverse gears 1 transfer drive box
**Fuel tank:** 129 litres

**USE**
General purpose lorry equipping Infantry battalions
**Other models:** Albion, Austin, Fordson.
*Note.* There was also a mobile workshop version for the REME and the RAOC, and a radio and liaison version for the RCS.

## 4 x 4 3-Ton Troop Carrier

**SPECIFICATION**
Bedford QLT
**Engine:** Bedford 6-cylinder 3.5 litre petrol
**Transmission:** 4 forward and one reverse gears; 1 transfer drive box
**Fuel tank:** 129 litres
The specially converted body enabled 30 infantrymen to be transported.

**USE**
Equipped the Royal Army Service Corps detached to the Infantry brigades

# 6. Recovery Vehicles

## M1 Wrecker Model 1000, Series 2 & 3
Ward La France 6 x 6
### SPECIFICATIONS
**Lifting Capability:** 4,500 kg
**Total weight ready for action:** 13,300 kg
**Total length:** 7 m
**Width:** 2.70 m  **Height:** 3 m
**Engine:** Continental 6-cylinder
**Transmission:** 5 forward and one reverse gears; 1 transfer drive box
**Fuel tank:** 380 litres
### USE
Heavy recovery lorry used by units of the Royal Electrical and Mechanical Engineers.

## Scammel, 6 x 4 Recovery Truck
### SPECIFICATIONS
**Engine:** Garner 6 LW, 6-cylinder, 8.4 litre diesel
**Transmission:** 6 forward and one reverse gears
**Fuel tank:** 245 litres
### USE
Recovery version of the Scammel TRMU/30 tractor with a modified cabin and a hoist mounted at the rea; used by the REME

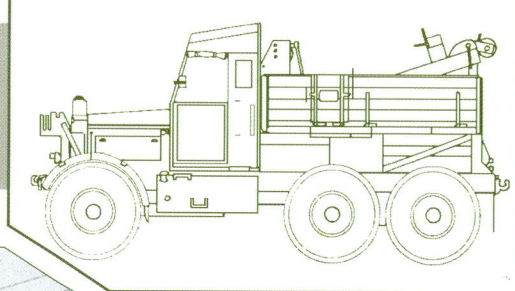

## T M 20 Diamond Type 980 & 981 Tractor 6 x 4
### SPECIFICATIONS
**Towing load:** 45,000 kg
**Total weight ready for action:** 12,410 kgs
**Total length:** 7,10 m. **Width:** 2,58 m
**Height:** 2,54 m
**Engine:** Hercules 6-cylinder 185 hp, diesel
**Transmission:** 4 forward and one reverse gears
### USE
Towing the Rogers 45-ton M9 24-wheel trailer. It can carry a Sherman or a Churchill tank, and was used by units of the REME and by the RASC, the RASC Tank Transporter Company. The Diamond Ton the picture at left belongs to the 21st Army Group ( number code 862 on a green and red background with diagonal white stroke).

## 30-ton 6 x 4 - 8 Tank Transporter Recovery
Scammel Tractor TRMU/30 with a TRCU/30 Trailer
### SPECIFICATIONS
**Weight empty with trailer:** 17,190 kg
**Payload:** 30,000 kg
**Engine:** Garner 6 LW 6-cylinder, 8.4 litre diesel
**Transmission:** 6 forward and one reverse gears
**Fuel tank:** 245 litres
### USE
Transport and recovery of medium tanks (eg Sherman). Equipped units of the REME.

## GMC, DUKW 353, 2.5-Ton 6 x 6 Amphibian

An amphibious vehicle based on the GMC 353 6 x 6 truck propelled in the water by propellers engaged by means of a transfer drive box and steered with a rudder.

### SPECIFICATIONS
**Total weight ready for action:** 8 800 kg
**Payload:** 2 250 kg
**Total length:** 9,70 m.
**Width:** 2,80 m.
**Height:** 2,69 m
**Engine:** GMC 6-cylinder 104 hp petrol
**Transmission:** 5 forward and one reverse gears; one transfer drive box
**Fuel tank:** 150 l
**Max. Speed:** (on land) 50 mph (on water): 6 knots (8 mph)

### USE
Unloading ships, crossing rivers. Used by the Royal Engineers and the RASC.

# 7. Amphibious vehicles

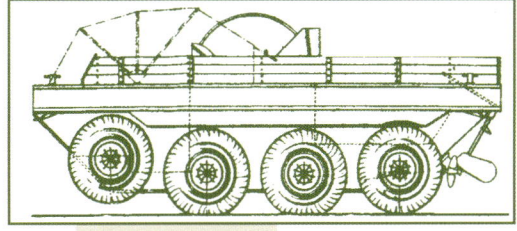

## Terrapin Mark I 8 x 8

Amphibian driven in the water by two propellers.

### SPECIFICATIONS
**Made by:** Morris Commercial
**Total weight ready for action:** 12 000 kg
**Payload:** 4 000 kg
**Total length:** 5,84 m. **Width:** 2,26 m. **Height:** 2,46 m
**Engine:** Ford 85 hp V8
**Transmission:** 3 forward and one reverse gears; one transfer drive box
**Max. speed:** (on land): 15 mph, (on water): 5 mph

### USE
Troop and material transport, used by the Royal Engineers and the RASC at the end of 1944. *(DR)*

## Amphibious 4 x 4 1/4-Ton Jeep

An amphibious vehicle using the principal mechanical elements of the jeep, moving across water by means of a propeller fixed at the rear of the hull and engaged by a clutch. Steering was done by means of a rudder and the front wheels.

**Total weight ready for action:** 1900 kg
**Total length:** 4,56 m.
**Width:** 1,62 m.
**Crew:** 5

### USE
Beach Groups, Royal Engineers, Royal Army Service Corps

# CHAPTER 7 VEHICLE and MACHINE MARKINGS and CAMOUFLAGE

## Formation Sign

This insignia was painted on the front and the rear in a standard surface not exceeding 21.6 cm by 24.10.

## Unit Serial Numbers

According to the regulations, the unit serial numbers were placed on the front and the rear either as a 24.5 cm by 21.6 cm plate of painted steel, or painted directly on to the bodywork.

Whatever their number, all divisions of the same type committed on the same front use identical markings, both for the background colour or for the unit serial numbers. These figures were not connected in any way with the unit's number. They only indicated the type of arm or service the vehicle or the machine belonged to.

In order to identify a unit with the help of the tables on page 14-27, it is necessary to know the following:

**1.** The number of the Division - or any other formation - with the help of the insignia (formation signs) presented in volume 1, as seen on the vehicle or on the sleeves of the men of the unit

**2.** The detailed organogram of the division where the different units were always presented in the same position: within each Brigade and from top to bottom in the order of precedence for Infantry Battalions and Armoured Cavalry (see tables at the end of this volume)

### Examples

— 3rd Infantry Division, Unit serial number 69 on a light brown base = 2nd King's Shropshire Light Infantry

— 11th Armoured Division, unit serial code 54 on a red base = 9th Battalion, the Rifle Brigade

— 51st Highland Infantry Division Unit serial number 60 on a green base = 5th Black Watch

— 7th Armoured Division, unit serial number 51
*(continued on p.127)*

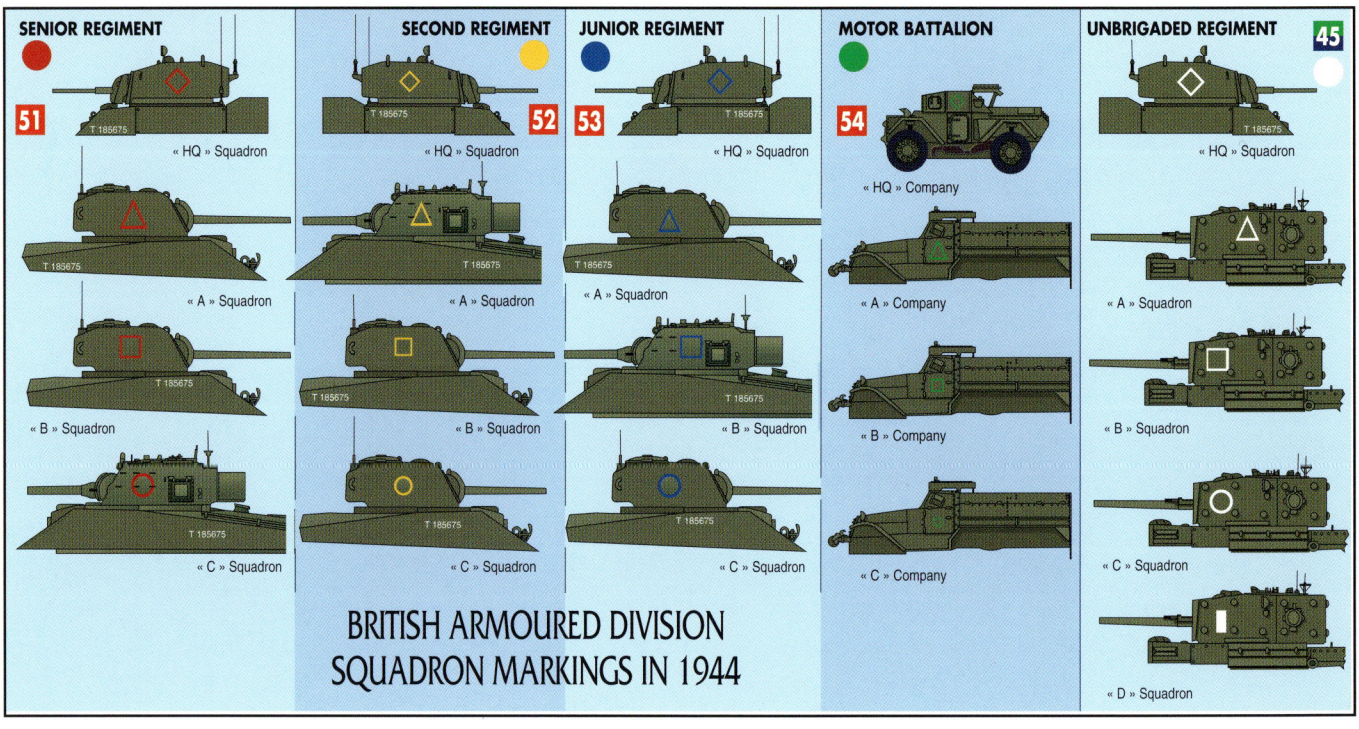

**MODEL of a VEHICLE PLATE and its UNIT SERIAL NUMBER**

**UNIT SERIAL NUMBERS**
The position of the white stripe indicated that the unit belonged to a higher command than the division.

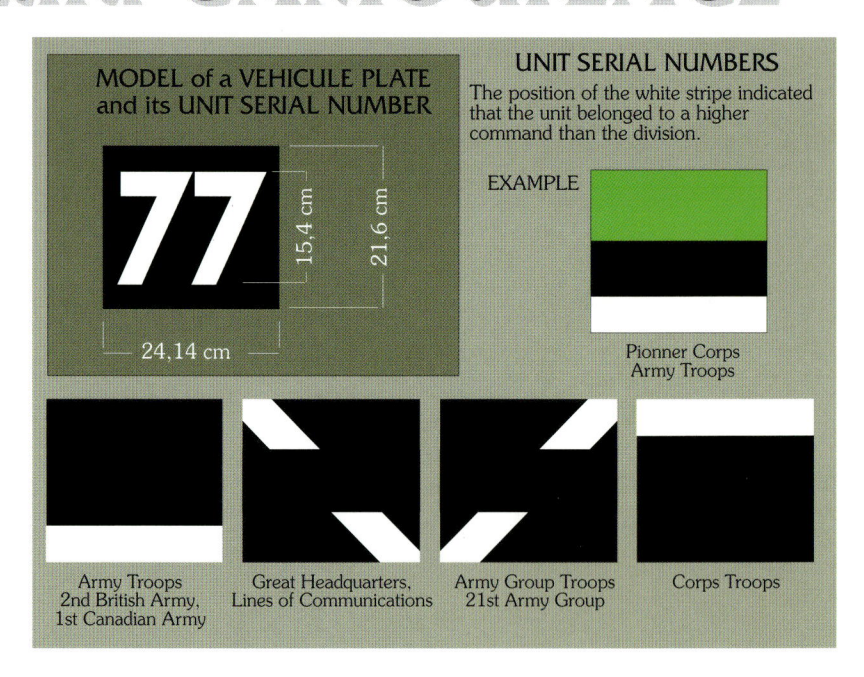

EXAMPLE — Pionner Corps Army Troops

Army Troops 2nd British Army, 1st Canadian Army | Great Headquarters, Lines of Communications | Army Group Troops 21st Army Group | Corps Troops

*Opposite left.*
**A column of Shermans including several Flails of the 79th Armoured Division, stopped on a small road in Normandy during Operation Goodwood.**
*(IWM)*

*Below.*
**This table presents the colours attributed in the order of precedence to the regiments in the Armoured Brigade and the symbols attached to each squadron within the regiment.**

**BRITISH ARMOURED DIVISION SQUADRON MARKINGS IN 1944**

122

## PLATES AFFIXED to the VEHICLES of GENERALS and BRIGADIERS

American specifications adopted by the British Army in 1944.

★★★★ General
★★★ Lieutenant-General
★★ Major-General
★ Brigadier

## MAXIMUM SPEED SIGN

**40 MPH** — 5,1 cm

This sign was placed on the rear of vehicles to indicate in miles per hour the maximum permitted speed, according to the type of vehicle. The sign was optional.

① Divisional Insignia
② Unit Serial Number
③ Bridge classification number
④ Serial Number
⑤ Identification star

### Markings placed on the rear offside of vehicles with left-hand drive

50 ②
Z 55117869 ①
CAUTION LEFT HANDRIVE NO SIGNALS ④ — 5,1 cm
Z 55117869 ①
▲ ③
50 ②

## The MAIN TYPES of IDENTIFICATION STARS for ALLIED VEHICLES

---

## Lettering and the IDENTIFICATION PREFIX LETTERS

A B C D E F G H I J K L
M N O P Q R S T U V W X Y Z
1 2 3 4 5 6 7 8 9

Examples of letters and numbers used for registration plates.

Some examples of registration plates taken from period photographs.

Z5250838   L3812186
P346438    F196184

**Sherman Firefly VC**
Prefix T (identifying Tanks and armoured personnel carriers)

**Humber Mk I.**
Prefix F (identifying Armoured Cars and reconnaissance vehicles)

**Half-track M3.**
Prefix T (identifying Tanks and armoured personnel carriers)

### PREFIX LETTERS

A. Ambulances
C. Motorcycles
F. Armoured Cars and reconnaissance vehicles
H. Tractors
L. Lorries of more than one ton
M. Cars and light utility vehicles (Jeeps)
P. Amphibious vehicles
S. Self-propelled guns
T. Tanks and armoured personnel carriers
V. RASC Vans
X. All types of trailers
Z. Lorries of less than one ton
E. Bulldozers and caterpillars
REC. Armoured Recovery vehicles

**Humber FWD 4 x 4.**
Prefix M [identifying Cars and light utility vehicles (Jeeps)]

**Bedford QL.**
Prefix L (identifying Lorries of more than one ton)

**Morris C8/GS15-cwt 4 x 4.**
Prefix Z (identifying Lorries of less than one ton)

123

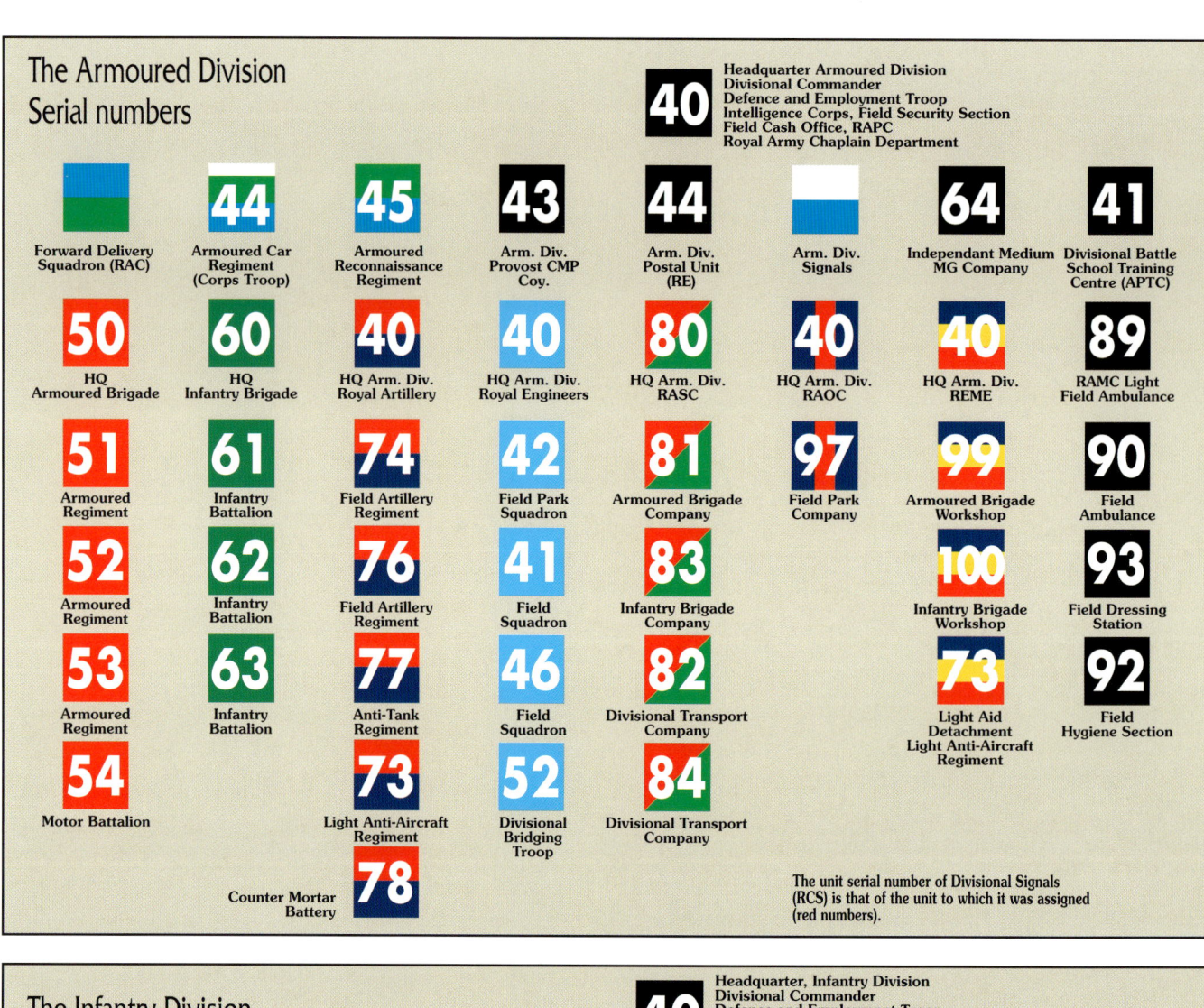

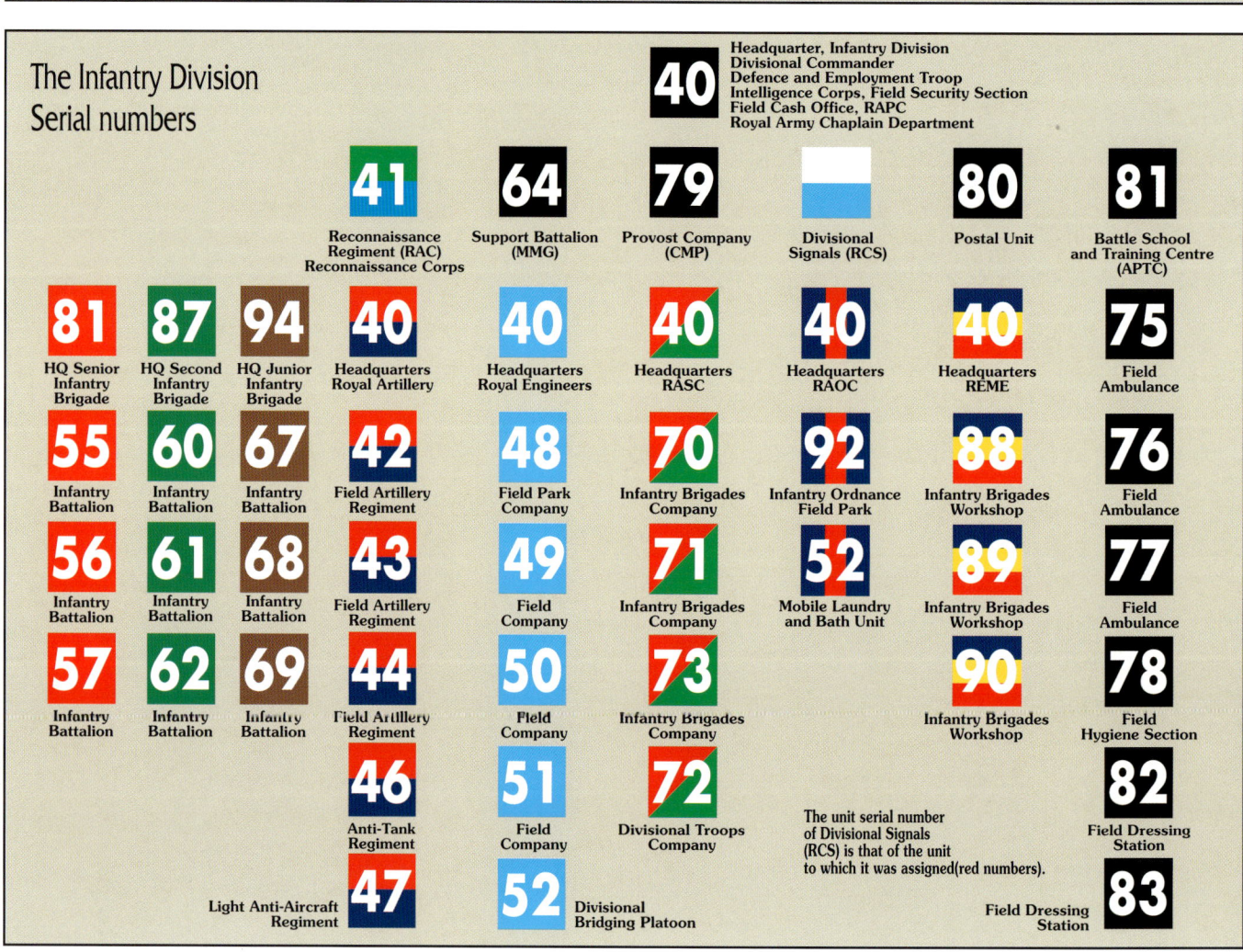

## The Armoured Division Serial numbers

**40** — Headquarter Armoured Division; Divisional Commander; Defence and Employment Troop; Intelligence Corps, Field Security Section; Field Cash Office, RAPC; Royal Army Chaplain Department

| Serial | Unit |
|---|---|
| (blue/green flag) | Forward Delivery Squadron (RAC) |
| 44 | Armoured Car Regiment (Corps Troop) |
| 45 | Armoured Reconnaissance Regiment |
| 43 | Arm. Div. Provost CMP Coy. |
| 44 | Arm. Div. Postal Unit (RE) |
| (white/blue flag) | Arm. Div. Signals |
| 64 | Independant Medium MG Company |
| 41 | Divisional Battle School Training Centre (APTC) |
| 50 | HQ Armoured Brigade |
| 60 | HQ Infantry Brigade |
| 40 | HQ Arm. Div. Royal Artillery |
| 40 | HQ Arm. Div. Royal Engineers |
| 80 | HQ Arm. Div. RASC |
| 40 | HQ Arm. Div. RAOC |
| 40 | HQ Arm. Div. REME |
| 89 | RAMC Light Field Ambulance |
| 51 | Armoured Regiment |
| 61 | Infantry Battalion |
| 74 | Field Artillery Regiment |
| 42 | Field Park Squadron |
| 81 | Armoured Brigade Company |
| 97 | Field Park Company |
| 99 | Armoured Brigade Workshop |
| 90 | Field Ambulance |
| 52 | Armoured Regiment |
| 62 | Infantry Battalion |
| 76 | Field Artillery Regiment |
| 41 | Field Squadron |
| 83 | Infantry Brigade Company |
| 100 | Infantry Brigade Workshop |
| 93 | Field Dressing Station |
| 53 | Armoured Regiment |
| 63 | Infantry Battalion |
| 77 | Anti-Tank Regiment |
| 46 | Field Squadron |
| 82 | Divisional Transport Company |
| 73 | Light Aid Detachment Light Anti-Aircraft Regiment |
| 92 | Field Hygiene Section |
| 54 | Motor Battalion |
| 73 | Light Anti-Aircraft Regiment |
| 52 | Divisional Bridging Troop |
| 84 | Divisional Transport Company |
| 78 | Counter Mortar Battery |

The unit serial number of Divisional Signals (RCS) is that of the unit to which it was assigned (red numbers).

## The Infantry Division Serial numbers

**40** — Headquarter, Infantry Division; Divisional Commander; Defence and Employment Troop; Intelligence Corps, Field Security Section; Field Cash Office, RAPC; Royal Army Chaplain Department

| Serial | Unit |
|---|---|
| 41 | Reconnaissance Regiment (RAC) Reconnaissance Corps |
| 64 | Support Battalion (MMG) |
| 79 | Provost Company (CMP) |
| (white/blue flag) | Divisional Signals (RCS) |
| 80 | Postal Unit |
| 81 | Battle School and Training Centre (APTC) |
| 81 | HQ Senior Infantry Brigade |
| 87 | HQ Second Infantry Brigade |
| 94 | HQ Junior Infantry Brigade |
| 40 | Headquarters Royal Artillery |
| 40 | Headquarters Royal Engineers |
| 40 | Headquarters RASC |
| 40 | Headquarters RAOC |
| 40 | Headquarters REME |
| 75 | Field Ambulance |
| 55 | Infantry Battalion |
| 60 | Infantry Battalion |
| 67 | Infantry Battalion |
| 42 | Field Artillery Regiment |
| 48 | Field Park Company |
| 70 | Infantry Brigades Company |
| 92 | Infantry Ordnance Field Park |
| 88 | Infantry Brigades Workshop |
| 76 | Field Ambulance |
| 56 | Infantry Battalion |
| 61 | Infantry Battalion |
| 68 | Infantry Battalion |
| 43 | Field Artillery Regiment |
| 49 | Field Company |
| 71 | Infantry Brigades Company |
| 52 | Mobile Laundry and Bath Unit |
| 89 | Infantry Brigades Workshop |
| 77 | Field Ambulance |
| 57 | Infantry Battalion |
| 62 | Infantry Battalion |
| 69 | Infantry Battalion |
| 44 | Field Artillery Regiment |
| 50 | Field Company |
| 73 | Infantry Brigades Company |
| 90 | Infantry Brigades Workshop |
| 78 | Field Hygiene Section |
| 46 | Anti-Tank Regiment |
| 51 | Field Company |
| 72 | Divisional Troops Company |
| 82 | Field Dressing Station |
| 47 | Light Anti-Aircraft Regiment |
| 52 | Divisional Bridging Platoon |
| 83 | Field Dressing Station |

The unit serial number of Divisional Signals (RCS) is that of the unit to which it was assigned (red numbers).

## The Special Service Group's Serial numbers (Royal Marines, Army Commandos)

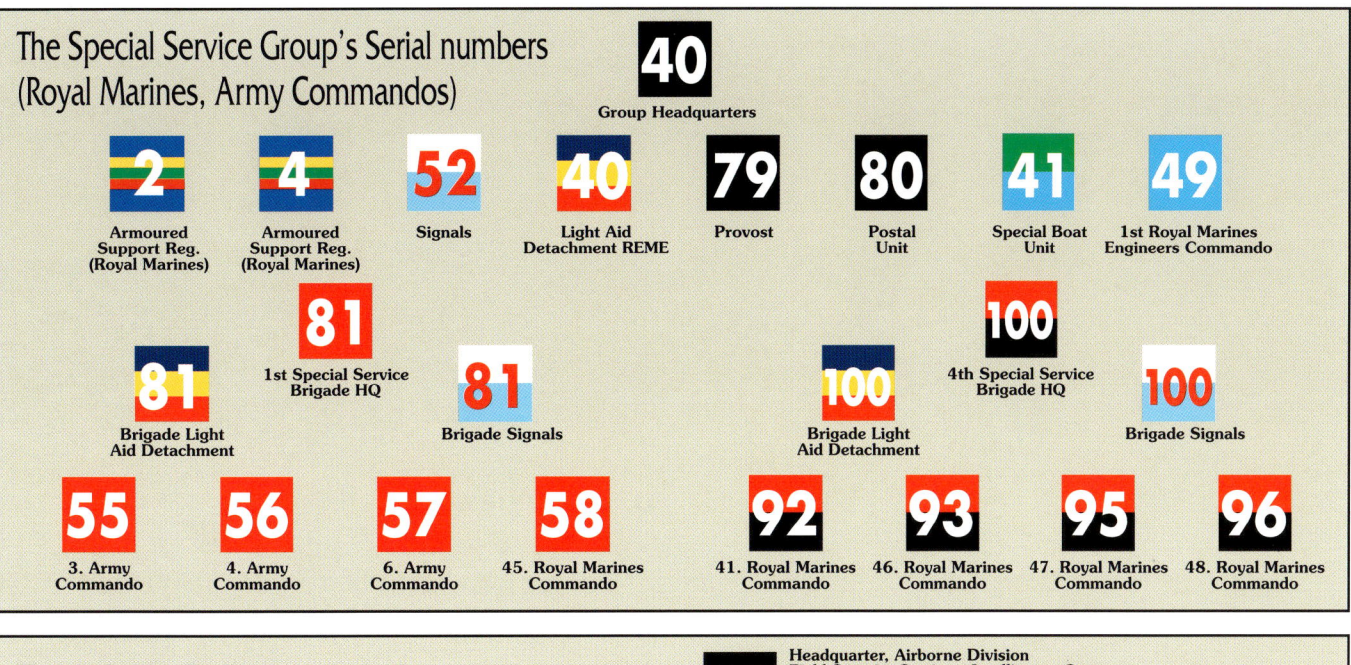

**40** — Group Headquarters

- **2** — Armoured Support Reg. (Royal Marines)
- **4** — Armoured Support Reg. (Royal Marines)
- **52** — Signals
- **40** — Light Aid Detachment REME
- **79** — Provost
- **80** — Postal Unit
- **41** — Special Boat Unit
- **49** — 1st Royal Marines Engineers Commando

- **81** — 1st Special Service Brigade HQ
- **81** — Brigade Light Aid Detachment
- **81** — Brigade Signals
- **100** — 4th Special Service Brigade HQ
- **100** — Brigade Light Aid Detachment
- **100** — Brigade Signals

- **55** — 3. Army Commando
- **56** — 4. Army Commando
- **57** — 6. Army Commando
- **58** — 45. Royal Marines Commando
- **92** — 41. Royal Marines Commando
- **93** — 46. Royal Marines Commando
- **95** — 47. Royal Marines Commando
- **96** — 48. Royal Marines Commando

## The Airborne Division Serial numbers

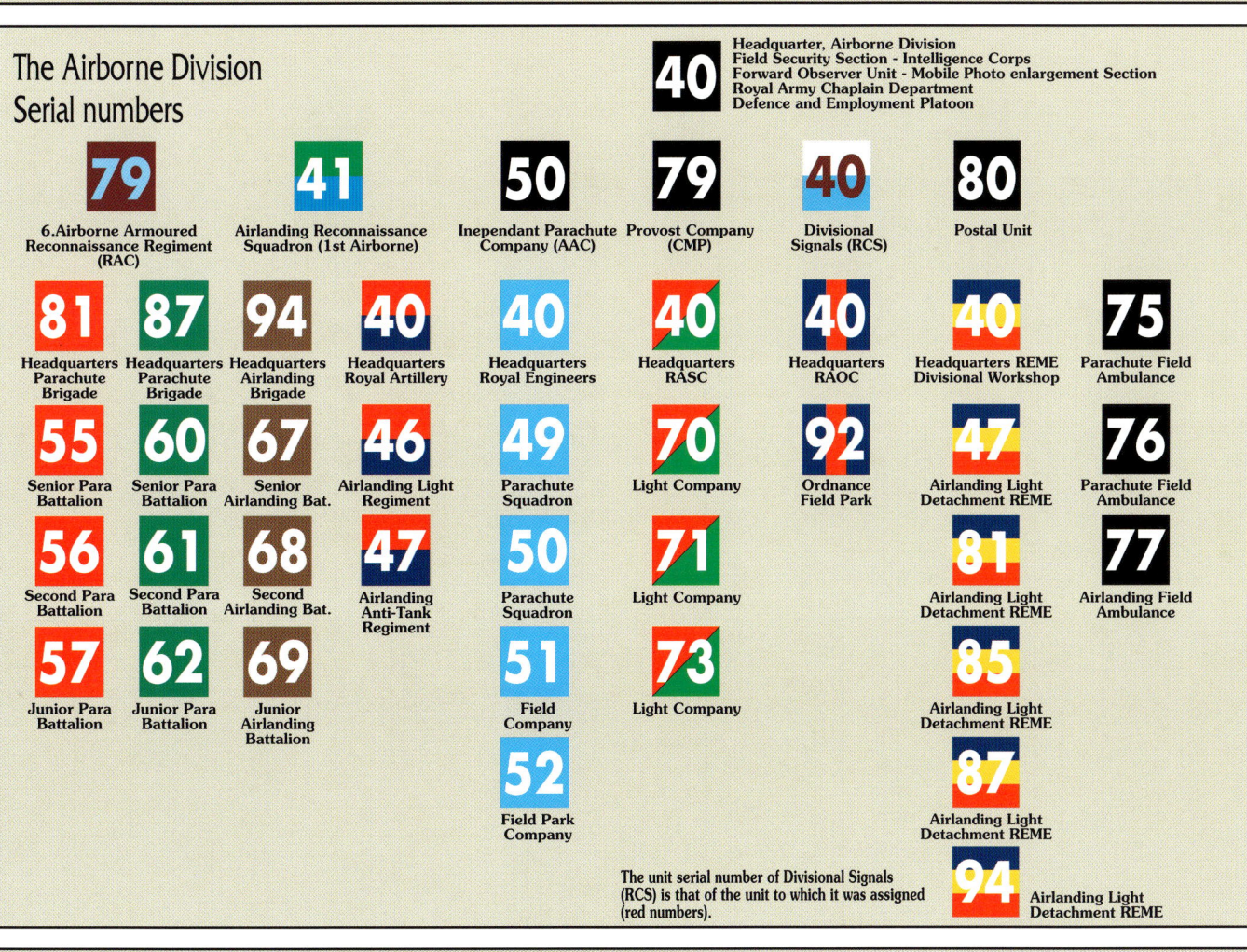

**40** — Headquarter, Airborne Division; Field Security Section - Intelligence Corps; Forward Observer Unit - Mobile Photo enlargement Section; Royal Army Chaplain Department; Defence and Employment Platoon

- **79** — 6. Airborne Armoured Reconnaissance Regiment (RAC)
- **41** — Airlanding Reconnaissance Squadron (1st Airborne)
- **50** — Inependant Parachute Company (AAC)
- **79** — Provost Company (CMP)
- **40** — Divisional Signals (RCS)
- **80** — Postal Unit

- **81** — Headquarters Parachute Brigade
- **87** — Headquarters Parachute Brigade
- **94** — Headquarters Airlanding Brigade
- **40** — Headquarters Royal Artillery
- **40** — Headquarters Royal Engineers
- **40** — Headquarters RASC
- **40** — Headquarters RAOC
- **40** — Headquarters REME Divisional Workshop
- **75** — Parachute Field Ambulance

- **55** — Senior Para Battalion
- **60** — Senior Para Battalion
- **67** — Senior Airlanding Bat.
- **46** — Airlanding Light Regiment
- **49** — Parachute Squadron
- **70** — Light Company
- **92** — Ordnance Field Park
- **47** — Airlanding Light Detachment REME
- **76** — Parachute Field Ambulance

- **56** — Second Para Battalion
- **61** — Second Para Battalion
- **68** — Second Airlanding Bat.
- **47** — Airlanding Anti-Tank Regiment
- **50** — Parachute Squadron
- **71** — Light Company
- **81** — Airlanding Light Detachment REME
- **77** — Airlanding Field Ambulance

- **57** — Junior Para Battalion
- **62** — Junior Para Battalion
- **69** — Junior Airlanding Battalion
- **51** — Field Company
- **73** — Light Company
- **85** — Airlanding Light Detachment REME

- **52** — Field Park Company
- **87** — Airlanding Light Detachment REME
- **94** — Airlanding Light Detachment REME

*The unit serial number of Divisional Signals (RCS) is that of the unit to which it was assigned (red numbers).*

## BRIDGE CLASSIFICATION NUMBERS

22,8 cm

- **30** — Painted bridge classification number for a Sherman Mk I
- **70/18** — Painted bridge classification numbers for a Diamond T 980 tractor and its tank recovery trailer
- **15** — Screw-on Bridge classification number plate

- Churchill — **40**
- Carrier AOP — **5**
- Bedford QLT — **7**

*Above and below. Some examples of tonnage plates taken from period photographs.*

- **5** — Bren carrier of the 1st Dorset, variant
- **3** — Bren carrier, variant
- **4** — Bren carrier of the 15th Scottish Division, 1944

125

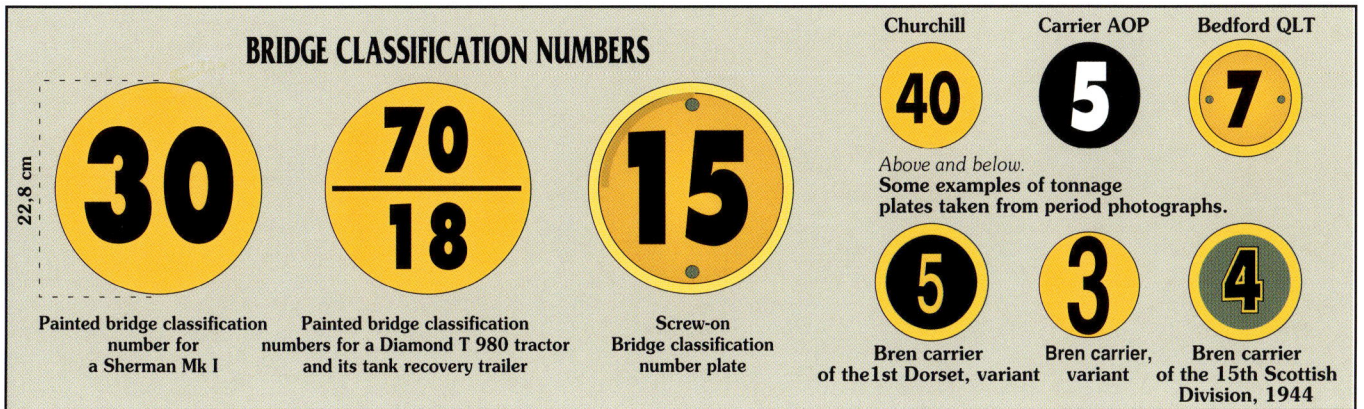

## British Vehicle and Machine Paint and Camouflage schemes

**Olive Green Drab**

**Bronze green**

**Special Camouflage for the barrels of the Firefly**

1. Vehicles put into service in 1943
2. Vehicles and machines of American and Canadian origin
3. Vehicles and Machines put into service in 1944

Note.
When machines of American and Canadian origin went away for repairs or conversion, they were repainted bronze green (3). During the Winter period, vehicles and machines were whitewashed.

**Black and bronze green**

**Bronze green and black scheme**

**Earth Brown and black scheme**

---

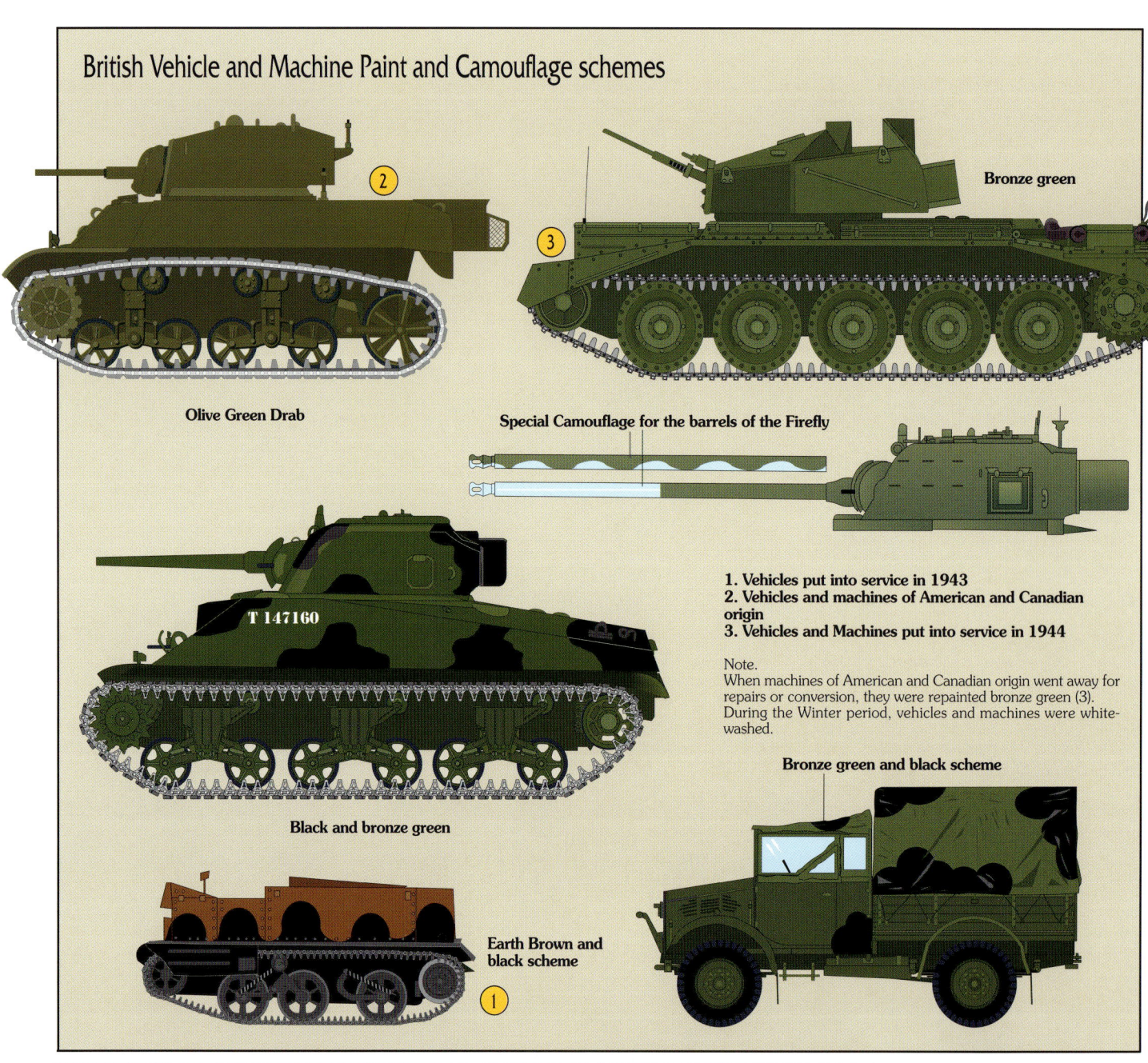

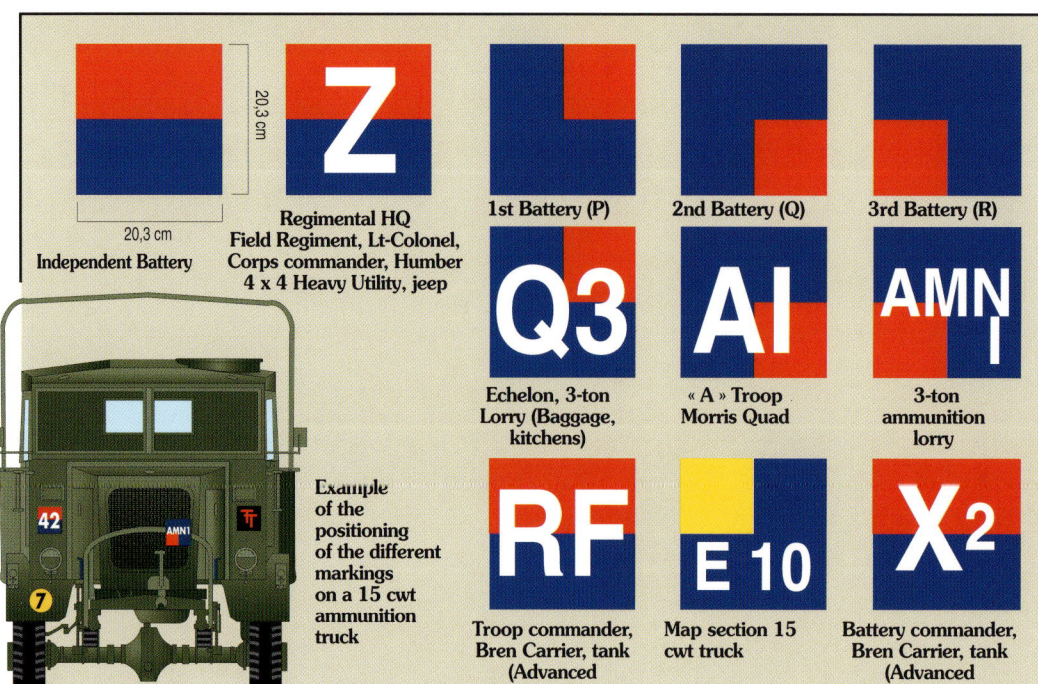

**Independent Battery**

**Z** — Regimental HQ Field Regiment, Lt-Colonel, Corps commander, Humber 4 x 4 Heavy Utility, jeep

**1st Battery (P)** | **2nd Battery (Q)** | **3rd Battery (R)**

**Q3** — Echelon, 3-ton Lorry (Baggage, kitchens)

**A1** — « A » Troop Morris Quad

**AMN1** — 3-ton ammunition lorry

**RF** — Troop commander, Bren Carrier, tank (Advanced observation post)

**E 10** — Map section 15 cwt truck

**X2** — Battery commander, Bren Carrier, tank (Advanced observation post)

Example of the positioning of the different markings on a 15 cwt ammunition truck

*Above.* **Chevrolet Canada C15 A 4 x 4 15 cwt** (Letter code «z») of the second battalion of a Junior Infantry Brigade (number code 68 on a brown base), 20th July 1944. (IWM)

## Royal Artillery Special Unit Serial Numbers

As well as the Unit Serial Numbers, the artllery used a series of plates and codes enabling the assignment of vehicles and machines to be identified very precisely

*(see next page for examples)*

on red base = 1st RTR. The vehicles and machines belonging to units of a higher level than that of a division (Army Corps, Army, Army Group) had unit serial numbers whose base colour was the same as the divisional markings, but which were modified by adding a white stripe, horizontally or diagonally. Numbering was also different and used normally, 3 or 4 digit numbers ranging from 100 to 900 or from 1000 to 2700.

## Registration Numbers (War Department Number)

Painted in white numbers, 8.9 cms high and 5.1 cms wide at the rear and the sides of every vehicle or machine, sometimes on the front if the shape of the vehicle prevented painting them on the sides. This number was always preceded by a letter which indicated the type; this letter was preceded by a "C" if the vehicle was Canadian.

**Registration number letter prefixes**
- **A.** Ambulances
- **C.** Motorcycles
- **E.** Engineering vehicle
- **F.** Armoured Cars and reconnaissance vehicles
- **H.** Tractors
- **L.** Lorries of more than one ton
- **M.** Cars and light utility vehicles (Jeeps)
- **P.** Amphibious vehicles
- **S.** Self-propelled guns
- **T.** Tanks and armoured personnel carriers
- **V.** RASC Vans
- **X.** Vehicle with trailer
- **Z.** Lorries of less than one ton

## Bridge Classification Plate

A 22.8cm disk positioned on the right at the front. Painted yellow, it had a black number indicating the laden weight category.

This number had to be the same or less than the numbers indicated on the approaches to an engineering site (bridge, etc). Vehicles pulling a trailer had two numbers painted on the yellow disk, one on top of the other, separated by a horizontal bar; only the number above the line was to be taken into consideration when the trailer was loaded.

**Examples**
- **2.** Jeep (3/2 with trailer)
- **4.** Daimler «Dingo»
- **5.** 15 cwt Lorry
- **7.** 3 ton Lorry
- **9.** Daimler Armoured Car
- **15.** Staghound armoured Car
- **30.** Sherman
- **40.** Churchill

## Armoured Units' Tactical Markings

These geometrical shapes indicated the position of the armoured squadron within the regiment and its colour indicated the position of the regiment within the brigade (the number of the troop was sometimes written inside the shape)

The tactical markings were painted on the sides of the turret or on the hull of tanks (on the front or rear if the shape of the vehicle was not suitable).

## Other Markings

Apart from particular names given to some machines (towns, regions, women's names, etc.), several tank regiments used large sized numbers enabling the vehicle to be identified within the squadron.

For example in the 13/18th Hussars or in the 1st Northamptonshire Yeomanry, large red numbers edged with white were painted on the turrets; in the 144th RAC, white numbers were painted on the turret.

### Examples of markings and insignia painted on British trucks and vans

1. Bedford OYD of the 6th Airborne Division, Divisional Ordnance Park RAOC
2. Bedford 1.5 ton Water tanker, 53rd 'Welsh' Infantry Division, 158th Infantry Brigade, 7th Royal Welsh Fusiliers.
3. Humber 51st Highland Infantry Division, Headquarters
4. Bedford QLT, 49th Infantry Division, 6th Battalion Duke of Wellington's.

There was a special disposition for certain transport convoys of the Royal Army Service Corps assigned to the transport of Infantry Brigades: the unit serial number of the RASC Company was superimposed over that of the battalion being transported.

127

## Examples of markings and insignia painted on British Scout Cars and Armoured cars

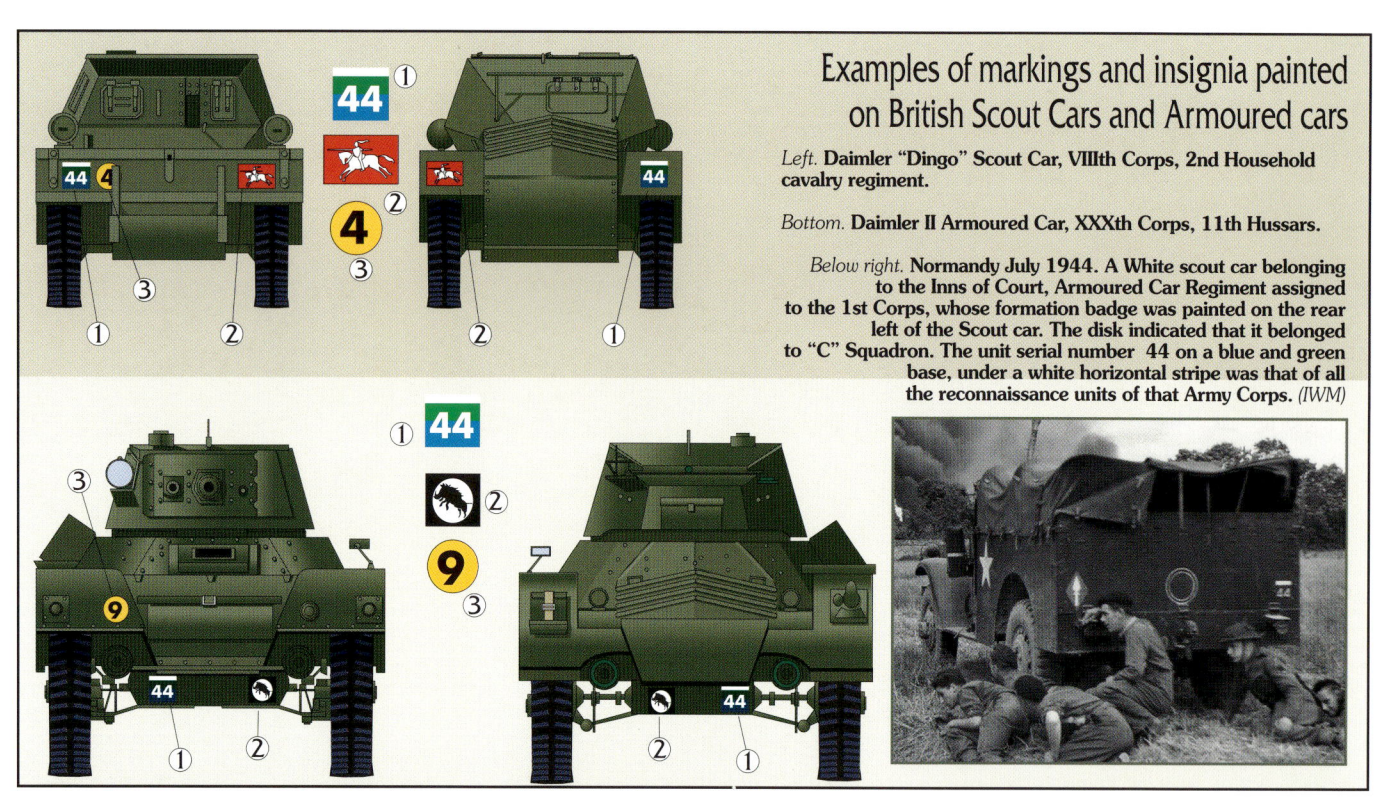

*Left.* **Daimler "Dingo" Scout Car, VIIIth Corps, 2nd Household cavalry regiment.**

*Bottom.* **Daimler II Armoured Car, XXXth Corps, 11th Hussars.**

*Below right.* Normandy July 1944. A White scout car belonging to the Inns of Court, Armoured Car Regiment assigned to the 1st Corps, whose formation badge was painted on the rear left of the Scout car. The disk indicated that it belonged to "C" Squadron. The unit serial number 44 on a blue and green base, under a white horizontal stripe was that of all the reconnaissance units of that Army Corps. *(IWM)*

## Examples of markings and insignia painted on British Half-Tracks

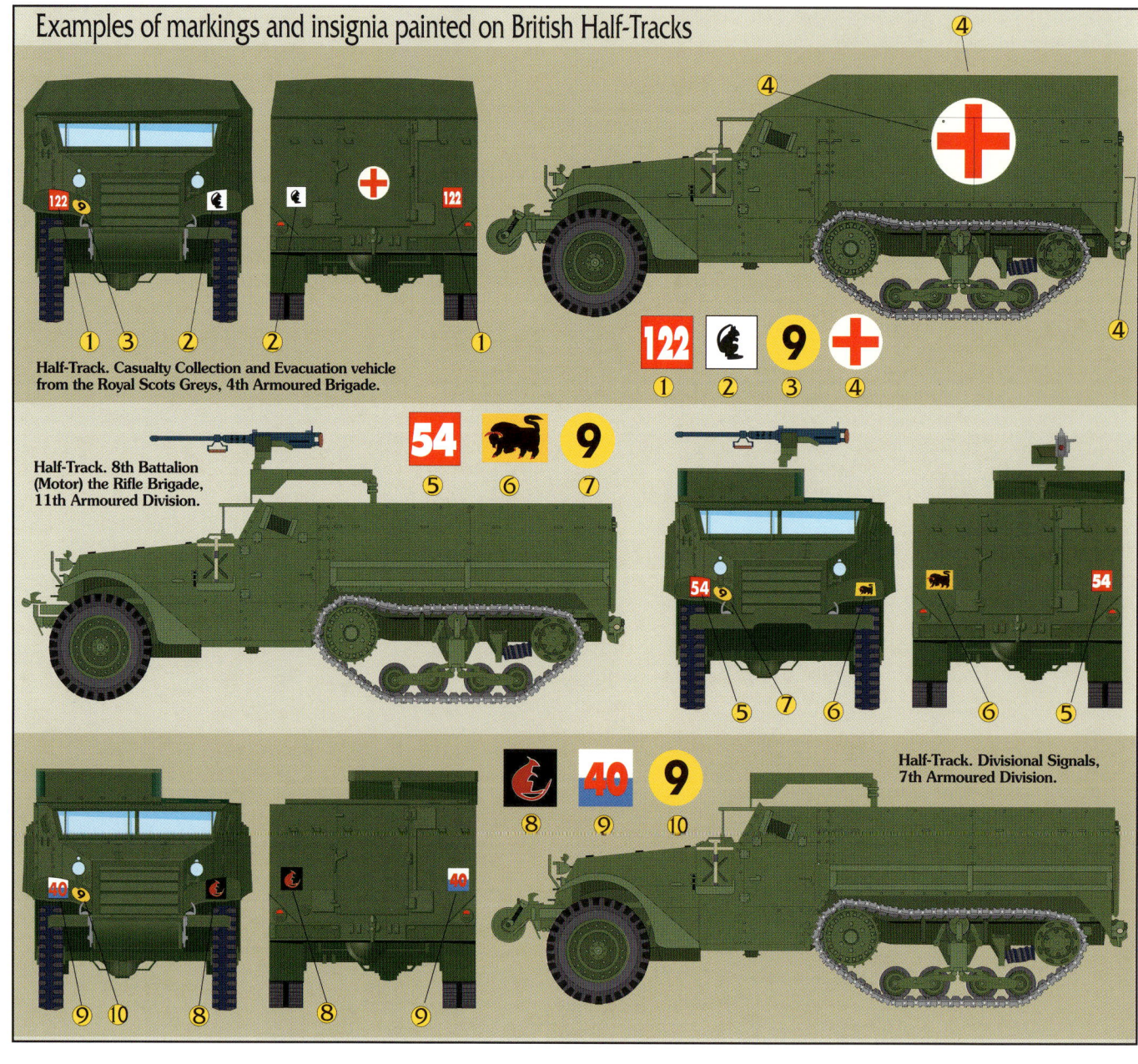

**Half-Track. Casualty Collection and Evacuation vehicle from the Royal Scots Greys, 4th Armoured Brigade.**

**Half-Track. 8th Battalion (Motor) the Rifle Brigade, 11th Armoured Division.**

**Half-Track. Divisional Signals, 7th Armoured Division.**

128

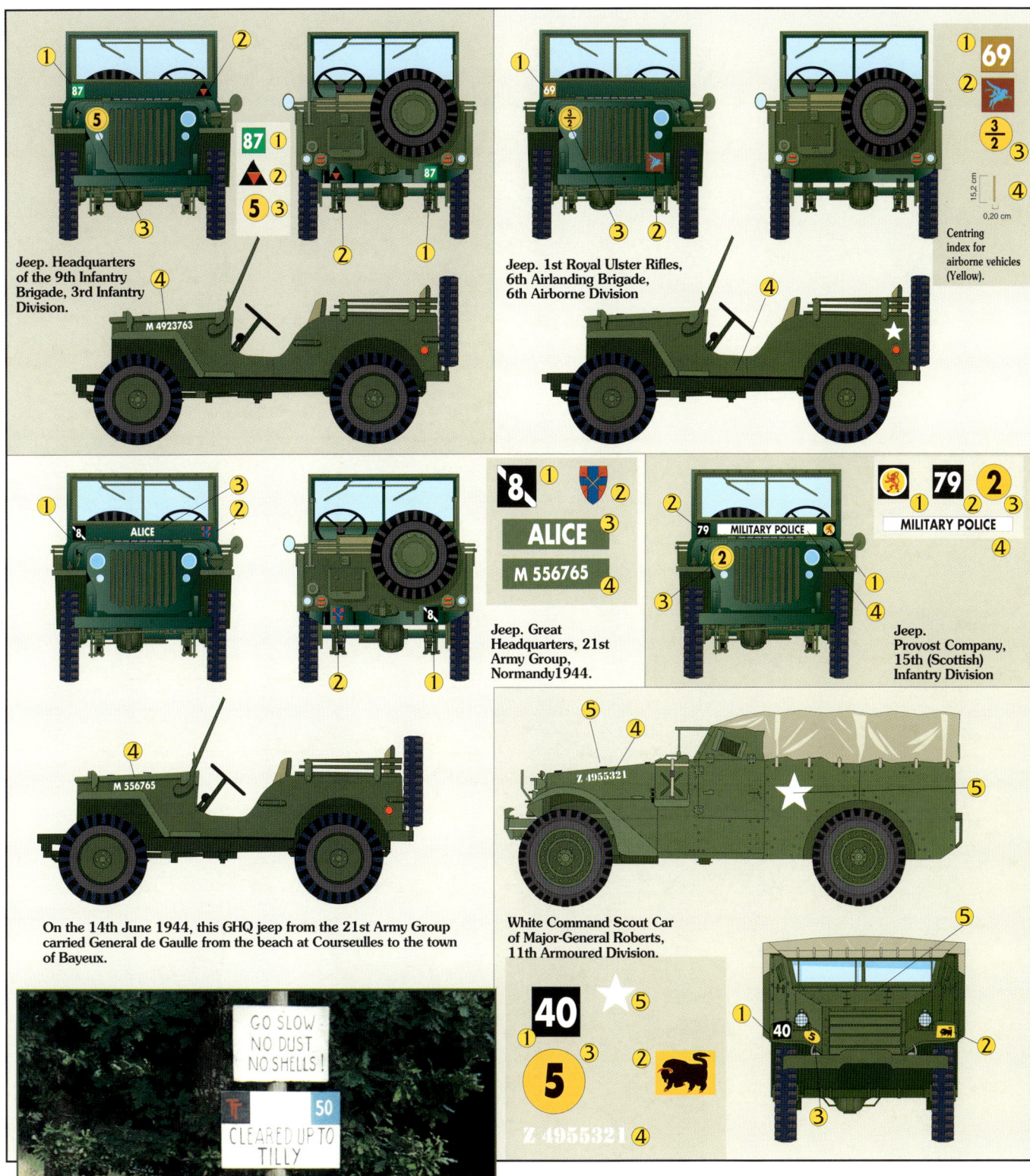

Jeep. Headquarters of the 9th Infantry Brigade, 3rd Infantry Division.

Jeep. 1st Royal Ulster Rifles, 6th Airlanding Brigade, 6th Airborne Division

Centring index for airborne vehicles (Yellow).

Jeep. Great Headquarters, 21st Army Group, Normandy 1944.

Jeep. Provost Company, 15th (Scottish) Infantry Division

On the 14th June 1944, this GHQ jeep from the 21st Army Group carried General de Gaulle from the beach at Courseulles to the town of Bayeux.

White Command Scout Car of Major-General Roberts, 11th Armoured Division.

*Opposite left.*
**Signposts in front of the jeep placed on the side of the road by the 295th Field Company, Royal Engineers, 50th Infantry Division. The lower sign indicates that the road has been cleared of mines to Tilly-sur-Seulle.**
*(DR)*

## Unit serial numbers

The positioning of the white mark indicated that the vehicle belonged to a command structure higher than that of the division.

## Recognition Signs

From July 1943 onwards and for all Allied armies, the white stars, circled or not, were adopted for all vehicles and machines.

Depending on the different units, the size and the position of these stars varied.

They were especially placed on the top of the vehicles for easier aerial identification, and rarely on the sides of armour.

129

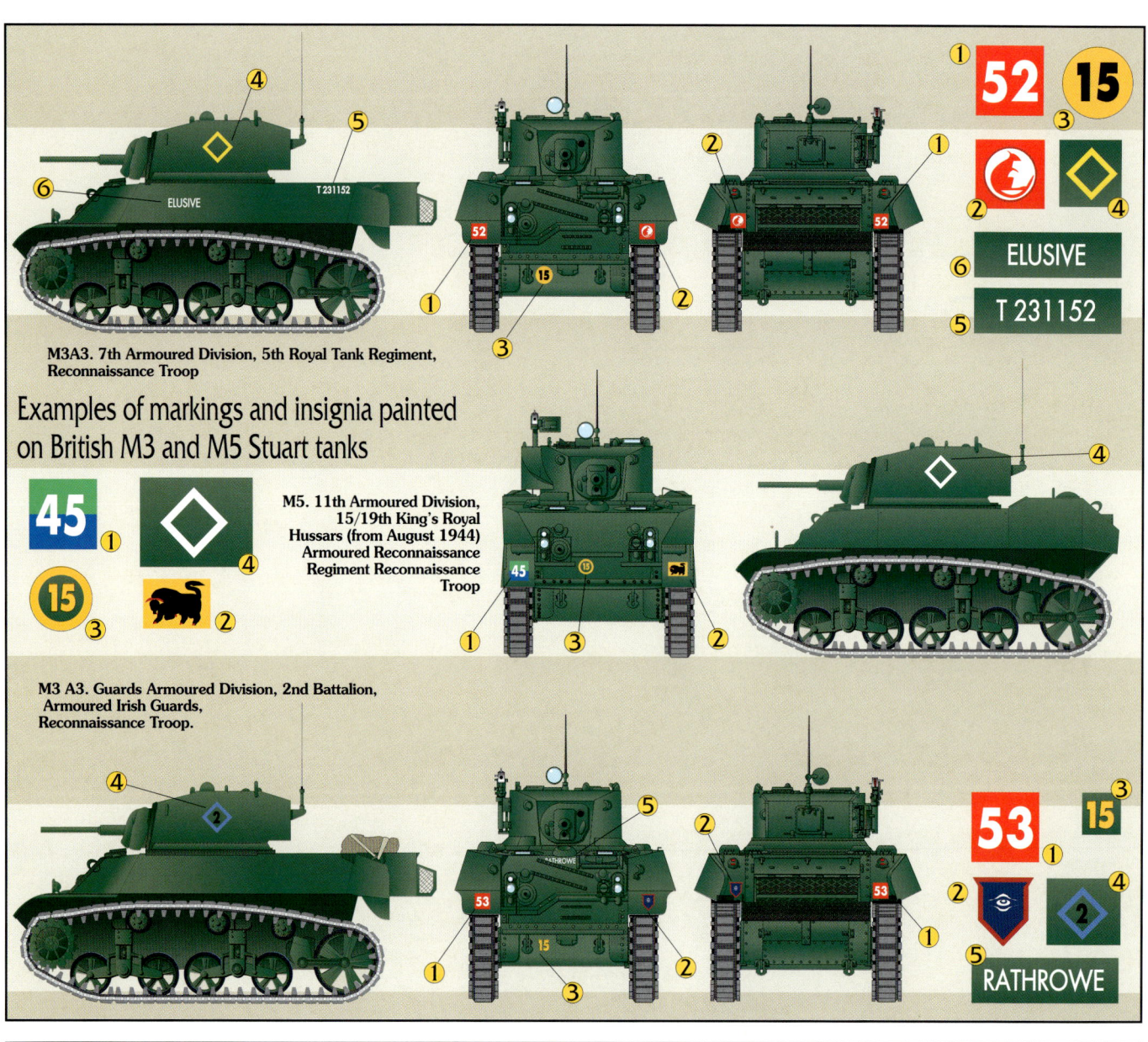

M3A3. 7th Armoured Division, 5th Royal Tank Regiment, Reconnaissance Troop

**Examples of markings and insignia painted on British M3 and M5 Stuart tanks**

M5. 11th Armoured Division, 15/19th King's Royal Hussars (from August 1944) Armoured Reconnaissance Regiment Reconnaissance Troop

M3 A3. Guards Armoured Division, 2nd Battalion, Armoured Irish Guards, Reconnaissance Troop.

**Examples of markings and insignia painted on British Cromwell tanks**

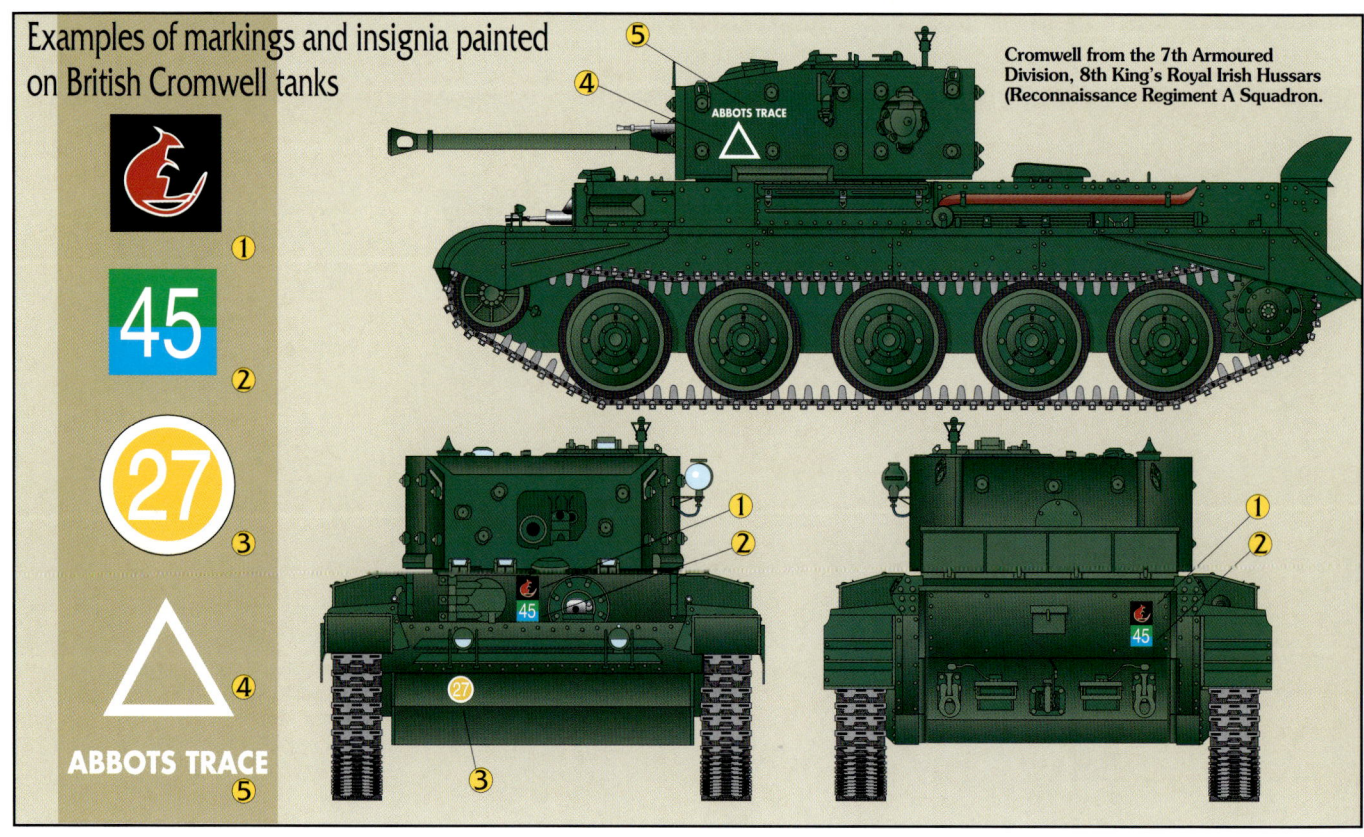

Cromwell from the 7th Armoured Division, 8th King's Royal Irish Hussars (Reconnaissance Regiment A Squadron.

ABBOTS TRACE

130

# Examples of markings and insignia painted on British Sherman tanks

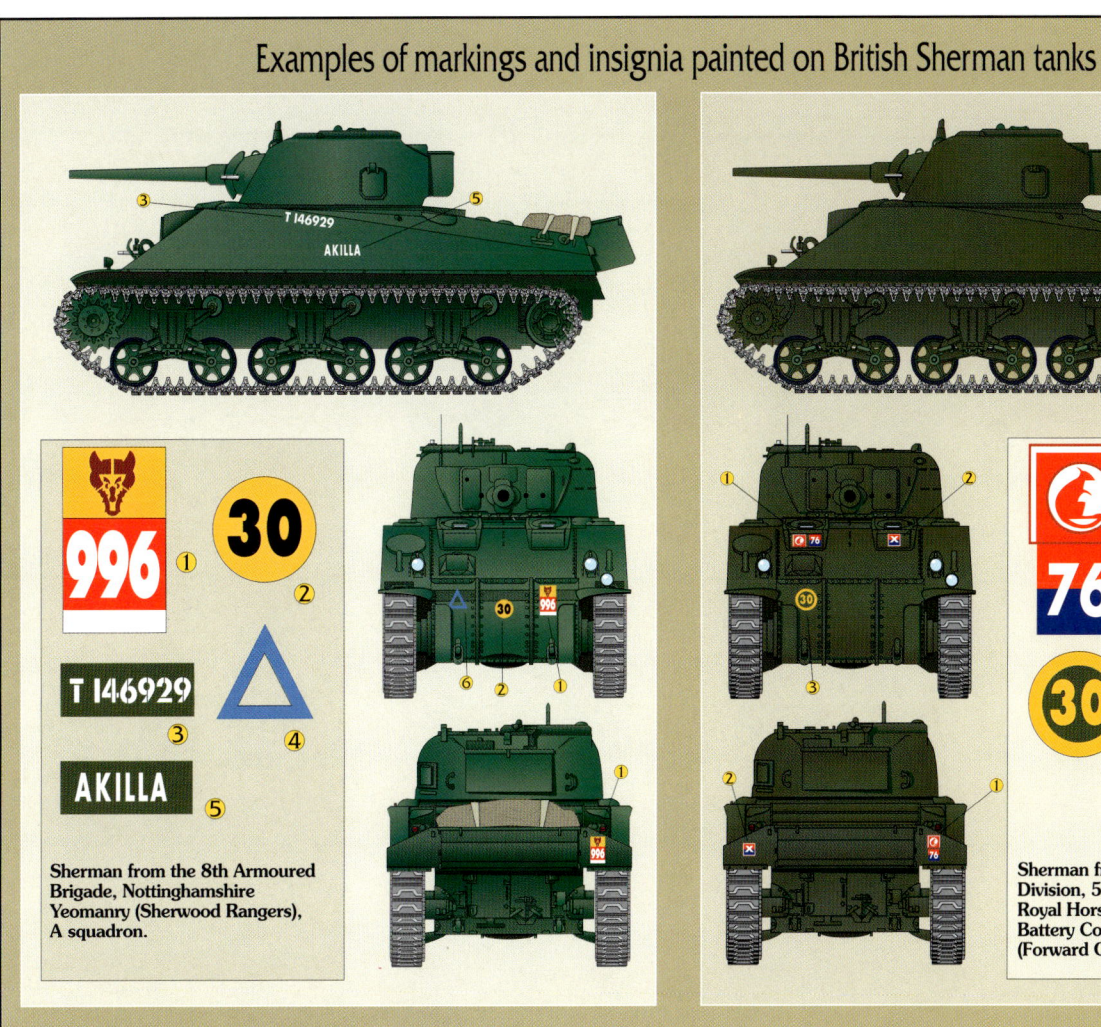

**Sherman from the 8th Armoured Brigade, Nottinghamshire Yeomanry (Sherwood Rangers), A squadron.**

T 146929
AKILLA
996

**Sherman from the 7th Armoured Division, 5th Field Regiment, Royal Horse Artillery Battery Commander (Forward Observation)**

76
30

**Sherman from the 27 Armoured Brigade, 13/18 Hussars, Regimental Headquarters.**

10
BALACLAVA
T 147161
51
30

**Sherman from the Guards Armoured Division, 2nd Battalion Armoured Grenadiers Guards, A Squadron.**

23
51
30
2

131

## Examples of markings and insignia painted on British TD M10 tanks

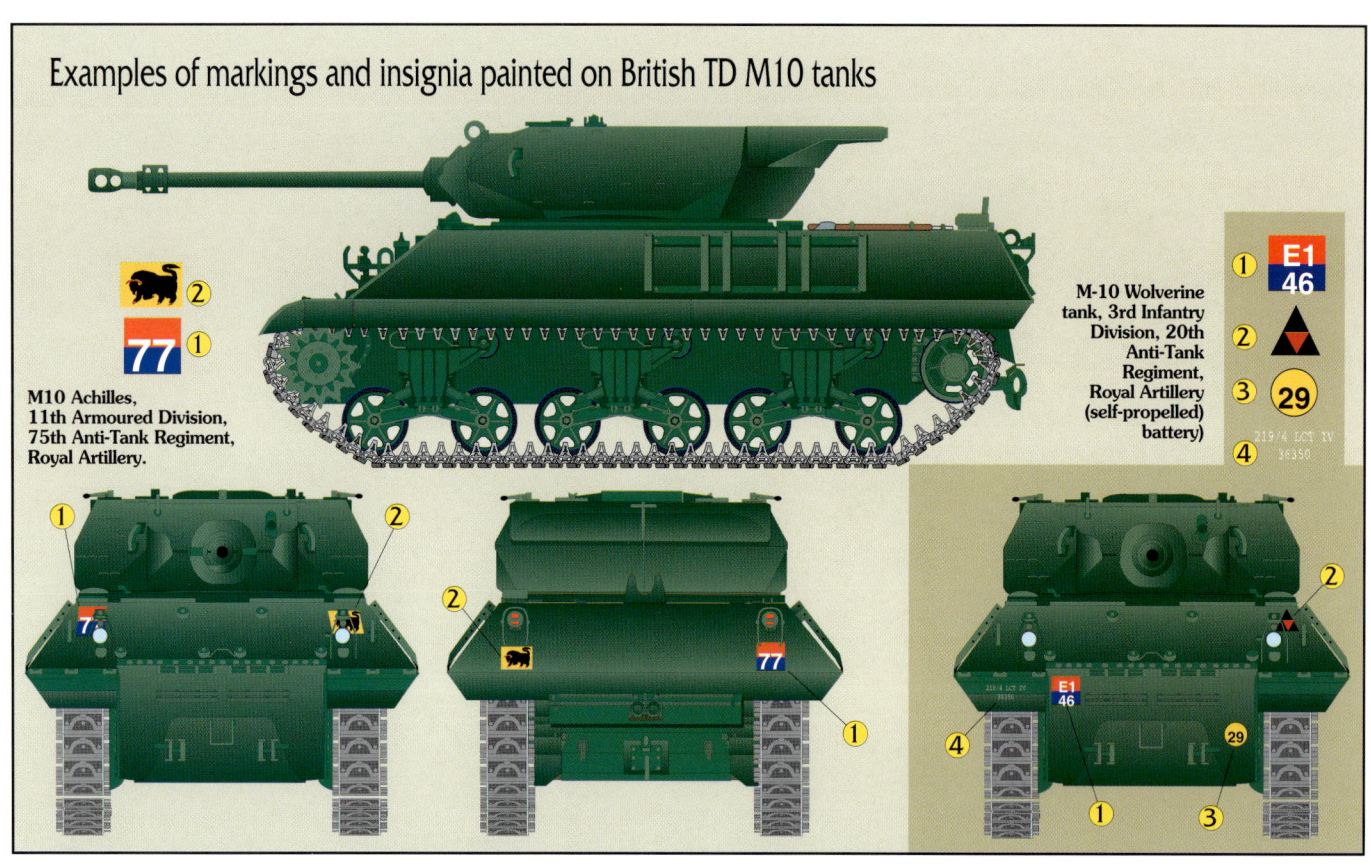

M10 Achilles, 11th Armoured Division, 75th Anti-Tank Regiment, Royal Artillery.

M-10 Wolverine tank, 3rd Infantry Division, 20th Anti-Tank Regiment, Royal Artillery (self-propelled) battery)

## Markings and insignia painted on British Churchill tanks

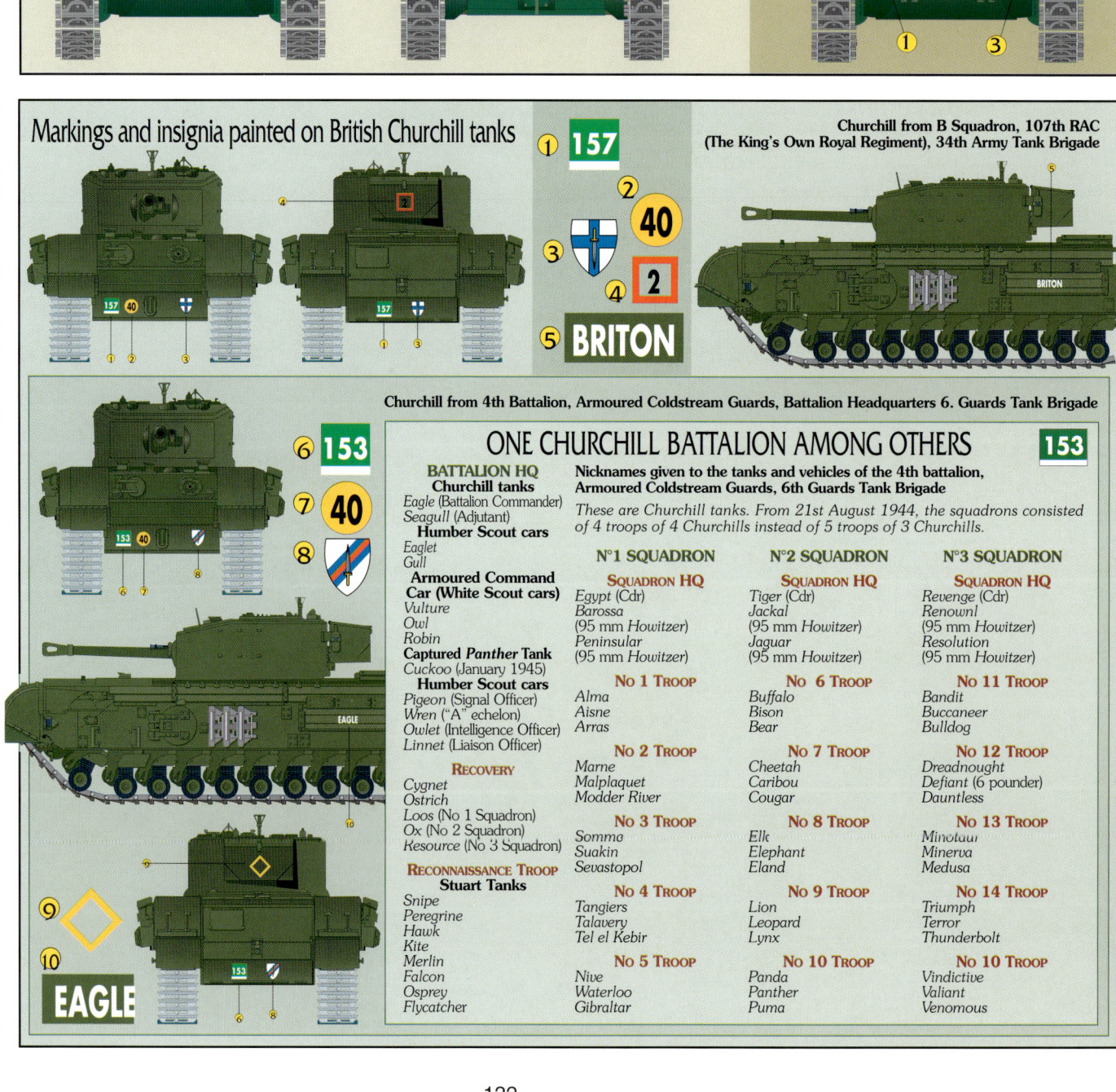

Churchill from B Squadron, 107th RAC (The King's Own Royal Regiment), 34th Army Tank Brigade

BRITON

Churchill from 4th Battalion, Armoured Coldstream Guards, Battalion Headquarters 6. Guards Tank Brigade

EAGLE

## ONE CHURCHILL BATTALION AMONG OTHERS

Nicknames given to the tanks and vehicles of the 4th battalion, Armoured Coldstream Guards, 6th Guards Tank Brigade

These are Churchill tanks. From 21st August 1944, the squadrons consisted of 4 troops of 4 Churchills instead of 5 troops of 3 Churchills.

**BATTALION HQ**
Churchill tanks
*Eagle* (Battalion Commander)
*Seagull* (Adjutant)
Humber Scout cars
*Eaglet*
*Gull*
Armoured Command Car (White Scout cars)
*Vulture*
*Owl*
*Robin*
Captured *Panther* Tank
*Cuckoo* (January 1945)
Humber Scout cars
*Pigeon* (Signal Officer)
*Wren* ("A" echelon)
*Owlet* (Intelligence Officer)
*Linnet* (Liaison Officer)

**RECOVERY**
*Cygnet*
*Ostrich*
*Loos* (No 1 Squadron)
*Ox* (No 2 Squadron)
*Resource* (No 3 Squadron)

**RECONNAISSANCE TROOP**
Stuart Tanks
*Snipe*
*Peregrine*
*Hawk*
*Kite*
*Merlin*
*Falcon*
*Osprey*
*Flycatcher*

**N°1 SQUADRON**
SQUADRON HQ
*Egypt* (Cdr)
*Barossa*
(95 mm *Howitzer*)
*Peninsular*
(95 mm *Howitzer*)

No 1 TROOP
*Alma*
*Aisne*
*Arras*

No 2 TROOP
*Marne*
*Malplaquet*
*Modder River*

No 3 TROOP
*Somma*
*Suakin*
*Sevastopol*

No 4 TROOP
*Tangiers*
*Talavery*
*Tel el Kebir*

No 5 TROOP
*Nive*
*Waterloo*
*Gibraltar*

**N°2 SQUADRON**
SQUADRON HQ
*Tiger* (Cdr)
*Jackal*
(95 mm *Howitzer*)
*Jaguar*
(95 mm *Howitzer*)

No 6 TROOP
*Buffalo*
*Bison*
*Bear*

No 7 TROOP
*Cheetah*
*Caribou*
*Cougar*

No 8 TROOP
*Elk*
*Elephant*
*Eland*

No 9 TROOP
*Lion*
*Leopard*
*Lynx*

No 10 TROOP
*Panda*
*Panther*
*Puma*

**N°3 SQUADRON**
SQUADRON HQ
*Revenge* (Cdr)
*Renownl*
(95 mm *Howitzer*)
*Resolution*
(95 mm *Howitzer*)

No 11 TROOP
*Bandit*
*Buccaneer*
*Bulldog*

No 12 TROOP
*Dreadnought*
*Defiant* (6 pounder)
*Dauntless*

No 13 TROOP
*Minotaur*
*Minerva*
*Medusa*

No 14 TROOP
*Triumph*
*Terror*
*Thunderbolt*

No 10 TROOP
*Vindictive*
*Valiant*
*Venomous*

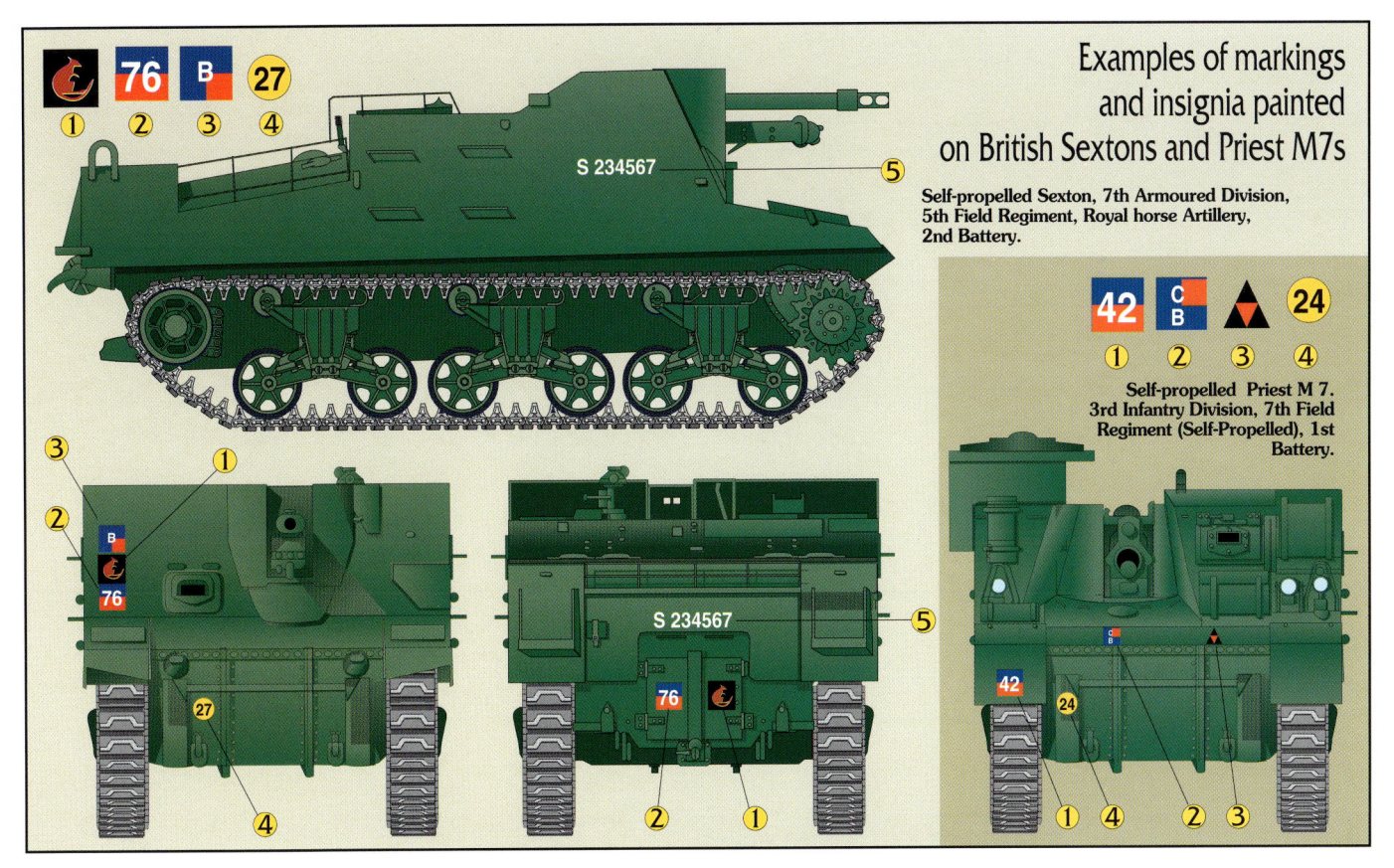

## Examples of markings and insignia painted on British Sextons and Priest M7s

Self-propelled Sexton, 7th Armoured Division, 5th Field Regiment, Royal horse Artillery, 2nd Battery.

Self-propelled Priest M 7. 3rd Infantry Division, 7th Field Regiment (Self-Propelled), 1st Battery.

*Opposite right*
**December 1944 in Holland. A party was organised by the 11th Armoured Division on the occasion of St-Nicholas' Day. The unit serial number 89 on a black base indicates that this jeep belonged to the 18th Light Field Ambulance, Royal Army Medical Corps.**
*(IWM)*

# Appendix 1 — HOW ARMOURED and INFANTRY UNITS PRESENT in the ORDER OF BA[TTLE]

| | CORPS TROOPS | ARMOURED DIVISION | TANK OU INDEPENDANT ARMOURED BRIGADE | OTHER SECTORS OF OPERATIONS |
|---|---|---|---|---|
| **CAVALRY** | | | | |
| 1st Household Cavalry Regiment — Life Guards and Royal Horse | | | | Italy |
| 2nd Household Cavalry Regiment — Guards *(régiments amalgamés)* | VIIIth Corps | | | |
| **DRAGOON GUARDS** | | | | |
| 1st King's Dragoon Guards | | | | Italy |
| Queen's Bay — 2nd Dragoons Guards | | | | Italy |
| 3rd Carabiniers — Prince of Wales Dragoon Guards | | | | Burma |
| 4/7 Royal Dragoon Guards | | | 8th Ind. Arm. Brig. | |
| 5th Royal Inniskilling Dragoon Guards | | 7th Arm. Div. | | |
| **DRAGOON S** | | | | |
| Royal Dragoons — 1st Dragoons | XIIth Corps | | | |
| Royal Scots Greys — 2nd Dragoons | | | 4th Ind. Arm. Brig | |
| 22nd Dragoons | | 79th Arm Div | | |
| 25th Dragoons | | | | India - Burma |
| **HUSSARS** | | | | |
| 3rd King's Own Hussars | | | | Italy |
| 4th Queen's Own Hussars | | | | Italy |
| 7th Queen's Own Hussars | | | | Italy |
| 8th King's Royal Irish Hussars | | 7th Arm. Div. | | |
| 10th Royal Hussars — Prince of Wales Own | | | | Italy |
| 11th Hussars — Prince Albert Own | XXXth Corps | | | |
| 13/18th Royal Hussars (Queen Mary Own) | | | 27th Ind. Arm. Brig. | |
| 14/20th King's Hussars | | | | Italy |
| 15/19th King's Royal Hussars | | 11th Arm. Div. | | |
| 23rd Hussars | | 11th Arm. Div. | | |
| **LANCERS** | | | | |
| 9th Queen's Royal Lancers | | | | Italy |
| 12th Royal Lancers — Prince of Wales | | | | Italy |
| 16/5th Lancers | | | | Italy |
| 17/21st Lancers | | | | Italy |
| 24th Lancers | | | 8th Ind. Arm. Brig. | |
| 27th Lancers | | | | Italy |
| **YEOMANRY** | | | | |
| 2nd County of London Yeomanry — Westminster Dragoons | | 79th Arm. Div. | | |
| 3rd County of London Yeomanry — Sharpshooters | | | 4th Ind. Arm. Brig. | |
| 4th County of London Yeomanry — Sharpshooters | | 7th Arm. Div. | | |
| 1st Derbyshire Yeomanry | | | | Italy |
| 2nd Derbyshire Yeomanry - | Reconnaissance Regiment de la 51st Infantry Division | | | |
| East Riding (of Yorkshire) Yeomanry | | | 27th Ind. Arm. Brig.. | |
| 1st Fife and Forfar Yeomanry | | 79th Arm. Div. | | |
| 2nd Fife and Forfar Yeomanry | | 11th Arm. Div. | | |
| 1st Lothians and Border Horse | | 79th Arm. Div. | | |
| 2nd Lothians and Border Horse | | | | Italy |
| 1st Northamptonshire Yeomanry | | | 33rd Ind. Arm. Brig. | |
| 2nd Northamptonshire Yeomanry | | 11th Arm. Div. | | |
| Nottinghamshire Yeomanry — Sherwood Rangers | | | 8th Ind. Arm. Brig. | |
| Royal Wiltshire Yeomanry | | | | Italy |
| Staffordshire Yeomanry — Queen's Own Royal Regiment | | | 27th Ind. Arm. Brig. | |
| Warwickshire Yeomanry | | | | Italy |
| Inns of Court Regiment | Ist Corps | | | |
| North Irish Horse | | | | Italy |
| Lovat Scouts | | | | Italy |
| **ROYAL TANK REGIMENT** | | | | |
| 1st Battalion | | 7th Arm. Div. | | |
| 2nd Battalion | | | | Italy |
| 3rd Battalion | | 11th Arm. Div. | | |
| 4th Battalion [1] | | 79th Arm. Div. | | |
| 5th Battalion | | 7th Arm. Div. | | |
| 6th Battalion | | | | Italy |
| 7th Battalion | | | 31st Army Tank Brigade | |

## WERE AFFECTED in 1944-1945, at the MOMENT of their ENGAGEMENT — Appendix 1

|  | CORPS TROOPS | ARMOURED DIVISION | TANK OU INDEPENDANT ARMOURED BRIGADE | OTHER SECTORS OF OPERATIONS |
|---|---|---|---|---|
| 8th Battalion | | | | Italy |
| 9th Battalion | | | 31st Army Tank Brigade | |
| 11th Battalion | | 79th Arm. Div. | | |
| 12th Battalion | | | | Italy |
| 40th Battalion | | | | Italy - Greece |
| 42nd Battalion | | 79th Arm. Div. | | |
| 43rd Battalion | | | | Great Britain - Burma |
| 44th Battalion | | | 4th Ind. Arm. Brig. | |
| 46th Battalion | | | | Italy - Greece |
| 48th Battalion | | | | Italy |
| 49th Battalion | | 79th Arm. Div. | | |
| 50th Battalion | | | | |
| 51st Battalion | | | | Italy |
| **ROYAL ARMOURED CORPS,** Régiments blindés issus d'Infantry Battalions transférés | | | | |
| 107th RAC. 5. King's Own Royal Regiment | | | 34th Army Tank Brigade | |
| 116th RAC. 9. Gordon Highlanders | | | | Burma |
| 141st RAC. 7. Buffs | | 79th Arm. Div. | | |
| 142nd RAC. 7. Suffolk (2) | | | | Italy |
| 144th RAC. 8. East Lancashire (3) | | | 33rd Ind. Arm. Brig. | |
| 145th RAC. 8. Duke of Wellington | | | | Italy |
| 146th RAC. 9. Duke of Wellington | | | | Burma |
| 147th RAC. 10. Hampshire | | | 34th Army Tank Brigade | |
| 148th RAC. 9. Loyals | | | 33rd Ind. Arm. Brig. | |
| 149th RAC. 7. King's Own Yorkshire Light Infantry | | | | Burma |
| 150th RAC. 10. York and Lancaster | | | | Burma |
| 153rd RAC. 8. Essex (4) | | | 34th Army Tank Brigade | |

(1) Reformed in March 1945 by transfer of the 144th RAC
(2) Disbanded in January 1945
(3) Disbanded in march 1945, forms the 4th RTR
(4) Dissolved in August 1944

|  | 21st ARMY GROUP LINES OF COMMUNICATION | ARMOURED DIVISION | INFANTRY DIVISION | INDEPENDANT ARMOURED. BRIG. | INDEPENDANT INFANTRY. BRIG. | AIRBORNE DIVISION |
|---|---|---|---|---|---|---|
| **FOOT GUARDS** | | | | | | |
| Coldstream Guards | | Guard | | 6th Guards Ar. Tk. Brig. | | |
| Grenadier Guards | | Guard | | 6th Guards Ar. Tk. Brig. | | |
| Irish Guards | | Guard | | | | |
| Scots Guards | | Guard | | 6th Guards Ar. Tk. Brig. | | |
| Welsh Guards | | Guard | | | | |
| **INFANTRY (par odre alphabétique)** | | | | | | |
| Argyll and Sutherland Highlanders — Princess Louise's | | | 15th - 51st | | | |
| Bedfordshire and Hertfordshire Regiment | | | | | | |
| Black Watch — Royal Highland Regiment | | | 51st | | | |
| Border Regiment | * | | | | | |
| 1st Brecknockshire Battalion (South Wales Borderers) | * | | | | | |
| Buckinghamshire Battalions (Oxs and Bucks Light Infantry) | * | | | | | |
| Buffs — Royal East Kent | | | | | | |
| Cameronians — Scottish Rifles | | | 5th - 15th- 52nd | | | |
| Cheshire Regiment | | | 11th | 5th - 50th | 115th | |
| Devonshire Regiment | | | 50th | | | 6th |
| Dorsetshire Regiment | | | 43rd - 50th | | | |
| Duke of Cornwall Light Infantry | | | 43rd | | | |
| Duke of Wellington Regiment | | | 49th | | | |
| Durham Light Infantry | * | | 49th - 50th | | | |
| East Lancashire Regiment | | | 53rd - 59 th | | | |
| East Surrey Regiment | | | | | | |
| East Yorkshire Regiment — Duke of York Own | * | | 3rd - 50th | | | |
| Essex Regiment | | | 5th - 49th | | 56th | |
| Glasgow Highlanders, (HLI) | | | 15th - 52th | | | |
| Gloucestershire Regiment | | | 49th | | 56th | |
| Gordon Highlanders | | | 15th - 51st | | | |
| Green Howards | | | 5th 50th | | | |
| 4th Hallamshire Battalion, (York and Lancaster Regiment) | | | 49th | | | |

135

# Annexe 1 — HOW ARMOURED and INFANTRY UNITS PRESENT in the ORDER OF BATTLE

| 21st ARMY GROUP | ARMOURED LINES OF COMMUNICATION | INFANTRY DIVISION | INDEPENDANT DIVISION | INDEPENDANT ARMOURED. BRIG. | AIRBORNE INFANTRY. BRIG. | DIVISION |
|---|---|---|---|---|---|---|
| **INFANTRY** | | | | | | |
| Hampshire Regiment | | | 43rd - 50th | | | |
| Herefordshire Regiment, KSLI | | 11th | | | | |
| Hertfordshire Regiment | * | | | | | |
| Highland Light Infantry — City of Glasgow | | | 15th- 52nd-53rd | | | |
| Kensington Regiment, Middlesex Regiment | | | 49th | | | |
| King's Own Royal Regiment — Lancaster | | | | | | |
| King's Own Scottish Borderers | | | 3rd-15 th-52th | | | 1st |
| King's Own Yorkshire Light Infantry | | | 5th - 49th | | | |
| King's Regiment — Liverpool | * | | | | | |
| King's Royal Rifle Corps | | | | 4th - 8th | | |
| King's Shropshire Light Infantry | | 11th | 3rd | | | |
| Lancashire Fusiliers | | | 59th | | | |
| Leicestershire Regiment | | | 49th | | | |
| Lincolnshire Regiment | | | 3rd - 49th | | | |
| London Irish Rifle (Royal Ulster Rifles) | | | | | | |
| London Scottish (Gordon Highlanders) | | | | | | |
| Loyal Regiment — North Lancashire | | | | | | |
| Manchester | | | 52nd - 53rd | | | |
| Middlesex Regiment — Duke of Cambridge Own | | | 3rd - 15th - 43rd - 51st | | | |
| Mommouthshire Regiment | | 11th | 53rd | | 115th | |
| Northamptonshire Regiment | | | 5th | | 115th | |
| North Staffordshire Regiment — Prince of Wales | | | 59th | | | |
| Oxfordshire and Buckinghamshire Light Infantry | | | 53rd | | | 6th |
| Queen's Own Cameron Highlanders | | | 51st | | | |
| Queen's Own Royal West Kent Regiment | | | | | | |
| Queen's Royal Regiment — West Surrey | | 7th | | | | |
| Rifle Brigade — Prince Consort Own | | 7th - 11th | | | | |
| Royal Berkshire Regiment — Princess Charlotte of Wales | * | | | | 115th | |
| Royal Fusiliers — City of London | | | | | | |
| Royal Inniskilling Fusiliers | | | | | | |
| Royal Irish Fusiliers — Princess Victoria's | | | | | | |
| Royal Norfolk Regiment | | | 3rd - 59th | | | |
| Royal Northumberland Fusiliers | * | G - 7th - 11th | 59th | | | |
| Royal Scots — Royal Regiment | | | 15th - 52th | | | |
| Royal Scots Fusiliers | | | 5 -15 - 49 - 52 | | | |
| Royal Sussex Regiment | | | | | | |
| Royal Ulster Rifles | | | 3rd | | | 6th |
| Royal Warwickshire Regiment | | | 3rd - 59th | | | |
| Royal Welch Fusiliers | | | 53th | | | |
| Seaforth Highlanders — Ross-Shire Buffs, Duke of Albany's | | | 5 - 15 -51 | | | |
| Sherwood Foresters | | | | | | |
| Somerset Light Infantry — Prince Albert's | | | 43rd | | | |
| South Lancashire Regiment — Prince of Wales Volunteers | | | 3rd | | | |
| South Staffordshire Regiment | | | 59th | | | 1st |
| South Wales Borderers | | | | | 56th | |
| Suffolk Regiment | | | 3rd | | | |
| Tyneside Scottish (Black Watch) | | | 49th | | | |
| Welch Regiment | | | 53rd | | | |
| West Yorkshire Regiment — Prince of Wales Own | | | | | | |
| Wiltshire Regiment — Duke of Edinburgh's | | | 5th - 43rd | | | |
| Worcestershire Regiment | | | 43rd | | | |
| York and Lancaster | | | 5th | | | |

▪ Regiments not having any constituted units engaged in the North West Europe Campaign, but in the Italian Theatre of operations.

▪ Regiments not having any constituted units engaged in the North West Europe Campaign, but in the Far-East, India and Burma.

▪ Regiments not having any constituted units engaged in the North West Europe Campaign. Personnel from these regiments were present in the Army Commandos and in isolated depots supplying reinforcements to the 21st Army Group.

**Note.** *In order to find out the affectation of any one unit in the North West Europe campaign, see the page where the organogram of the larger unit is set out above, in the chapter entitled II. The 21st Army Group (pp 10 to 27).*

**Example.**
*Royal Scots Greys:* 4th Independant Armoured Brigade, see p. 26
or *Highland Light Infantry:* 15th, 52nd, 53rd Infantry Divisions, see pages 15, 17, 18.

## WERE AFFECTED in 1944-1945, at the MOMENT of their ENGAGEMENT — Annexe 1

| PARACHUTE REGIMENT | AIRBORNE DIVISION | OTHER AFFECTATIONS AND SECTORS OF OPERATIONS |
|---|---|---|
| 1st Battalion | 1st | |
| 2nd Battalion | 1st | |
| 3rd Battalion | 1st | |
| 4th Battalion | | 2. Para Brigade (Italy, Provence, Greece) |
| 5th Battalion | | 2. Para Brigade (Italy, Provence, Greece) |
| 6th Battalion | | 2. Para Brigade (Italy, Provence, Greece) |
| 7th Battalion | 6th | |

| PARACHUTE REGIMENT | AIRBORNE DIVISION | OTHER AFFECTATIONS AND SECTORS OF OPERATIONS |
|---|---|---|
| 8th Battalion | 6th | |
| 9th Battalion | 6th | |
| 10th Battalion | 1st | |
| 11h Battalion | 1st | |
| 12th Battalion | 6th | |
| 13th Battalion | 6th | |
| 15th Battalion | | India, Burma |
| 16th Battalion | | India, Burma |
| 156th Battalion | 1st | |

## Appendix 2 — OFFICIAL ABBREVIATIONS — Appendix 2

### OFFICIAL ABBREVIATIONS OF THE ARMS', SERVICES' AND REGIMENTAL NAMES OF THE BRITISH ARMY

| Designation | Abbréviation |
|---|---|
| **CAVALRY AND SCOUTS** | |
| Life Guards | LG |
| Royal Horse Guards (The Blues) | RHG |
| Lovats Scouts | LOVATS |
| **ROYAL ARMOURED CORPS** | RAC |
| Regiments, Royal Armoured Corps | 107 (etc) RAC |
| Regiments, Reconnaissance Corps | 48 (etc) Recce Regt |
| **DRAGOON GUARDS** | |
| 1st King's Dragoon Guards | KDG |
| Queen's Bays (2nd Dragoon Guards) | BAYS |
| 3rd Carabiniers (Prince of Wales's Dragoon Guards) | 3 DG |
| 4th/7th Royal Dragoon Guards | 4/7 DG |
| 5th Royal Inniskilling Dragoon Guards | 5 DG |
| **DRAGOONS** | |
| 1st Royal Dragoons | ROYALS |
| Royal Scots Greys (2nd Dragoons) | GREYS |
| 22nd Dragoons | 22 DGNS |
| 25th Dragoons | 25 DGNS |
| **HUSSARS** | |
| 3rd King's Own Hussars | 3 H |
| 4th Queen's Own Hussars | 4 H |
| 7th Queen's Own Hussars | 7 H |
| 8th King's Royal Irish Hussars | 8 H |
| 10th Royal Hussars | 10 H |
| 11th Hussars (Prince Albert's Own) | 11 H |
| 13th/18th Royal Hussars | 13/18 H |
| 14th/20th King's Hussars | 14/20 H |
| 15th/19th King's Royal Hussars | 15/19 H |
| 23rd Hussars | 23 H |
| Yorkshire Hussars (TA) | YORKS H |
| Royal Gloucestershire Hussars (TA) | RGH |
| **LANCERS** | |
| 9th Queen's Royal Lancers | 9 L |
| 12th Royal Lancers (Prince of Wales's) | 12 L |
| 16th/5th Lancers | 16/5 L |
| 17th/21st Lancers | 17/21 L |
| 24th Lancers | 24 L |
| 27th Lancers | 27 L |
| **ROYAL TANK REGIMENT** | R Tks |
| Battalions Royal Tank Regiment | 48 (etc) R Tks |
| **YEOMANRY** | |
| County of London Yeomanry (Sharpshooters) (TA) | SHARPSHOOTERS |
| 2nd County of London Yeomanry (Westminster Dragoons) (TA) | W DGNS |
| Derbyshire Yeomanry (TA) | DERBY YEO |
| East Riding Yeomanry (TA) | E RIDING YEO |
| Fife and Forfar Yeomanry (TA) | FF YEO |
| Lothians and Border Yeomanry (TA) | LOTHIANS |
| Northamptonshire Yeomanry (TA) | N YEO |
| Nottinghamshire Yeomanry (TA) | N YEO |
| Royal Wiltshire Yeomanry (TA) | R WILTS YEO |
| Staffordshire Yeomanry (TA) | STAFFS YEO |
| Warwickshire Yeomanry (TA) | WARWICK YEO |
| Inns of Court Regiment (TA) | INNS OF COURT |
| North Irish Horse (SR) | NIH |
| **FOOT GUARDS** | |
| Coldstream Guards | COLDM GDS |
| Grenadier Guards | GREN GDS |
| Irish Guards | IG |
| Scots Guards | SG |
| Welsh Guards | WG |

| Designation | Abbréviation |
|---|---|
| **INFANTRY** | |
| Argyll and Sutherland Highlanders | A & SH |
| Bedfordshire and Hertfordshire Regiment | BEDFS HERTS |
| Black Watch (Royal Highland Regiment) | BW |
| Border Regiment | BORDER |
| Brecknockshire Battalion, South Wales Borderers | BRECKNOCCK |
| Buckinghamshire Battalion, Oxfordshire and Buckinghamshire Light Infantry (TA) | BUCKFS |
| Buffs (Royal East Kent Regiment) | BUFFS |
| Cambridgeshire Regiment (TA) | CAMB |
| Cameronians (Scottish Rifles) | CAMERONIANS |
| Cheshire Regiment | CHESCHIRE |
| Devonshire Regiment | DEVON |
| Dorsetshire Regiment | DORSET |
| Duke of Cornwall's Light Infantry | DCLI |
| Duke of Wellington's Regiment (West Riding) | DWR |
| Durham Light Infantry | DLI |
| East Lancashire Regiment | E LAN R |
| East Surrey Regiment | SURREYS |
| East Yorkshire Regiment (Duke of York's Own) | E YORKS |
| Essex Regiment | ESSEX |
| Glasgow Highlanders (TA) | GLAS H |
| Gloucestershire Regiment | GLOSTERS |
| Gordon Highlanders | GORDONS |
| Green Howards (Alexandra, Princess of Wales's Own Yorkshire Regiment) | GREEN HOWARDS |
| Hallamshire Battalion, York and Lancaster Regiment (TA) | HALLAMS |
| Hamphire Regiment | HAMPS |
| Herefordshire Regiment (TA) | HEREFORD |
| Hertfordshire Regiment (TA) | HERTS |
| Highland Regiment | HIGHLAND I |
| Highland Light Infantry (City of Glasgow Regiment) | HLI |
| Kensington Regiment (TA) | KENSINGTONS |
| King's Own Royal Regiment (Lancaster) | KING'S OWN |
| King's Own Scottish Borderers | KOSB |
| King's Own Yorkshire Light Infantry | KOYLI |
| King's Regiment (Liverpool) | KINGS |
| King's Royal Rifle Corps | KRRC |
| King's Shropshire Light Infantry | KSLI |
| Lancashire Fusiliers | LF |
| Leicestershire Regiment | LEICESTERS |
| Lincolnshire Regiment | LINCOLNS |
| Liverpool Scottish (TA) | LIVPL SCOT |
| London Irish Rifles (TA) | LIR |
| London Scottish (TA) | LOND SCOT |
| Lowland Regiment | LOWLAND R |
| Loyal Regiment (North Lancashire) | LOYALS |
| Manchester Regiment | MANCH |
| Middlesex Regiment (Duke of Cambridge's Own) | MX |
| Monmouthshire Regiment (TA) | MO, |
| Northamptonfihire Regiment | NORTHAMPTONS |
| North Staffordshire Regiment (The Prince of Wales's) | N STAFFS |
| Oxfordshire and Buckinghamshire Light Infantry | OXF BUCKS |
| Queen's Own Cameron Highlanders | CAMERONS |
| Queen's Own Royal West Kent Regiment | RWK |
| Queen's Royal Regiment (West Surrey) | QUEENS |
| Rifle Brigade (Prince Consort's Own) | RB |
| Royal Berkshire Regiment (Princess Charlotte of Wales's) | R BERKS |
| Royal Fusiliers (City of London Regiment) | RF |
| Royal Inniskilling Fusiliers | INNISKS |
| Royal Irish Fusiliers (Princess Victoria's) | R IR F |
| Royal Norfolk Regiment | NORFOLK |

| Designation | Abbréviation |
|---|---|
| Royal Northumberland Fusiliers | NF |
| Royal Scots (The Royal Regiment) | RS |
| Royal Scots Fusiliers | RSF |
| Royal Sussex Regiment | R SUSSEX |
| Royal Ulster Rifles | RUR |
| Royal Warwickshire Regiment | WARWICK |
| Royal Welch Fusiliers | RWF |
| Seaforth Highlanders (Ross-shire Buffs, The Duke of Albany's) | SEAFORTH |
| Sherwood Foresters (Nottinghamshire and Derbyshire Regiment) | FORESTERS |
| Somerset Light Infantry (Prince Albert's) | SOM LI |
| South Lancashire Regiment (The Prince of Wales's Volunteers) | S LAN R |
| South Staffordshire Regiment | S STAFFORDS |
| South Wales Borderers | SWB |
| Suffolk Regiment | SUFFOLK |
| Tyneside Scottish (TA) | TYNE SCOT |
| Welch Regiment | WELCH |
| West Yorkshire Regiment (The Prince of Wales's Own) | W YORKS |
| Wiltshire Regiment (Duke of Edinburgh's) | WILTS |
| Worcestershire Regiment | WORC R |
| York and Lancaster Regiment | Y & L |
| **OTHER REGIMENTS AND CORPS** | |
| Army Air Corps | AAC |
| Glider Pilot Regiment | Glider P Regt |
| Parachute Regiment | Para Regt |
| Special Air Service Regiment | SAS Regt |
| Army Catering Corps | ACC |
| Army Dental Corps | AD Corps |
| Army Educational Corps | AEC |
| Army Physical Training Corps | APTC |
| Corps of Military Police | CMP |
| Corps of Royal Engineers | RE |
| General Service Corps | GSC |
| Intelligence Corps | Int Corps |
| Military Provost Staff Corps | MPSC |
| Non-Combatant Corps | NCC |
| Pioneer Corps | Pnr Corps |
| Royal Army Chaplains' Department | RA Ch D |
| Royal Army Medical Corps | RAMC |
| Royal Army Ordnance Corps | RAOC |
| Royal Army Pay Corps | RAPC |
| Royal Army Service Corps | RASC |
| Royal Army Veterinary Corps | RAVC |
| Royal Corps of Signals | R Sigs |
| Royal Electrical and Mechanical Engineers | REME |
| Royal Regiment of Artillery | RA |
| Small Arms School Corps | SASC |
| **WOMEN'S SERVICES** | |
| Auxiliary Territorial Service | ATS |

**Women's Services ATS Abbreviations of ATS - Officers' ranks**

| | |
|---|---|
| Chief Controller | C contr |
| Senior Controller | S contr |
| Controller | Contr |
| Chief Commander | C comd |
| Senior Commander | S comd |
| Junior Commander | J comd |
| Subaltern | Sub |
| Second Subalten | 2 sub |
| Queen Alexandra's Imperial Military Nursing Service | QAIMNS |
| Territorial Army Nursing Service | TANS |

# Appendix 3

# OFFICIAL ABBREVIATIONS

## A

| Designation | Abbreviation |
|---|---|
| Accommodation | accn |
| Acknowledge, acknowledged, or acknowledgement | ack |
| Addressed | addsd |
| Adjutant | adjt |
| Administration or administrative | adm |
| Advance or advanced | adv |
| Advanced ammunition depot | AAD |
| Advanced dressing station | ADS |
| Advanced landing ground | ALG |
| Advanced ordnance depot | AOD |
| Advanced workshop detachment | AWD |
| Airbone troops | airtps |
| Air liaison officer | ALO |
| Air liaison section | Al sec |
| Air officer commanding | AOC |
| Air raid precautions or ammunition refilling point | ARP |
| Air support signal, unit | ASSU |
| Ambulance | amb |
| Ammunition | amn |
| Ammunition point or armour piercing | AP |
| Ammunition railhead | ARH |
| Ammunition refilling point or air raid precautions | ARP |
| Ammunition sub depot | ASD |
| And so on or and the rest | etc |
| Annexure | annx |
| Animal transport | AT |
| Anti-aircraft or Army Act | AA |
| Anti-gas | AG |
| Anti-personnel | A per |
| Anti-tank | A tk |
| Appendix | appx |
| Approximately or approximate | approx |
| Armoured | armd |
| Armoured car | armd C |
| Armoured command vehicle | ACV |
| Armoured fighting vehicle | AFV |
| Armoured piercing or ammunition point | AP |
| Armoured replacement group | ARG |
| Army Act or anti-aircraft | AA |
| Army book | AB |
| Army Council Instruction | ACI |
| Army form | AF |
| Army group, Royal Artillery | AGRA |
| Army group, Royal Engineers | AGRE |
| Army Order | AO |
| Army photographic interpretation section | APIS |
| Army post office | APO |
| Army routine order | ARO |
| Army Training Instruction | ATI |
| Army Training Memorandum | ATM |
| Army Troops | A tps |
| Artillery | arty |
| Artillery reconnaissance | arty R |
| Artizan works company | art wks coy |
| Assault | aslt |
| Assault vehicle, Royal Engineers | AVRE |
| Attach, attached, or attachment | att |
| Australia or Australian | Aust |
| Auxillary or auxiliaries | aux |

## B

| Designation | Abbreviation |
|---|---|
| Base ammunition depot | BAD |
| Base depot or bomb disposal | BD |
| Base ordnance depot | BOD |
| Base supply airfield | B sup airf |
| Base supply depot | BSD |
| Base workshop | B wksp |
| Bath unit | BU |
| Battalion | bn |
| Battery | bty |
| Battery commander | BC |
| Battery quarter-master-serjeant | BQMS |
| Battery serjeant-major | BSM |
| Beach maintenance area | BMA |
| Bomb disposal or base depot | BD |
| Bombardier | bdr |
| Bombing report | bomrep |
| Boundary | bdy |
| Bridge or bridging | br |
| Brigade | bde |
| Brigade ordnance warrant officer | BOWO |
| British | Brit |
| Bulk breaking point | BBP |

## C

| Designation | Abbreviation |
|---|---|
| Camouflage or camouflaged | cam |
| Canada | Cda |
| Canadian | Cdn |
| Captain | capt |
| Casualty (ies) | cas |
| Casualty clearing station | CCS |
| Casualty collecting post | CCP |
| Cavalry | cav |
| Centre line | CL |
| Chaplain to the forces | CF |
| Chemical | chem |
| Chemical warfare | CW |
| Chief ordnance officer | COO |
| Civil or civilian | civ |
| Civil affairs or coast artillery | CA |
| Close Support | CS |
| Coast artillery or civil affairs | CA |
| Coast defence | CD |
| Colonel | col |
| Column | coln |
| Command, commanded, commandant, or commander | comd |
| Cornmand driver increment | CDI |
| Commanding Officer | CO |
| Commando | cdo |
| Communication | comm |
| Company | coy |
| Company quarter-master-serjeant | CQMS |
| Company Serjeant-major | CSM |
| Composite | comp |
| Concentrate, concentrated, or concentration | conc |
| Confinement to barracks or counter-battery | CB |
| Construct, constructed, or construction | constr |
| Contact reconnaissance | con R |
| Co-ordinate, co-ordinated, co-ordinating, or co-ordination | coord |
| Corporal | cpl |
| Corps troops | C tps |
| Counter-battery or confinement to barracks | CB |
| Counter-battery officer | CBO |
| Craftsman or craftsmen | cfn |
| Cross-roads | X rds |

## D

| Designation | Abbreviation |
|---|---|
| Decontamination | decn |
| Defend, defended, defence, or defensive | def |
| Defensive fire or direction finding | DF |
| Deliver, delivered, or delivery | del |
| Delivery point | DP |
| Depot | dep |
| Despatch rider or motor-cyclist | DR |
| Despatch rider letter service | DRLS |
| Detach, detached, or detachment | det |
| Detail issue depot | DID |
| Diesel engined road vehicle fuel | derv fuel |
| Direction finding or defensive fire | DF |
| Dispersal point | dis P |
| District | dist |
| Division or divisional | div |
| Dressing station | DS |
| Driver | dvr |
| Dropping zone | DZ |

## E

| Designation | Abbreviation |
|---|---|
| East Africa, East African or enemy aircraft | EA |
| Echelon | ech |
| Electrical mechanical engineer | EME |
| Embarkation staff officer | ESO |
| Employ, employed, or employment | emp |
| Enemy aircraft, East Africa, or East African | EA |
| Engineer | engr |
| Equipment | eqpt |
| Establish, established, or establishment | est |
| Evacuate, evacuated, or evacuation | evac |
| Exclude, excluded, excluding, or exclusive | excl |
| Expeditionary force | EF |

## F

| Designation | Abbreviation |
|---|---|
| Field | fd |
| Field bakery | fd bky |
| Field butchery and cold storage depot | fd bchy |
| Field dressing station | FDS |
| Field force or fire fighting | Ff |
| Field general court-martial | FGCM |
| Field service or field security | FS |
| Field service pocket book | FSPB |
| Field surgical unit | FSU |
| Field transfusion unit | FTU |
| Fire fighting or field force | FF |
| Fixed signal service | FSS |
| Flash spotting | F sp |
| Flight | flt |
| Folding boat equipment | FBF |
| Foot or feet | ft |
| For example | eg |
| Formation | fmn |
| Forming up place | FUP |
| Forward or forwarded | fwd |
| Forward defended locality | FDL |
| Forward maintenance area | FMA |
| Forward observation officer | FOO |
| Frequency | freq |
| Fusilier(s) | fus |

## G

| Designation | Abbreviation |
|---|---|
| Gallon | gal |
| Garrison | grn |
| General | gen |
| General court-martial | GCM |
| General Headquarters | GHQ |
| General routine order | GRO |
| General service or general staff | GS |
| General transport company | GT coy |
| Gridded vertical air photograph | photogrid |
| Group | gp |
| Guard | gd |
| Guardsman or guardsmen | gdsm |
| Gunner | gnr |

## H

| Designation | Abbreviation |
|---|---|
| Harassing fire or high frequency | HF |
| Headquarter(s) | HQ |
| Heavy | hy |
| Heavy Anti-aircraft | HAA |
| High explosive | HE |
| High frequency or harassing fire | HF |
| High power or horse power | HP |
| High tension or horsed transport | HT |
| Home defence or horse drawn | HD |
| Home Guard | HG |
| Horse drawn or home defence | HD |
| Horse Power or high power | HP |
| Horsed transport or high tension | HT |
| Hospital | hosp |
| Hour | hr |
| Howitzer | how |
| Hundredweight(s) | cwt |
| Hygiene | hyg |

## I

| Designation | Abbreviation |
|---|---|
| Inch | in |
| In charge of or internal combustion | IC |
| Include, included, including, or inclusive | incl |
| Independent | indep |
| India or Indian | Ind |
| Indan Army | IA |
| Infantry | inf |
| Inform informed, or information | infm |
| Inland water transport | IWT |
| Inspecting ordnance officer | IOO |
| Instruct, instruted, instruction, or instructor | instr |
| Intelligence | int |
| Intelligence officer | IO |
| Intercornmunication | intercomn |
| Internal combustion or in charge of | IC |
| Internal Security | IS |

## J

| Designation | Abbreviation |
|---|---|
| Junction | junc |

## L

| Designation | Abbreviation |
|---|---|
| Laboratory or labour | lab |

## OFFICIAL ABBREVIATIONS — Appendix 3

| Designation | Abbreviation |
|---|---|
| Lance-bombardier | L bdr |
| Lance-corporal | L cpl |
| Lance-serjeant | L sjt |
| Landing | ldg |
| Landing zone | LZ |
| Liaison officer | LO |
| Lieutenant or light | lt |
| Light or lieutenant | lt |
| Light aid detachment | LAD |
| Light Anti-Aircraft | LAA |
| Light machine gun | LMG |
| Line, or lines, of communication | L of C |
| Line telegraphy or low tension | LT |
| Lorried or lorryborne | lor |
| Lorry, command | CV |
| Lorryborne or lorried | lor |
| Low tension or line telegraphy | LT |

### M

| Designation | Abbreviation |
|---|---|
| Machine gun | MG |
| Magazine or magnetic | mag |
| Magnetic or magazine | mag |
| Maintain, maintained, or maintenance | maint |
| Major | maj |
| Mark | mk |
| Mechanical transport | MT |
| Mechanic, mechanical, or mechanized | mech |
| Medical officer | Mo |
| Medium or medical | med |
| Medium machine gun | MMG |
| Meeting point or military police | MP |
| Message | msg |
| Meteorolooical or meteorology | met |
| Miles in the hour | mih |
| Miles in two hours | mi2h |
| Miles per hour | mph |
| Military | mil |
| Military assistant or Military Attaché | MA |
| Military forwarding officer | MFO |
| Military police or meeting point | MP |
| Military Training Pamphlet | MTP |
| Minute | min |
| Mobile or mobilization | mob |
| Mobile field photographic section | MFPS |
| Mobile laundry and bath unit | MLBU |
| Motor or motorized | mot |
| Motor ambulance convoy | MAC |
| Motor-cycle or movement control | MC |
| Motor-cyclist or despatch rider | DR |
| Mountain | mtn |
| Mounted | mtd |
| Movement | mov |
| Movement control or motor-cycle | MC |

### N

| Designation | Abbreviation |
|---|---|
| Namely or that is to say | ie |
| Newfoundland | Nfld |
| New Zealand | NZ |
| Non-commissioned officer | NCO |

### O

| Designation | Abbreviation |
|---|---|
| Observation post | OP |
| Officer | offr |
| Officer commanding | OC |
| Officer-in-charge (of) | OIC |
| Operate, operated, operation, operational, or operator | op |
| Operation order or ordnance officer | OO |
| Ordnance | ord |
| Ordnance beach detachment | OBD |
| Organize, organized, or organization | org |
| Other rank(s | OR |
| Ounce(s) | oz |

### P

| Designation | Abbreviation |
|---|---|
| Parachute or paragraph | para |
| Paragraph or parachute | para |
| Park | pk |
| Passive air defence | PAD |
| Paymaster | pmr |
| Petrol | pet |
| Petrol, oil and lubricants | POL |
| Petrol point | PP |
| Petrol railhead | PRH |
| Petrol refilling point | PRP |
| Photograph or photographic | ph |
| Photograph, vertical air, gridded | photogrid |
| Photographic reconnaissance | ph R |
| Pioneer | pnr |
| Platoon | pl |
| Point | pt |
| Position | posn |
| Post office | Po |
| Pound(s | lb |
| Pounder | pr |
| Prisoner(s) of war | PW |
| Private | ptc |
| Provost | pro |
| Provost marshal | PM |

### Q

| Designation | Abbreviation |
|---|---|
| Quarter-master | QM |
| Quarter-master-serjeant | QMS |

### R

| Designation | Abbreviation |
|---|---|
| Radio telephony | RT |
| Railhead | RH |
| Railhend, or roadhead, maintenance area | RIIMA |
| Railhead, or roadhead, ordnance officer | ROO |
| Railhead, or roadhead, supply officer | R sup O |
| Railway | rly |
| Railway traffic officer | RTO |
| Rear maintenance area | RMA |
| Reconnaissance or reconnoitre | recce |
| Recover, recovered, or recovery | rec |
| Reference | ref |
| Reffilling point, regimental police, or Rules of Procedure | RP |
| Regiment or Regimental | regt |
| Regimental aid post | RAP |
| Regimental police, refilling point, or Rules of Procedure | RP |
| Regiment quarter-master-serjeant | RQMS |
| Regimental serjeant-major | RSM |
| Regulate, regulated, regulating, or regulation | reg |
| Reinforcement | rft |
| Reinforcement holding unit | rft HU |
| Reinforcement sub-unit | rft SU |
| Relief driver increment | RDI |
| Rendezvous | RV |
| Repeated | rptd |
| Represent, represented, or representative | rep |
| Reserve(s) | res |
| Returned stores depot | RSD |
| Rifleman or riflemen | rfn |
| Road | rd |
| Roadhead, or railhead, maintenance area | RHMA |
| Roadhead, or railhead, ordnance officer | ROO |
| Roadhead, or railhead, supply officer | R sup O |
| Rounds per gun (per minute) | rpg (pm) |
| Routine order | RO |
| Royal Horse Artillery | RHA |
| Royal Warrallt for Pay and Promotion | RW |
| Rules of procedure, refilling point, or regimental police | RP |

### S

| Designation | Abbreviation |
|---|---|
| Salvage or salvaged | sal |
| Sapper | spr |
| Searchlight or start line | SL |
| Seater or strength | str |
| Second or Section | sec |
| Second in command | 2IC |
| Section or second | sec |
| Self-propelled or starting point | SP |
| Senior medical officer | SMO |
| Senior supply officer | S sup O |
| Serjeant | sjt |
| Shellillg report | shelrep |
| Signal | sig |
| Signalman or Signalmen | sigmn |
| Situation report | sitrep |
| Small arms, South Africa, or South African | SA |
| Small arms ammunition | SAA |
| Small box girder | SBG |
| Sound ranging | S rg |
| South Africa, South African, or small arms | SA |
| Squadron | sqn |
| Staff officer | SO |
| Staff, or squadron, quarter-master-serjeant | SQMS |
| Staff sergeant | S sjt |
| Staff, or squadron, serjeant-major | SSM |
| Starting point or self-propelled | SP |
| Start line or searchlight | SL |
| Station | sta |
| Sten machine carbine | SMC |
| Stereoscope or stereoscopic | stereo |
| Strategical reconnaissance | strat R |
| Strength or seater | str |
| Stretcher bearer | SB |
| Supply or supplied | sup |
| Supply dropping point | SDP |
| Supply landing point | SLP |
| Supply loading airfield | SLA |
| Supply point | sup P |
| Supply railhead | SRH |
| Support or supported | sp |
| Survey | svy |
| Switchboard | swbd |

### T

| Designation | Abbreviation |
|---|---|
| Tactical reconnaissance | tac R |
| Tank | tk |
| Technical | tech |
| Telegraph or telegraphic | tg |
| Telephone | tele |
| Tentacle. | tcl |
| Territorial Army | TA |
| That is to say or namely | ie |
| Thompson machine carbine | TMC |
| Traffic | tfc |
| Traffic control | TC |
| Traffic post | TP |
| Training | trg |
| Transport | tpt |
| Transported | tptd |
| Transport officer | TO |
| Transportation | tn |
| Transporter | tptr |
| Troop | tp |
| Troop carrying vehicle | TCV |
| Trooper | tpr |

### U

| Designation | Abbreviation |
|---|---|
| Unexploded bomb(s) | UXB |
| United Kingdom | UK |
| United States of America. | USA |
| Urgent memorandum | UM |

### V

| Designation | Abbreviation |
|---|---|
| Vehicle | VEH |
| Vehicle reserve depot | VRD |
| Vehicles to the mile | VTM |
| Vertical air photograph, gridded | photogrid |
| Veterinary | vet |
| Visual signalling | VS |
| Vulnerable point | VP |

### W

| Designation | Abbreviation |
|---|---|
| Wagon line | WL |
| Walking wounded collecting post | WWCP |
| War establishment | WE |
| War substantive, warlike stores, or wireless set | WS |
| Warlike stores, war substantive, or wireless set | WS |
| Warrant Officer | WO |
| Water point | Wp |
| Waterproofing | wpfg |
| Weapon training or wireless telegraphy | WT |
| West Africa or West African | WA |
| Wheel or wheeled | wh |
| Wireless | wrls |
| Wireless set, warlike stores, or war substantive | WS |
| Wireless telegraphy or weapon training | WT |
| With effect from | wef |
| Workshop | wksp |

### Y

| Designation | Abbreviation |
|---|---|
| Yard | yd |

# HISTORICAL BIBLIOGRAPHY

Works in French dealing with British Army Operations from 6th June 1944 to 8th may 1945 in the North West Europe theatre of operations

— **Adelin, Louis** « La neutralisation de la batterie de Merville-Franceville »*
14810 - Merville Mairie
— **Ambrose, Stephen** « Pegasus Bridge »*
Horizon 1987, France
— **Belfield & Essame** « Normandie. Eté 1944 »
Presses de la Cité, 1966
— **Bernard, Georges** « Le pont d'Arnhem »
Editions Heimdal, 1977
— **Buffetaut, Yves** « Les Blindés alliés en Normandie »
« 6 Juin 1944. La première vague »
« La bataille du bocage »
« Le choc des blindés »
« Au cœur du Reich »
« Opération Goodwood » *
Histoire &Collections, 1992, 1993, 1994, 1995, 1997
— **Blond, Georges** « Le débarquement »
A Fayard, 1960
— **Boussel, P. & Florentin, E.**
« Guide des plages du Débarquement et des champs de bataille de Normandie »
Presses de la Cité, 1984
— **Brisset Jean** « La Charge du Taureau » *
Bates Book,1989
— **Baldewyn, Herman & Lemoine**
« Les Batteries de Walcheren » *
Rossel Editions
— **Chauvet, Maurice** « Mille et un jours pour le Jour-J » *
Michel Laffon 1994).
— **Churchill, Winston** « Mémoires de la Seconde Guerre » *
Plon, 1951
— **Croockenden, Napier** « Les paras du 6 Juin »
Albin Michel, 1994
— **Edwards, Kenneth** « Opération Neptune »
La Jeune Parque, 1946
— **Florentin, Eddy** « Stalingrad en Normandie »
« Opération Paddle »
« La Ruckmarsh »
« Le Havre à Feu et à Sang » *
« Montgomery franchit la Seine » *
Presses de la Cité, Editions révisées 1994-1995
— **G. Golley John** « La nuit des canons de Merville » *
Presses de la Cité, 1983
— **Grandais, Albert** « La Bataille du Calvados » *
Presses de la Cité, 1973

— **Ingersoll, Ralph** « Ultra Secret »
La Jeune Parque, 1947
— **Keegan, John** « Six Armées en Normandie »
Albin Michel, 1989

— **Commandant Kieffer, Phillipe**
« Les bérets verts français du 6 Juin » *
Présentation par Eddy Florentin, France - Empire, 1994
— **La Sierra, Raymond** « Le Commando du 6 Juin » *
Presses de la Cité, 1983
— **Mac Kee Alexander** « La Bataille de Caen » *
Presses de la Cité, 1965
— **Montgomery (Maréchal)**
« De la Normandie à la Baltique »
Editions Lavauzelle, 1948
« Mémoires »
Plon, 1958
— **Pipet, Albert** « Mourir à Caen » *
Presses de la Cité, 1974
— **Perrault, Gilles** « Le Grand Jour »
Lattès, 1984
— **Ryan, Cornelius** « Le Jour le plus Long
Robert Laffont, 1960
« Un Pont trop loin »
Robert Laffont, 1974
« La dernière bataille »
Robert Laffont, 1966
— **Ruge, Friedrich (Amiral)**
« Rommel face au Débarquement »
Presses de la Cité, 1960
— **Shulman, Milton** « La défaite allemande à l'Ouest »
Payot, 1948
— **Speidel, Hans** « Invasion 1944 »
Berger-Levrault 1950
— **Stacey, CP (colonel)** « La campagne de la Victoire » *
Ministère canadien de la Défense, Ottawa, 1960
— **Toland, John, F.** « Les 100 derniers jours »
Calmann-Levy 1967).
— **Turner, John, F.** « Histoire du débarquement »
Arthaud, 1960
— **Wilmot, Chester** « La lutte pour l'Europe »
Arthème Fayard, 1953
— **Ouvrages Collectifs**
« Overlord. Jour-J en Normandie »
« La bataille de Caen »*
« La bataille de Normandie »
« 12. SS Panzer Division Hittlerjugend »
« La Panzer Lehr Division »
« 6 juin 1944. La Cornemuse du D-Day » *
« Villers-Bocage. Tigres au combat »*
« La Garde contre la Hohenstauffen »*
« Pegasus Bridge. 6th Airborne » *
Editions Heimdal, 1984-1997

* Operations concerning the 21st Groups only

140

# TECHNICAL BIBLIOGRAPHY

**INSIGNIA, MEDALS, UNIFORMS, EQUIPMENT**

— **Gaylor, John** « Military Badge collecting »
A Leo Cooper Book, Secker & Warburg, London, 1983
— **Cox, Reginald, H. W.** « Military Badges of the British Empire, 1914-1918 »
Ernest Benn Ltd, London, 1982
— **Alderson, G. L. D.** « Cap Badges of the British Army, 1939-1945 »
G.L.D. Alderson Pool Lane Brocton, Stafford, 1989
— **Edwards, Major** « Regimental Badges »
Gale & Polden, 1953
— **Westlake, Ray** « Badge Backings & Special Embellishments of the British Army »
The Ulster Defence Regiment Benevolent Fund, 1990
— **Cole, Howard** « Formation Badges of World War Two »
Arms and Armour Press, 1973
— **Litchfield, Norman, E. H.** « The Territorial Artillery, 1908-1988
— **Davis, Brian, L.** « British Army Uniforms and Insignia of World War Two »
Arms & Armour Press, 1983
— **War Office** « The Pattern 1937 Web Equipment »
Army Council Instruction, 25 October 1939
— **Cotton, Marcus** « Les casques d'acier britanniques »
Militaria Magazine, Histoire & Collections, 1989
— **Tariel, Yves** « Le parachute Type X »
Militaria Magazine n° 59-60, Histoire & Collections, 1994
— **Chappell, Mike** « Battledress, 1939-1960 »
Wessex Military Publishing
— **Chappell, Mike** « British Battle Insignia, 1939-1945 (2) »
Osprey Publishing, Men at Arms Series
— **Cassin Jack & Fabb, Scott and John**
« Military Bands and their Uniforms »
Blandford Press Ltd, 1978
— **Abbot, P. E. & Tamplin, J. M. A.**
« British Gallantry Awards »
Guinness Superlatives Ltd, Cecil Court, London Road, Enfield, Middlesex
— **Tapnel Dorling, H.** « Ribbons and Medals »
Osprey Publishing Ltd
— **Joslin, E. C. & Litherland, A. R. & Simkin, B. T.**
« British Battle Medals »
Spink & Sons Ltd, London
— **Rosignoli, Guido** « Ribbons of Orders, decorations and medals »
Blandford Press
— **War Office** « Campaign Stars and Commemoratives Medals institued for the 1939-1345 War
Code No 199, 11 June 1948
— **War Office** « Medals, Campaign Stars and Clasps and Defence Medal, Condition of Award »
Army Council Instruction No 829, 14 July 1945.

**UNIT ORGANISATION**

— **Ellis, L. F., Major** « Victory in the West, part I & II »
The Imperial War Museum, Department of Printed Books
— **Joslen H. F., Lt. Col.** « Orders of Battle, Part I & II »
The Majesty's Stationery Office, London, 1960
— « Administrative History of 21st Army Group, 6 june 1944 - 8 May 1945 »
— **War Office** « Infantry Training, The Infantry Battalion, 1944 »
Army Council Instructions, 1943-1944, Field Service Books
— **Bellis, Malcolm, A.** « 21st Army Group, Organization and Markings »
Malcolm, A., Bellis, 1992
— **Ladd, James** « Commandos and Rangers of World War II »
Mac Donald and Janes, 1978
— **Griffin, David** « British Army Regiments »
Thomsons Publishing Group
— **Chant, Christopher** « Handbook of British Regiments »
Routledge, 1988
— **Horrocks, Sir Brian, General**
« Famous Regiments » (série)
— **Bellis, Malcolm, A.** « British Armoured & Infantry Regiments, 1939-1945 »
Malcolm A. Bellis, Datafile Series
— **Collectif** « Historiques régimentaires et divisionnaires divers »
**Bibliothèque de documentation internationale contemporaine, Universitéde Paris**

— « Notices sur l'armée britannique »
Ministère des armées, 1945
— « Combined Operations, Beach Organization and Maintenance »
Pamphlet No2, March 1944
— **Hallows, Ian, S.** « Regiments and Corps of the British Army »
Arms and Armour Press, 1991
— **Bellis, Malcolm, A.** « Regiments of the British Army, Artillery»
Military Press, London, 1995
— **Ellis, John** « The World War two Databook »
Aurum Press, 1993
— « Handbook on the British Army, Technical Manual TM 30-410, September 1943 »
United States Government Printing Office, Washington 1943

**ARMAMENT**
— **Smith, J. E.** « Small Arms of the World »
8th Edition revisited, Stackpole Books, Harrisburg, USA, 1966
— **Barker, A. J.** « British & American Infantry Weapons of World War II »
Cox & Wyman Ltd, London, 1978
— **Skennerton, Ian** « British Small Arms of World War II »
Greenhill Books, London
— **Skennerton, Ian** « The Lee Enfield story »
Greenhill Books, London
— **Collectif** « Notices du centre d'instruction d'armes britanniques »
3e division d'infanterie coloniale, 1945
— « L'artillerie britannique »
Ministère de la guerre, état-major de l'armée, 1945

**VEHICLES, MISCELLANEOUS MACHINES, MATERIAL**
— « Churchill Tank »
London, Her Majesty's Stationery Office
— « Cromwell Tank »
London, Her Majesty's Stationery Office
— « Army Transport, 1939-1345 »
Tank Museum, London, Her Majesty's Stationery Office, 1983
— **Vanderveen, Bart, H.** « The Observer's Fighting Vehicles Directory World War II »
— **White, B. T.** « British Tanks and Fighting Vehicles, 1914-1945 »
Ian Allan, 1970
— **White, B. T.** « British Tanks Markings and Names »
Arms & Armour Press, 1978
— **Wise, Terence** « D-Day to Berlin »
Arms & Armour Press, 1979
— **Wise, Terence** « Military Vehicles Marking World War II »
— « British Military Transport World War II »
Ryton Publications, 1994
— **Hodges, Peter** « British Military Markings, 1939-1945 »
Almark Publications, 1978 (Revised Edition, 1995)
— « Royal Air Force, Airborne Forces Manual »
Arms & Armour Press, 1979
— « Assault Crossing Equipment, Part III »
War Office, January 1944
— « The Bailey Bridge, Military Engineering Volume II, Part III »
War Office, 1944
— **Conniford, Mike** « British Light Military Trucks, 1939-1945 »
Bellona, 1976
— **Boniface, Jean-Michel & Jeudy, Jean-Gabriel**
« Les véhicules américains de la Seconde Guerre mondiale »
Editions EPA
— **Boniface, Jean-Michel & Jeudy, Jean-Gabriel**
« Scout-Cars et Half-Tracks »
Editions EPA, 1986
— **Collectif** « Véhicules automobiles militaires, Manuel technique (French) TM 9-2800 »
Ministère de la Guerre, septembre 1943
— **Forty, George** « M4 Sherman »
Blandford Press, 1987
— **Schreier Jr, K.** « Tanks & Artillery, Standard Guide to US World War II »
Krause Publications, 1994

## ACKNOWLEDGEMENTS

I should like to thank Jean-Marie MONGIN, Patrick LESIEUR and Morgan GILLARD for the care that they have taken with the production of this work. Philippe CHARBONNIER and Robert LE CHANTOUX for their precious help during the proof reading, and all the staff of Histoire & Collections who took part in the making of this book.

The curators of the museums for their help:

David FLETCHER of the Bovington Tank Museum, Great Britain; Jean MENARD of the Musée de la Bataille du Bocage, Saint-Martin des Besaces, Calvados, France; Marc JACQUINOT of the Musée des troupes aéroportées britanniques, Benouville, Calvados, France; Colonel M. YDE of the Musée du Canon et des Artilleurs de Draguignan, Var, France; Michel LELOUP of the Musée de la bataille de Falaise, Calvados, France; Jean-Marc COMBE of the Railway Museum at Mulhouse, Haut Rhin, France; W. BOERSMA of the Airborne Museum of Hartenstein, Holland; Miss Diana ANDREWS of the Airborne Forces Museum at Aldershot, Great Britain.

Thanks to the *Medical Doctor*, T. J. RENOUF, *Medical Officer*, The Black Watch, veteran of the North West Europe Campaign.

Thanks to André JOUINEAU for the realisation of the plate on the British Infantry Combat Group.

Thanks also to all the collectors and the specialists for the help they brought at all times to the realisation of this work. Louis ADELIN, Didier BAULAND, Pierre BESNARD, Robert d'ELIA, Frédéric FINEL, Marc LANDRY, Bruno LAURENS, Christophe HEBACKER, Patrick NONZERVILLE, Pascal PEREZ, Yves SACLEUX, Yves TARIEL.

Thanks to my two sons Patrice and François BOUCHERY.

Thanks finally to the Paris shops specialising in military souvenirs and memorabilia: *Overlord*, *Poussières d'Empire* and *Le Poilu*.

---

**PICTURE ACKNOWLEDGEMENTS**
**Imperial War Museum.** pp. 3, 6, 7, 9, 21, 23, 25, 29, 35, 36, 36, 37, 38, 39, 41, 45, 46, 47, 48, 49, 50, 51, 53, 54, 56, 57, 58, 59, 62, 66(c), 68(br), 70(b), 73(t), 75(t), 76(t), 77(t,c), 80(b), 82, 83, 84, 86(c,b), 89(t,b), 90(b), 91(t,b), 92(t), 93(t), 94, 97(t,b), 98(t),99(cb,br), 100, 101(t), 102(t,c), 103(t,b), 104(b), 105(t,b), 106(t,b), 108(h,h), 109(t,b), 110(t,b), 111, 113(b,c), 114(b), 115(c,b), 116(b,b), 120(b,c), 121(t), 122(c), 126, 128.
**Bovington Tank Museum.** pp. 85, 87(t,c,b), 88(t,d), 89(c), 93(b), 95(t),96, 98, 99(t,cr,c), 102(b), 103(c), 110(c), 112(t), 115(t,c), 118, 119, 120(t).
**Militaria magazine/Philippe Charbonnier.** pp. 55, 55, 57, 60, 63, 64, 65, 66(t,bl), 67(t), 68, 69, 70, 71, 72(t,b), 78 (b), 79(t), 81 (b,r), 114 (t,c,c,c).
**Reserved rights.** pp. 37, 38(b), 39(tl,b), 55(h), 66(br), 67(c,b), 68, 69, 70(b), 72(c), 73(b), 74(t,b), 75(b), 76(b), 77(b), 78(h), 79(b), 80(t), 81(t), 83(cr), 86(t), 101(c,b), 104(t), 107, 109(c), 110(b),112(c), 113(t,c), 114(b), 116(t,c), 117(x6), 120(c), 121 (c,c,b), 133.

# COMPANION VOLUME

# THE BRITISH TOMMY
## IN NORTH WEST EUROPE, 1944-1945

### VOLUME 1 - TABLE OF CONTENTS

| | |
|---|---:|
| 1 - HEADGEAR<br>Berets, helmets, caps, traditional headgear | 6 |
| 2 - CAP BADGES<br>Cavalry, Infantry, arms and services | 21 |
| 3 - UNIFORMS<br>Battledress and the issue set clothing | 32 |
| 4 - CLOTH SLEEVE INSIGNIA, RANK INSIGNIA | 56 |
| 5 - MEDALS and DECORATIONS | 88 |
| 6 - AIRBORNE TROOPS CLOTHING and EQUIPMENT | 92 |
| 7 - INDIVIDUAL EQUIPMENT<br>Web equipment, intrenching tools and sleeping gear | 104 |
| 8 - PERSONAL ITEMS | 116 |
| 9 - FIELD RATIONS | 122 |
| 10 - OPTICAL INSTRUMENTS, CARTOGRAPHY and SIGNALS | 128 |
| ANNEXES | 138 |
| BIBLIOGRAPHY | 142 |

Drawings, design and lay-out by Jean-Marie MONGIN, © *Histoire & Collections*

All rights reserved. No part of this publication can be transmitted or reproduced without the written consent of the Author and the Publisher.

ISBN : 2 908 182 742

Publisher's number : 2-908182

© Histoire & Collections 2001

A book published by
HISTOIRE & COLLECTIONS
SA au capital de 1 200 000 francs
5, avenue de la République
F-75541 Paris Cédex 11

Phone 01 40 21 18 20
Fax    01 47 00 51 11

This book has been designed, typed, laid-out and processed
by *Histoire & Collections*,
fully on integrated computer equipment.

*Second print*
Printed by KSG-Elkar / KSG-Danona, Spain, European Union.
*31 May 2001*